ROMAN AFRICA

THE THREE TEMPLES AT SUFETULA (SBEITLA)
(Restored).

ROMAN AFRICA

By
ALEXANDER GRAHAM

The Black Heritage Library Collection

 BOOKS FOR LIBRARIES PRESS
FREEPORT, NEW YORK
1971

First Published 1902
Reprinted 1971

Reprinted from a copy in the
Fisk University Library Negro Collection

INTERNATIONAL STANDARD BOOK NUMBER:
0-8369-8807-8

LIBRARY OF CONGRESS CATALOG CARD NUMBER:
70-157369

PRINTED IN THE UNITED STATES OF AMERICA

ROMAN AFRICA

AN OUTLINE OF THE

HISTORY OF THE ROMAN OCCUPATION OF NORTH AFRICA

BASED CHIEFLY UPON
INSCRIPTIONS AND MONUMENTAL REMAINS
IN THAT COUNTRY

BY

ALEXANDER GRAHAM

F.S.A., F.R.I.B.A.

WITH THIRTY REPRODUCTIONS OF ORIGINAL DRAWINGS
BY THE AUTHOR, AND TWO MAPS

LONDON, NEW YORK AND BOMBAY
1902

TO THE READER

THE inscriptions in the following pages have mostly been published in various forms and at different periods, especially during the latter half of the last century. From the time of Shaw, whose volumes were first published in 1738, so many travellers in North Africa have recorded their interpretations of inscribed lettering that it is difficult, in some cases, to assign credit where credit is due. And since the French occupation of Algeria and Tunisia opportunities have been offered of publishing these interpretations in many noteworthy periodicals, such as the *Revue Africaine*, commenced in 1856, and the *Annuaire de la Société archéologique de la Province de Constantine*, which was issued as far back as 1853. To collate and systematise the great mass of inscriptions has been the laborious work of such well-known epigraphists as Léon Renier, Gustavus Wilmanns, and others, whose names appear in footnotes in the following pages. Most of them can be better studied in the volumes of inscriptions mentioned on pp. 32 and 33, and referred to hereafter under the letters *C.I.L.* and *I.R.A.* Incompleteness of lettering, arising either from exposure or destruction, has given rise to difference of opinion in filling up many omissions of importance, but it is satisfactory to note that a general agreement prevails on most of the inscriptions of historic value. Whenever an alternative reading is admissible, the titles of the books that may be referred to are given in the text or in one of the footnotes.

PREFACE

FOR many generations the interest attached to the progress of civilisation in Central and Southern Africa has diverted men's minds from a somewhat analogous process which was being evolved nearly 2000 years ago in the Northern regions of this great Continent. History very often repeats itself in an unaccountable way. The methods of civilisation adopted in one age differ in a marked degree from those of another, varying with the habits of national life, and governed by the insuperable natural laws affecting climate or race. But the outcome of human progress is invariably the same, exhibiting respect for and obedience to ruling authority, a mute recognition of the unwritten rules of social life, and greater regard for personal preservation. The gradual development of North Africa as a great Roman colony was spread over a period of more than 500 years, and culminated in an era of peace and prosperity to a vast population enjoying the highest civilisation of the time. Asia and Africa took rank as the greatest of Rome's colonial possessions, and it is a question whether the latter did not take the lead, in the third and fourth centuries, in all matters affecting the maintenance of the Empire and the general welfare of its citizens. However successful Roman rule may have proved in the Asiatic provinces, we have in Africa indisputable testimony to the wealth and resources of this fair appendage of the Empire, to the growth of municipal life, the spread of education, and the high attainments of many of its citizens in literature, philosophy, and art.

To the archæologist no country in the world possesses greater attraction, or offers a more useful field for his researches, than this vast region on the southern shores of the Mediterranean, known to the ancients by the simple word Africa.[1] Its long and chequered career, the rise and progress of national life, the spread of civilisation amongst hordes of barbarians whose origin still remains an unsolved problem, and the romantic lives of the chief actors in its eventful history are mainly recorded on imperishable stone or exhibited in the ruined monuments which still greet the traveller's eye on the hillsides or deserted plains of North Africa. From the borders of Egypt to the Atlantic Ocean, from the shores of the Mediterranean to the trackless plains of the Great Desert, marble and stone are there in abundance, telling their own tale of nations and communities long passed away, of deeds of heroism and benevolence, of thoughtful men and kindly women. The history of the country may truly be said to be written on stone. The untameable Libyan, the enterprising Phœnician, the crafty Carthaginian, and the indomitable Roman, followed by the destructive Vandal, the half-civilised Byzantine, and the wandering Arab, have all left enduring marks of their occupation. But the mark of the Roman predominates everywhere. And interwoven with the declining years of the greatest Empire the world had yet seen we have records of the early career and struggles of the Christian Church in North Africa. For the illustration of this period there is abundant material—a period when temples and basilicas were to become the home of a new

---

[1] The Greeks, in the days of Homer, only knew of North Africa as Libya, and in the time of Herodotus would not believe that Africa had been circumnavigated by Phœnicians. The Persians, however, believed it, and it is recorded that Xerxes pardoned Sataspes, who was condemned to death, on condition that he made a voyage round Africa. Sataspes, we are told, returned quickly, owing, as he said, to fabulous obstacles that he encountered in the Straits of Gades. Xerxes declined to accept such excuses, and ordered him to be beheaded. (*L'Univers pittoresque*.) The earliest mention of Africa is by the poet Ennius, B.C. 239–169, who styled himself the Homer of Latium. Suidas says that Africa was the ancient name of Carthage itself.

ritual, when sculptured deities were to be overthrown, when symbols of a despised creed were to be carved on post and lintel, and when the names of Tertullian, St. Cyprian, and St. Augustine were to add new lustre to a country entering upon the last stages of imperial decay.

From the time when the first adventurers from the Syrian coast entered the sheltered inlets of the African shore—a remote period, even before Saul was made king of Israel and while Priam sat on the throne of Troy—down to the seventh century of the Christian era, when the Arabs passed over it like a whirlwind, this fair land has been the battle-field where destinies of nations have been sealed, and where heroes and warriors have sought their last resting-place. The myths that surround its earlier development and shed a halo of romance over the career of its primitive races are somewhat obscured by the sterner facts of later times—by wars innumerable, wars of invasion and local disturbances, succeeded by a long period of piracy and power misused, and finally by neglect, abandonment, and decay. The legend of Dido still hangs over Carthage hill, the spirit of Hannibal haunts the fateful Zama, and the banks of the Medjerda hold in everlasting memory the story of Regulus and his affrighted army. The air is full of myths and old-world stories which faithfully represent the traditions of the country in its varying fortunes; and slight as may be their connection with events in pre-historic times, yet they serve as foundations for an historic superstructure of never-failing interest. The earlier records are fragmentary, but we learn that the library of the Carthaginians, written in Phœnician characters, was presented by the Romans, after the fall of Carthage, to the kings of Numidia; and that Sallust, as pro-consul of that province in the time of Julius Cæsar, borrowed largely from it while writing his history of the Jugurthine war. In all probability Sallust was unacquainted with either the Libyan or the Phœnician tongue (the former being the language of the primitive inhabitants of the country), and consequently obtained much of his information through interpreters. Moreover, he must have felt little interest in a people who had been for so many centuries the sworn enemies of Rome. Punic literature was probably limited, Greek being usually spoken by educated Carthaginians. Hannibal, we are told, wrote in Greek. There is little doubt, however, that most of the earlier records passed to Alexandria, which became the rival of Athens as a seat of learning. With the burning of its library by fanatical Arabs in the seventh century many a link between the old world and the new was severed, and reliable information concerning the laws and traditions, and the manners and customs of a people, who were the fathers of navigation and the founders of commerce, was swept away.

Writers of antiquity who have recorded their impressions of North Africa are numerous enough, but their statements are not always accurate, and their descriptions of localities and monumental remains too frequently untrustworthy. Many of them derived their knowledge from various sources, especially from enterprising navigators, Phœnician or Greek, who sailed to various commercial ports on the shores of the Mediterranean. They wrote without personal knowledge of the country or its extent, and had limited acquaintance with its inhabitants or the Libyan tongue which then prevailed. Herodotus, Polybius, Sallust, Strabo, Pliny the Elder, Plutarch, and the Spanish geographer Pomponius Mela are the chief authorities down to the close of the first century.[1] These were followed by Suetonius, the favoured secretary and friend of the Emperor

---

[1] As an instance of looseness of statement, Strabo the geographer, in the time of Augustus, says it was the general impression that the sources of the Nile were not far off the confines of Mauritania, crocodiles and other animals found in the Nile being indigenous in the rivers of that country (lib. xvii. p. 454). Dion Cassius also says: 'I have taken particular care to inform myself about the Nile. It visibly takes its rise from Mount Atlas. This mountain, which is near the ocean on the west side, is infinitely higher than all the rest upon earth, which gave the poets occasion to feign that it supported the heavens. Never did anybody ascend to the top. The foot of this hill is marshy, and from these morasses proceeds the Nile.' (*Vide* Dion Cassius, abridged by Xiphilin, Manning's translation, 1704, vol. ii. p. 277.)

Preface

Hadrian, Apuleius of Madaura, Ptolemy the renowned geographer of Alexandria, Dion Cassius the Bithynian, and Aurelius Victor, a Roman biographer of the fourth century In later times we have Procopius, the Greek secretary attached to the army of Belisarius; Leo Africanus, an Arab of Granada in the sixteenth century; and numerous African authors, among whom El-Bekri and El-Edrisi, who flourished in the eleventh and twelfth centuries, are the most conspicuous. Then, after a long interval, we have a succession of European travellers, whose voluminous notes paved the way for more systematic research. The most noticeable are Shaw, an Oxford divine; Peysonnel, a professor of botany; Bruce, British consul at Algiers; and Sir Grenville Temple, a cavalry officer. It seems invidious to select a few names in more recent times where so many are worthy of recognition, but the labours of those who have best served the cause of archæology, and whose names are inseparably associated with the literature and monumental remains of North Africa, cannot be passed over. The contributions of Berbrugger, De la Mare, Guérin, Ravoisié, Pellissier, Cherbonneau, Léon Renier, and Charles Tissot in the last century, supplemented in our own days by a long array of valuable notes by our late Consul-General Sir Lambert Playfair, have added largely to our knowledge of the topography and antiquities of the country. To De la Mare we are indebted for an illustrated, though unfortunately incomplete, work on monumental Algeria; to Ravoisié we owe some careful measurements and restorations (on paper) of the principal remains in the northern regions; and to Renier, Wilmanns, and others a wealth of deciphered inscriptions which constitute in themselves a fair outline of many centuries of national life in this great Roman colony. The researches also of officers attached to the 'Bureau Arabe,' as well as the expert knowledge of many curators of local museums, have filled up numerous gaps in the general history of Roman Africa. And in the present generation the establishment of a 'Commission des Monuments historiques' has not only resulted in more intimate acquaintance with matters of topography, but has brought into the field of African literature many French authors of known repute. Again, the bibliography of the entire country, including Morocco, Algeria, Tunisia, and Tripoli, has also been the subject of much thoughtful and enlightened labour. Some idea of the extent of the literature associated with North Africa may be gathered from the fact that the five English volumes devoted entirely to its bibliography comprise no less than 1215 pages.[1]

The rise and progress of Roman Africa are necessarily interwoven with the history of the Roman people, and form some of its most interesting chapters during the long period which elapsed between the close of the second Punic war, B.C. 201, and the fall of Rome, A.D. 455. Gibbon's scholarly pages treating of this branch of his subject are masterpieces of erudition, and are the outcome of diligent investigation of the works of Greek and Roman authors. But he wrote at a time when archæological inquiry was hardly recognised as a branch of knowledge, when little assistance could be given by observant travellers, who hesitated to explore a trackless region inhabited by barbarian hordes, and when the historian had to rely on his own interpretation of many conflicting statements by authors of antiquity. Mommsen has lived in a more favoured age. He has had at his disposal the notes of a long array of modern travellers and antiquaries, and has been able to correct or substantiate the statements of ancient authors by the light of recent research.

It is difficult for the traveller, as he journeys across the now

[1] *A Bibliography of Algeria.* By Sir R. Lambert Playfair. Pp. 430. London: John Murray. 1888. A supplementary volume by the same author and publisher. Pp. 321. 1898.

A Bibliography of Tunisia. By Henry Spencer Ashbee, F.S.A. Pp. 144. London: Dulau & Co. 1889.

A Bibliography of Tripoli and the Cyrenaica. By Sir R. Lambert Playfair. Pp. 58. London: 1889.

A Bibliography of Morocco. By Sir R. Lambert Playfair and Dr. Robert Brown. Pp. 262. London: John Murray. 1892.

Preface

deserted plains of North Africa, to realise, in these far-off days, the extent and completeness of Roman colonisation. No other nation has left so many enduring marks of its presence as the Roman, and in no other country, outside Italy, is there such a wealth of inscriptions as in North Africa. Stone and marble, bearing the impress of human agency, are scattered over the land, and the familiar lettering is there also as a mute memorial to widespread contentment and prosperity.

It is not within the scope of this outline of historic inquiry to trace the methods by which the Romans achieved success in colonisation where other nations have failed. This branch of the subject has proved attractive to many authors of high repute, especially in the present generation, and still presents an unexhausted field for further critical investigation. Nor does the writer of the following pages claim originality in the treatment of this subject, or any ability to impart special information not open to students of Roman history, who may care to pursue their inquiries in some of the more remote regions of Northern Africa. Notes and observations during frequent journeys in various parts of the country,[1] and a study of the inscriptions and monumental remains of the Roman occupation, have supplied a large proportion of the material embodied in this volume. Archæology is the willing handmaid of history. Without such help the history of the Romans in Africa would be less attractive, and our acquaintance with their progress and decline more fragmentary. Every week the spade of the explorer contributes something to our knowledge; either some undiscovered monument on the plains, or an inscribed stone to tell its own unvarnished tale of place or person long passed away. The chief aim of the present work is to trace as far as possible the extent of the Roman occupation, the degree of civilisation attained in the first four centuries of the Christian era, and to show how conspicuous a part was played by North Africa in the building up of a great Empire.

[1] *Travels in Tunisia.* By Alexander Graham and Henry Spencer Ashbee. London: 1887.

CONTENTS

CHAPTER	PAGE
I. CARTHAGE AND ROME. B.C. 201–46	1
II. AFRICA UNDER THE CÆSARS. B.C. 46–A.D. 96	19
III. AFRICA UNDER TRAJAN. A.D. 97–117	55
IV. AFRICA UNDER HADRIAN. A.D. 117–138	103
V. AFRICA UNDER ANTONINUS PIUS. A.D. 138–161	120
VI. AFRICA UNDER MARCUS AURELIUS. A.D. 161–180	155
VII. AFRICA UNDER SEPTIMIUS SEVERUS. A.D. 193–211	196
VIII. AFRICA UNDER ALEXANDER SEVERUS. A.D. 222–235	209
IX. AFRICA UNDER THE GORDIANS. A.D. 236–244	220
X. AFRICA UNDER THE LATER EMPERORS. A.D. 244–454	235
CONCLUSION	297

APPENDICES.

I. LIST OF ABBREVIATIONS USUALLY FOUND IN ROMAN INSCRIPTIONS	309
II. LIST OF THE PRINCIPAL KNOWN TOWNS IN THE AFRICAN PROVINCES OF THE ROMAN EMPIRE, OR THE SITES OF OTHERS WHICH HAVE BEEN IDENTIFIED BY INSCRIPTIONS.	311
III. CHRONOLOGY OF THE PRINCIPAL EVENTS IN NORTH AFRICA DURING THE ROMAN OCCUPATION AND, SUBSEQUENTLY, TILL THE INVASION OF THE COUNTRY BY ARABS	316
INDEX	321

LIST OF ILLUSTRATIONS

THE THREE TEMPLES AT SUFETULA (SBEITLA), RESTORED	*Frontispiece*
VIEW OF UTICA (BOU CHATER)	*To face p.* 22
MOSAIC IN THE BRITISH MUSEUM, REPRESENTING THE WALLS OF ROMAN CARTHAGE	,, 24
TOMB OF JUBA II.	,, 27
PLAN OF TOMB OF JUBA II.	,, 28
ENTRANCE TO TOMB OF JUBA II.	,, 29
TOMBS OF NUMIDIAN KINGS, RESTORED	,, 30
PLAN OF BASILICA AT THEVESTE (TEBESSA)	,, 46
THE QUADRIFRONTAL ARCH OF CARACALLA AT THEVESTE	,, 48
TEMPLE OF MINERVA AT THEVESTE, RESTORED	,, 50
VIEW OF BULLA REGIA (HAMMÂM DARRADJI)	,, 71
TRAJAN'S BRIDGE AT SIMITTU (CHEMTOU)	,, 72
MONUMENT AT SCILLIUM (KASSERIN)	,, 81
ARCH OF TRAJAN AT THAMUGAS (TIMEGAD), RESTORED	,, 96
AQUEDUCT OF CARTHAGE	,, 109
CISTERNS OUTSIDE KAIROUAN	,, 111
AQUEDUCT OF CARTHAGE IN THE MEDJERDA PLAIN, SHOWING CONSTRUCTION	,, 114
VIEW OF MOUNT ZAGHOUAN	,, 116
ENTRANCE TO THE HIERON AT SUFETULA	,, 122
THE BRIDGE AT SUFETULA (SBEITLA)	,, 127
VIEW OF SUFETULA (SBEITLA)	,, 128
THE CAPITOL AT THUGGA (DOUGGA)	,, 171
THE PRÆTORIUM AT LAMBÆSIS (LAMBESSA)	,, 186
AMPHITHEATRE AT THYSDRUS (EL-DJEM)	,, 228
,, ,, ,, ,,	,, 230
THE FOUR PRINCIPAL AMPHITHEATRES COMPARED	232, 233
AMPHITHEATRE AT UTHINA (OUDENA)	,, 234
FRONT OF A MARBLE CIPPUS IN THE MUSEUM AT PHILIPPEVILLE	,, 296
MOSAIC SLAB IN THE MUSEUM AT CONSTANTINE (BYZANTINE PERIOD)	,, 308

MAPS

NORTH AFRICA	*To face p.* 4
NORTH AFRICA AT THE CLOSE OF THE THIRD CENTURY	*At end*

ROMAN AFRICA

CHAPTER I

CARTHAGE AND ROME

B.C. 201-46

THE history of Roman Africa commences at the close of the second Punic war, B.C. 201. The fall of Pyrrhus, the adventurous king of Epirus, B.C. 272, whose ambition was to surpass Alexander the Great in warlike achievements, had made the Romans masters of Southern Italy, and brought them face to face with the Carthaginians in the fair island of Sicily. For nearly two centuries and a half these rival nations had been watching each other's movements across the sea with jealousy and dismay. Success to the Romans on the first encounter on land mattered little to a maritime people like the Carthaginians, whose fleets were to be found in every port and inlet of the Mediterranean, and who reigned supreme as the one commercial people of the known world. The career of these ancient rulers of North Africa, illustrious from their spirit of adventure, unflagging energy, and wondrous commerce, is a chapter of romance. Hemmed in originally between mountain and sea on the Syrian coast, a little colony of Phœnicians spread itself in a comparatively short period along the whole seaboard of the Mediterranean; then passing the Pillars of Hercules it reached Sierra Leone in the south, eastward it touched the coast of Malabar, and northward skirted the inhospitable shores of the German Ocean. It seems strange that these Canaanites or Phœnicians, the scorn of Israel, and the people against whom Joshua bent all his powers, should have enjoyed such an unchecked career, making themselves sole navigators of every sea, and finally founding a city which stood unrivalled for more than 700 years. Through their hands, as Mommsen has observed, passed grain, ivory, and skins from Libya, slaves from the Soudan, purple and cedar from Tyre, frankincense from Arabia, copper from Cyprus, iron from Elba, tin from Cornwall, wine from Greece, silver from Spain, and gold and precious stones from Malabar. As a nation of traders and navigators they established themselves on the coast, and wherever they settled depots and factories of various kinds were erected. We do not find them in the interior of a country. Neither do we hear of alliances with the people with whom they came into contact, nor of their impressing barbarian tribes with any notions of the advantages of civilisation. In the field of intellectual acquirements the Carthaginian, as the descendant of the Phœnician, has no place, and his skill in the gentler arts of life has no recognition. We find no native architecture, nor do we hear of any industrial art worth recording. Carthage, it is true, became the metropolis of their widespread kingdom, and one of the wealthiest cities of the world. But this was due, in a great measure, to its central position, and its convenience as an outlet for the vast produce of North Africa. Temples and stately edifices adorned its streets, and the remains of great constructional works still attest the solid grandeur of the city. But the architecture was the work of Greek, and not of Punic, artists; and the few sculptures of note, which may be assigned to a period anterior to the last Punic war, have nothing in common with the rude carvings which bear the impress of Carthaginian origin. On the other hand the art of navigation, the science of agriculture, the principles of trading, and a system of water supply combined with the construction of gigantic cisterns, which may still be seen at Carthage and on the outskirts of many towns in North Africa, became Rome's heritage from Phœnicia. The distinguishing characteristic of Phœnician architecture, or rather of building construction, is its massive and imposing strength, singularly deficient in fineness of detail, as M. Renan has observed, but with a general effect of power and grandeur. The few Phœnician buildings existing are constructed with immense blocks of stone, such as the ramparts of Aradus, the foundations of the temple at Jerusalem, and the earlier portions of the great temple at Baalbec.

From the day when the two nations crossed arms in the vicinity of Syracuse a kind of fatality hung over them. It seemed as if there were no room in the world for two such ambitious rivals; and that, the struggle having once commenced, it should continue till one or the other ceased to exist. The want of an efficient fleet to enable them to do battle with the Carthaginians in their own element preyed heavily upon the Romans in their Sicilian campaign. But Rome was not discouraged. With that strength of will which always characterised her people, she set to work to create a navy. In sixty days, we are told, a forest of timber was cut down, and 140 galleys, fully manned and provisioned, sailed out under M. Attilius Regulus to attack the Carthaginian fleet on their own coasts.[1] This intrepid general, inspired by the temporary success of Agathocles[2] the Sicilian, in his invasion of Carthaginian territory, contemplated a similar adventure. He captured more than 200 towns and villages and, landing Italian troops for the first time on African soil, paved the way for a more permanent occupation which was to take place after the lapse of nearly 100 years.[3] Then came the close of the first Punic war. Carthage retreated. All Sicily, except the little kingdom of Syracuse, then wisely governed by the renowned Hiero II., was abandoned to the Romans. Sardinia, which the Cartha-

[1] Polybius, i. 66. The Romans began to build ships (or rather coasting vessels) B.C. 338, and seventy years later the maritime services had assumed such importance that four quæstors of the fleet, stationed at different ports of Italy, were appointed. This provoked the jealousy of Carthage, whose supremacy at sea had for so long a period remained undisputed. (Rawlinson's *Manual of Ancient History*.) The Romans occupied the old Phœnician ports on the coast of Africa, and did not attempt, till a much later period, to form any new ones.

[2] Agathocles, an adventurous Sicilian and tyrant of Syracuse, invaded North Africa B.C. 306 and nearly ruined Carthage, either destroying or taking possession of nearly all the towns. Recalled to Sicily, he left the war in the hands of his son Archagathus, who was unsuccessful. The Carthaginians regained all they had lost. The army of Agathocles consisted of 6,000 Greeks, about the same number of European mercenaries, 10,000 Libyan allies, and 1,500 horse. (*L'Univers pittoresque*.)

[3] There is nothing on record to indicate that the Roman people, so little accustomed to maritime warfare and with a superstitious dread of the sea, encouraged so hazardous an undertaking. Regulus followed the banks of the Bagradas, laid siege to Uthina, and subsequently took Tunis. The Carthaginians engaged Greek mercenaries, led by Xantippus the Lacedemonian, who brought the war to a close. The Romans were defeated, and their fleet destroyed by a tempest. Polybius (i. 66) says that the Romans had 330 galleys and 140,000 men, and that the Carthaginian fleet consisted of 350 galleys and 115,000 men.

ginians had held for 400 years, shared the same fate. Peace was declared, or rather a respite was agreed upon by the two rivals, utterly wearied and worn out by continuous warfare of twenty years, preparatory only to a trial of strength on a more extended scale. The twenty-three years' interval of watchful unrest which preceded the outbreak of the second Punic war was among the most eventful in the whole history of the struggle. It is this period, prior to the renewal of hostilities when the fate of Carthage and her people was to be decided, which is peculiarly attractive, partly on account of the events that preceded the fall of a great nation, and partly from the dramatic career of the chief native rulers of Africa.

In order to form an idea of the vast extent and limits of Africa of the ancient world, it is necessary to glance at a map of the southern shores of the Mediterranean, to note how the country was then divided, and to sketch, as briefly as possible, the history of the tribes who contributed by their endless rivalries to hasten the Roman occupation of the entire region. Commencing westward of Cyrene[1] (a Greek colony founded about B.C. 630, and though afterwards part of the Roman Empire yet never recognised as part of North Africa) we come to Africa proper, the little corner afterwards known as Africa Provincia, of which the capital was Carthage.[2] Westward of this was the country of a people whom Greeks and Romans were accustomed to call Nomades or Numidians, divided between the Massylians on the east and the Massæsylians on the west. Beyond was the land of the Mauri, stretching round the shores of the Atlantic. Now all this vast region, from Cyrene to the Atlantic, with a seaboard of not less than 2,000 miles, had been for many centuries under the control of Carthage, furnishing large bodies of troops in time of war and contributing to the preservation of the kingdom of their enterprising masters.

[1] Cyrene was founded by Greeks from the island of Thera, one of the Sporades group in the Ægean Sea, now called Santorin. It became the capital of the region known as Pentapolis, whose five cities were Cyrene, Apollonia, Ptolemais, Arsinoe, and Berenice.

[2] Sallust divides North Africa into four regions: (1) Cyrenaica and the country of the Syrtes, the modern Barca: Tripoli, with the Fezzan in the interior; (2) the territory of Carthage, now known as Tunisia; (3) Numidia, now corresponding to Algeria; and (4) Mauritania, the modern Morocco. (*Vide* Vivien de Saint-Martin, *Nord de l'Afrique dans l'antiquité.*)

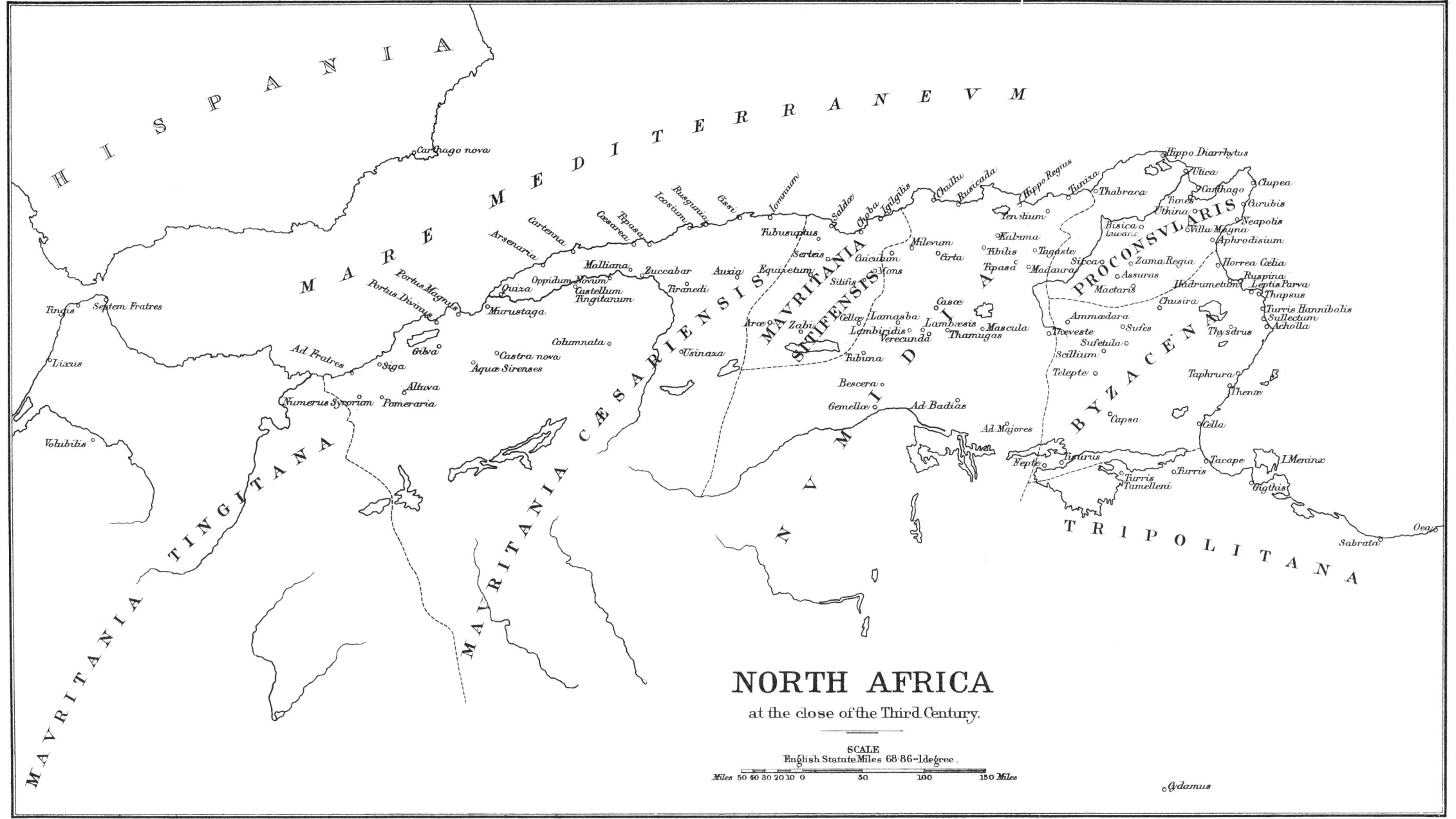

The boundaries of Punic territory appear to have been determined at a very remote period, when the neighbouring country of Cyrene had attained power and prosperity, and when the tribes of North Africa had recognised the supremacy of the Phœnician colony settled at Carthage. The river Tusca, separating Carthage on the west from the land of the Massylii, formed a natural boundary. The borders of the Desert were also a natural boundary on the south, peopled at all times, even at the present day, by numerous tribes wandering from place to place and living in incessant rivalry.[1] But the limitation of the eastern frontier, separating the Carthaginians from the Greek colony of Cyrene, did not admit of easy solution. No river or watercourse was there to mark the line of territory. No fortress or earthwork had been raised in testimony of a settlement of ancient claims. Nothing was there but shifting tracts of sand and an undefined coastline. Physical force was at last resorted to for the purpose of deciding a long-pending controversy, not the force of arms or skill with weapons, but strength of limb and endurance in a long and harassing journey. And this was the simple expedient. Two deputies on either side, probably athletes, were to leave home at a given hour, and the spot where they met should be the boundary between the two States. The names of two brothers, deputies on the Carthaginian side, are recorded; but those despatched from Cyrene have not been handed down. Neither have we any description of the race, or circumstances attending the journey. All we know is that the spot where the race terminated is designated in most charts of the ancient world as *Philænorum Aræ*, and we are told that the Cyrenians, having covered but a small distance compared with their opponents, accused them of having started before the time agreed upon. Like many a schoolboy, who is worsted in a youthful encounter, they endeavoured to account for their defeat by imputing to their adversaries that

---

[1] The country in the south between Mount Atlas and the Sahara, as far as the Niger, was inhabited by the Getuli and Melanogetuli, the Moslem Tuariks, or, as they are now called, Touaregs. (Niebuhr's *Lectures*.) Pliny also speaks of the inhabitants of the south as Getulians. They are a distinct people in African ethnology. Owing to their geographical position they were not subject to external influences. Their neighbours, the Garamantes, who occupied the country south of Tripoli as far as Ghadames, may be classed with them. (*Vide* Tissot, *Géogr. comparée de l'Afrique*, i. 447.) The limits of the country occupied by either of them are not known.

they had not played fair. A quarrel ensued, but the Philæni brothers, as the representatives of Carthage, stood firm, rooted, as it were, to the spot. To end the dispute without resorting to arms, the men of Cyrene said, 'You shall be buried alive on the spot which you claim as the boundary for your people, or we, on the same condition, shall be allowed to proceed on our journey to whatever point we may think proper.' The Philæni, it is said, accepted the terms imposed upon them, and, sacrificing themselves in the interest of their country, were forthwith buried alive. If we are to assume that the Carthaginians started from Carthage and the Greeks from the city of Cyrene, the whole story may be regarded as a fable, for the two mounds that once marked the legendary spot are not midway, but about seven-ninths the distance between the alleged starting-points. We may be permitted to suppose that the wind favoured the Philæni, and that a sand-storm, such as is prevalent in those parts, blew into the faces of their opponents and retarded their progress. To give the tale an appearance of reality we may imagine that the Carthaginians started from Leptis[1] and not from Carthage, for the mounds or altars consecrated to these heroic brothers were nearly midway between that city and Cyrene. Now Leptis was, at that period, a city of wealth and magnitude, and took rank with Utica as one of the chief Phœnician colonies. Founded by Sidonians in a prehistoric age, it grew into importance long before Carthage had attained the climax of its prosperity, and was regarded by the Carthaginians as one of their choicest possessions. Whether this old-world story of the Philæni is to be read in the light of a fable, or is based upon some incident in the settlement of a long-disputed boundary, matters little after a lapse of more than 2,500 years. The historian and the geographer have accepted the legend, and honoured it with a place in their records which time will never obliterate. But whether true or not we may receive the narrative in the form in which it has been handed down. It is good for us to think that the spirit of patriotism inspired men, in the old world as in the new, in the exercise of

[1] Leptis Magna, now Lebda, was one of the earliest Phœnician settlements in Africa. The fertility of the soil favoured colonisation, and the inhabitants, under Roman rule, were allowed to retain their old laws and customs. Commercial intercourse and intermarriage with Numidians forced them to alter their language and to adopt the Numidian tongue. (Sallust, *Jug.* lxxviii.)

Carthage and Rome

heroic deeds, and that self-sacrifice in a country's honour has never been found wanting in the hour of need.[1]

The territory occupied by Carthaginians formed only a small portion of North Africa, as we have already observed. At the time of the Roman invasion, which may be regarded as the opening of the last chapter in the history of the second Punic war, the country west of Carthage was under the rule of Gala, the tribes beyond being governed by Syphax, the most powerful of African kings at that period. The rivalry of these two potentates and their wavering policy contributed largely to the success of the Romans in the impending war. It was impossible for both these kings to form simultaneous alliances with either Roman or Carthaginian. Traditional policy seems to have inspired them with perpetual animosity; and so soon as it was known that one favoured the invading Roman, the other immediately, without any settled line of action or forecast of the consequences, formed an alliance with the Carthaginian. Both were jealous of the supremacy of Carthage, and both awaited the coming of the Roman that they might eventually participate in spoiling the Carthaginians. Syphax was at first inimical to Carthage, and subsequently a friend in an hour of need. But he changed sides again and made a treaty with Publius Scipio, who commanded the invading force. The conditions were the support and good will of the Roman Senate and people in exchange for his assistance in the field of battle. A small embassy, consisting of three centurions, was despatched from Rome with instructions to remain in Africa till a formal treaty was concluded with this potent but wayward Numidian. Syphax was flattered by the attention, entertained the ambassadors with princely hospitality, and requested that one of the centurions should be allowed to instruct his soldiers in the Roman methods of warfare. 'Numidians,' he said, 'are only horsemen. They know nothing about infantry. Teach them.' The request was complied with, and bodies of Numidians, drilled after the manner of Roman infantry, were at once formed for the purpose of defeating Carthage in the plains when the next war broke

---

[1] Strabo says that a tower called Euphrantas was the boundary between Cyrene and Carthaginian territory. The altars of the Philæni were a little to the east of this. They fell to ruin about B.C. 350. These mounds or altars, if they ever existed, may have had some resemblance to the tombs of the two Horatii near Alba, erected B.C. 673–640. These had a *podium* or wall of stone surmounted by a cone of earth.

out. Carthage was thunderstruck at these proceedings, and, nothing daunted, sent envoys to King Gala, who responded in a spirit of friendship, and at once entered into an alliance, offensive and defensive, more for the purpose of crushing his old antagonist Syphax than of maintaining the integrity of the Punic kingdom. Now Gala had a son who had just attained his seventeenth year when the embassy was despatched. This fearless youth, who lives in history as Masinissa, the hero of Numidia, was a warrior from his cradle. Without hesitation he seized the first opportunity of offering battle to Syphax. Not once only but twice he defeated him, but on the third occasion his rival was victorious. To commemorate his success over so redoubtable a warrior as Masinissa, Syphax vowed eternal friendship with Rome. Forthwith ambassadors were despatched to Italy, and in return officers of state were sent by the Roman Senate to his capital at Cirta, bearing costly presents of various kinds, including a toga, a purple tunic, an ivory throne, and a gold cup. But Syphax's happiness was of short duration. In an evil hour he fell in love with Sophonisba, the fair daughter of Hasdrubal, the Carthaginian general, and, to prove his affection for the country of his bride, thoughtlessly deserted the Roman alliance, and quartered his army in the opposing camp. This step was not lost on Masinissa, who immediately favoured the Roman cause and encamped his troops with the army of Scipio. Such a powerful alliance laid the foundation of Masinissa's fortune, and to his credit it should be said that throughout a long career he never swerved from the attachment, but remained to the close of his active life a loyal friend to Rome. The sad story of Sophonisba is soon told. On the defeat of Syphax by the all-conquering Masinissa, the victor hastened to take possession of Cirta, the capital and stronghold of his rival. At the gates he was met by the unfortunate queen, whose love and beauty had tempted the amorous Syphax to commit an act of the grossest perfidy. On bended knees and with tearful eye she implored the conqueror not to suffer her to fall into the hands of the Romans, dreading the fate that might befall her as a captive in the streets of Rome. Love and pity combined sealed her fate. Masinissa, we are told, was so struck with the beauty of Sophonisba that he sent her to his camp, and, with that impetuosity which characterises Orientals in their relations with the fair sex, married her forthwith. But love and pity had, in this case, a direful termination. Masinissa was summoned before Scipio for having taken to wife the daughter of their sworn enemy, the Carthaginian general. It may be that the Roman desired to claim Sophonisba for himself as part of the spoils of war, but history is silent on this point. All we know is that Scipio, regarding her presence in the camp as a stumbling-block to success, demanded her immediate dismissal. Such was Masinissa's dread of the exercise of Roman authority that he dared not disobey. With a tearful face he entered Sophonisba's tent, and, telling her he was powerless to deliver her from the jealousy of the Romans or the dread captivity that might befall her, besought this ill-fated bride, in pledge of his love for her and her person, to die in the manner worthy of the daughter of Hasdrubal. Silently and unmoved Sophonisba obeyed, and swallowed the poison which Masinissa ordered to be conveyed to her tent at the close of their interview.[1]

The success of Scipio, aided by his brilliant Numidian ally, had placed Carthage in sore distress. Syphax was taken prisoner to Italy, and soon closed his career ingloriously. The fleet, which had once reigned supreme, was of little service, and the army, largely composed of mercenaries, was sadly reduced in numbers and without a reliable commander. An armistice was agreed upon, and the conditions imposed by Scipio, heavy as they may seem to modern ideas, were accepted. Carthage had to surrender her territories in Spain and her island possessions in the Mediterranean, to hand over all her war vessels except twenty ships, to pay a money fine equivalent to nearly one million sterling, and finally to transfer to Masinissa the kingdom of his adversary Syphax. The events which followed, terminating on the fatal day when Scipio and Masinissa were to crush the Carthaginian army on the plain of Zama, and to close the career of one of the greatest generals in ancient or modern times,

[1] Corneille's dramatised version of this tragic story is little in accord with the statements of ancient authors. The Sophonisba of the stage had been married by Hasdrubal her father to Masinissa, but the Carthaginians, ignoring this husband, married her afresh to Syphax. Such was her affection for him that she declined to forsake his cause, although he had been twice defeated, and was prepared to bury herself with him in the ruins of his capital, even if he had suffered defeat a third time. Her attachment to her country was no less sincere than her avowed hatred of Rome.

have been so ably described by historians of all ages from Livy to Mommsen that they need only brief recapitulation in these pages. But it should be observed that the rise of Numidia at this period, as a powerful nationality under such a potentate as Masinissa, introduces a new factor in the history of Roman Africa. For fifty years Numidia is destined to play a leading part in the affairs of the country, and to contribute in a larger measure to the ultimate success of Roman arms than Latin historians are wont to acknowledge. It might be thought that researches in recent years, coupled with the diligent investigations of so many learned archæologists, would have thrown additional light on this period of African history, and cleared up many doubtful points in ancient records. But neither stone nor marble has yet been unearthed to tell its own unvarnished tale, nor has any writer succeeded in refuting the descriptive account by our great Roman historians of the last pitched battle between Carthage and Rome. The recall of Hannibal, who for thirty-six years had not set foot on his native land, and who was then devastating the plains of Italy and threatening Rome with destruction, was the signal for Rome and her allies to prepare for battle. Scipio and his army were then encamped in the valley of the Bagradas, not far from Carthage. Hannibal, who had landed at Hadrumetum, was arranging his forces, and securing, by the magic of his name, the aid of the tribes who had recently fought under the banner of Syphax. The opposing armies met at Zama, which was then a large city and stronghold of the king of Numidia, and continued to remain so at a later period. Sallust informs us that it was built on a plain, and was better fortified by art than by nature. The same authority tells us that the city existed as the bulwark of that part of the kingdom a century after the battle, for Metellus, the Roman commander, laid siege to it during the Jugurthine war. We also read of it as Zama *regia*, the capital of Juba I. in the time of Julius Cæsar. It is difficult, after a lapse of more than 2,000 years, to mark the exact site of the city, for destruction and neglect have left no tangible remains. The geography of Ptolemy, the chart of Peutinger, and the Itinerary of Antoninus where distances are given, form the only clue to the position of the battlefield, which appears to have been between the towns of El-Kef, Taoura, and Kalaat-es-

Saan. Bruce, who traversed the country in 1766, says that in proceeding in a north-easterly direction after leaving Zanfour, and traversing the plain a distance of twelve miles, 'we came to Djebel Mesaood, on the other side of which upon an eminence is a small town built from the fragments of a larger and ancient one, whose name is still called Zama, and was probably the ancient capital of Juba I.' So decisive a victory enabled the Roman general to name the conditions of peace. Had Scipio been prompted to subject Carthage to the same fate that only a few years previously Hannibal had desired to inflict on Rome, there was nothing to prevent him. He granted peace, but on heavy conditions. Carthage was to pay, in addition to the penalties previously enforced, a sum of money equivalent to 48,000*l.* sterling annually for a term of fifty years, and not to engage in arms with Rome or her allies, either in Africa or elsewhere, without the permission of Rome. It was not without grave discussion in the Senate, or the expression of many conflicting opinions, that these conditions were agreed to. As usual on such momentous occasions, when the very existence of a nation trembles in the balance, there was a peace party and a war party. The former, headed by Scipio, whose valour was only equalled by his magnanimity, prevailed. Carthage was allowed to exist for another fifty years as a tributary of Rome. But the ill-fated city was doomed to a long period of unrest and disturbance as soon as the treaty was signed and the Roman army had been withdrawn. The adversary was no longer the Roman but the powerful Numidian, who had contributed so largely to her defeat on the decisive field of Zama.

There is no name in African records which is so conspicuous, or exercised so extraordinary an influence on the career of Numidia and its people, as that of Masinissa. Fearless in action, a steadfast friend or a merciless foe, unscrupulous and of unbounded ambition, this powerful chieftain ruled for more than sixty years over a conglomeration of tribes who knew no will but his, and recognised his authority as though he were a god from Olympus. In the whole range of ancient history there was no one ever invested with kingly power who enjoyed such a career of unchequered good fortune as this remarkable man. Sober in habit and, after the manner of his race, never drinking anything but water, his physical powers were extraordinary. Riding without saddle, sometimes for twenty-four consecutive hours, and jumping on his horse like an athlete, even after he had atttained his ninetieth year, there is little wonder that history should have claimed him as the hero of Numidia. Generous in disposition, a firm ruler, and skilled in the crafty statesmanship of his time, he was free from crimes so common among uncivilised tribes. Of his domestic life we have no record, but we are told that he had forty-four children, and at his death, when he had passed his ninetieth year, his youngest son was only four years old. But his boundless activity proved disastrous to Carthage, and in later years contributed to the downfall of his own kingdom. So restless a spirit could not remain satisfied with the large territory which Rome had transferred to him. The policy of Rome was to preserve antagonism between Carthage and Numidia and to give tacit encouragement to Masinissa in his encroachments upon Carthaginian territory. Not content with appropriating the rich lands which lay in the upper valley of the Bagradas, to which he had no legal claim, he must needs occupy the old Sidonian city of Leptis Magna in Tripoli, and ultimately hem in the Carthaginian within the tract of country now represented by Tunisia. There is little doubt that, if opportunity had offered to shake off the Roman yoke without a disturbance of friendly relations, this enterprising Numidian would have occupied Carthage and made it the capital of an extended kingdom. So irritating a procedure, which continued for nearly forty years, became at last unbearable to a people who, in spite of all their shortcomings as a governing power, and their absence of respect for treaties with other countries, desired only to exist peacefully as a commercial nation, and to carry on unrestricted trade in every part of the world. An appeal to Rome was at first disregarded. Subsequently commissioners were despatched to Carthage by the Senate for the purpose of settling the long-pending disputes, and to determine the boundaries of Carthage and Numidia, but without result. Carthage was exasperated, and, not being able to make terms with either friend or foe, took the field against Masinissa, and on the first encounter suffered defeat. This action, being in direct contravention of the treaty entered into after the defeat of Hannibal, gave the Romans a pretext for declaration of war. It is but just to the Carthaginians to observe that the sacrifices they were prepared to make to avert a conflict were unlimited in respect of ships, war material of all kinds, and personal weapons. But the decree of the Senate and people of Rome was irresistible. Carthage must be destroyed, and the city must cease to exist. The events which followed the issue of this terrible edict, terminating the third and last Punic war and erasing the metropolis of the Phœnician world from the book of nations, are too well known to need recapitulation.[1] They form the last chapters of African history prior to the Roman occupation.

In the opening paragraph of this chapter it was said that the history of Roman Africa commences with the close of the second Punic war, B.C. 201; and, in support of this assertion, it may be fairly added that, till the fall of Hannibal and the recognition of Carthage and Numidia as powerful States subject to the will of Rome, Africa held no place in the Roman mind as a country adapted either for the establishment of military strongholds or for the future settlement of a civil population. To keep Carthage in subjection, to destroy her fleet, and to force her to supply the Roman army with money and provisions, seem to have met the immediate requirements of the Senate. Continuous wars in other parts of the world had decimated the Italian army, and caused sad havoc in the ranks of the male population. Colonisation on any organised plan was not even contemplated, nor do we hear of any attempt, so far as African possessions were concerned, till Julius Cæsar set the example. It is true that inhabitants of Rome and of the Italian provinces, prompted by a love of change and adventure, had migrated to towns on the African coast, and had even located themselves at Cirta, the capital of Numidia. But they were not the representatives of any organised system. All we know is, that when Jugurtha laid siege to the town, B.C. 107, he found it mainly defended by Italians, who were put to death by his orders on the surrender of the place.[2] Indeed, after the destruction of Carthage, when the ploughshare had passed over the site, and merchants from Italy crossed the Mediterranean in search of new fields for commercial enterprise, we hear of little

---

[1] To use the words of Polybius, the Carthaginians, at the suddenness of their fall, perished from off the face of the earth. Their annihilation as a people made them insensible of their misfortunes. The whole subject is admirably treated in Mr. R. Bosworth Smith's *Carthage and the Carthaginians*, London, 1877.

[2] Sallust, *Jug.* xxvi.

movement in the direction of permanent settlement in the newly acquired country. It satisfied the Roman Senate to take actual possession of the diminished territory of the Carthaginians, extending from the river Tusca in the north (now known as the Oued-ez-Zan, River of Oak-trees, or Oued-el-Kebir, the Great River) to Thenæ on the south-east (the modern Zina, not far from Sfax), and to appoint a Roman governor, whose headquarters were to be at Utica. In order to define the boundary of this territory, a ditch was cut round it on the land frontier, extending from Thabraca in the north to Thenæ on the coast. Towns and villages, which had shown loyalty to the Carthaginians, were razed to the ground, and the inhabitants sold as slaves. Confiscated lands were divided into three classes. The first became the property of the State, who let it to the inhabitants on payment of rent, or to censors who farmed the revenues. The second was sold to adventurous individuals, giving rise to the formation of extensive *latifundia*, and laying the foundation of a system of land-grabbing which excited the ire of Horace, Pliny, and other writers.[1] The third was at first held by the State, but was subsequently apportioned to the colonists of Caius Gracchus. It is stated on reliable authority[2] that no less than six thousand indigent persons, including women and children, were shipped to Carthage from Rome and the Italian provinces by this intrepid demagogue. So noble an enterprise, conducted at a time when colonisation was unknown, has given the name of Gracchus a place in history, for having established on a proper basis the principles of emigration beyond the sea. This benevolent undertaking was not attended with immediate beneficial results, and gave little encouragement to a furtherance of the scheme on a larger scale. So slow, indeed, was the progress of colonisation that, as a recent writer has observed,[3] it was not seriously commenced till two years after the battle of Actium, B.C. 29. 'The idea was one which Cæsar and his successors inherited from the democratic party, and of which the restoration of Carthage and Corinth by the dictator were the first-fruits. The objections felt to any such

---

[1] Horace, *Carm.* i. 1, 10, iii. 16, 31; Pliny, *Hist. Nat.* xviii. 6; Frontinus, *Geom.* p. 53.
[2] Appian, *Bella Civil.* i. 24; Plutarch, *C. Gracchus*, 10, 14.
[3] J. Toutain, *Les Cités Romaines de la Tunisie*, p. 27.

scheme of colonisation were founded on foolish jealousy and a fear of creating possible rivals to the world-ruling Romans.'[1]

The short period of rest, resulting from a more peaceful attitude of the native tribes, enabled the Romans to establish themselves securely at Utica, and to construct fortified posts on the line of frontier. But it soon came to an end. The kingdom of Numidia, which had been powerful and united under the firm rule of the great Masinissa, was destined to crumble away almost as rapidly as it had been formed. Amongst his numerous family there were only three sons having legitimate claim to his possessions. Their names were Micipsa, Mastanabal, and Gulussa. The two last died, or were removed early in life, leaving Micipsa in sole possession. This potentate had two sons, Adherbal and Hiempsal. He also took under his charge an illegitimate son of his brother Mastanabal, named Jugurtha, whom he educated and trained in the arts of war, and subsequently adopted, making him joint heir with his own children. The name of Jugurtha has been immortalised by the pen of Sallust, and figures largely in the early history of Roman Africa. A true Numidian, knowing neither fear nor fatigue, unscrupulous and cunning, and skilled in the arts of war and diplomacy, he stands conspicuously in the pages of the Roman historian, more on account of his heroism and endurance in the field of battle than for his conduct as the prince of a great country. The skill and generalship of Quintus Metellus and Caius Marius, combined with the treachery of his father-in-law Bocchus, king of Mauritania, brought about his downfall, after having carried on war against Rome uninterruptedly for nearly six years. There are few characters with which the schoolboy is taught to be more familiar, and which more readily excite transient admiration, than that of Jugurtha. The manly form and fair countenance of this Numidian prince, his vigour and intelligence, his wisdom in council, his skill with weapons, and a certain youthful modesty of demeanour, bearing out the statement of Sallust that 'he performed very much but spoke very little of himself,' gained for him the affection of his people and the admiration of his adversaries.

It is at this period that Mauritania, the land of the Moors, begins to occupy a place in Roman history. At the

[1] *Quarterly Review*, 1879.

commencement of the Jugurthine war, B.C. 112, the country was governed by Bocchus, who (to use the words of Sallust) 'was ignorant of the Romans except by name, and who, prior to this time, was as little known to us, either in peace or war.'[1] The immediate result of the war was that all Numidia lay at the mercy of the Romans. So vast a territory could only be held by a large army and the establishment of fortified posts on the southern and western frontiers. Rome was not prepared for so great an undertaking, preferring to reduce the strength of the country by dividing the kingdom of Masinissa into territories or provinces. The western portion of Numidia was transferred to Bocchus as the reward of treachery to his kinsman. Tripoli and the adjacent parts, that had formerly belonged to Carthage, were appropriated by the Romans. The rest of the country, still retaining the title of Numidia, was placed under the rule of an imbecile prince named Gauda, the grandson of Masinissa and the rightful heir to the throne. At the close of his brief reign Numidia was divided between his two sons Hiempsal and Hierbas, whose joint career was one of lifelong war and interminable rivalry. In the civil wars of Sylla and Marius they took opposite sides. Hierbas joined the Marian party, was besieged in the city of Bulla by the combined forces of Sylla and Pompey, defeated and put to death B.C. 81. Hiempsal, the ally of the victors, was thus established on the throne of Numidia, and had every prospect of preserving, by the exercise of tact and good government, the splendid heritage of his great grandfather Masinissa. But ill-fortune tempted him in his later days into the wrong camp, and prompted him to oppose the invading army of the all-conquering Cæsar. The sovereignty of the world was then in dispute between two noble Romans. At the outset the parties seemed fairly matched, the one, headed by Cneius Pompeius, upholding the maintenance of the authority of the Republic; the other, under the leadership of C. Julius Cæsar, advocating the principles of democracy and foreshadowing a revolution in Roman policy. During the first

---

[1] Bocchus died about B.C. 91. He left the western portion of his dominions to his eldest son Bogud, and the newly annexed portions to his second son Bocchus. Fifteen years later the names of the kings were reversed, Bogud ruling in the east and Bocchus in the west. (Vide *Rev. Afr.* xiv. 45.)

triumvirate, when Cæsar, Pompey, and Crassus divided the provinces among themselves, Africa fell to the lot of Pompey. And when the final rupture terminated in the signal defeat of Pompey in the plains of Pharsalus, Cæsar crossed the Mediterranean and invaded Africa. His first attempt to land an army at Leptis Parva (Lemta), B.C. 47, was successfully prevented. But in the following year, when the opposing forces met at Thapsus[1] (Dimas), the army of Pompey, commanded by his father-in-law Metellus Scipio and Marcus Cato, acting in conjunction with the Numidian forces under Juba I., son of Hiempsal, was utterly routed. Scipio killed himself rather than fall into the hands of Cæsar. Cato fled to Utica, and on the approach of Cæsar's army to lay siege to the city, perished by his own hand. Juba, attended by one companion, fled to Zama, where he had left his household and all his treasures. The gates of the city were closed against him by the terrified inhabitants, so the poor king, deserted and broken-hearted, fled to the woods and made away with himself. Numidia thus fell into the hands of the Romans, and became a province of the great Empire which was then being established by the first of the Cæsars.[2] The battle of Thapsus changed the whole aspect of African affairs, and enabled the conqueror to apportion the country in the manner best adapted to serve the Roman cause. For valuable assistance rendered during the campaign by Bogud, king of Eastern Mauritania (afterwards designated Mauritania Cæsariensis), the eastern boundary of his kingdom was extended as far as the river Ampsaga (Roumel); and for the services of P. Sittius Nucerinus, whose valour was conspicuous on the

[1] Shaw says that Thapsus was the largest city on the coast south of Carthage, judging by the extent of the ruins. Portions of the old harbour can still be traced, and the lines of the concrete retaining walls give indications of exceptionally massive construction. Thapsus has had a long history, and was noted as a commercial port in the earlier days of Carthaginian rule.

[2] The early history of Numidia is somewhat obscure and involved in mystery. Eusebius tells us that Hercules, after his conquest of the giant Antæus, about fifty years before the foundation of Utica and 287 years before that of Carthage, founded the town of Capsa; and that Iarbas, king of the nomadic Libyans or Numidians, sought the hand of Dido at the time that Carthage became the capital of the State. Sallust describes the Numidians as a mixture of Persians and Getulians. The word *Numidians* is the same as *Nomades*, or wanderers, a term applied in ancient times to pastoral nations without fixed abode. When the Romans took possession of Numidia they made it into a province entitled *Africa nova*, to distinguish it from Carthaginian territory, which was styled *Africa vetus* or *Africa Provincia*.

battle-field, and to whom the fall of Cirta (Constantine), the capital and stronghold of Numidia, was mainly due, Cæsar allotted the towns of Milevum (Mila), Chullu (Collo), and Rusicada (Philippeville), as well as the capital itself and the adjacent country. In the same year the little kingdom of Cyrene, which had been subservient to Rome since B.C. 74, and had been regarded as a Roman province, was handed over by the ruling king, Ptolemy Apion. All North Africa, from the borders of Egypt to the Atlantic Ocean, was now under the control of the Romans. Mauritania was preserved as a separate kingdom, remaining for nearly a century in quasi-independence. With this new order of African affairs a form of government had to be inaugurated which should prove acceptable to the native tribes and their rulers, which should respect their ancient forms of religion, and should hold in check the turbulent spirit of the populous tribes of the south. With the fall of the Roman Republic and the dawn of imperial rule commences a fresh chapter in the history of Roman Africa.

In the foregoing pages an outline of the principal events which paved the way for Roman occupation gives a fair idea of the difficulties which had to be surmounted at each successive stage. They form a prelude to a long career of peace and prosperity, disturbed at intervals by harassing warfare with untameable tribes on the Desert frontier, of successful colonisation, of progress in civil life, of encouragement of the arts of peace, and of decline in later years when the great Empire was tottering to its fall.

CHAPTER II

AFRICA UNDER THE CÆSARS

B.C. 46–A.D. 96

THE long interval between the destruction of the capital of the Carthaginians and the building of Roman Carthage is frequently lost sight of. After the fall of Punic Carthage a century elapsed before Julius Cæsar landed on the shores of Africa, and another century and a half passed before the reconstructed city became of sufficient importance to be recognised as the metropolis of the new colony. It is during the latter part of this interval that the old Tyrian settlement at Utica, founded about B.C. 1200, played a prominent part in political and commercial life. At first an *emporium* on the coast, then a walled town with a large mercantile population, governed by a Senate and suffetes, it became the chief Phœnician colony in Africa long before the foundation of Carthage. Utica retained its independence as a free republic for many centuries, but at last, being dragged unwillingly into the Sicilian wars which preceded the first encounter between Rome and Carthage, it closed an independent career by acknowledging the supremacy of its more powerful countrymen. Such was the strength of its walls and magnificent fortifications at the outbreak of the second Punic war that not even the genius of Scipio nor the gallantry of his soldiers could effect an entry into the city till after four years' protracted siege. In the troublous times that preceded the last Carthaginian war, Utica, forecasting the result of further opposition to the Romans, threw open its gates to the invading army. This step was the commencement of nearly 200 years' revived prosperity. Utica became the residence of the Roman proconsul and the metropolis of Africa Provincia. Under Augustus it obtained the rank of a *municipium*, and had a population of 40,000 within the walls. The ruined monuments covering a large tract of land bear testimony to the wealth of the city in Roman times, even at a period subsequent to the recognition of Carthage as the metropolis of Africa at the end of the first century. Under Hadrian it became a *colonia*. In its last days it was an important centre of Christianity, and the bishop of Utica held a conspicuous position among the prelates of the African Church. One of the chief causes which contributed to its final extinction as a place of renown, and which any traveller can attest, were the vagaries of the Bagradas (Medjerda) which once skirted its walls. This remarkable river, which rises in the beautiful valley of Khamisa in Algeria, and winds in a devious way across the Medjerda plain for a length of about fifty miles, has altered its course more than once. After crossing a marsh it now falls into the sea south of the lake at Porto-Farina, which is a little to the north of Utica, and about eighteen miles farther in that direction than at the period when Carthage was destroyed. The wayward action of the stream, cutting through the banks at one place and depositing its slime at another, has been a source of wonderment to many generations of men inhabiting the Medjerda plains. Legendary history, or rather tradition, asserts that on the banks of the Bagradas the great combat between the army of Attilius Regulus and a monstrous serpent took place, B.C. 225. Pliny repeats the fable, and tells us that the Romans attacked the creature with *balistæ* and other weapons of war, laying siege to it as though it were a city. It was 120 feet long, and the skin and jaws were preserved in a temple at Rome till the outbreak of the Numantian war, B.C. 133. To the vagaries of the river may be attributed this old-world legend :—at one time a sluggish stream easily traversed at any part, at another time a swollen torrent deluging the adjacent country and carrying with irresistible force sheep and oxen, houses and trees, and anything that happens to be on the verge of its troubled waters.[1] The silting up of the Gulf of Utica, which is now four miles inland, may be assigned as another reason for the decline of the city. These geographical changes appear to have occurred in the

[1] *Turbidus arentes lento pede sulcat arenas*
Bagrada, non ullo Libycis in finibus amne
Victus limosas extendere latius undas
Et stagnante vado patulos involvere campos.
Silius Italicus, vi. 141 et seq.

latter days of the Empire, for we learn that Genseric, the Vandal king, A.D. 440, used the harbour of Carthage for the purposes of the fleet with which he contemplated ravaging the coast of Sicily. One may therefore suppose that the harbour of Utica, which was so renowned for its facilities of access and so adapted for warlike purposes, was at that time useless. Again, we find no traces of Byzantine constructions, or reconstruction of Roman work so common throughout North Africa, clearly proving that Utica had lost its value as a mercantile town and a stronghold for defence.

The melancholy interest attaching to the site of any city of the old world is experienced in a marked degree when we contemplate and study the Phœnician and Roman remains of Utica. The town was built on a promontory, and appears to have been divided into two parts, one occupying a series of heights, the other, which was washed by the sea, being probably the commercial centre. Plutarch, in his life of Cæsar, says that the place was very strong and well defended, that Cato strengthened the fortifications considerably, raised the towers, and surrounded the walls with a deep ditch. Hirtius, who accompanied Cæsar in his African campaign, also informs us that the fortifications were magnificent, that the walls were twenty feet thick, with a height up to the battlements of thirty-four feet. In many respects the arrangement of the city was similar to that of Punic Carthage, and was not disturbed by the Romans when they took possession. There was a war-port of monumental character, similar to the *Cothon*[1] at Carthage and other coast towns, a palace for the admiral situated on an islet in the centre, a commercial harbour of great extent, a *Byrsa* or acropolis, and cisterns of vast dimensions. Among the buildings of Roman date were a hippodrome, a magnificent theatre, an amphitheatre and museum, temples and baths. It is difficult, in the present day, to trace the lines of all these monumental structures, many of which are indicated by undulations of the ground rather than by masses of ruined masonry. According to M. Daux, the hippodrome or circus

[1] The term *cothon* may be regarded as of Phœnician origin. We may accept the meaning attached to it by Latin commentators, and as used by the Greek historian Appianus, A.D. 123 : ' Cothones appellantur portus in mari arte et manu facti.' (M. J. Toutain, *Les Cités Romaines de la Tunisie*, p. 150 ; also cf. Ch. Tissot, *Géographie comparée de la Province Romaine d'Afrique*, p. 603.)

was 1,730 feet long and 250 feet wide. The amphitheatre, which is clearly defined, was hollowed out of a plateau on the summit of a hill. The great cisterns are six in number, side by side, each measuring 135 feet by 20 feet, with a height to the crown of the vault of 24 feet. Three of these cisterns are in good condition, and are occupied as farm-stables. Their construction is Phœnician, but the vaulting is Roman. The streets of the city were narrow, not exceeding fourteen feet, and they were paved. Servius says that the Romans borrowed the idea of street-paving from the Carthaginians—a statement which is borne out by Isidore of Seville and other writers. 'The adjacent country,' says Cæsar in his Commentaries, 'is of great fertility. The trees supply quantities of timber. The fields are covered with corn, and there is water in abundance.' To testify his appreciation of the commercial wealth of the inhabitants, Cæsar, we are told, mulcted three hundred merchants of the city in a sum equivalent to one million sterling. Plutarch also informs us that, on his return from Africa after a campaign of three whole years, Cæsar spoke of his triumph in magniloquent terms. He said that the country he had just conquered was so extensive that the Roman people might draw from it every year two hundred thousand Attic bushels of corn and three million pounds of oil.

The remains of Utica, as well as of other towns on the coast, present opportunities of comparing the Punic and Roman methods of building, in the use of stone and rubble, as well as the application of concrete or rammed earth commonly known as *pisé*. At Utica the distinction is very marked. The earliest walls, which are massive, are entirely of rubble, but the stones being small and the lime being made from the same stone, they have the appearance of concrete construction. The vaulting of Punic times is with the same materials, but the art of constructing arches by voussoirs, or of vaults on the same principle, was unknown to these Phœnician builders. The inner faces of walls appear to have been coated with thin lime, and from the absence of cut stones, the bold rounding of angles, and the prevalence of rounded forms, it would appear that implements for the dressing and squaring of stone were then unknown. The remains of the admiral's palace, which form a conspicuous mass among the ruins of Utica, are a good example of this kind of building with

VIEW OF UTICA (BOU CHATER).

rubble. At Thapsus (Dimas) the Punic sea-wall, nearly a quarter of a mile long, not yet quite destroyed, was built up in frames with small pebbles and mortar, like modern concrete construction. To use the words of Shaw, the traveller, 'the walls are so well cemented and knit together that a solid rock cannot be more hard or durable.' In walking over the ploughed fields and marshy lands of Bou-Chater, as Utica is now called, from which the sea has receded several miles, it is difficult to believe that some thirty or more feet under the surface lie the paved streets and foundations of one of the oldest known cities in the world. Although the plough literally turns up marble, it is the marble of the Roman city. Older Utica lies below. The investigations of the late M. Daux and of M. le Comte d'Hérisson, and their researches into the origin and development of Phœnician *emporia*,[1] are of comparatively recent date. A tribute of gratitude is certainly due to them for having, under great difficulties and with little information at their command, made a careful study of Utica and of the remains of other coast towns prior to the Roman occupation. Homeric Troy has been unearthed, and Mycenæ has given up its treasures. Perhaps old Utica, which flourished 3,000 years ago, may engage the attention of a future Schliemann, and throw additional light on the history of an ancient people.

A few words must suffice for the Carthage of the Romans, which has been ably described by so many writers of note. Built on the site of the older city but occupying a smaller area, it attained the climax of its prosperity early in the second century. Some idea of its magnificence can be obtained from the borrowed remains in marble and porphyry which still enrich the principal mosques and palaces in North Africa, which help

[1] M. A. Daux, *Recherches sur l'Origine et l'Emplacement des Emporia phéniciens dans le Zeugis et le Byzacium, faites par ordre de l'Empereur*, Paris, 1869; Le Comte d'Hérisson, *Relation d'une Mission archéologique en Tunisie*, Paris, 1881. The tract of country designated the *Emporia* comprises the coast of the lesser Syrtes, with the towns located there. The principal city was Leptis Minor (Lemta), where there was a considerable mercantile population. Under Carthaginian rule Leptis paid tribute to Carthage amounting to one talent a day. Another important town and port was Tacape (Gabes). Zeugitania or Zeugis, so called by Pliny and other ancient geographers, is the old Phœnician territory, afterwards peopled by Carthaginians. Byzacium or Byzacena included the country between Zeugis and Lake Triton, together with the *emporia*, on the coast. Both these regions constitute modern Tunisia.

to make Cordova one of the wonders of the Western world, and to which the sumptuous beauty of Pisa is chiefly due. El-Bekri, the Arab writer of the eleventh century, says : 'Marble at Carthage is so abundant that, if all the inhabitants of Africa were to assemble to carry away the blocks, they could not accomplish the task;' and speaking of the columns of the amphitheatre he quaintly adds : 'Two men could sit on one of the capitals cross-legged with plenty of room for a table in the middle. The shafts are fluted, white as snow, and shining like crystal.' And now of all this monumental grandeur not one stone remains on another. But it is some satisfaction to know that, if the later Carthage with its wealth of marble and mosaic no longer exists, yet the paved streets of the Punic metropolis still await the spade of the explorer some forty feet below the present surface. The few sculptures and mosaics appertaining to Roman Carthage that may be seen in the local museum, as well as those deposited some years ago by the late Mr. Davis in the British Museum, represent only a small portion of discovered remains. The majority have served to enrich many private collections. Among the mosaics recovered by Mr. Davis is one which represents some dwelling-houses apparently built against or near the city walls. This mosaic, which is of the fourth century, is a portion of a large composition representing a hunting scene, the figures being nearly half life-size. Judging from the appearance of the roofs and the general scale, these houses could not have been less than seven stories high. We know that buildings in Rome were erected of an enormous height before the time of the Empire, that during the reign of Augustus a law was promulgated by the Senate which restricted the height of buildings in the streets of Rome to 60 feet, and that subsequently in Trajan's time a limit of 70 feet was allowed, without regard to the widths of the streets. It is quite possible that the Augustan law prevailed in the rebuilding of Carthage, which was commenced during his reign, and that the Senate was powerless to impose restrictions in later times, when building ground within the city walls was of abnormal value.[1]

---

[1] Appianus, the Greek historian, who flourished in the time of Hadrian, says that the streets of Roman Carthage were narrow and irregular, and that they were paved with large flat stones. He also adds that some of the houses were six stories

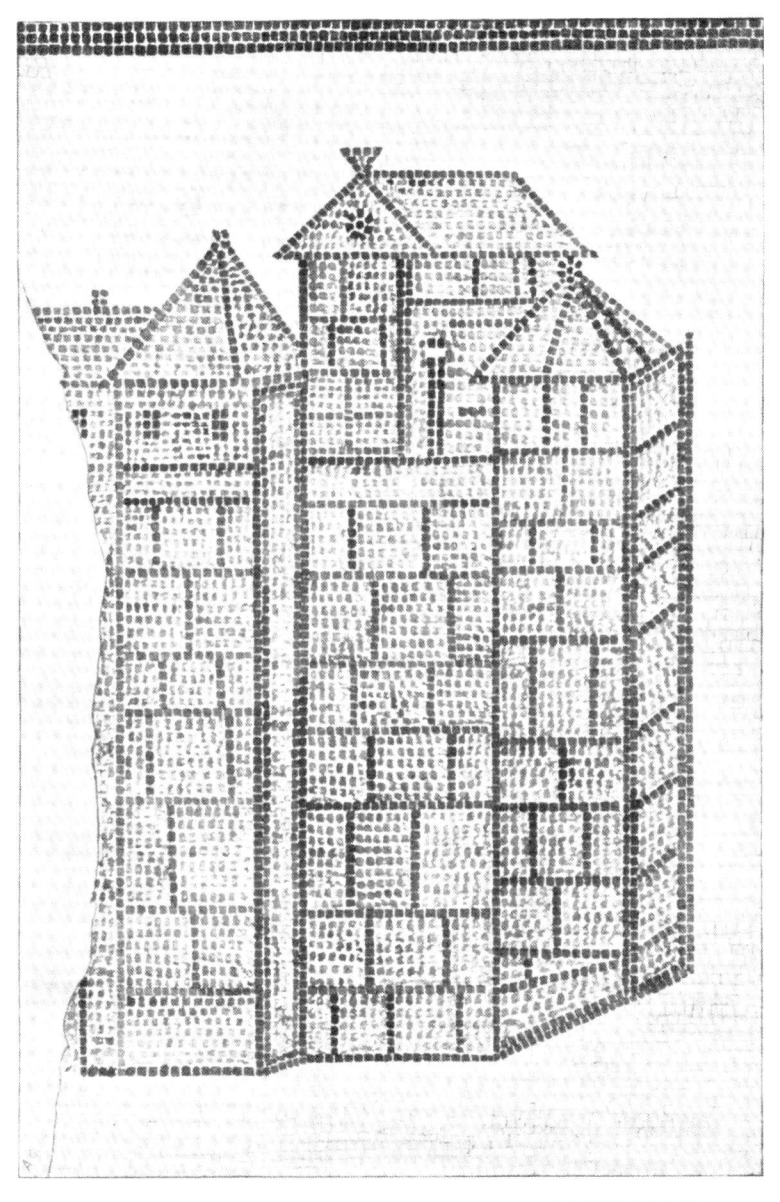

MOSAIC IN THE BRITISH MUSEUM REPRESENTING THE WALLS
OF ROMAN CARTHAGE.

The establishment of the principles of monarchy, dating from the time when Cæsar and Pompey acted in unison to overthrow the aristocratic constitution of Rome, became permanent after Cæsar's decisive victory at Thapsus. The new order of things, far from interfering with the liberty enjoyed by the native races, left them undisturbed in nearly everything except a recognition of their dependence upon Rome. Numidia, the latest acquired territory, became a Roman province under the title of *Africa nova* to distinguish it from Africa Provincia, which was now called *Africa vetus*. And as a first step towards establishing a permanent form of government, a proconsul of Numidia was appointed to reside at Cirta, the old capital of Eastern Numidia and of Masinissa's kingdom. Cæsar, in the exercise of his monarchical powers, appointed Sallust, the historian, to the post for one year, 'nominally,' says Dion, 'to govern it, but in reality to ravage and plunder it.' His recall to Rome to answer the charges of extortion made against him by Numidian chiefs was followed almost immediately by the assassination of his imperial patron. No successor was appointed. On the accession of Augustus Numidia was handed over to its rightful heir, the son of Juba I., and the direct descendant of Masinissa. This step was taken with a view to conciliating the people of the country, but chiefly for the purpose of making their king subservient to the will of Rome. The incidents in the life of this last native ruler of the Numidian kingdom are very touching, and shed unusual lustre on the closing pages of its history. This young prince, afterwards known as Juba II., was but a child when his father terminated his career so ingloriously after his defeat at Thapsus. Taken captive to Rome, he followed the chariot wheels of Cæsar in his triumphal entry into the city, and might have perished in a dungeon or met with that summary injustice which was too often meted out to the conquered in war. But a better fate was in store for him. The comely looks of the lad and his marked intelligence attracted the attention of the great Augustus, who committed him to the charge of his sister Octavia, the discarded wife of the ill-fated Antony. Devoting himself to literature and

---

high, especially in the oldest part of the town, and that the external walls, where exposed to the sea, were coated with tar.

According to Livy, Roman Carthage was twenty-three (Roman) miles in circuit. *Carthago in circuitu viginti tria millia passus patens.* (Liv. Epit. li.)

the arts of peace, the young Juba became one of the most learned men of his time. On arriving at man's estate, Augustus seated him on the throne of his ancestors, and bestowed on him the hand of Cleopatra Selene, the daughter of Antony and his Egyptian queen. Shortly afterwards the Emperor, finding it necessary, mainly on military grounds, to occupy the eastern portion of the country as a Roman province, and to establish a seat of government at Cirta, transferred Juba to the western portion, the capital being the old Phœnician city of Iol, and for a short period the capital of Mauritania.[1] This was renamed Julia Cæsarea, and is now known by its Arab name of Cherchel. Here, on this beautiful spot, washed by the shores of the Mediterranean, Juba II. reconstructed the city on a magnificent scale and embellished it with works of art from Greece and Rome. Here, during a prosperous rule of nearly fifty years, he gathered around him all the celebrities of his time in literature and art, introducing into his kingdom elements of civilisation unknown to the unruly tribes of North Africa. His only son Pompey, who succeeded him, took up arms against Cæsar, and paid the penalty of his rashness by the sacrifice of his kingdom. His daughter Drusilla, who died in a foreign land, married Felix, the governor of Judæa, before whom Paul was arraigned.[2] Had Juba II. lived in other times, his career would have entitled him to a far more conspicuous position, but the dazzling rule of the Cæsars and the stirring events in other parts of the world at the dawn of the Christian era cast into the shade the unobtrusive labours of so peaceful a monarch, affording but few materials for the historian. Such was his popularity throughout a long reign that the Athenians raised a statue in his honour, and the tribes of the

---

[1] The origin of the word Iol is uncertain, attempts having been made to associate the word with Iola, the name of one of the reputed wives of Hercules. As a Carthaginian port it was well known; but the town itself, according to Pomponius Mela, does not appear to have been of any importance in his time. He speaks of it as *Iol ad mare aliquando ignobilis* (P. Mela, iii. c. vi). At a later date Pliny refers to it as *oppidum celeberrimum*, and Procopius, in the sixth century, makes special reference to the splendour of the city and its numerous population. Vide 'Life and Writings of Juba,' by l'Abbé Sevin, in the *Mémoires de l'Académie des Inscriptions*, iv. 457.

[2] According to Suetonius, Felix married two princesses bearing the name of Drusilla, the first being the daughter of Juba, and the second a Jewess, the daughter of Agrippa. (Suet. *in Cl.* 18. Tacit. *Ann.* xii. c. 14.)

TOMB OF JUBA II

Africa under the Cæsars

Desert worshipped him as a deity : *Et Juba, Mauris volentibus, deus est.* Of his numerous literary works fragments only remain. It is enough that Strabo, Pliny, and other less prolific writers bear testimony to the value of his researches, and quote freely from his histories of Rome and Arabia, as well as treatises on various subjects. And it is enough for us that the monumental edifice which he erected to contain the ashes of himself and his Egyptian queen is still standing, though in a ruined condition, on the summit of a lonely mountain some ten miles east of his capital—an enduring memorial of the most learned, if not the greatest, of Numidians.

The form of this tomb is polygonal, surmounted by a truncated cone composed of a series of steps each 22 inches high, and terminating in a platform. The diameter of the polygon, which appears to be cylindrical, is 198 feet. It stands on a square stone platform measuring 210 feet each way. Around the polygon or podium of the structure are 60 engaged columns of the Ionic order, with Attic bases and capitals of a Greek type, and surmounted by a frieze and cornice which, as far as one can gather from the scattered fragments, had only a slight projection. The total height of the monument was originally about 130 feet, but the top courses of masonry having been thrown down it is now about 110 feet. At four places in the colonnade, corresponding to the cardinal points, are false stone doors about 14 inches thick and 20 feet high. The entrance to the tomb, which is *under* the eastern false door, was discovered by MM. Berbrugger and MacCarthy in 1866. The plan of the monument, shown on the accompanying illustration, with its spiral gallery and sepulchral chambers, is taken from the elaborate notices and measurements by those eminent Algerian scholars. After descending seven steps the gallery commences, averaging 6 feet 6 inches wide and 7 feet 10 inches high, with a total length of nearly 500 feet. The gallery terminates in two vaulted chambers 15 feet high. The first, measuring 13 feet by 4 feet 9 inches, is commonly known as 'The Chamber of Lions,' on account of a rudely sculptured lion and lioness on the doorhead. The second or central one measures 13 feet by 9 feet 6 inches. Stone doors formed of single stone slabs, fitting loosely and moving in grooves in the jambs, shut off the two chambers as well as the gallery. There are niches at intervals in the walls of the gallery to receive lamps, and in the central chamber are two niches for similar purposes or for cinerary vases. Outside and about 10 feet in front of the entrance are indications of a raised stone platform, where the ceremony of cremation was probably performed, and where the funeral urn or *cinerarium* was deposited. The external masonry of the monument is of coarse hard limestone, but the interior filling is of tufa, solidly constructed. The courses of stone are laid with great regularity, breaking bond from top to bottom. They were put together with metal cramps which have long since disappeared, though the mortices in the blocks to receive them are very conspicuous. The masonry of the gallery and the chambers is still in good preservation, having been constructed with large blocks of squared and dressed limestone, and finely jointed. Mortar, if used at all, must have been very thin, and the gallery was apparently faced with thin plaster. The dilapidated condition of the monument externally is attributable to numerous unsuccessful attempts to penetrate the interior in search of treasure, more than once with the aid of artillery. So solid is the construction that, even in its exposed situation, it might have resisted the wear of nineteen centuries and remained fairly perfect to the present day if the destructive Arab had never passed over the land.

During a long period succeeding the Roman occupation of North Africa, when the country was overrun successively by Vandals, Byzantines, and Arabs, the traditions associated with this gigantic tomb and the purposes of its erection seem to have been forgotten. So recently as the time of Shaw it was known by the Arab name of Maltapasi, or Treasure of the Sugarloaf. How it came to receive the absurd appellation by which it is now universally known, 'Le Tombeau de la Chrétienne,' is not difficult to explain. Hear what Dr. Judas, a learned Orientalist, says on the subject. The term Kubr-er-Roumiah of the Arabs is the ancient Phœnician designation which, taken in its original sense, means 'Tombeau Royal.' The natives, instead of translating this foreign word Roumiah, as they ought to have done, have given it the same meaning as a similarly sounding word in their own language, Roumi, viz. 'Strangers of Christian origin,' the feminine being Roumiah. And the French mistranslation originated in a misinterpretation of a feature in the

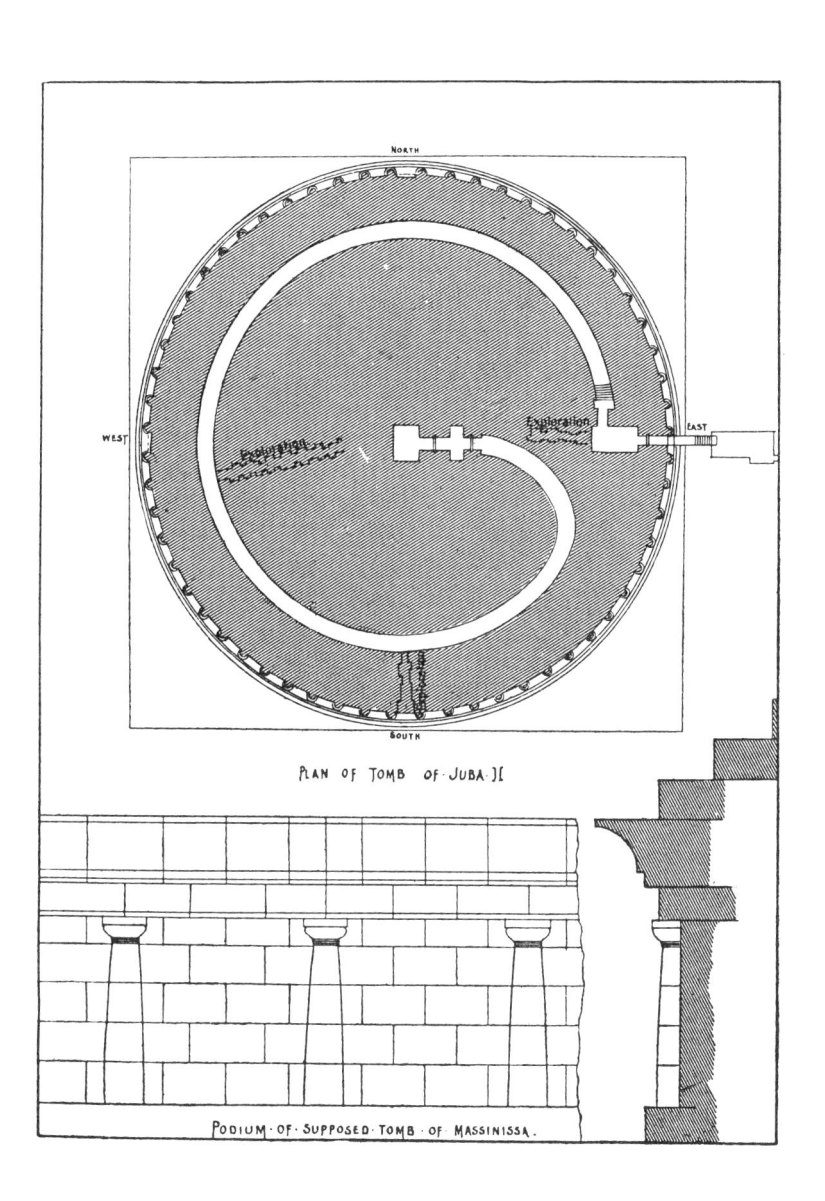

PLAN OF TOMB OF JUBA II

PODIUM OF SUPPOSED TOMB OF MASSINISSA.

Ionic Capital

Entrance to Tomb of Juba II.

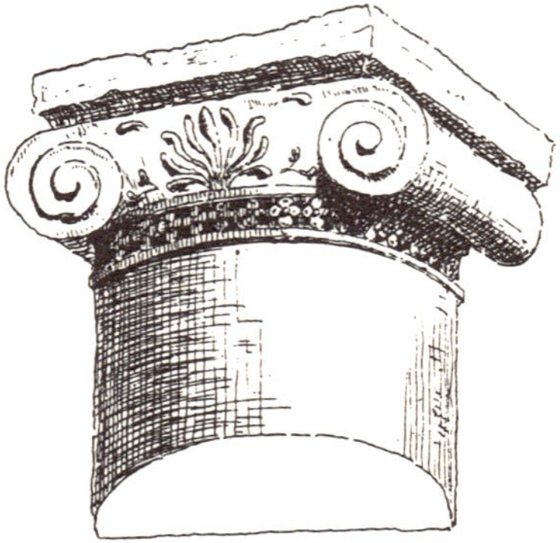

architecture, the stiles of the four-panelled stone doors being mistaken for crosses. Hence it was inferred that such a tomb must have been that of a Christian! 'The name is preserved,' says Dr. Judas, 'but nevertheless we must protest against its absurdity.' Leaving this tangle of French and Arabic, we turn with satisfaction to the pages of Pomponius Mela, a geographer of the first century who had seen this monument, probably in the lifetime of Juba II., and we find it described in simple language as '*Monumentum commune regiæ gentis.*' That it was intended as the common sepulchre of Juba and his descendants is clear enough; but his dynasty, as we have said, was short-lived. It is worthy of mention, in concluding an account of this edifice, that vegetation is so luxuriant on its conical top that some years ago M. Jourdain, the naturalist, found ample matter for a pamphlet entitled *Flore murale du Tombeau de la Chrétienne.*

Mention should here be made of a similar tomb about fifty-two miles south of Constantine, called by the Arabs the Medrassen, probably after a tribe known as the Madres, who occupied a neighbouring territory on the northern slopes of the Aures mountains. By some it has been thought to be the sepulchre of Syphax, and there is a tradition that the monument was raised by the Emperor Probus in honour of the African chief Aradion, who fell bravely in his last struggle with the soldiers of the Empire. We may pass by these conjectures, for it is tolerably certain that the edifice was built by Masinissa as a sepulchre for himself and his descendants, or by his son and successor Micipsa. Its situation in the centre of his kingdom, and at a convenient distance from his new capital Cirta, favours this supposition. There is no sufficient ground for supposing it to have been built by Syphax, for it must be remembered that, till the last year of his reign, his capital was at Siga, on the western frontier of his dominions. Moreover, Syphax was led captive to Rome and died in prison.

The form of the tomb is cylindrical, surmounted by a truncated cone composed of a series of steps, each being 21 inches high. The cylinder, having a diameter of about 190 feet, is ornamented by 60 engaged columns with a frieze and cornice, and stands on three steps forming a base to the entire monument. The material of the facework is a fine sandstone, but the mass of the structure is formed of thin slabs of inferior stone in regular courses, having at a distance the appearance of bricks. The columns and cornice are Egyptian in character. The capitals are Greek. The monument, in fact, is one of the few existing buildings in North Africa which mark the transition between Egyptian and Greek art, and was probably the work of an architect from the neighbouring colony of Alexandria towards the close of the second Punic war, B.C. 201. The entrance to the sepulchral chamber, which is nearly in the centre of the monument, is above the cornice on the west side, and is approached by a series of steps and a straight narrow gallery. The tomb has been ransacked from time to time in search of treasure, and, from the charred appearance of some of the masonry, attempts must have been made to set it on fire. It was not till 1873 that the French engineers succeeded in finding and effecting an entry, and, after much patient labour, discovered the sepulchral chamber measuring 10 feet 3 inches by 4 feet 7 inches. Nothing of value is stated to have been found during the exploration. The points of resemblance between these two monuments, the Medrassen and the so-called Tombeau de la Chrétienne, are very striking, leaving no room for doubt that one furnished the idea for the other. Their value must be estimated, not on the ground of any special artistic merit, but as links in a long chain of architectural history, and as memorials of two men whose names will be for ever associated with that old-world country Numidia.[1]

The remains of Juba's renowned capital, *splendidissima colonia Cæsariensis*, as it is designated in one of the numerous inscriptions, are very extensive. Sacked by Firmus in the fourth century, it was razed to the ground by the Vandals a century later. Under Barbarossa it regained something of its former splendour, but the city was almost entirely overthrown by an earthquake in 1738. After such vicissitudes it is not surprising to find the remains in a fragmentary condition.

[1] A somewhat similar monument is that of El Djedar in Oran. And in Western Algeria, not far from the village of Frenda, is a group of smaller tombs in the form of low pyramids supported on square, instead of circular or polygonal, podiums. The largest is about forty-three feet high, the podium being about ten feet. The entrance was from the top of the podium, descending by a flight of steps to a vaulted corridor communicating with the sepulchral chambers in the centre of the monument.

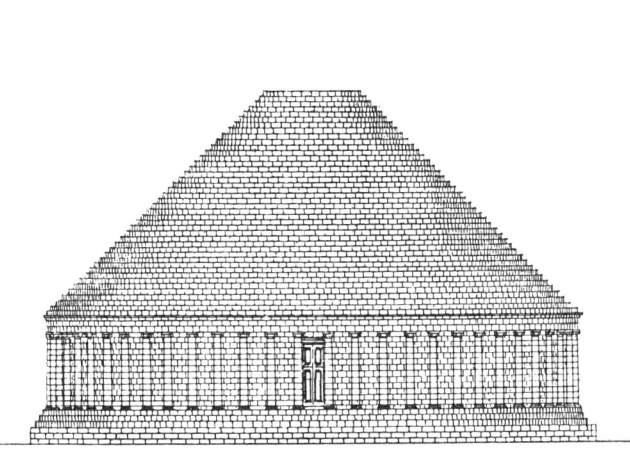

TOMB OF JUBA II.
(RESTORED.)

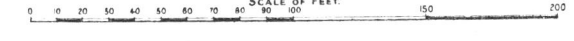

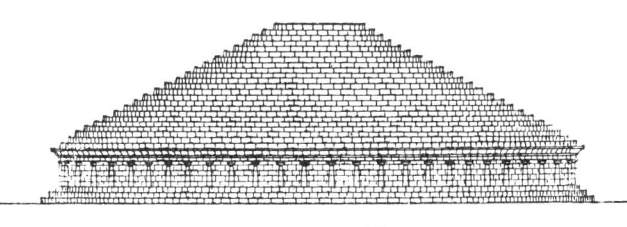

SCALE OF FEET
0 10 20 30 40 50 60 70 80 90 100   150   200

SUPPOSED TOMB OF MASSINISSA.
(RESTORED.)

'Nothing,' says Shaw in 1730, 'could have been better contrived, either for strength or beauty, than the situation of this city. A strong wall, forty feet high, buttressed, and winding nearly two miles along the shore, secured it from all encroachments from the sea.' The outlines of the amphitheatre, choked with some twelve feet of earth, may still be traced in the middle of a ploughed field. Nearly all the steps have disappeared, and the blocks of stone and marble with which the edifice was constructed have been regarded as a quarry for many centuries past. The great cisterns, storing more than four million gallons, are still used as reservoirs, and in connection with the same system of supply as the ancient city. The principal *thermæ*, the façade of which was more than 300 feet long, are scarcely traceable in outline, though the huge masses of solid walls still standing give a fair idea of the magnificence of the edifice. There were at one time two other palatial baths, the remains of one of them being still visible by the seashore. The hippodrome, which some seventy years ago was in fair preservation, with its portico and columns of marble and granite, is now a mere undulation of its surface. The blocks of stone have been removed, and the débris accumulated during this long interval has almost obliterated the outline. There is little doubt that Julia Cæsarea remains to be unearthed. Whenever excavations have been made, architectural fragments have been brought to light: columns of black diorite, shafts of white marble, busts and broken statuary, many of them replicas of Greek statuary ordered by Juba for the embellishment of his city. Some of them are still stored in the little museum at Cherchel, sufficiently attesting the splendour of Juba's capital and his appreciation of the work of Greek artists. Outside the city are the remains of the aqueduct which conveyed the waters of Djebel Chennoua. Eighteen arches only remain. When Bruce visited Cherchel in 1765 he found the aqueduct in much better condition. A drawing made by him has been preserved, showing a triple series of arches, rising in one part to the height of 116 feet.[1]

[1] The construction of this aqueduct, which is a conspicuous object in the landscape, is very irregular, and will not bear comparison with the great aqueduct of Carthage. The span of the arches is about nineteen feet, and the thickness of the piers averages fourteen feet.

The administration of the provinces which constituted Roman Africa in the early days of the Empire presented many difficulties, owing to the uncivilised and restless character of the natives in the interior, and the uncertain attitude of the tribes on the Desert frontier. Prior to the accession of Caligula, A.D. 37, the general commanding the Roman army in Africa was proconsul of Africa and Numidia, but that emperor separated the civil establishment from the military. Under his successor Claudius the system of government was definitely organised, and the older province, *Africa vetus*, was administered by a proconsul nominated by the Senate and selected from that body. His functions were both civil and military. He was chosen for his merits as a ruler and for his high social position, much in the same way as the governor of a colony of the British Empire. He held office for one year, resided at Carthage, and received a fixed salary equivalent to 8,000*l*. sterling. The newer province of Numidia, *Africa nova*, was administered by a *legatus*, or lieutenant-general, selected from the Senate and approved by the Emperor. He resided at Cirta, had the command of the Roman troops permanently stationed in Africa, and was responsible for the security of both provinces, as well as the maintenance of order on the frontiers. He held command at the pleasure of the Emperor, and was called *legatus Augusti pro prætore legionis III Augustæ*, abbreviated generally to *legatus Augusti pro prætore*.[1] Beyond Numidia, extending from the river Ampsaga (Roumel), lay Mauritania, which was divided by Claudius (after the murder of Ptolemy, son of Juba II, by his predecessor) into two provinces, the eastern portion being called Mauritania Cæsariensis, with Cæsarea for its capital, and the western portion Mauritania Tingitana, deriving its name from the chief town in that region, Tingis (Tangiers). Each of these provinces was governed by a

---

[1] (*C. I. L.*) No. 10165. *Ann. de Const.* 1858-59, p. 181.

Corpus Inscriptionum Latinarum (*C. I. L.*), vol. viii. part 1, entitled *Inscriptiones Africæ Latinæ*, Gustavus Wilmanns, Berlin, 1881.

A supplement entitled *Inscriptiones Africæ Proconsularis Latinæ*, Renatus Cagnat and Johannes Schmidt, Berlin, 1891.

Vol. viii. part 2, entitled *Inscriptiones Africæ Latinæ*, Gustavus Wilmanns, Paris, 1881.

A supplement entitled *Inscriptiones Provinciæ Numidiæ Latinæ*, Renatus Cagnat, Johannes Schmidt, and Hermannus Dessau, Berlin, 1894.

procurator,[1] who, according to Dion Cassius, was of equestrian rank.[2] This continued till the third century, when the title *procurator* was superseded by *præses*. These four Roman provinces of Africa constituted four gradations of civilisation, the first bidding fair to rival Rome and Alexandria in wealth, culture, and general prosperity, and the last scarcely removed from barbarism, inhabited by tribes whose petty rivalries were the cause of constant disturbance.

The Roman occupation of Mauritania dates from the fall of Ptolemy, A.D. 39. In contrast with the career of his distinguished father, the short reign of this unworthy prince was marked by misgovernment and debauchery.

It is to be regretted that the name of Juba II does not appear on any inscribed stone yet discovered, but the name of the son is recorded on a slab of marble at Saldæ (Bougie) :[3]

REGI · PTO
LEMAEO
REG · IVBAE · F

Another discovered at Algiers and deciphered by Renier runs thus :

Regi Ptolemæo, regis Jubæ filio, Lucius Cæcilius Rufus, Agilis filius, honoribus omnibus patriæ suæ consummatis de sua pecunia faciendum curavit et consecravit.[4]

The earliest attempts at colonisation in Africa by C. Gracchus, after the destruction of Carthage, proved, as already remarked, unsuccessful, and *Colonia Junonia*, as it was called, was abandoned. To Julius Cæsar and his successor must be accorded the honour of establishing on a permanent basis a system of colonisation which soon spread through the Roman provinces. By imperial order 3,000 Italian colonists were located in Carthaginian territory, and under the protection of Rome and Carthage throve with amazing rapidity. Utica, hitherto the capital and principal commercial city in the province, had already received the privilege of Latin rights as some compensation for the favours shown to its distinguished competitor, and was in a position to reassert its claims as one of the chief ports of the Mediterranean.[5] In Numidia an advance

[1] *C. I. L.* Nos. 9362, 9363.   [2] Dion Cassius, lx. 9.   [3] *C. I. L.* No. 8927.
[4] *Inscriptions Romaines de l'Algérie* (*I. R. A.*), par Léon Renier, Paris, 1858 ; *I. R. A.* No. 4049. Berbrugger, *Rev. Afr.* i. p. 57.
[5] Mommsen's *History of Rome*, iv. 544.

was made by conferring the rights and privileges attached to Roman military colonies upon Cirta the capital, as well as on other towns which had been assigned to Publius Sittius and his troops, for great services rendered to the State. Many towns in the interior, which the insane fury of Juba I had rendered desolate, were not revived till a later period, but the great Julian colonies, Carthage and Cirta, became at once the centres of Africano-Roman civilisation.

From the date of the decisive battle of Actium, B.C. 31, to the latter days of the reign of Tiberius, an interval of more than sixty years, North Africa enjoyed a period of rest which helped forward the cause of civilisation. The gentle rule of Juba II in the western province, and the endearing regard with which he was held by turbulent tribes on the frontier, checked insurrection and spread the arts of peace among a lawless population scarcely removed from barbarism. But no sooner had his worthless son Pompey ascended the throne of Mauritania, and commenced a career of misgovernment and debauchery, than a revolution broke out. Tacfarinas, a Numidian and a deserter from the Roman army, where he held command of an auxiliary force—a bandit rather than a warrior—raised the standard of revolt, and drew to his camp a motley herd of miscreants, adventurers, and cut-throats. Amongst them was a Moor named Mazippa, to whom Tacfarinas gave the command of the scum of his army, with permission to carry on the war with fire and sword, and to show no mercy to town or village in his march of destruction. Reserving for himself the better disciplined troops, whom he trained and armed after Roman methods, this daring Numidian drew the Roman legions after him, sometimes in the plains, at others on the hillsides, in the vain hope of tiring them out with the fatigue of constantly shifting their camp and countermarching in a difficult country. For seven whole years Tacfarinas carried on this predatory warfare with varying success, and, in the words of Tacitus, *sparsit bellum*. Rome was alarmed for the safety of her African possessions, for we are told that the Emperor Tiberius, in addressing the Senate, implored them to select for proconsul a man of military experience, blessed with a vigorous constitution, and capable of bringing this disastrous war to a close. Tacfarinas was at last taken by surprise near Tubusuptus (Tiklat) by the army of

P. Cornelius Dolabella, proconsul of Africa; and, finding his forces decimated and no hope of retreat, he rushed fearlessly into the fight and died like a true Numidian. The war was over, and a cry of deliverance went through the land: *is demum annus populum Romanum longo adversum Numidam Tacfarinatem bello absolvit.*

To encourage growth of population and to promote assimilation of the Roman with native races, the first Emperors established on the old Carthaginian highways colonies of veterans, as they were called, all men of approved military experience. They were exempt from taxation and had many privileges, but held themselves in readiness to bear arms in times of war or local disturbance. Some of the native towns, which had been partly deserted after the overthrow of the Carthaginians, were peopled with Italians, and fortified villages were built at points of vantage near the frontiers. There are records of nearly fifty such towns at this period, many of which had been Punic or Numidian. These were renamed by order of the Emperors. It may be assumed that the principal ones were occupied by colonies of soldiers who had done good service in battle, or had lost their substance in the service of the State. Among the most noticeable were Uthina (Oudena), Maxula (Mascula), Thuburbo major (Tebourba), and Sicca Veneria (El-Kef). Their monumental remains bear ample testimony to the prosperity they attained at this remote period.

The constitutional difference between *municipia* and *coloniæ* has given rise to much controversy, and it is only by a comparison of the opinions expressed by able authorities that a clue can be found to a fairly accurate interpretation of these terms. Suetonius says that *municipia* were foreign towns which had obtained the rights appertaining to Roman citizens. They were of different kinds. Some enjoyed all the rights of Roman citizens, except those which could not be held without residing in Rome, while others were invested with the right of serving in the Roman legions, but could not hold civil office, nor had they the privilege of voting. The *municipia* had their own laws and customs, and they were not obliged to accept Roman laws unless they chose. Gibbon is quite explicit on the subject, He tells us that 'a nation of Romans was gradually formed in the provinces, by the double expedient of introducing colonies, and of admitting the most faithful and deserving of the provincials to the freedom of Rome. Throughout the Empire districts were reserved for the establishment of colonies, some of which were of a civil, and others of a military nature. In their manners and internal policy the colonies formed a perfect representation of their great parent; and as they were soon endeared to the natives by the ties of friendship and alliance, they effectually diffused a reverence for the Roman name, and a desire, which was seldom disappointed, of sharing, in due time, its honours and advantages. The municipal cities insensibly equalled the rank and splendour of the colonies; and in the reign of Hadrian it was disputed which was the preferable condition of those societies which had issued from, or those which had been received into, the bosom of Rome.'[1] Liddell, another able authority, says that, in considering this question of *coloniæ*, we must dismiss from our minds those conceptions of colonisation which are familiar to us from the practice of ancient Greece or of the maritime States of modern Europe. Roman colonies were not planted in new countries by adventurers who found their old homes too narrow for their wants or their ambition. The colonies of Roman citizens consisted usually of 300 men of approved military experience, who went forth with their families to occupy conquered cities of no great magnitude, but important as military positions. The 300 families formed a sort of patrician caste, while the old inhabitants sank into the condition formerly occupied by the plebeians at Rome. The heads of these families retained all their rights as Roman citizens, and might repair to Rome to vote in the popular assemblies.[2] The same author says with regard to *municipia* that 'they furnished certain contingents of troops, which they were obliged to provide with pay and equipments while on service, provisions being found by the Romans. Their privileges consisted in freedom from all other taxes, and in possessing more or less completely the right of self-government. They were thus exempt from all tribute or toll paid to Rome, except military service. They administered their own laws. They exercised the civil or private rights of Roman citizens; but none, without special

---

[1] Gibbon's *Decline and Fall of the Roman Empire*, vol. i. p. 172.
[2] Liddell's *History of Rome*, vol. i. B. 3, c. 27.

grant, had any power of obtaining political or public rights. There was considerable diversity of condition among the *municipia.*' Another writer [1] defines a colony as 'part of the Roman State. There were Roman colonies and Latin colonies. The members of a Roman colony, *colonia civium Romanorum*, must have always had the same rights which, as citizens, they would have at Rome,' but the conquered people among whom the Romans sent their colonists were not Roman citizens. The power of Rome over her colonies was derived, says Niebuhr, 'from the supremacy of the parent State, to which the colonies of Rome, like sons in a Roman family, even after they had grown to maturity, continued unalterably subject.' On the subject of *municipia* a well-known writer [2] says they 'had a narrower import after B.C. 90, and signified the *civitates sociorum* and *coloniæ Latinæ*, which then became complete members of the Roman State. Thus there was really no difference between *municipia* and *coloniæ*, except in their historic origin and in their original internal constitution. The Roman law prevailed in both.' M. J. Toutain, the most recent writer on the subject, says that the terms *colonia* and *municipium*, used as the official titles of several African cities, had each its own meaning, and that the conditions of the *municipia* were inferior to those of the *coloniæ*.[3] But he adds that the words lost their respective significations at a later period of the Empire, and were employed indifferently.

The colonies sent out by Augustus and his immediate successors were essentially of a military character, and differed in many respects from those referred to by Tacitus a century later.[4] Whereas the former were composed of veterans commanded by military tribunes, the latter were chosen haphazard from the army, but not banded together by old associations or the ties of mutual interest. Tacitus speaks deploringly of this class of *coloniæ*, and almost refuses to mention them by that designation. We learn from Pliny, who speaks of colonies

[1] Smith's *Dict. of Class. Antiq.* art. 'Colonia.' [2] *Ibid.*
[3] Toutain, *Les Cités Romaines de la Tunisie*, Paris, 1895, p. 324.
[4] It is worthy of mention that *Londinium* (London) was not even a *colonia* when C. Suetonius Paulinus, the general, and afterwards governor of Britain, A.D. 60, marched through the town (Tacitus, *Ann.* lib. xiv. c. 33). Richard of Cirencester mentions nine *coloniæ* in Britain, of which *Londinium* was one ; and two *municipia*, *Eboracum* (York) and *Verolamium* (St. Albans).

in the province of Africa as *coloniæ*, and municipia as *oppida civium Romanorum*, that classification extended still further. There were *oppida libera*, which had the privilege of self-government, and there were *oppida* simply. These were probably inhabited entirely by natives having their own laws and preserving their own language. Pliny also mentions one *oppidum stipendiarium*, which paid a fixed tribute to Rome; one *oppidum Latinum*, which had only Latin rights; and one *oppidum immune*, which was free from tribute. In short, *coloniæ* were communities founded by genuine colonists, *municipia* were towns in which all the inhabitants had rights of Roman citizenship, *oppida Latina* were towns enjoying the same privileges as were formerly accorded to members of the Latin confederation, and the rest were provincial communities and towns with varying privileges.

The spread of colonisation and municipal life was restricted to towns on the coast or a few fortified cities in the interior, till about the time of Vespasian. Absence of roads, general ignorance of the country and its inhabitants, and the want of fortified outposts checked the enthusiasm of the Cæsars in their eagerness for the entire subjugation of Africa. The peculiar configuration of Africa, from Tripoli westward to the Atlantic, and from the Mediterranean southward to the Great Desert, has always been a bar to permanent civilisation. Until the arrival of the Romans no one of the native tribes, however successful in predatory warfare or distinguished for those daring qualities which were so conspicuous in Masinissa and Jugurtha, had ever contemplated the conquest of the inhabitants of mountainous regions. On the southern frontier it was as impossible then as it has proved to be after a lapse of 2,000 years. Looking southward from the Mediterranean we have the coast country, known as the Tell of modern Algeria, a region of undulating fertile soil, v aryingin width from fifty to a hundred miles, intersected by ravines and attaining considerable altitude in those parts now occupied by Khabyles. Behind are the high plateaux, mostly lying between two long crests of mountain ranges, where the soil is variable, some highly productive, but hardened by a tropical sun, dotted with salt-marshes and rising in terraces till they attain an altitude of nearly 7,600 feet. These table-lands, which once contributed largely to the wheat supply of Rome, were in high

Africa under the Cæsars

cultivation long before the arrival of the Romans. The general aspect must have been much the same as in the present day. Road communication had been established by the Carthaginians along the coast and to a few towns in the interior, but it was not till the time of Trajan that impetus was given to any organised system of road construction. When the southern territory of the Carthaginians, extending from Thenæ on the coast to the borders of Tripoli, had been handed over to Masinissa by the Romans at the close of the second Punic war, that enterprising Numidian attempted to alter the nomadic lives of his people by settling them in small towns or villages, linked together by a chain of roads. We have no record of the success of his scheme. All these roads formed part of a network of military highways which traversed the country in all directions early in the second century, and portions of which still unexpectedly greet the traveller's eye in journeying through regions which are apparently trackless. From Carthage, the new metropolis of Africa, there were only two roads. One went in a north-westerly direction to Utica, and then by way of Membro to Hippo-Diarrhytus (Bizerta). The other, skirting the north side of the Lake of Tunes (Tunis), had two branches. One went direct west to the banks of the Bagradas (Medjerda), and, crossing the river at a place called Djedeida, went to Teburbo minus (Tebourba), Bulla Regia (Henchir Hammam Darradji) and Simittu (Chemtou), terminating at Hippone (Bone). The other branch, after passing the salt lake of Tunis, now called Sebkha es-Sedjoumi, continued as far as Theveste on the southern frontier. From Cæsarea (Cherchel) one road followed the shore, and another passed through the valley between the Great and Little Atlas. But the principal highway from this city traversed the banks of the Chelif and went by way of the plains to Sitifis (Setif) and Cirta (Constantine), the capital of Numidia. From Cirta there was a road to the coast at Rusicada (Philippeville), and from Kalama (Guelma) in the interior two roads—one to Hippo Regius, and the other by way of Naragarra and Sicca Veneria (El-Kef) to Bulla Regia, and so on to Utica and Carthage. A southern road went through Zama to Hadrumetum (Susa) on the coast, continuing to Thysdrus (El-Djem) and Thenæ; whilst another highway of considerable importance linked together the well-known towns of Lambæsis (Lambessa),

Thamugas (Timegad), Theveste (Tebessa), Ammædara (Hydra), and Telepte. Still further south, some few leagues north of Lake Triton, there was a road from Capsa (Gafsa) binding together a long line of military outposts, and extending eastward as far as Cyrene. Hippo Regius was the starting-point of seven roads, and Lambæsis, the great military centre of the country, was provided with three highways, one going north to Sitifis, another to Cirta, and a third to Theveste. This last town was the junction of not less than eight roads, and, during the first century of the Christian era, took rank as one of the most important towns in North Africa. Of any highways in Mauritania west of Cæsarea we have no mention till a later period. The *Tabula Itineraria Peutingeriana*, as it is termed, now in the library at Vienna, makes no reference to them, and the Itineraries of Antoninus, in the form handed down to us, throw no light upon the course of any military highways in the western provinces. A dearth of inscriptions in the days of the Cæsars leaves us in considerable doubt as to the actual course of many of the roads in more elevated regions, and the absence of milliary columns, so numerous in the time of Trajan and the Antonines, has made it difficult to ascertain the correctness of statements by ancient authors and geographers. Still there is sufficient evidence of the thoughtfulness of the Romans, as a great road-making nation, in covering the country, wherever practicable, with a network of roads, and constructing the chief military highways with such imperishable materials that portions of them remain to the present day. Roman roads in North Africa were of two kinds, either paved with flat stones or macadamised. The paved roads were constructed with stone slabs in squares, or laid diamond-wise. The others were made with broken rubble or gravel, differing from English roads of that type by being laid with cement, and having kerbs of cut stone at the sides.

Although the rule of the Cæsars may be regarded as experimental, yet it laid the foundations of a system of government which resulted in a long era of wealth and prosperity. Few of the Cæsars had personal acquaintance with this splendid appendage to the Empire. Carthage claims the distinction of having been the first Roman colony established out of Italy, and Hadrian was the first of the emperors to make a systematic tour through nearly every part of his dominions; and, consequently, personal acquaintance with the native races he was called upon to govern contributed largely to his success as a ruler of mankind. It is true that Julius Cæsar spent three entire years in Africa, but this was in the declining years of the Republic, prior to his assumption of the dictatorship. Many of his successors, too, were acquainted with Africa, having filled the office of proconsul in the earlier portion of their career. The work of Augustus consisted in maturing a system of government, both civil and military, on the lines laid down by his predecessor, quelling disturbances on the frontier, and forming an African army which was destined to play an important part as the third Augustan legion. We are told that this legion was first quartered in Asia, but, by the orders of Tiberius, was removed to the neighbourhood of Theveste (Tebessa) at the time of the insurrection of Tacfarinas. It appears to have been encamped there till Theveste was rebuilt by Vespasian. Caligula's work in Africa seems to have been restricted to the murder of Ptolemy, the misguided son of Juba II., and the last of a line of Numidian kings. The only act of Claudius worth mentioning was the division of Mauritania into two provinces, but this was an imperial necessity. The record of Galba, like that of Nero, is a blank, although it must be admitted that, as proconsul of Africa, his career was distinguished for great activity, and by the exercise of sound judgment in the discharge of the duties of his high office. Vitellius also was proconsul in his earlier years, and, notwithstanding the ignominy attached to his name as an emperor, governed Africa with singular integrity for two years, acting in the latter year as deputy for his brother who succeeded him as proconsul. Vespasian's active career of ten years proved of great service in the cause of good government. During his reign the third Augustan legion was established at Theveste, and the town rebuilt and enlarged. Among the principal places associated with his name Icosium is worthy of passing mention, especially as its modern representative, the city of Algiers, has played so great a part in the life and progress of North Africa. A modest inscription on a stone built into the wall of a house in Algiers attests the existence of the old Roman town.[1] Beyond this it has no value.

[1] *I. R. A.* No. 4052. Berbrugger, *Notice sur les Antiquités Romaines d'Alger*, fig. H.

P · SITTIO · M · F · QVIR	
PLOCAMIAN	
ORDO	*Publio Sittio, Marci filio, Quirina*
ICOSITANOR	*tribu, Plocamiano, ordo Icositanorum,*
M · SITTIVS · P · F · QVR	*Marcus Sittius, Publii filius, Quirina*
CAECILIANVS	*tribu, Cæcilianus pro filio pientissimo*
PRO · FILIO	*honore recepto impensam remisit.*
PIENTISSIMO	
H · R · I · R	

The short rule of Titus, which was conspicuous for propriety and restraint, was followed by the persistent cruelty of his brother Domitian, who brought to a disgraceful end the reign of the twelve Cæsars.

It has been already observed that there is a dearth of inscriptions in North Africa relating to the earlier emperors. Most of those which have been discovered are so fractured as to be scarcely legible, but mention may be made of a slab found at Ain Khenchla, the ancient Mascula, on which is recorded a simple dedication to the Emperor Augustus by the Roman colonists and the natives of that city.[1]

DIVO AVGVSTO
SACRVM
CONVENTVS
CIVIVM ROMANOR
ET NVMIDARVM QVI
MASCVLAE HABITANT

Another inscription of about the same date was found near the ruins of the supposed city of Zama, and is of special interest as a memorial of the celebrated Empress Livia, who exercised her powers of fascination over Augustus, and ultimately became his third wife.[2] As Livia died A.D. 29 at the advanced age of eighty-six, it is probable that the dedication is of that year.

IVNONI · LIVIAE · AVGVSTI · SACRVM
L · PASSIENO · RVFO · IMPERATORE
AFRICAM . . . . OBTINENTE
CN · CORNELIVS · CN · F · COR · RVFVS
ET · MARIA · C · F · GALLA · CN
CONSERVATI
VOTA · L · M · SOLVONT

[1] *C. I. L.* No. 15775.

[2] *C. I. L.* No. 16456. The proconsul L. Passienus Rufus was honoured with a triumph on account of his successful rule, and the title of *Imperator*.

Africa under the Cæsars

Further interest is attached to this inscription, as it records the name of Rufus Passienus, who achieved great success in the subjugation of Numidia.

Tiberius also is represented in the form of a dedication by C. Vibius Marsus, who was proconsul for the third time.[1] The slab bearing the inscription was discovered by M. Tissot on a bridge over the river Badja near Vicus Augusti. The date would be A.D. 29-30.

```
       TI · CAESAR · DIVI
       AVG · F · AVGVSTVS
       PONTIF · MAX · TRIB
       POTEST · XXXI · COS IIII
              DEDIT
       C · VIBIVS · MARSVS · PRO
          COS · III · DEDIC
```

Another dedication to this Emperor is on a *milliarium* at Tacape (Gabes) on the road to Capsa, the date, A.D. 14, being the year of his accession on the death of Augustus.[2]

```
       IMP CAES AVG
       TIF AVGVSTVS TRI
       POT . . . . . XVI
       L ASPRENAS COS
       PROCOS VII VIR
       EPVLONVM VIAM
       EX CASTR HIBER
       NIS TACAPES MVNI
       ENDAM CVRAVIT
          LEG III AVG
          CIX . . . . . . .
```

A similar one has been brought to light on the same highway, some fifty miles beyond Gabes. The two dedications to the Emperor Claudius have no special interest, and the name of Nerva appears only on one inscription. Of the other Cæsars, the names of Titus and Vespasian may be traced on a few much-worn *milliaria*, and a dedication to the latter by a *flamen perpetuus* of Chusira, in the province of Byzacene, may still be read on the base of an altar, bearing the date A.D. 70-71.

---

[1] *C. I. L.* No. 14386.

[2] *C. I. L.* No. 10018, deciphered by Temple and Wilmanns. Sir Grenville Temple, *Excursions in the Mediterranean*, London, 1835, vii. p. 321.

The history of Theveste is so associated with the Emperor Vespasian that it seems fitting, in this stage of inquiry, to give some little account of its progress and of its many interesting monumental remains. We have no record of its early career, except that it was not occupied by Carthaginians till the first Punic war; but its situation, so well adapted for a commercial centre as well as for a military station, induced the Emperor to make Theveste the head-quarters of the African legion.[1] The subjugation of this part of the country was attended with many difficulties, chiefly on account of the lawless character of adjacent tribes; and consequently the presence of a large number of disciplined troops was absolutely necessary for the security of its inhabitants. Neither Sallust, nor Tacitus, nor Pliny makes mention of Theveste, its name appearing for the first time in the geography of Ptolemy.[2] The oldest inscriptions are of the reign of Vespasian, but, with the exception of its being for more than fifty years the chief military centre of Africa, Theveste was of little importance till the close of the second century, when it became one of the richest and most populous of Roman colonies. Among the ruined monuments of the city, none have attracted more attention than the Basilica. Built not later than the end of the first century, and probably commenced during the reign of Vespasian, it appears to have been almost destroyed, with the city itself, during the incursions of the Moors and wild tribes of the Aures in the sixth century. When Solomon, the successor of Belisarius, arrived at the gates of Theveste he found the whole place in ruins; and we learn from an inscription on a triumphal arch assigned to the third year of Justinian's reign, A.D. 539, that *Theveste civitas a fundamentis ædificata est.*[3] The interpretation by Renier fully attests the rebuilding of the city, and, as Sir Lambert Playfair has observed, this Byzantine inscription is the

---

[1] In the reign of Tiberius the imperial army, irrespective of native troops raised in the different provinces, consisted of 25 legions. In the time of Trajan there were 30, and under Septimius Severus 32. Each legion comprised 10 companies, the first company having a full strength of 1,105 infantry and 132 cavalry. In each of the nine other companies there were 555 infantry and 66 cavalry, altogether 6,600 foot-soldiers and 726 mounted. Each legion was accompanied by 10 great military engines, and 55 catapults for discharging stones and arrows. From Trajan to Constantine companies were divided. (Duruy, *Histoire Romaine*, vol. v., also Vegetius, *Mil.* 4, 22.)

[2] M. Letronne, *Ann. de Const.* 1858, p. 29.

[3] *I. R. A.* No. 3089.

only one yet found in Africa, which makes direct allusion to the expulsion of the Vandals.

> *Nutu divino felicissimis temporibus
> piissimorum dominorum
> nostrorum Justiniani et Theodoræ
> Augustorum post abscissos ex Africa
> Vandalos extinctamque per Solomonem
> gloriosissimo magistro militum ex
> consulte Præfecto Libyæ ac patricio
> universam Maurusiam gentem
> providentia ejusdem æminentissimi
> viri Theveste civitas a fundamentis
> ædificata est.*

This Roman Basilica stood on the north side of a *forum*, approached through two lofty gateways, one of which is still standing. A broad flight of thirteen steps, now partly destroyed, gave access to an open court, 65 feet by 60 feet, surrounded by an arcade. The Basilica had a nave and aisles separated by piers and engaged shafts in two superimposed orders, the whole being arcaded. The nave had an apsidal end, and the aisles had galleries. The material of the walls is a finely grained limestone, in large stones of regular size, the courses being about 20 inches high, and the stones bedded in very little thin mortar. The columns were of granite and grey marble, not fluted, and the capitals of both stages were of the Corinthian order of pure white marble, the carving showing great delicacy of form and execution. The simplicity of the arch construction is remarkable. There were no archivolts, and the faces of the voussoirs were polished like marble. The entire floor surfaces were covered with beautiful mosaics, portions of which are still in fair preservation.

It has been suggested that the Basilica of Theveste, as we now see it in ruined condition, was a work of the sixth century, and that Solomon rebuilt it, as well as the city, *a fundamentis*. Had this been the case, the stones of the older Roman work would have been re-used, and the facework, like other masonry at Theveste of the Byzantine period, would have been irregular. It should be observed that when Constantine removed the seat of empire to Byzantium, A.D. 328, the basilica form of plan, which had been adopted for the purposes of the early Christian Church, underwent many changes, the most noticeable being the introduction of the cupola, which received its full development under Justinian, two centuries later. And it so happens that the Byzantine restorations at Theveste were commenced the same year that Justinian laid the foundations of the great Basilica of Sta. Sophia. At Theveste the Byzantine additions are clearly distinguishable, the masonry being of a different character and not even attached to the old work. The quatrefoil chapel on the east side, with its adjoining chambers, and approached from an aisle of the Roman basilica by a descent of thirteen steps, was one of these additions. The eight internal shafts of the chapel were of green marble, and the walls to a considerable height were faced with marble. Large quantities of gilt and coloured tesseræ having been found on the site favour the supposition that the vaulting, as well as the upper parts of the walls, was decorated with mosaic. The entire floor surface was of mosaic, large fragments still remaining in one of the apses. In the centre of the floor appears to have been a tomb, the enclosing walls being constructed with stones of the Roman period. South of the chapel is a large burial-chamber, in which several tombs were found, bearing inscriptions of the sixth and seventh centuries.

Having restored the Basilica, Solomon surrounded it on three sides with shops or small dwellings, portions of which are still standing. He then enclosed the entire ranges of buildings with a wall about 25 feet high, strengthened with numerous towers. This wall of defence is irregularly built with blocks and slabs of stone in great variety, and the presence of tombstones in the construction seems to indicate that the edifices round the *forum* had been recklessly destroyed and the materials used for building purposes. The object of Solomon's fortification is not quite clear. He had already enclosed a large portion of the city by a high wall with ramparts, and in the centre had constructed a citadel of great strength. Most of these are still in existence. One may assume, therefore, that in time of siege this fortified Basilica and its surrounding buildings would serve as an additional refuge for the inhabitants of the adjacent settlements. Procopius, in his work entitled 'War with the Vandals,' throws light upon this subject. He tells us that 'inside the walls of Carthage is a church, under the charge of men devoted to the service of God, whom we call monks. Solomon, who had built this church a

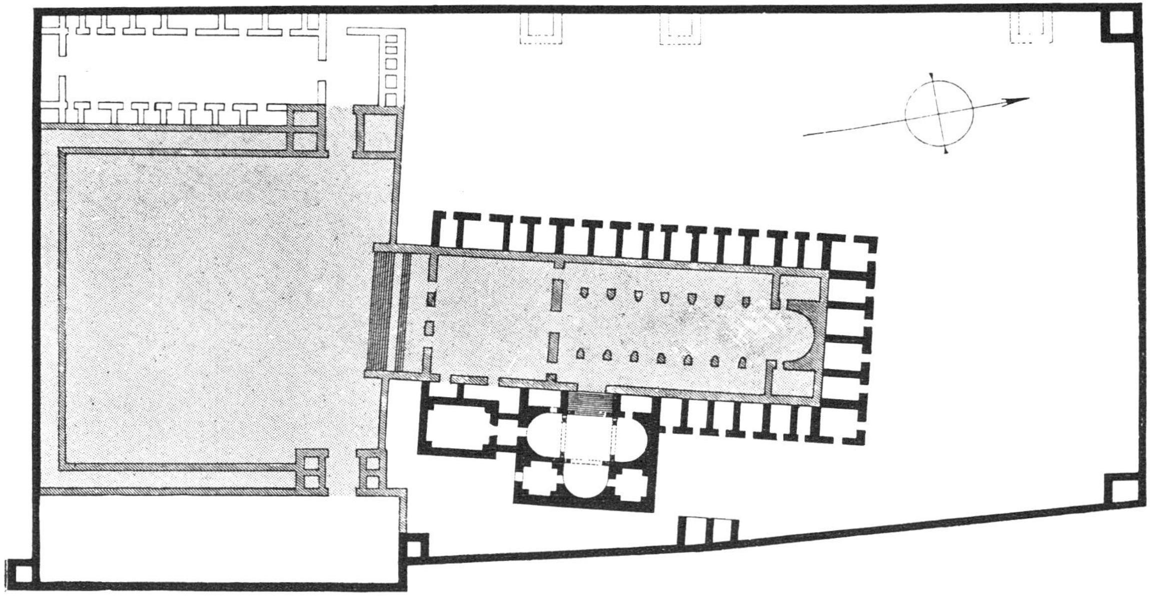

PLAN OF BASILICA AT THEVESTE.
FROM MEASUREMENTS TAKEN BY CAPT. MOLL AND PUBLISHED IN THE ANNUAIRE DE CONSTANTINE
SCALE OF FEET.

little time before, surrounded it with walls in order that, in case of necessity, it might serve as a fortress. Areobindas, governor of Africa, took refuge there, having previously sent his wife and his sister.' The work at Theveste fully bears out this description.

Among other monumental remains of this city the quadrifrontal arch of the time of Caracalla is a conspicuous object, and demands notice on account of the rarity of this form of architectural composition. It will compare favourably with the arch of Janus at Rome, but is in every way inferior to a similar edifice at Tripoli. From inscriptions we learn the complete history of the structure, how the youngest of three brothers, members of a wealthy family at Theveste, bequeathed all his property to his two brothers on condition of their erecting a triumphal arch in his native town, to be surmounted by two tetrastyles [1] enclosing statues of the two Augusti. This Caius Cornelius Egrilianus, who commanded the 14th legion Gemina, quartered in Pannonia, must have been a man of considerable substance, for in addition to this munificent bequest he enjoined his brothers to place in the *forum* statues of Juno and Minerva, to appropriate a sum of 250,000 sesterces for the purpose of affording free baths to the inhabitants in the public *Thermæ*, and lastly 170 pounds weight of silver and 14 pounds weight of

[1] A tetrastyle is a square edifice, adorned with four columns, surmounted by a dome or cupola (*tholus*). It was sometimes called *ædicula tetrastyla*, and frequently a statue of marble or bronze was placed within it. Here is an inscription found at Constantine relating to the dedication of a tetrastyle with a *tholus* (*Archæolog. Journ.* vol. xxix. 1882):—

    C · IVLIVS
    Q · F · QVIR
    POTITVS
    TETRASTV
    LVM · ET
    THOLVM
    D · E · D

The word *tholus* is correct Latin, signifying a round roof or a cupola. The word cupola is of Arabic origin. *Tholus* is applicable to a building of circular form, having the same meaning as θόλος, which was used with reference to the round chamber or *rotunda* at Athens, in which the *Prytanes* dined. Cupola, like alcove and the verb 'to cove,' is derived from the Arabic word *gobba*, which was originally applied to the hump on a camel's back, and afterwards to the cup-shaped tents of nomadic tribes. This word is now pronounced 'koubba,' and is applied generally to native tombs roofed with a cupola. The Italian language retains the word, in its primitive signification, in *gobbo*, a hunchback.

gold were to be deposited in the Capitol for purposes that this much-worn inscription fails to enlighten us about. The rendering of the inscription, that may still be read on the left side as one passes out of the modern town (Tebessa), has proved an attractive study to many eminent epigraphists, including Renier, Wilmanns, and Mommsen.[1] According to the last two the wording is as follows :—

Ex testamento C. Corneli Egriliani, præfecti legionis XIIII Geminæ : quo testamento ex HS CCL millibus nummum arcum cum statuis Augustorum in tetrastylis duobus cum statuis Junonis et Minervæ, quæ in foro fieri præcepit, præter alia HS CCL millia nummum, quæ rei publicæ ita ut certis diebus gymnasia populo publice in thermis præberentur legavit, datasque ad Kapitolium argenti libras CLXX, id est lances IIII . . . et auri libras XIIII, id est pihalas (sic) III, scyphos II fieri iussit ; quæ omnia diligenter secundum voluntatem eius in contione . . . Corneli Fortunatus et Quintus fratres et heredes consignaverunt et opus perfecerunt.

The reading by Renier varies in a few particulars, the most noteworthy being in the third line, *cum statuis divi Severi et Minervæ*. The substitution of the goddess Juno for the Emperor Septimius Severus is immaterial, though it should be observed that the defaced portion of the stonework at this part of the inscription would admit the insertion of the words *divi Severi*. This monument is commonly known as the Arch of Caracalla, the two Augusti referred to in the testament being Caracalla and his brother Geta. It appears to have been built just after the murder of Geta by his brother, A.D. 212. The eastern façade has an inscription dedicated to Severus, father of the Augusti,[2] and on the keystone of the arch is the head of an emperor enclosed in a medallion and resting on the head of Medusa.

DIVO · PIO · SEVERO · PATRI
IMP · CAES · M · AVRELI · SEVERI · ANTONINI
PII · FELICIS · AVG · ARAB · ADIAB · PARTH · MAX · BRIT ·
MAX · GERM · MAX · PONT · MAX · TRIB · POT · XVII · IMP II
COS IIII · PROCOS · P · P ·

On the frieze of the west façade is a dedication in honour of Julia Domna, wife of Severus and mother of the Augusti.[3] The bust sculptured on the keystone, representing a young

---
[1] *C. I. L.* No. 1858 ; *I. R. A.* No. 3085.
[2] *I. R. A.* No. 3087. [3] *I. R. A.* No. 3088.

THE QUADRIFRONTAL ARCH OF CARACALLA AT THEVESTE.

female surmounting an eagle on a thunderbolt, cannot be intended for the Empress, who at the date of the erection of this monument had already passed middle age. It was probably a symbol of Theveste as a young and rising city.

IVLIAE · DOMNAE · AVG ·˙ MATRI
CASTRORVM · ET · AVG · ET · SEN
ET · PATRIAE

The inscription on the south façade is illegible, and on the northern side no longer exists, this part of the edifice having been restored in recent times. Both these inscriptions were probably in honour of Caracalla and Geta. The peculiarities of this architectural composition are the exceptional width of the frieze, and the absence of an attic—a marked feature in triumphal arches. For the latter, two tetrastyles, as a crowning feature of the edifice, are substituted. It has been suggested that there were similar tetrastyles on each of the four façades, but there is no mention of that number on any inscription or document, nor is there any indication on the monument itself of there having been more than the two mentioned in the testament of Caius Cornelius Egrilianus.

Triumphal arches form a class of monuments that is exclusively Roman. The Greeks raised columns in honour of men distinguished in war and intellectual attainments, bearing out a statement by Pliny the Elder, *Columnarum ratio erat attolli supra ceteros mortales, quod et arcus significant novitio invento.* Arches came in with the Empire as permanent structures. In the days of the Republic they were made of wood, after the manner of the Etruscans, and, like similar erections of our own time, were taken down on completion of a public ceremony.[1] These monumental gateways, which generally served as ap-

[1] It may be as well to quote the opinion expressed by Gibbon on Roman triumphs, which is generally accepted: 'A Roman triumph could only be obtained by the conquerors of nations who had never previously acknowledged the authority of the Romans; the reduction of a revolted province did not suffice; the Senate took no account of victories which did not extend the frontiers of the Empire. This seems to have been the rule; but when Titus and his father triumphed over the Jews, and when the Senate commemorated their victories by medals and that triumphal arch which has subsisted to the present day, they did nothing more than triumph over a revolted province, which had been subdued by the arms of Pompey, and governed by Roman magistrates for the space of fifty years.' (Gibbon, *Miscellaneous Works, Classical*, vol. iv. p. 369.)

proaches to cities and towns, are very numerous in North Africa. It would be safe to assert that one or more are to be found in every town, however remote or little known. At Lambæsis for instance, no less than forty arches were traced by Peysonnel 150 years ago, and fourteen were then still standing. There is no reason to suppose that they formed part of the enclosure of a walled town. Those that have been discovered in Africa are all isolated structures, though in some instances the defensive walls built during the Byzantine occupation have been brought close up to them on both sides. This remark is equally applicable to triumphal arches generally in the various provinces of the Empire. The cost of their erection was sometimes defrayed by the inhabitants of a town who wished to honour a victorious emperor, and sometimes by private individuals. At Seressitanum, for instance, a small town in the interior, long forgotten and now a mass of ruins, there are the remains of four triumphal arches. One of these, according to an inscription found some fifty years ago, was the gift of a citizen, the cost being borne by himself, his mother, and his sister; and the edifice, when completed, was surmounted, as the two last lines inform us, by a *quadriga* at the public expense.[1]

```
. . . . . . . . . . . . .   TESTAMENTO
C · M . . . . . . . . . .   FELICIS ARMENIANI
EQVO · PVBLICO · ADLECTI · OPTIMAE
. . . . . . . . . . . .   IAE · CIVIS · ARCVS
. . . . . . . . . . .   AD · CVIVS · ORNAMENTA
ARMENIA · AVGE · MATER · ET · BEBINIA · PAVLIANA
SOROR · LIBERALITATE · SVA HS X̅X̅V̅ MIL N̅
EROGAVERVNT · ET · DIE · DEDIC · SPORTVLAS · DECV
RIONIS · ET · EPVLVM · ET · GVMNASIVM · MVNICIPIB
                    DEDERVNT
ITEM · MVNICIPIVM · SERESSITANVM · AD · AMPLIANDA
ORNAMENTA · QVADRIGAM · PVBLICA · PEC · FEC
```

Another edifice at Theveste worthy of a notice is a little tetrastyle temple, apparently dedicated to Minerva or Jupiter. The date of its erection is about A.D. 300. Although in a ruinous condition externally, its portico being kept standing by the aid of iron straps and rods, modern ingenuity has utilised the building for a variety of purposes never dreamt of by its pious

[1] *C. I. L.* No. 937. Victor Guérin, *Voyage archéologique dans la Régence de Tunis*, Paris, 1862, vol. ii. p. 354.

TEMPLE OF MINERVA AT THEVESTE
(Restored).

founders. It was at one time a soap factory, then converted into a prison, and at a subsequent date did duty as a canteen. Lastly, as a bit of irony that could not be exceeded, this temple of the gods was converted into a parish church, and fitted up for that purpose in the worst possible taste. Little wonder that, after undergoing so many vicissitudes, a doubt has been expressed as to the name of the deity in whose honour this sanctuary was founded! But it is an interesting edifice, and, like the triumphal arch of Caracalla, shows a departure from the recognised proportions and treatment of a Classic order. It stands on a *podium*, twelve feet high, and is approached by a broad flight of stone steps. Originally there was an enclosing wall, the space in front of the temple being about 80 feet and at the sides 50 feet.

Like other large Roman towns, Theveste had a *forum civile* and a *forum venale*. The former, according to Vitruvius, was usually surrounded by public buildings, such as the basilica, the curia, the mint, or the prison. At Theveste the open court on the south of the basilica, measuring about 180 feet by 165 feet, was undoubtedly the *forum civile*, but all traces of buildings at the southern end have disappeared. The other *forum* was probably removed by Solomon, on account of its obstructing his lines of defence. It occupied the open space, now planted with trees, in front of the modern citadel.

The beneficent rule of the aged Nerva, who succeeded the last and worst of the twelve Cæsars, was too short for the display of any activity in the African provinces. But it was marked by the establishment of a colony of veterans in a town of old Numidia, which has retained to the present day its name and prosperity. The ancient Sitifis (Setif), as Ptolemy the geographer informs us, was an important mercantile town long before the arrival of the Romans. Its admirable situation on high table-land, 3,570 feet above the sea-level, in the midst of fertile plains, with a soil capable of producing cereals and fruit and oil in abundance, and at the junction of no less than nine highways communicating with every part of the country, made Sitifis a commercial centre at a very early period. The discovery of more than 250 inscribed stones on the site of the old town gives an insight into its long career of prosperity and the lives of its inhabitants. The very few memorials of soldiers or their families seem to indicate that the population was civil, and not military, during the Roman occupation. From one of the inscriptions we learn that Nerva conferred on the town the title of *Colonia Nerviana Augusta Martialis Veteranorum Sitifensium*. There are inscriptions also relating to the erection of a theatre, an amphitheatre, and several temples ; also the dedication of statues of the Emperors Trajan, Hadrian, Antoninus, M. Aurelius, and L. Verus. The town was embellished with noble monuments, and marble and mosaic were freely used in its public buildings. Many of the votive tablets were enriched with sculpture, and, from the character of the inscriptions generally, we may assume that a high tone of culture prevailed among the inhabitants. One memorial in the public gardens is worth noticing. It is a dedication by one Maurusius, apparently a Moor, to his two beloved children, Prætorianus and Prima, a boy and a girl. The father indicates with precision and loving care the exact time of their decease. He educates his son for a *notarius* (secretary), and sends him to Rome, where he died, A.D. 225, at the age of seventeen.[1]

MEMORIAE
PRAETORIANI
FILI DVLCISSI
MI HOMINI
INGENIOSIS
SIMO NOTA
RIO V · AN · XVII
M · VIII · D · XVII · ROMAE
DECESSIT · XV · K · NOV · A · P · CLXXXVI.

MEMORIAE
PRIMAE
FILIAE DVL
CISSIMAE
V · AN · VIII · M · V.
DECESSIT V KAL
SEPT · A · P · CLXXXVII

MAVRVSIVS FILIS

At all times an agricultural town, it is not surprising to find that Saturn, the deity of agriculture of the Latins, figures largely in many dedications, and the names of Saturus and Saturninus given to many residents in the city and the neighbourhood. Sitifis has had a long history, but during its occupation as a Roman colony was not associated with any great movement, nor with any change in its constitution, till the time of Diocletian at the close of the third century. At that period a great increase in the population of Mauritania Cæsariensis rendered a division of the province necessary. Diocletian, therefore, gave

[1] *C. I. L.* No. 8501. *Mauritanie Césarienne*, par Ed. Cat, Paris, 1891, p. 164.

the name of Mauritania Sitifensis to the eastern portion, with Sitifis for a capital, and retained the old name for the western portion, with Cæsarea for its capital as heretofore. But the separation must have been more nominal than real, for the two provinces had the same troops, and sometimes they were both administered by the same governor. Sitifis suffered during the insurrection of Firmus, the chief of a powerful Moorish tribe, A.D. 369, and was partly destroyed by an earthquake, A.D. 419. Like most of the cities and towns in North Africa, it fell a victim to the Vandal and Arab invasions, but recovered its position at a later period. In the Middle Ages it was still prosperous, for El Bekri speaks of Sitifis as in a flourishing condition and thickly populated. But in his time the city walls, which had been noted for great solidity and thoroughly restored during the Byzantine occupation, no longer existed.

The history of the rise, progress, and decline of a people is generally divided into periods, sometimes dynastic, at other times tribal or accidental. Roman history, after the fall of the Republic, is divisible into several periods. We have the Empire under the Cæsars, including the Flavian epoch, which covers twenty-seven years under the reigns of Vespasian, Titus, and Domitian. The line of the so-called twelve Cæsars terminates with Domitian, but Nero, as the last representative of the Julian family, should be the sixth and last of the Cæsars, his successors, Galba and Otho, who preceded the Flavian family, being created emperors for their services to the State, and not for dynastic or family reasons. After the twelve Cæsars we have the rule of the Emperors Nerva, Trajan, and Hadrian, all raised to the purple for distinguished services, civil or military. Then came the age of the Antonines under the imperial rule of Antoninus Pius, Marcus Aurelius, Lucius Verus, and Commodus. And lastly a long line of emperors, selected sometimes on the score of distinction in the Senate or on the field of battle, but generally as nominees of party factions. This last period covers more than 263 years, commencing with the death of Commodus and terminating with the occupation of Carthage by Genseric, A.D. 439, and the sacking of Rome, A.D. 455.

In the first chapter of this outline of North African history, an attempt has been made to trace the causes which contributed to the invasion of the country and its occupation by the Romans.

Its progress under the Cæsars, the successful establishment of a form of government adapted to the traditional habits of the native races, and the permanent settlement of a military force on the frontier, have been the subject of inquiry in this second chapter. We have now reached a period which demands more than one chapter for its special consideration—a long era of peace and prosperity, of good government, and of a higher tone prevailing in municipal as well as in domestic life. Verily for Africa this was the Golden Age of Empire.

CHAPTER III

AFRICA UNDER TRAJAN

A.D. 97-117

THE history of North Africa, during the eighty-three years that Trajan and his three successors sat on the throne of the Cæsars, may truly be said to be written on stone. In nearly every province of the Empire, which extended almost to the gates of India, the names of these illustrious rulers figure largely on ruined monuments in far distant lands. In Africa this is especially the case. Were it not for inscriptions on panel or frieze, on milliary stone or votive pedestal, we should have but a poor record of Trajan's magnificence as a ruler, or of his solicitude for the welfare of his colonists and protection of native tribes. Nor should we have reliable information about the honours bestowed upon him by all classes of his subjects for deeds of thoughtfulness and beneficence. Among the first acts of Trajan's reign was the regulating the supply of corn from Africa, and framing edicts for the administration of justice to the producer and the merchant in their commercial transactions with Rome. For a long period not only Rome, but Italy also, had depended upon large shipments of corn from abroad, and had looked to Egypt and Africa for one third at least of their annual requirements, equivalent to about six million bushels. Italy and Spain provided the rest. The African provinces were called upon to deliver a certain amount of produce in the form of imperial tribute, under the superintendence of a high functionary who resided at Carthage. Some years ago M. Renier discovered at Kalama (Guelma) an inscription of the time of Trajan, which clearly showed that this important officer of state was charged with the control of the wheat supply to the metropolis. The small amount produced in Italy was only sufficient for the soldiers. War in Africa meant famine in Rome, and this was an evil to be guarded against at all costs. Historians inform us of scarcity and distress in the reigns of Augustus and Tiberius. Under Claudius there was dearth of corn for three consecutive years, and famine caused great hardship in various parts of the Empire during the rule of Domitian and some of his successors. Under the later emperors there are records of several others, but one may reasonably suppose that the admirable system of corn storage in years of plenty, inaugurated by Trajan, lessened the evil in a time of need. During his struggles with Cæsar Pompey stopped the export. Such was the distress in the capital that the populace implored Cæsar to terminate his differences with his rival. A treaty was then arranged, the chief condition being that grain-ships were to be allowed to leave the African ports and to cross the Mediterranean unmolested.

It is difficult in these days of abundant food supply, and with the control of so large a portion of the earth's surface to meet the growing requirements of mankind, to measure the anxiety of the Roman people when the days of harvesting were drawing near. Their very existence was at one period at the mercy of the waves, and tempestuous weather off the ports of Africa or on the coasts of Sicily and Spain was too often the cause of deep anxiety in the metropolis.[1] As far back as the time of Caius Gracchus, the socialist of his time and hero of the hour, poor citizens were allowed their doles of wheat at half the current prices in the market, and what were known as *tesseræ frumentariæ*, equivalent to modern soup and coal tickets, were distributed freely by civil functionaries to all persons in need. So pauperising a measure attracted to the capital the idle and worthless from all parts of Italy, and ultimately created an evil which the earlier emperors had great difficulty in checking. It was not likely that the populace would remain satisfied till they had ultimately acquired the right of demanding bread unstinted and without payment, nor was it possible for the resources of the treasury to be equal to supplying a demand which was both arbitrary and impolitic. In the last days of the Republic no less than 320,000 persons claimed their weekly doles, and it required all the popularity of a Cæsar and the combined efforts

---

[1] Tacitus, *Ann.* iii. 54 : *Vita populi Romani per incerta maris et tempestatum quotidie volvitur.*

of the Senate and the wealthier classes to reduce the number to 150,000. This number was increased to 200,000 by Augustus, who, according to Suetonius, was personally inclined to abolish for ever this objectionable custom.[1]

The general fertility and capabilities of the soil of North Africa are attested by numerous authors. According to Plutarch, the town of Leptis alone, after Cæsar's decisive victory at Thapsus, was condemned to a fine of 2,500,000 pounds of oil ; and Hirtius, who accompanied Cæsar on this expedition, tells us that this was a very moderate demand. The use of oil was indispensable for lamps as well as for baths. For the latter purpose the consumption in the days of the Cæsars was enormous, and the production of this article, imposed as a tax on Africa for the benefit of Rome, amounted annually to about 300,000 English gallons. Tacitus also mentions that Vespasian, in disputing the throne with Vitellius, conceived the project of invading Africa by sea and land, and seizing the granaries. On the death of his rival he charged with wheat every ship of the Empire. At Rusicada (Philippeville) may still be seen the remains of enormous granaries ; and we learn that when Cæsar's army landed in the neighbourhood of Leptis, an immense wheat supply stored at Thysdrus (El-Djem) was placed at the service of the troops.

Pliny the Elder is profuse in his praises of Africa, and tells us that the climate is so good, so kind, and so beneficial, that after the seed is sown the land is not visited for nine months, and then the corn is cut down and laid on the threshing-floors ; the reason being that the drought keeps down all weeds, and the dews that fall by night are sufficient to refresh and nourish the corn. In another of his comments [2] he says that there is a city called Tacape (Gabes) in the midst of the sands, the neighbourhood of which is so fruitful that it passes wonder and is incredible. There may be seen a mighty date-tree under which grows an olive, under that a fig-tree, and that overspreads a pomegranate under the shade whereof is a vine, and under the compass thereof they sow corn and then herbs, all in one and the same year. The vines in the neighbourhood bear twice a year and yield ripe grapes for a double vintage. Once again,

---

[1] Suetonius, *Aug.* 42.   [2] Pliny, *Hist. Nat.* xviii. 22.

Pliny refers to the land of Byzatium or Byzacene,[1] which was represented on Roman coins in the guise of a young girl with her arms full of wheatsheaves, and says that when the season is dry the strongest team of oxen cannot plough it, but that after one good shower one poor ass with the help of a silly old woman will be enough, as he has observed many a time and often.

The Emperor Commodus, whose reign was not remarkable for acts of munificence or utility, built a fleet of ships especially for the grain supply. He had an African and an Alexandrian fleet. It was in a ship of the latter, whose sign was Castor and Pollux, that St. Paul embarked from Malta when he was journeying to Syracuse. In the fourth century, especially during the reign of Constantine, wheat from Egypt was shipped entirely to Constantinople, and wheat from Africa supplied the Roman markets. In the time of Cæsar a maximum price of wheat was fixed in Rome, and certain ports were named on the coast of Italy to which it should be exclusively shipped. This arbitrary measure, which appears to have been in force more than a century, was little in accord with the statesmanlike views which characterised the Emperor Trajan in all his public acts. He abolished restrictions, declined to fix a legal price for any articles of production, and allowed shippers and merchants to adopt their own methods in all commercial transactions. The merits of this enlightened policy were put to a severe test on one occasion during his reign. The waters of the Nile had refused to rise, and famine in the land of Egypt seemed imminent. But wheat from Africa and Sicily came of their abundance to the ports of Italy, and there was enough to spare for the distressed population of Alexandria. We cannot wonder at the interest taken in those days in the shipment of grain,

---

[1] The region called Byzacene was originally inhabited by a Libyan people called Byzantes, and comprised the southern portion of Africa Provincia. At a later date it became a distinct province, with the title of Provincia Byzacena. It was separated from Tripolitana by the river Triton, and the marshes *Palus Tritonis*, with a stretch of desert on the south and south-west, formed a natural boundary. Hadrumetum (Susa) was the capital. Other important towns on the coast were Acholla (no existing remains), Leptis minor (Lemta), Ruspina (Monastir), Thapsus (Ras Dimas), add Thenæ (Henchir Tina). In the interior of the country were Assuras (Zanfour), Capsa (Gafsa), Sufetula (Sbeitla), Terebintha (no existing remains), and Thysdrus (El-Djem). All these were flourishing towns till the fall of the Empire.

nor can we be surprised at reading that the safe arrival of the fleet at a certain period of the year was a matter of grave anxiety to the people of Rome. From Seneca we have a graphic description of the arrival of the Alexandrian fleet in the port of Puteoli, how the population mounted the hill-tops in expectation, how they scanned the broad waters for the first glimpse of the convoy, and how great the rejoicing when the laden vessels were brought safely into harbour. Similar scenes occurred at the still more important port of Ostia at the mouth of the Tiber. Any one who has visited in recent times this almost deserted sand-choked region, with its silent waters and still more silent plains, experiences a difficulty in conjuring up from these mute surroundings a picture of Ostia of old times— the port of Rome, and the pride of the Emperors. Undulations of the surface and fragments of marble and pottery upturned by the plough or spade are the chief indication of the old city buried far below. The harbour which Claudius caused to be made for his increasing fleet, and the splendid pentagonal basin of Trajan's time, may still be traced on the marshy land which has swallowed up the Mediterranean on these inhospitable shores. And the foundations of the great granaries which stored the wheat supply of Northern Africa are there to tell their own tale of a period of marked prosperity and great commercial activity.[1]

From the epistles of Pliny the Younger and his panegyric on his noble patron we obtain an insight into the principles which actuated Trajan in his government of the provinces of the Empire. Africa and Asia were the two senatorial provinces of the first rank, and, as Roman colonies were more numerous in Africa, we may assume that this enlightened ruler adopted a large-minded policy in so important an adjunct of his dominions. Had Pliny been governor of a province of Mauritania in Africa instead of Bithynia in Asia, we should have been acquainted with many subjects which can only be in-

[1] Ostia and its remains have been an attractive field for archæologists of many countries. The intelligent labours of Visconti, Canina, and Texier have thrown considerable light on the history and value of Ostia and its harbours in the days of the Empire. And so eminent an authority on all questions of Roman archæology as Signor Lanciani has cleared up many points in numerous papers on the subject, fully attesting the splendour of Ostia at the commencement of the second century. (*Vide* Lanciani, *Ancient Rome*, pp. 235-246.)

differently explained by an interpretation of fragmentary inscriptions found in the country. Anyhow, the letters addressed to Trajan and the Emperor's replies to his dear 'Secundus' are of special interest, because they convey a faithful impression of the manners of the time and the honest attempts to do justice to every subject of the Empire. It must, however, be borne in mind that Pliny was not only the governor or proconsul of Bithynia, but that he acted as the Emperor's own lieutenant with extraordinary powers, and was privileged to hold direct communication with his august master on all matters relating to his office. From the time of Augustus the proconsuls had ruled over the provinces more or less despotically. When any of the Emperors exercised arbitrary powers in Rome by exorbitant demands, or exacted heavy tribute from the more prosperous colonies, the proconsuls, after satisfying the needs of the imperial treasury, did not hesitate to serve their own interests. To plunder the towns seemed to be one of the duties of their high office, till at last the title of proconsul became identified with robbery and extortion. So long as the farmers of taxes throughout the Empire paid certain fixed sums into the treasury at Rome, and gave security for the payment, the proconsuls did not trouble themselves about the way in which taxes were collected. If the collector succeeded in enriching himself at the expense of the people, the proconsul expected to share the plunder. As a governor invested with almost despotic powers he could prevent extortion, but ultimately found it to his interest to promote it; and as a senator he was not amenable to the ordinary laws, but was responsible to the Senate only for his actions. Tacitus tells us that in the western provinces of Mauritania Cæsarea and Tingitana, plunder and depredation were tacitly recognised. Nero placed the former under the governorship of Albinus, who was master of a considerable body of troops, with numerous auxiliary companies raised in the country, all of whom lived more or less by rapine and depredation.[1] Nerva was the first Emperor to initiate a better order of things, but to Trajan may be credited the establishment of a form of provincial government, which was honourable in the demands made upon his subjects, progressive in its policy, and inimical to all kinds

[1] Tacitus, *Hist.* ii. 58–59.

of corruption and bribery. An outcry against the exactions of a provincial governor reached its climax during his reign, when the Emperor was petitioned by his African subjects to bring to trial Marius Priscus, the proconsul of Africa, and his lieutenant Hostilius Firmanus, on the ground of their cruel and extortionate demands. Both Pliny and Tacitus held briefs for the unfortunate provincials, and the hearing of the case, which lasted three days before the Senate in Rome, was under the presidency of the Emperor Trajan himself, as Consul. From Pliny we learn that his speech for the plaintiffs occupied five hours, and from the graphic description of the trial in two of his letters we may assume that he acted as his own special reporter. Anyhow, the petitioners won their case. M. Priscus was mulcted in a heavy fine and was banished; and H. Firmanus was declared incapable of serving as a proconsul. To wind up the whole matter, Pliny tells us with pardonable pride that both he and Tacitus received the congratulations of the Senate for their successful impeachment of two such distinguished officers. The trial was remarkable on account of the high position of M. Priscus, who had been Consul, and was a person of great distinction. Similar proceedings, we are told, were taken against Julius Barrus, governor of Bithynia, and Rufus Varenus.[1]

Such praiseworthy endeavours to administer justice to all classes in every part of the Empire are fully corroborated in the correspondence between Trajan and his friend the proconsul of Bithynia. When Pliny petitioned the Emperor to sanction the introduction of Roman methods of local government to displace the irregular systems in operation in various parts of the province, Trajan replied that it seemed best, and was even the safest way, to leave each city to exercise its own peculiar laws. On another occasion when Pliny complained to the Emperor of the ruinous condition of the bath at Prusa (Broussa), and asked his approval of its being rebuilt, 'Yes,' said Trajan, 'provided no new tax be levied for this purpose, nor any of those taken off which are appropriated to necessary services.' Only once did the Emperor appear to show any signs of irritation with his exacting correspondent. 'The theatre and gymnasium in course of construction at Nicæa,'

[1] Pliny. These names appear in several letters.

said Pliny, 'are being built on marshy ground, and the walls are already cracked. The gymnasium is not only of irregular shape, but it is badly planned. The present architect, who is a rival of the one first engaged on the work, tells me that the foundations, which are twenty feet thick and loosely built, are unequal to support the superstructure. Send me some architects from Italy to advise me in the matter, which is urgent.' Trajan's reply was very brief. 'As to architects,' said the Emperor, 'there is no province which has not trained men of skill and ingenuity to do what you require. Such experts are not produced in Italy. We have several in Rome, but they come to us from Greece.'[1]

The confidence inspired by the just and beneficent rule of Trajan soon spread to the more distant parts of the Empire. The magic of his name, associated with unbounded success as a warrior, checked the turbulent tribes on the frontiers of his African provinces; and the native races subject to the will of Rome were left to cultivate their fields in peace, or change a nomadic life for one of settlement in towns and villages. Public works were in progress everywhere, roads were multiplied or repaired, and harbours constructed or enlarged. With the aid of the renowned Apollodorus of Damascus, the great architect of his time, rivers were spanned by stately bridges far exceeding in magnificence anything the world had ever seen; triumphal arches—tributes of gratitude to a wise and thoughtful Emperor—graced the entry of provincial towns; and temples and theatres, baths and aqueducts, rose, as if by magic, to do honour to the Emperor in his lifetime. But the name of Trajan, as a patron of architecture and a man of princely tastes, will for ever be associated with the great forum at Rome which bears his name, and with the stately column which has happily defied the ravages of time. When the Emperor Constantius II. made his triumphal entry into Rome A.D. 356, he stood amazed at the beauty and grandeur of the forum, with its splendid embellishments in marble and stone. In despair of ever doing anything that would rival such magnificence, he said, as he turned away, that he would be content to match the horse which figured in the equestrian statue of Trajan. 'You can

[1] This letter of Trajan's testifies to the widespread influence of Hellenic art, and the indebtedness of the Roman world to the more cultured Greek.

imitate the horse,' said the Persian prince Hormisdas, who accompanied him, 'but how about the stable?' It is also stated that when the Persian was asked on a subsequent occasion what he thought of Rome, he replied, 'I am trying to forget that men are but mortal.' In his epitome of the history of Rome Eutropius speaks of Trajan as *orbem terrarum ædificans*, but he might have coupled his name with that of Hadrian, his successor, as his equal in the encouragement given to the building of public monuments worthy of a great Empire. To the honour of Trajan it may be said that he raised these costly edifices for the people and not for himself, and that during the twenty years he sat on the throne of the Cæsars not one single gallery or room of state was added to the imperial palace on the Palatine hill. But his name, inscribed on marble or stone, was so much in evidence everywhere that Constantine, two centuries later, humorously compared it to the pellitory on the wall. Yet with all this magnificence Art in Trajan's time was not the Art of the Augustan age. It had lost its vitality, and the high ideal inherited from the Greeks had departed. Human thought, said Plutarch, had descended from its throne and had wings no longer. 'Poetry did not hold the same place in the Roman mind,' says an intelligent French author. 'Eloquent prose was heard where song was once triumphant. The gods had departed, and mortals only remained. In art as in policy the era of Trajan was one of truth, but not of the ideal; of good sense, but not of genius.'[1]

There were several cities and towns in Roman Africa which became associated with Trajan's name on account of some public work or act of watchful benevolence. Leptis Magna, for instance, was favoured by his notice, and coins were struck in his honour bearing the words *Colonia Ulpia Traiana Leptis*.

Mention should also be made of Hippo Diarrhytus or Hippo Zarytus (Bizerta), which was founded by some Phœnician colonists from Tyre at an early date, and subsequently became a commercial port under the rule of Carthage. Its importance for strategic purposes attracted the attention of Agathocles, who invaded Africa B.C. 309. He remained there long enough to fortify the town and construct a harbour, of which the lines

---

[1] Le Comte de Champagny, *Les Antonins*, Paris, 1875, vol. i. p. 387.

can still be traced. According to Pliny, Hippo was a well-known colony in his time: *est in Africa Hipponensis colonia mari proxima*. And he adds, *Adjacet ei navigabile stagnum, ex quo in modum fluminis, æstuarium emergit quod, vice alterna, prout æstus aut repressit aut impulit, nunc infertur mari, nunc redditur stagno*.[1] With reference to this latter quotation, M. V. Guérin remarks that the statement is perfectly correct. Any one who has visited Bizerta must have noticed the currents spoken of by Pliny, as moving sometimes one way and sometimes the other. The sea enters the lake by two branches of a canal when the wind is westerly, and when it is in a contrary direction the current is reversed. The monumental remains of Hippo have entirely disappeared, the materials having been re-used in the construction of the uninteresting Arab town of Bizerta. Two inscriptions were discovered here about forty years ago by M. Guérin, one being on a milliary column dedicated to Marcus Aurelius, and the other on a block of marble from some edifice presented to the colony by the inhabitants of an adjacent colony styled Julia Carpitana, near Carthage.[2]

IMP · CAES	GENIO · COL · IVLIAE
M · AVRELIVS	HIPP · DIARR · SACR
ANTONINVS	COLONI · COL · IVLIAE
PIVS · FELIX · AVG	CARPIT . . . .
PARTHICVS · MAX	GVLV . . . .
GERMANICVS · MAX	QVIS . . . .
TRIB · POT · XVIII	IVSTISSIMIS
COS · IIII · P · P	D · D · P · P
RESTITVIT	
XLIX	

This town still preserves its ancient name of Carpis, pronounced by the Arabs Kourbis. The city of Hippo received the affix of Zarytus to distinguish it from Hippo Regius (Bone), the word Zarytus being translated by the Greeks into διάρρυτος (diarrhytus), on account of a canal which passed through the town.

Hadrumetum (Susa) is another town of importance which bears testimony to the beneficence of Trajan and to its rank as a colony, *Coloni Coloniæ Concordiæ Ulpiæ Trajanæ Augustæ*

---

[1] Pliny, *Epist.* ix. 33.   [2] V. Guérin, vol. ii. pp. 22-23.

Frugiferæ Hadrumetinæ. According to Sallust it existed as a Phœnician colony before Carthage, and its original name is supposed to have been Adrymès or Adramytos. It was the capital of Byzacene and suffered terribly during the campaign of Julius Cæsar. As a city of wealth it was condemned to pay a heavy fine at the close of the war. Procopius speaks of Hadrumetum in the sixth century as a large and populous town. It was destroyed by the Vandals, but rebuilt and fortified by the Byzantines. For a short period it changed its name to Justiniana in compliment to the Emperor, and in later times became conspicuous as a seat of Christianity and the residence of a bishop. It is difficult, in the present day, to trace the lines of the *Cothon* or harbour mentioned by Hirtius, or the position of the eight gates described by El-Bekri, as well as of the immense tower at the entrance of the harbour called Dar-es-Senaâ (signifying arsenal, and from which our word is probably derived). M. Daux, who made a special study of Phœnician remains at Hadrumetum, as well as of other places and *emporia* on the coast already referred to, says that the Byzantine occupation was most destructive. The exactions of Justinian, under pretence that money was wanting for reconstructing the defences of the country, while it really went to swell the coffers of the insatiable Emperor at Byzantium, drove away the population. Procopius, the historian of the time, says that five millions left the country, but this is probably an exaggeration. During the Byzantine occupation, which was purely military, the incursions of the Moors proved a source of considerable trouble. The Christian population was roused to action, and for protection they constructed a class of buildings outside the towns, answering the double purpose of convents and fortresses, of which mention has been already made. The occupants were soldier-monks, and the buildings, which were enclosed by surrounding walls of defence, were called *Monasteria*. Several of these still exist. There is one at Leptis Parva (Lemta) ; another at Ruspina (actually Monastir, to which it gave the name) ; and another at Hadrumetum called Kasr-er-Ribat, mentioned by El-Bekri. This was partly reconstructed by a prince of the Aghlabite dynasty A.D. 827, and converted by the disciples of Mahomet into a place of retirement for marabouts. There are also the remains of two other *monasteria* on the coast between

Hadrumetum and Carthage. The internal arrangement of these buildings was similar, and for the most part consisted of a series of vaulted chambers, which were originally occupied by foreign mercenaries in the pay of Carthage. These chambers were afterwards converted into cells for monks. This hybrid institution was the origin of orders of a similar kind so celebrated in the Middle Ages, and especially familiar to us under the names of Templars and Knights of St. John.

Among the many useful arts which are associated with the Roman name, and received direct encouragement from Trajan, that of road-making stands pre-eminent. In the days of the Republic the maintenance and repair of public highways and streets were under the charge of censors, the highest rank in the magistracy of Rome. From the time of Augustus roads were of three classes: *publicæ*, sometimes designated as *consulares*, *militares*, or *prætoriæ*; *privatæ*, sometimes called *agrariæ*; and *vicinales*. The first were under the charge of men of prætorian rank, to whom two lictors were assigned. To give additional weight to their high office, the Emperor appointed them for life, instead of for a term of five years which had hitherto been the rule, and nominated men of senatorial or equestrian rank according to the relative importance of the roads committed to their care. According to Isidore of Seville, the kind of roads supposed to have been borrowed from the Carthaginians were called *viæ munitæ*, which were paved with rectangular blocks of any hard local stone, or with polygonal blocks of lava.[1] From Ulpian[2] we learn that there were several different kinds of roads known to the Romans. There was the *via terrena*, which had an ordinary surface of levelled earth. A second kind was the *via glareata*, having a gravelled surface, referred to by Livy,[3] who speaks of the censors of his time as being the first to contract for paving the streets of Rome with flint stones, for laying gravel on the roads outside the city, and for forming raised footpaths at the sides. A third kind was the *via munita*, which in course of time became identical in meaning with *via publica*.[4]

[1] *Orig.* xv. 16, 6. *Primum Pœni dicuntur lapidibus vias stravisse; postea Romani per omnem pæne urbem disposuerunt, propter rectitudinem itinerum et ne plebs esset otiosa.*
[2] Ulpian, *Dig.* 43, 11, 2.   [3] Livy, xli. c. 27.
[4] Smith's *Dict. of Gr. and Rom. Antiq.* art. 'Viæ.' According to Signor Lanciani, *munita* means levelled, straightened, and macadamised. *Vide* Livy, ix. 29.

During the Empire the office of superintendent of public roads was of such honour and distinction that it became the custom to confer it upon those who had been consuls. Julius Cæsar is mentioned by Plutarch as curator or superintendent of the Appian Way, and we learn that he spent his own money on its maintenance. Augustus also, we are told, personally accepted the office of curator in the vicinity of Rome. The roads extended to a considerable distance from the capital, the length of the Appian Way being computed at 350 miles. A recent traveller, speaking of this great highway, remarks that though it is much broken in several places and travelling over it very uncomfortable, it is wonderfully well preserved. So hard indeed is the material that it may be said to be polished rather than worn, and in some parts the entire width appears to have been paved with single slabs.[1] Siculus Flaccus, who lived in the reign of Trajan, designates the public roads as *viæ publicæ regalesque*, under the charge of *curatores*, and says that they were repaired at the public expense by *redemptores* (contractors), a fixed contribution being levied from adjacent landowners. The use of the word corresponding to *regales* may be traced to Herodotus, who speaks of the ὁδοὶ βασίλειοι of the Persians, probably the first organisers of the system of public highways. In the book of Numbers we read of the children of Israel asking permission to 'go by the king's highway,'[2] and in our own time we constantly use such expressions as the king's highway and the royal road. There is sufficient evidence from the Geography of Ptolemy, who lived in the reigns of Hadrian and Antonine, and from the Itinerary of Antoninus, which was written in the form handed down to us prior to the time of Constantine, that extraordinary attention was bestowed on the service of the public roads in the provinces of the Empire, as well as in Italy.

Among the inscriptions found in Africa relating to *curatores viarum*, the following dedication on a pedestal at Tiddis[3] (Kheneg) of the time of Hadrian possesses some interest. It gives an idea of the high distinction attached in those days to a seat on a highway board, *quatuorviro viarum curandarum*.

---

[1] Smith's *Dict. of Gr. and Rom. Antiq.* art. 'Viæ.'   [2] Numbers xx. 17.
[3] *I.R.A.* No. 2322. Vide *Annuaire de Constantine*, art. by General Creuilly, 1853, p. 87.

```
         Q · LOLLIO · M · FIL
         QVIR · VRBICO · COS
         LEG · AVG · PROVINC · GERM
         INFERIORIS · FETIALI · LEGATO
         IMP · HADRIANI · IN · EXPEDITION
         IVDAICA · QVA · DONATVS · EST
         HASTA · PVRA · CORONA · AVREA · LEG
         LEG · X̄ · GEMINAE · PRAET · CANDIDAT
         CAES · TRIB · PLEB · CANDIDAT · CAES · LEG
         PROCOS · ASIAE · QVAEST · VRBIS · TRIB
         LATICLAVIO · LEG · X̄X̄ĪĪ · PRIMIGENIAE
         ĪĪĪĪ · VIRO · VIARVM · CVRAND
                  PATRONO
         D · D                P · P
```

Quinto Lollio, Marci filio,
Quirina tribu, Urbico, consuli,
legato Augusti provinciæ Germaniæ
inferioris, fetiali, legato
Imperatoris Hadriani in expeditione
Judaica, qua donatus est
hasta pura, corona aurea, legato
legionis decimæ Geminæ, prætori candidato
Cæsaris, tribuno plebei candidato Cæsaris, legato
proconsulis Asiæ, quæstori Urbis, tribuno
laticlavio legionis vicesimæ secundæ Primigeniæ,
quatuorviro viarum curandarum,
           patrono.
Decreto decurionum. Pecunia publica

A long score of indebtedness to the Roman world tempts us to ignore our obligations in such small matters as the placing of milliary columns or milestones on our highways, and to forget that Caius Gracchus, 120 years before the Christian era, was the first to recognise their utility for civil as well as military purposes. The system which he adopted was afterwards brought to perfection by Augustus, and from his time no public road in the Empire was without them. The *milliaria* in general use were short columns, generally of marble, but sometimes of stone. The inscriptions upon them gave the distance from a capital or town expressed in paces, a thousand paces (*mille passus*) representing a Roman mile, equivalent to 4,854 English feet. Sometimes the initial letters M.P. were omitted. The inscription further gave the name of the constructor of the road, coupled with that of the emperor in whose honour it was dedicated.

Africa under Trajan

As a central mark in Rome, Augustus set up a gilt bronze column in the Forum, called the *Milliarium Aureum*, near a flight of steps which led up to the Temple of Saturn.[1] On this column were inscribed the names and distances of the chief towns on the roads mentioned by Pliny as radiating through the thirty-seven gates of Rome.[2] Outside the city walls the respective measurements were taken from the gates. It may be inferred that each city in the province had a similar *milliarium*, though not necessarily *aureum*. Ordinary *milliaria* abound in North Africa, and by many of them we obtain a clue to several lines of roads which would otherwise have been lost, the date of their construction, and a reliable means of correcting loosely written statements by ancient authors. Few milliary columns of the period of the Cæsars have been discovered, but those inscribed with the names of Trajan and his successors have been brought to light in nearly every part of the country occupied by the Romans.

The port of Thabraca (Tabarca), which lies on the northern coast midway between Utica and Hippo Regius, and the road running direct south connecting the town with the main highway from Carthage, received the attention of Trajan in the early part of his reign. Pliny speaks of Thabraca as a Roman city on the river Tusca, which forms the eastern boundary of Numidia, and quaintly adds that besides Numidian marble and wild beasts 'there is nothing worth noting.'[3] The port was evidently used for the shipment of wild animals to Ostia for the service of the amphitheatre in Rome, for the export of the rich products of the Medjerda plains, and for the transport of timber for building purposes, and possibly firewood. The Roman remains at Tabarca are scattered over a large area, but, from the absence of refinement in any architectural or decorative work yet discovered, the town may be regarded as having been purely commercial. The chief interest of the place in modern times is centred in a rocky island about half a mile from the mainland, crowned by a citadel of picturesque aspect and considerable strength, constructed by Charles V. on the

---

[1] Middleton's *Ancient Rome in* 1885, p. 166. Otho and the Prætorian conspirators who murdered Galba met *ad Milliarium Aureum sub æde Saturni*. (Plutarch, *Galba*, 24.)

[2] Pliny, *Hist. Nat.* iii. 5.   [3] *Ibid.* v. 3.

completion of his expedition against Tunis in 1535. The edifice, with the walls of defence, has been partly built with the stones of old Thabraka, but no inscriptions relating to the occupation of the island by the Romans have yet been discovered. When Peysonnel visited the spot in 1724 the castle was occupied by Genoese troops, and the fortifications were armed with bronze guns bearing the arms of the Lomellini, a noble family of Genoa. He speaks of the island as strong and safe, and in a condition neither to fear the Turk nor the Arabs of Barbary. The old road into the interior, which followed for a considerable distance the banks of the ancient river Tusca, now known as the Oued-el-Kebir (the Great River) or the Oued-es-Zan (the River of Oak-trees), appears to have been reconstructed by Trajan. Close to the southern boundary at Fernana, about 32 miles from Tabarca, is a milliary column, and 12 miles further south, at the foot of the mountains, another is still existing.

This region lying between the Mediterranean and the Medjerda plains, occupying an area of about 480 square miles, with a seaboard of less than 16 miles, has been known for a long period as the country of the Khomair (*sing*. Khomiri). Prior to the French occupation, and dating back many centuries, it was practically an unknown country, avoided by travellers on account of the lawlessness of its inhabitants, and generally marked as a blank on maps of Northern Africa. A tribute in money was paid annually to the emissaries of the Bey of Tunis representing the Sultan of Turkey, but this was invariably done with the payment in one hand and the pistol in the other.[1] In fact, these uncivilised people refused to recognise the authority of the Bey on one side of their territory, or that of the Dey of Algiers on the other, preferring independence and a lawless life coupled with poverty and hardship to the doubtful advantages of living under Turkish rule. The configuration of the country, and the capabilities of the soil to produce a sufficiency of food with the smallest amount of labour, were all

---

[1] This historic spot, known as Fernana, where tribute was paid, derives its name from a gigantic cork oak, the branches of which spread considerably over 100 feet. It is a conspicuous object in the landscape, as there is no other tree within many miles. The story goes that, if any soldier of the Bey had attempted to advance beyond the tree, the taxes would have been paid in powder and shot.

VIEW OF BULLA REGIA (HAMMÂM DARRADJI).

in their favour, and so they have lived on through countless generations in penury and rags, without one thought of striving for a higher life, or the slightest regard for the beauty of the country they called their own. No part of North Africa has been more favoured by nature than this little-known land of the Khomair. Hill and dale clothed with soft verdure succeed each other in pleasant variety; mountain slopes rugged and picturesque; forests of cork and olive; an undergrowth of myrtle and juniper and wild rose; a land thinly peopled, but a landscape to charm the eye of poet or painter.[1]

Faint traces of the Roman road are apparent in traversing the country, and remains of farm establishments give sufficient indications of a civilised condition in the days of the Empire. It is probable that this road of Trajan's followed the course of a road or track used in earlier times by the kings of Numidia, because it lay in a direct line between the coast and their ancient capital Bulla Regia, now known as Hammam Darradji. It is unfortunate that we have so little knowledge of this old-world metropolis which has a history without records, and ruined monuments without inscriptions. A few years ago a triumphal arch elaborately ornamented was a conspicuous feature on the rising ground. The *Thermæ*, judging from their remains, were on a large scale and covered a considerable area of land. The theatre, the walls of which are still intact, built with large blocks of finely dressed stone, was beautifully situated on a spur of the mountain; and as the ground at the present time is on a level with the top of the proscenium, some idea may be formed of the alteration of the surface since the final destruction and abandonment of Bulla Regia by the Arabs in the seventh century. The amphitheatre is only indicated by undulations of the surface, and the entire site of the city, nearly a mile long, is so choked with weeds and undergrowth that recognition of the different public buildings is difficult. The Byzantines in their turn contributed largely to the destruction of Roman edifices here as elsewhere, and, as usual, paid no respect to monumental buildings, whether Roman or Numidian, but used them as a kind of quarry for the erection of fortresses and walls of defence. In the centre of the city are the remains of a large *Nymphæum*, semicircular in plan, a favourite form

[1] ' *Umbriferos ubi pandit Tabraca saltus.*' (Juvenal, *Sat.* x. 194.)

with the Romans. From the appearance of the fragments this was a work of great beauty, and was ornamented with colonnades, like other well-known examples in Italy and elsewhere. It is lamentable to add that an inexcusable concession of the stones in this district, for the purposes of the Tunisian railway completed some fifteen years ago, was followed by a destruction of numerous monuments, as well as of a number of inscribed stones which might have thrown some light on the early history of this royal city. According to M. Tissot,[1] who made careful investigations of the site in recent years, Bulla Regia appears to have long preserved its Punico-Libyan character, and coins discovered here bearing the crescent and the disc indicate the worship of Baal joined to that of the great goddess of the Carthaginians, Tanith or Virgo Cælestis.

The Numidian marble referred to by Pliny in his mention of Thabraka came from the quarries at Simittu (Chemtou), one day's journey west of Bulla Regia. Trajan's interest in the town and its beautiful products was marked by the erection of a colossal bridge over the Medjerda, two arches of which and the remains of a quay are still standing. Two hundred feet distant are the ruins of a much older bridge, carrying us back to the time of the Numidian kings. An immense slab of *gialloantico* marble lying in an adjoining meadow bears an inscription relating to Trajan's monumental structures.[2] The date of its erection is A.D. 112, when the Emperor was Consul for the sixth time, being the same year in which the stately column was raised in the Forum at Rome in honour of his Dacian victory.

```
           CAESAR DIVI
           VAE F NERVA
          AIANVS OPTIMVS
        G · GERM · DACIC PONT
       X TRIB POT · XVI IMP VI
          COS VI   P · P
      TEM NOVVM A FVNDAMENTIS
      ERA MILITVM SVORVM · ET
         PECVNIA      SVA
      ROVINCIAE AFRICAE FECIT
```

[1] C. Tissot, *Le Bassin du Bagrada et la Voie Romaine de Carthage à Hippone par Bulla Regia.* Paris, Imp. Nat. 1881.

[2] C. Tissot, *ibid.*

TRAJAN'S BRIDGE AT SIMITTU (CHEMTOU).

Africa under Trajan

*Imperator Cæsar Divi
Nervæ filius Nerva
Trajanus Optimus,
Augustus, Germanicus, Dacicus, Pontifex
Maximus, Tribunitia Potestate $\overline{XVI}$, Imperator $\overline{VI}$
Consul $\overline{VI}$. Pater Patriæ,
Pontem Novum a Fundamentis
Opera Militum suorum et
    Pecunia sua
Provinciæ Africæ fecit.*

The words *opera militum suorum* and *provinciæ Africæ fecit* show that the bridge was undertaken for the benefit of the provinces of Africa under the supervision of the Emperor as chief of the army, and *pecuniâ suâ* that it was paid for out of the imperial treasury.

The neighbouring town of Simittu became a colony in the reign of Augustus or one of the emperors of the Julian family, under the title of *Colonia Julia Augusta Numidica Simittu*, and its citizens, like those of Bulla Regia, were inscribed in the tribe of Quirina. It is described as a town on the high road from Carthage to Hippo Regius (Bone), and four days' journey from the former. The complete destruction of the roads in the vicinity of Simittu, and difficulty of access to this part of the country, were the chief causes of its neglect, and of its remaining unknown and unthought of for so many centuries. Fortunately an inscribed milliary column fixes the site of the Roman town, and gives the date of the construction of a road from Simittu to Thabraca A.D. 129.

```
            IMP · CAESAR
            DIVI · TRAIANI
            PARTHIC · FIL
            DIVI · NERVAE · NEP
            .  .  .  .  .  .  .
            HADRIANVS AVG
            PONTIFEX MAX
            TRIB · POT · XIII
                COS · III
            VIAM A SIMITTV
            VSQ · THABRACAM · F
                     I
```

The monumental remains cover a large area, but, with the exception of the bridge referred to, possess little interest. The workmanship generally is coarse and unrefined, and there is an absence of those decorative features in marble and stone which are generally to be found in the public buildings of prosperous communities. It is probable that Simittu owed its existence to the proximity of the marble quarries, and that its inhabitants were mostly connected with the working and transport of these valuable products. The marbles were quarried from a number of small hills, about 800 feet above the sea-level, and covering an area of not less than 220 acres. They are of different kinds, principally *giallo antico*; but there are many other varieties, especially of the *breccia* class, of a brownish hue and of beautiful shades of colour. There is no doubt that Simittu attained great celebrity under the Empire on account of the abundance of this rich material, which was worked here extensively and shipped to Rome. Hadrian, we know, valued these products very highly. An inscription informs us that he made the road to the coast to facilitate their transport, and used them freely in the embellishment of his villas at Tivoli and Antium.

The employment of marble by the Romans as a decorative material cannot be traced farther back than the commencement of the first century B.C. It seems to have been disfavoured on its first introduction, mainly on the ground that it was a Greek luxury ill suited to the taste of the commonwealth. The quarries of Italy had not then been opened, and the only known marbles were the white varieties imported from Greece. Pliny the Elder expresses an opinion on the use of marble, especially in private houses, in a violent diatribe, and vents his indignation against Marcus Scaurus for having set up in front of his house on Mount Palatine some lofty columns of black Lucullean marble.[1] 'Considering, then, this bad example,' says Pliny, 'so prejudicial to all good manners and so hurtful to posterity, would it not be better for the city to disallow such superfluities by wholesome laws and edicts than thus to permit such huge and proud pillars to be raised in front of a private house, even under the nose of the gods, whose images were but of earth and their temples as of potter's clay?' Lucius Crassus also, who built himself a house

---

[1] Middleton, p. 14. Lucullean marble was the product of an island on the Nile, but its position has not been identified, although mentioned by Pliny, *Hist. Nat.* xxxvi. 2. It was so called because it was specially used in Rome by the Consul L. Lucullus about B.C. 74.

on Mount Palatine about B.C. 95, was condemned by Pliny for his extravagance in erecting in the *atrium* six pillars of 'outlandish marble, although they were but quarried on Hymettus hill.' But the first Roman known to employ coloured Numidian marble was M. Æmilius Lepidus during his year of consulate with Q. Lutatius Catulus, B.C. 78.[1] Its use as a decorative material was probably encouraged by Sallust when governor of Numidia, B.C. 46. The term Numidian is, however, a misnomer, being applied to the products of Simittu near the eastern boundary of old Numidia, as well as those of Kleber in Algeria, about twenty-one miles north-east of Oran, in the ancient kingdom of Mauritania. Neither of these places has ever been in Numidian territory, but the term may have originated from the shipment of marble at the port of Thabraka, near the mouth of the Tusca, which formed, as previously observed, the eastern boundary of Numidia proper. It is quite certain that what is known as Numidian marble was not found in Numidia, although some quarries at Filfila, near Philippeville, produce a white marble, but no coloured varieties. Seneca, in his 'Epistles,' refers to slabs of Numidian in conjunction with marble from Alexandria: *Nisi Alexandrina marmora Numidicis crustis distincta sunt.* And Suetonius makes passing mention of a column nearly twenty feet high, raised in the Forum at Rome in honour of Cæsar, in the following words: *Postea solidam columnam prope viginti pedum lapidis Numidici in foro statuit scripsitque Parenti Patriæ.* A later writer also mentions these products as distinguished for patches of saffron colour: *Numidicum marmor Numidia mittet, ad cutem succum dimittet croco similem.*

The quarries at Chemtou are much in the condition in which they were left by the Romans at the time of the Vandal invasion of the country in the fifth century. Half-quarried blocks lie side by side in the yawning chasms of the rocks, with the mason's marks still legible, and far down the cavernous abyss can be seen the preparations for working one of those lordly monoliths, which still excite our admiration in Rome and elsewhere.[2] One thing very noticeable at the quarries of Simittu is

[1] Pliny, *Hist. Nat.* xxxvi. 6.
[2] The excavations conducted systematically in Rome during recent years under the able supervision of Signor Lanciani are continually bearing testimony to the lavish use of African marble under the Empire. In exploring the site of the cele-

the absence of economy in the extraction and working of marble. But it must be remembered that imperial edicts overruled laws of economy, and that, if an order were given for so many columns from any particular quarry, they had to be produced regardless of cost. Of the use of marble at Simittu there are no indications, except in the construction of the aqueduct which conveyed the water to the town, a distance of about five miles, and this is mostly built with waste marble from the quarries. Some portions have been reconstructed, probably during the Byzantine occupation in the sixth century; and it is lamentable to add that a number of inscribed stones with their faces inwards have been built into the piers. Some years ago these quarries were actively worked by a Belgian company, and operations were conducted on a large scale. It is a matter of regret that success did not attend their efforts, and that further proceedings were stopped. The increasing demand for coloured marbles as a material will probably lead to a reopening of the works. The products are unusually varied, bearing Italian names well known to marble merchants, such as marmor bianco, giallo avorio, giallo canarino, giallo paonazzo, rosa carnagione, breccia dorata, breccia sanguigna, bianco e nero antico.

The other quarries at Kleber in Mauritania Cæsariensis are far more extensive, comprising more than 1,500 acres at an altitude of nearly 2,000 feet above the sea. The products are varied. Breccias from dark brown to blood red; giallo antico of different hues; cipollino rosso, and more than one quality of white marble. One of the rose-tinted varieties is of so close a texture that trinkets resembling coral in appearance might be made of it, and the paonazzo variety, so called from its exquisite colouring after the manner of a peacock's plumage, is a reddish marble bearing a similarity to the far-famed variety known as rosso antico.

Another beautiful product of Mauritania, discovered shortly after the French occupation of Algeria, is that variety of alabaster known as Algerian onyx. The main source of supply is from

brated Basilica Emilia, tons upon tons of remains of columns of this beautiful material were brought out by the workmen. The pavement of the central hall or nave was found to be composed of slabs of *bigio* and *africano*. This basilica, measuring 300 feet in length, was nearly as large as its rival monument the Basilica Julia, which excited the admiration of the poet Statius, describing this noble edifice as *sublimis regia Paulli*.

Ain Tekbalet, near Tlemcen. Any one who has visited that remarkable Moorish city, which rivalled Granada for its wealth and civilisation in the twelfth and thirteenth centuries, and took high rank as the capital of a great and powerful nation, could not fail to notice the abundant use of this beautiful material in the chief mosques of the city. The coloured marbles of Mauritania are not to be seen, but Algerian onyx is everywhere.[1]

With such abundance of coloured marble in North Africa, and so many indications of extensive and laborious quarrying during the Roman occupation, one might expect to find it used in great profusion throughout the country. But this is not the case, for its employment was mostly restricted to the towns on or near the coast. The principal quarries were near the sea, and transmission from port to port was easy. Fragments of shafts or slabs of marble are rarely met with in the monumental Roman remains in the interior of the country. There was abundance of good stone, some of the limestone varieties being almost equal to marble in textdre and appearance. One might be induced to believe that Numidian marble was so highly prized in Rome and the chief cities of Italy that its use was almost forbidden in the African provinces, except for imperial purposes. Roman Carthage, according to Arab writers, was a city of marble. But Carthage was the metropolis of Africa, and was rebuilt, by the order of Augustus, on a scale of great magnificence. This is fully attested by El-Bekri and other authors. But the marble of Carthage is now elsewhere. It may be seen in the stately monoliths clustered in twos and threes in the prayer-chamber of the great Mosque at Kairouan, with their capitals and bases of white and grey marble, Greek, Roman, and Byzantine; in the court and gateway of the mosque; and in the palaces of the Beys. All these, noble as they are, pale

---

[1] The late Sir R. Lambert Playfair, H.B.M. Consul-General in Algeria and Tunisia, contributed many interesting reports on the marbles of North Africa, and strove to encourage the working and shipment of these beautiful products. In a paper read before the British Association in Aberdeen (1885), he adds : ' Were I a speculator I might reasonably be distrusted, but as I am performing merely an official duty, I hope I may be credited when I assert my belief that as regards quantity, beauty, and variety, the world contains nothing comparable to the treasures of Numidian marble in the mountain at Kleber. Every one who has visited it at my suggestion has admitted that, far from having exaggerated their importance, my account falls short of the reality.'

before two wondrous pillars which flank the *mihrab*. Tradition holds that they were brought to Carthage from Egypt when the city was being rebuilt. El-Bekri tells us that ' Hassan, governor of Africa replacing Loheir, who succeeded Okhbar, founder of Kairouan, brought there from an ancient building two red shafts tinged with yellow, of incomparable beauty.' It is recorded that a Byzantine emperor offered to purchase them at a price equivalent to their weight in gold.

The quarrying and shipment of Numidian marble, which had formed so important an industry during five centuries of Roman domination, may be said to have ceased when the Vandals passed like a firebrand over the land. The Byzantines, in their turn, were too much occupied with the erection of strongholds and works of defence to give a thought to works of embellishment. And their Arab successors, who brought with them a love of colour and a taste for Oriental splendour, found in Roman Carthage and other ruined cities such an abundance of marble already worked that the re-opening of the ancient quarries was not at any period a matter of necessity.

It is worthy of note that the favour shown by the Romans to what is known as the Composite Order, which towards the fall of the Empire showed great elasticity in its treatment, and considerable departure from so early an example as that familiar to us in the Arch of Titus, is apparent on examining the capitals in the mosque at Kairouan. Intermixed with them are several Corinthian capitals of the best type, both in form and ornamentation. These would be the work of Sicilian Greeks, who were largely employed in buildings at Carthage. Some few capitals are Byzantine, which must have been the spoil of other countries, for the occupation of Africa by Justinian and his successors was a short one, and was one long series of wars and feuds with the Desert tribes. Similar methods at Cordova produced similar results, Roman *Hispania* having to give up its treasures of marble to glorify a new creed.

Twenty years of peace and prosperity in Africa, under the rule of Trajan, had made the name of the Emperor honoured throughout the country. And this was especially the case towards the close of his active career, attested by numerous inscriptions bearing the date A.D. 117. Triumphal arches were conspicuous everywhere, sometimes gracing the principal en-

Africa under Trajan

trance of a town, at others prominently placed in the centre. This was so at Mactar, or *oppidum Mactaritanum* (Mukther), a large and important agricultural town on the high road from Carthage to Sufetuta (Sbeitla). Of the town of Mactar and its history we have no record. Its position on a broad elevated plateau, bounded on one side by the river Melian, and on the other by the precipitous banks of the Oued Sabon, or River of Soap, rendered it a conspicuous object from the fertile plains in its vicinity. The principal remaining arch, dedicated to Trajan, is an architectural composition of some merit, presenting an order within an order. It exhibits a departure from the usual treatment of this class of edifice, and, although very simple in its features, has an aspect of nobility befitting its purpose. The inscription on the lesser frieze facing south is much worn, but when Bruce visited Mukther in 1765 it was quite legible. The date is fixed by the mention of the twentieth year of the tribunate of Trajan, which was A.D. 117.

     IMP · CAES · DIVI · NERVAE · F
     TRAIANO · OPTIMO · AVG · GER ·
     DACIO · PARTHICO · P · M · TRIB
     POTEST · XX · IMP · XII · COS · VI
     . ... FAVSTIN · OS · DEDI · DD · PP

There are remains also of another triumphal arch, forming an approach to the town on the opposite side of the river, and giving indications of a monumental building of a very ornate character. It is now in a dilapidated condition, but, in the absence of any inscription relating to it, one may assign it to the reign of Hadrian, who was honoured in this town a few years later.[1] The hillside of the ancient Mactar is covered with tombs, some of them having been structures of a decorative character, sufficient to show that the town and its neighbourhood must have been in a very prosperous condition in the second century. Among the inscriptions in the cemetery is a lengthy one in verse, relating to a successful farmer who resided in the town, and who evidently desired that his name and his labours

---

[1] Drawings of this Arch, which was more than forty-four feet high, are given by Sir R. Lambert Playfair in his work entitled *Travels in the Footsteps of Bruce* (London, 1877), p. 201. It is an ornate composition of the Corinthian order, but has no special merit ; and as there are no remains of any inscription, the date of its erection is uncertain.

should be held in perpetual remembrance. He says: 'I was the son of a poor man who left me neither house nor money. But I was active and had plenty of pluck, which makes up for everything. I began life as a labourer in the fields. I worked early and late. When harvest commenced I was the first in the fields. Then I became the chief of the gang with whom I worked. I saved money and became owner of a house and farm that were wanting in nothing. I then became a town-councillor, and finally I, having begun life as a working man, ended by taking my seat in the very middle of the assembly over which I presided as chief magistrate. Follow my example by living a blameless life, and meriting by virtuous conduct a peaceful death.' Self-laudatory inscriptions were not uncommon in the days of the Empire. They may be regarded in the light of short memoirs or biographical notices of loyal citizens, who had played their part in the drama of life with benefit to others and much satisfaction to themselves. No other means of recording their labours was open to them. Journalism had not been created, and printer's ink had not been invented, but the mason and his chisel were ready to hand. It is a question whether human ingenuity will ever succeed in devising so enduring a method of perpetuating the actions of mankind as that of incised letters on imperishable stone. Another well-known inscription of a similar kind, from a tomb in the outskirts of Cirta (Constantine), was deciphered many years ago by M. Léon Renier. This monument, discovered in 1855 on the slopes of the cliff leading up to the city, was about 19 feet long and 10 feet wide, and had two stories, both paved with mosaic. Outside the tomb, extending along the façade, was also a pavement of mosaic. In the interior are niches in the walls for receiving the sarcophagi, one of which, when opened, contained a perfect skeleton. On one of the stone sides was a long inscription written in inelegant Latin, and somewhat difficult to decipher. It may be read as follows :

Hic ego qui taceo versibus mea(m) vita(m) demonstro
Lucem clara(m) fruitus et tempora summa,
Præcilius, Cirtensi lare, argentariam exibui artem.
Fydes in me mira fuit semper et veritas omnis.
Omnisbus (sic) communis ego ; cui non misertus ubique ?
Risus, luxuria(m) semper fruitus cum caris amicis,

MONUMENT AT SCILLIUM (KASSERIN).

Talem post obitum dominæ Valeriæ non inveni pudicæ
Vitam; cum potui gratam, habui cum conjuge sanctam.
Natales honeste meos centum celebravi felices
At venit postrema dies, ut spiritus inania mempra (sic) reli(n)quat;
Titulos quos legis vivus mee (sic) morti paravi,
Ut voluit Fortuna; nunquam me deseruit ipsa,
Sequimini tales; hic vos ex(s)pecto; venitæ (sic).

'Here I lie in silence, describing my life in verse. I have enjoyed a good reputation and great prosperity. My name is Præcilius. I reside in Cirta, and follow the art of a silversmith My honesty was extraordinary in everything, and I always spoke the truth. I was known to everybody, and my sympathies were with others. I was merry, and always enjoyed entertainments in the company of my dear friends. After the decease of the virtuous lady Valeria, I did not find life to be the same. As long as my wife lived I found life agreeable. I have celebrated a hundred happy birthdays in a becoming way. But the last day arrived when breath was to forsake this mortal body. The epitaph which you read I prepared while waiting for my death. Good fortune, which has never deserted me, wills it so. May fortune accompany you in a like manner through life! Here I await you. Come!'

Another inscription, too lengthy to repeat, may be read on the faces of a mausoleum in very fair preservation at Scillium, sometimes called *Scillitana Colonia*, but now known as Kasrin. This town was on the southern frontier and on the high road between Sufetala and Theveste. The monument is a conspicuous object amidst a mass of stones and fallen buildings, and is three stories in height, erected on a pyramid of steps now mostly hidden under the surface of the ground. The lowermost story, which is quite plain, is twelve feet square, and has two entrances, each three feet square. The next story, slightly receding from the bottom one, is ornamented with four Corinthian fluted pilasters, of great delicacy of workmanship, on each face (the two central ones on the principal side being spaced a little further apart in order to find room for a lengthy inscription). The top story consists at present of a large niche, square externally, and without any traces of ornamentation or of the statue which filled it. The height of the mausoleum may be estimated at 50 feet. At the summit, surmounting a pyramid common to edifices of this kind, of which there are many examples in Roman Africa, was a bronze cock, which, as the quaint inscription informs us, was placed 'above the clouds and so near to heaven that if nature had given it a voice it would have compelled all the gods by its morning song to get up early.'

> *In summo tremulas galli non diximus alas*
> *Altior extrema qui puto nube volat,*
> *Cujus si membris vocem natura dedisset*
> *Cogeret hic omnes surgere mane deos.*

The monument was erected by Flavius Secundus, in honour of his parents and other members of his family, who are fully described in a lengthy inscription nearly covering one entire face. In addition there are no less than ninety hexameters and twenty elegiacs in somewhat pretentious language, in which the charms of the city and the beauties of the neighbourhood are set forth in a graphic manner by a local poet. What constitutes the beauties of this remote spot, not easy of access in the present day, is difficult to discover. The city, delightfully situated on the verge of a plateau, and girt on three sides by the steep banks of a river, is a mass of ruins extending in one direction for nearly a mile and a half. The land is bare and treeless, and human habitations, as far as the eye can compass, have long ceased to exist. Clumps of juniper bushes clothe the sides of the ravines, and the river that once ran freely round the city is now a comparatively small stream, bubbling over the rocks and soon lost in the plains, like so many of the rivers of North Africa.[1] Nearly sixty years ago an intelligent traveller, who visited Kasrin, took special notice of this tomb of the Secundus family, and remarked that if the monuments 'still standing in a country now desolate attest a former prosperity which confounds our imagination, these verses, composed in a remote town scarcely known in history, prove how the civilising influence of Rome had awakened the intelligence and moral nature of a people once numerous and wealthy, but to-day without art or literature, or even settled inhabitants.'[2]

---

[1] Job vi. 15: 'My brethren have dealt deceitfully as a brook, and as the stream of brooks they pass away.' Also Jer. xv. 18.

[2] E. Pellissier de Reynaud, *Description de la Régence de Tunis* (Paris, 1853).

The first few lines of the inscription are worthy of mention.[1] They refer to the founder of the mausoleum and his wife, Flavia Urbana.

```
       T · FLAVIO · SECUN
       DO · PATRI · PIO
       MIL · AN · XXXIII
    VIX AN · CX · H · S · E
       FLAVIAE VRBANAE
       MATRI · PIAE · VIX
       AN · CV · H · S · E
```

From this we learn that the founder lived to the age of 110, and his wife 105. Strange to say, other lines in the epitaph savour of a complaint against the transitory nature of human life!

```
SINT · LICET · EXIGVAE · FVGIENTIA · TEMPORA · VITAE
PARVAQ · RAPTORVM · CITO · TRANSEAT · HORA · DIERVM
MERGAT · ET · ELYSIIS · MORTALIA · CORPORA · TERRIS
ADSIDVE · RVPTO · LACHESIS · MALE · CONSCIA · PENSO.
```

To live to an advanced age was an ordinary occurrence, and extreme longevity was not exceptional in a country proverbial for its salubrity. At Ammædara (Hydra) a woman who had lost her husband at the age of 82 years and 7 months inscribes on his tombstone, 'You died too soon. You ought to have lived to a hundred. And why didn't you?' Herodotus says that 'there are no people in the world so healthy as Africans,' and Sallust remarks that 'most of them die of old age (*plerosque senectus dissolvit*), except such as perish by the sword or beasts of prey; for disease finds but few victims.'[2] Epitaphs of centenarians, like those of the self-satisfied silversmith of Cirta or the two worthies of Scillium, are numerous, but the extreme of longevity seems to have been reached in the neighbourhood of Cirta (Constantine), where a citizen named M. Julius Abæus closed his career at 131. Close by we find an inscription recording the decease of Julius Gracililius, an old soldier, at the age of 120. Julius Pacatus lived as long, and Julia Gætula has a record of 125 years. In the ruined village of Temda in old Numidia we find the good life of the aged Sittia Helena still preserved in pleasant memory,[3] and at a place called Sila

---

[1] *C.I.L.* No. 211.   [2] Sallust, *Jug.* xvii.
[3] *C.I.L.* No. 20109.

in the same district another lady had the good fortune to live to the age of 111.[1]

```
     D · M · S                    D · M · S
   SITTIA · HE            C · IVLIVS · C · FIL · QVIR
   LENA · SPLEN           BARVARVS V · A · LXXXV
  DIDISSIMAE · ME         H · S · E · O · E · B · Q . . . .
  MORIAE · MATER          ENNIVS CELLINIANVS
    V · A · CIII · H      SITTIA FORTVNVLA
      S · O · B · Q       P · FILIA · QVIR · V · A · CXI
                          H · S · E · O · T · B · Q.
```

One other inscription is worth recording, in memory of a priestess at Sigus (Ziganiah), about twenty-four miles from Cirta.[2]

```
        D · M · S
      IVLIA · VRBA
       NA · SACER
       DOS · MAG
        NA · V · A
      CI · H · S · E
```

Of the history of Sigus we know nothing, except that it was a place of renown long before the Roman occupation, and was the residence of many of the Numidian kings. So complete has been its destruction that nothing has been left but foundations of walls and a few inscribed stones.

Some parts of the country were evidently not so salubrious, for there is an inscription at Auzia (Aumale) relating to a good woman who lived for twenty-six years without an attack of fever : . . . *piissima cultrix pudicitiæ, famæ, quæ vixit sine febribus annis viginti sex.*[3] Another excellent woman is recorded as having lived as long as she could, but without mentioning her length of years : *Diis Manibus Æsclepiæ, Matri carissimai, Zablutius posuit. Vixit annos quod potuit.*[4]

Among the many good qualities which marked Trajan's career as a ruler, thoughtfulness for the poor and distressed stands pre-eminent. Sculptured memorials on the numerous edifices raised to his honour are a striking testimony to that

[1] *C.I.L.* No. 19204.   [2] *C.I.L.* No. 19136.
[3] *I.R.A.* No. 3648.
[4] *I.R.A.* No. 1941. M. Tissot observes that the duration of life among the Touaregs averages 80 years. Centenarians are numerous, and instances are given of persons living to the advanced age of 115 to 130 years. (*Géographie de la Province d'Afrique*, p. 479.)

spirit of benevolence which contemporary writers freely acknowledge. The force of example, which did not fail to reach the most remote of his subjects, is borne out by an inscription at Sicca Veneria (El-Kef) in the early part of the reign of Marcus Aurelius, setting forth the terms of a charitable endowment on the lines of similar ones on a larger scale originating with Trajan himself. The inscription informs us that P. Licinius, son of Marcus, of the tribe Quirina, surnamed Papirianus, procurator of the Emperor Marcus Aurelius Antoninus, left in trust to his very dear fellow-citizens a sum of money, the interest of which should be expended for ever from year to year in the maintenance of three hundred boys from three to fifteen years of age, and two hundred girls from three to thirteen years of age.[1]

```
        MVNICIPIBVS MEIS CIRTHENSIBVS
        SICCENSIBVS CARISSIMIS MIHI DARE
        VOLO HS XIII VESTRAE FIDEI COMMITTO
        MVNICIPES CARISSIMI VT EX VSVRIS
        EIVS SVMMAE QVINCVNCIBVS QVODAN
        NIS ALANTVR PVERI CCC ET PVELLAE CC
                    PVERIS
        AB ANNIS TRIBVS AD ANNOS XV ET
                   ACCIPIANT
        SINGVLI PVERI ✻ IIS MENSTRVOS
                    PVELLAE
        AB ANNIS TRIBVS AD ANNOS XIII
```

It is pleasant to record the circumstances attending Trajan's benefaction, mainly on the ground that it serves as a prototype of unnumbered similar charitable institutions still increasing in all parts of the civilised world. In the latter days of the Republic the poor-law question remained an unsolved problem, and continued so under the Cæsars. Many attempts were made to promote a more equal distribution of property, but without success. Rome had become a city of millionaires and mendicants. The former had established themselves by rapacity as an oligarchy of wealth, the latter had been gradually attracted to the metropolis by the corn doles, which had become, by long usage, the established right of every Roman burgess settled in Rome. No emperor had dared to repeal so pernicious a regu-

---

[1] Berbrugger, *Revue Africaine*, i. 273.

lation. Revolution and anarchy would have been the result. So far from even hinting at its suppression, many of them encouraged it from self-interest, and, with a view to checking disorder in the streets, provided plenty of public entertainments for a dissolute herd of idlers. Public baths were at their service, theatres were enlarged, and exhibitions in the arena were multiplied for their benefit. The outcry for *panem et circenses* was heard and answered. To meet this costly expenditure the thrifty villager and the hard-working farmer were heavily taxed, with the result that children were too often turned adrift or neglected, and, as there was no law against infanticide, new-born babes were put out of the way or exposed, as a matter of cruel necessity. But the far-seeing Trajan came to their help, and, as it were with the stroke of a pen, gladdened the farmer's heart, and made every villager and every child rejoice in serving so benign a ruler. The form of charity which the Emperor established was novel in conception, and proved far-reaching in operation. Two instances have been handed down to us in the form of mortgage deeds, by which sums of money were lent by the Emperor to numbers of small proprietors, bearing interest at 5 per cent. in one case, and $2\frac{1}{2}$ in the other. The yearly amount of interest was to be devoted without deductions to the maintenance of poor boys and girls in the district. It is fair to assume that these two were not exceptional cases, but that throughout Italy at least similar endowments were made in accordance with the wants of the locality. The better known of the two instances relates to the district of Velleia, near Parma,[1] and from the descriptive account furnished by the inscribed stone we gather that Trajan advanced a sum of 23,619,580 sesterces (187,000*l*.) to fifty-one landowners, and the interest was deemed sufficient to support 300 children (264 boys and 36 girls). The other, also on an inscribed slab found at Beneventum, relates to a sinking fund of 414,930 sesterces (3,300*l*.) lent to sixty-seven proprietors at $2\frac{1}{2}$ per cent. interest. By such enlightened methods agriculture was promoted, labourers were

---

[1] The district to which the benefaction recorded in the inscription applies comprises Velleia, Parma, Placentia, and Libarna, equivalent to the entire duchy of Parma, and covering about one forty-seventh part of the kingdom of Italy. (Champagny, *Les Antonins*, i. 258. *Vide* J. C. von Orelli, *Inscript. Lat. Coll.* Turici, 1828-50.)

in demand to till the fields, an impetus was given to trade and manufacture in the smaller towns, and a generation of little children grew up bearing the additional name of Ulpiani in grateful memory of their imperial benefactor. It is gratifying to add that these little matters of Roman history, in Africa as well as in Italy, come down to us unaffected by the lapse of centuries. The records are not on parchment, nor are they the statements of contemporary authors, but inscriptions in indelible lettering on imperishable bronze or marble. This tablet, unearthed at Velleia in the middle of the last century, measures 10 feet by 6 feet, and weighs nearly four hundredweight. It was thoughtlessly broken up as old metal, but, after infinite labour, was put together, and is now an object of attraction in the Museum at Parma, bearing the title of the *Tabula Alimentaria* of Trajan. The inscription, one of the longest yet discovered, covers 670 lines, and gives the names of the several properties on which money was advanced, with the amount in each case and the names of the owners. It also specified in detail how the interest was to be applied, and how it was to be apportioned among a given number of poor children.

It was not long before Trajan was confronted with slight disturbances on the frontier, similar to those which had been recurrent under many of his predecessors. Although they were not of a nature to cause alarm, a feeling of unrest was created, and, consequently, the work of colonisation was retarded. The establishment of a permanent encampment at Theveste as the headquarters of a fully equipped Roman legion, and the erection of a line of fortified posts (*castella*) on the northern slopes of the Aurès mountains, had hitherto afforded sufficient protection in a thinly peopled district. But the feeling of security inspired by Trajan's name, and the many successes attending his earlier career, had tempted Roman farmers and small agriculturists to establish themselves in the more remote but fertile portions of old Numidia. Long stretches of arable land, a beautiful climate unequalled in any part of North Africa, abundant water supply, mineral wealth almost at their doors, and forests of cedar and oak, pine and juniper, which exist to the present day, offered attractions for permanent residences and the investment of capital. With this increase of population and local wealth came the demand for greater protection, and this was not difficult to meet. The military road which connected Theveste with Sitifis (p. 40), fortified at intervals, and following for the greater part of the distance the lower slopes of the Aurès, brought into communication the following towns: *Tinfadi, Vegesela, Mascula, Claudi, Thamugas,* and *Lambæsis*.[1] Of these towns, or rather settlements, Mascula, which was regarded as the key to the Sahara, was the most important from a strategic point of view. We learn that a town was built there at the commencement of the second century, and that it was garrisoned by the 7th company of Lusitanians. At a later period, when Christianity had been firmly established in Roman Africa, it had a brief era of prosperity. Numerous Christian ornaments have been found on the site, and the names of four bishops of Mascula have been preserved—Clarus in the third century, Donatus in the fourth, Januarius at the close of the fifth, and a fourth bearing the same name early in the sixth century. It appears to have suffered terribly about the middle of the fourth century from the incursions of barbarian tribes who banded together for its destruction. An inscription establishes the fact that Publilius Cæcina Albinus rebuilt the town about A.D. 370. *Pro splendore felicium sæculorum dominorum nostrorum Valentiniani et Valentis semper Augustorum . . . atæ . . . re . . . omni Masculæ . . . a fundamentis construxit (atque dedicavit) Publilius Cæionius Cæcina Albinus vir clarissimus consularis sexfasculis provinciæ Numidiæ Constantinæ.* During the Byzantine occupation Solomon the general converted Mascula into a garrison town with walls of defence, and finally, when the Arabs swept over the land, its history as a town came to a close.

The next station of importance on the southern frontier was Thamugas (Timegad), which, at the time of Trajan's accession, appears to have been merely a fortified post. Its charming situation on rising ground more than 3,000 feet above the level of the sea at the intersection of six roads, on the verge of a vast tract of fertile country, and presenting no difficulties in the way of abundant water-supply, induced Trajan to build a town, or rather a city, which should attract citizens of substance from other parts of Roman Africa. The imperial legate pro-prætor, L. Munatius Gallus, in command of the third legion Augusta, received the instructions of the Emperor, A.D. 100, to lay the

[1] *Revue Africaine,* vol. xxi.

Africa under Trajan

foundations, and to proceed with the work as rapidly as possible. At the close of Trajan's reign, A.D. 117, the principal buildings were completed, the town and the neighbourhood adequately peopled, and general prosperity prevailed. Thamugas was not fortified, nor did it cover a very large area, but it became conspicuous for the decorative character of its monuments, and for the sumptuousness which is always associated with a life of ease and prosperity. The town, better known by its modern name Timegad, was designated by the Romans as *Colonia Marciana Trajana Thamugas* or *Colonia Ulpia Thamugas*. The word *Marciana* commemorates the public and private virtues of the Emperor's amiable sister bearing that name. Her humanity and good offices to the poor and friendless are testified by all writers of every age, and her services to the Empire caused her name to be regarded with exceptional honour. This excellent princess, who died A.D. 113, was declared by the Emperor to be Augusta and Empress during his lifetime. The word *Ulpia* is supposed by M. Léon Renier to refer to the veterans of the thirtieth legion *Ulpia Victrix*. In recognition of their meritorious services in the Parthian war, Trajan located them at Thamugas, as a garrison for the protection of the town and the neighbourhood. The inscription referring to this legion exists in duplicate on two octagonal pedestals of white marble.

```
              VICTORIAE
              PARTHICAE
              AVG · SACR
         EX · TESTAMENTO
         M · ANNI · M · F · QVIR
         MARTIALIS . . . MIL
         LEG III AVG DVPLC
         ALAE · PANN · DEC · AL
         EIVSDEM > LEG III · AVG
         ET XXX . VLPIAE · VICTRIC
         MISSI . . . . . HONESTA
         MISSIONE . . . AB . . . . IMP
         TRAIANO . . . . OPTIMO
         AVG · · GER · DAC · PARTH
         SING · HS VIII XX PR · MIN
         ANNI · M · LIB · PROTVS
         HILARVS . . . . . EROS
         ADIECTIS · A · SE · HS · III
         PONEND . . . . CVRAVER
         IDEM · Q · DEDICAVER
                   D · D
```

It will be observed that the words LEG III on the seventh and ninth lines are enclosed by deeply incised lines forming an oblong border. This is equivalent to effacement, although in many inscriptions found in Numidia the words have been entirely effaced. This act was done by the order of Gordian III., A.D. 238, as a punishment to the legion for their adhesion to the cause of his brutal rival Maximinus, and aiding the revolt of Capellianus, at that time governor of Numidia and in command of the legion. Gordian not only disbanded the legion, but employed the troops in other services on the banks of the Rhine.

There is no spot in North Africa which has deservedly attracted so much attention as the site of this old Roman city. Its history may truly be said to be written on marble and stone. Inscriptions relating to its municipal government, with the names of its magistrates faithfully recorded, votive offerings of worthy men and benevolent women, dedications to the emperors who brought peace and prosperity to their doors, and memorials of loyal citizens who desired to be buried on the hillsides which had been so pleasant to them in their lifetime, are all there, in more or less mutilated condition, to tell their own tale of a quiet community long passed away, and, till recently, almost forgotten. Bruce the traveller, who visited the spot in 1765, was the first to make careful drawings of some of the monumental remains, and to decipher the leading inscriptions still standing above the surface. Many other explorers of a succeeding generation have furnished valuable notes as the result of personal investigation, which may be found in the pages of reviews and other periodicals relating to Algeria and Tunisia. But it was not till Professor Masqueray published his official report in 1875-76 that an opinion could be given on the remarkable character of the remains, or on the importance of Thamugas as a link in the long chain of Roman history in Africa. The next valuable contribution to the subject was from the pen of the late Sir R. Lambert Playfair, for many years H.B.M.'s esteemed Consul-General at Algiers. His work, undertaken in 1877, consisted for the most part in following Bruce's track, re-editing his 'Travels in Barbary,' and supplementing the author's notes by much additional information acquired during long residence in the country. The result of M. Masqueray's report was the placing the ruins of Thamugas under the control of the *Service des Monuments historiques*, and authorising a systematic exploration, which was commenced in 1880. Operations have been in progress almost uninterruptedly since that date, and have enabled the experts engaged on the work to publish from time to time descriptive accounts of their discoveries. From an historical point of view, our knowledge of the ancient city has not advanced much since the issue of the official report, nor is it probable that further investigations will throw any additional light on the history of a city which does not appear to have played any part in the political life of the period. But students of history and archæology gratefully recognise the patient, conscientious labours of a number of intellectual men, who have successfully explored a spot of such exceptional interest as the site of the Pompeii of North Africa.[1]

Our knowledge of Thamugas during the first three centuries of its existence is based upon inscriptions, and although it became a centre of Christianity at an early period when St. Cyprian was bishop of Carthage, A.D. 236, there is little written record of its activity till the end of the fourth century. The Church in North Africa was then split into factions, and Thamugas became the seat of religious agitation, the bishop, Optatus, taking part in revolt against the Emperor. The Vandal invasion was the prelude to its decline as a residential city, and when Solomon the general arrived there, A.D. 535, he found the place in a ruinous condition. Procopius tells us that on the approach of the Byzantine army the inhabitants of the mountains destroyed the place to prevent its occupation by the invaders. Solomon made no attempt to restore the city, but made use of the materials for the construction of a large fortress on the outskirts, and for other works of defence. This huge rectangular fortress forms at the present day one of the most conspicuous objects in the landscape. We also learn that Christianity flourished at Thamugas in the seventh century under the rule of Gregorius, governor of Africa, whose name appears on an inscription on the lintel of the entrance-door of a large church which he built there.[2]

---

[1] MM. Boeswillwald, Ballu, et Cagnat, *Timgad, une cité Africaine sous l'Empire Romain* (Paris, 1895-98). M. Albert Ballu, *Les Ruines de Timgad* (Paris, 1897). M. Gaston Boissier, *L'Afrique Romaine* (Paris, 1895). [2] *I.R.A.* No. 1518.

IN TEMPORIBVS CONSTANTINI IMPERATORIS
FL · GREGORIO PATRICIO JOANNES DVX
DE TIGISI OFFERET DOMVM DEI + ARMENVS

This edifice is in a ruined condition, but we may fix the date at A.D. 641, during the short reign of Constantine III. There are also the remains of six other churches, one of which, from its dimensions, was probably the cathedral. In all cases they are constructed with the materials of destroyed Roman buildings, put together with little thought or care, and designed to meet the present requirements of a new creed, rather than as public edifices for the embellishment of the city. There is reason to believe that after the overthrow of Gregorius by the Arabs, A.D. 647, Thamugas was deserted, and reduced by earthquakes[1] and centuries of neglect to its present ruined condition. The names of several bishops of Thamugas have been handed down: Novatus in the third century, Sextus and Optatus in the fourth, Faustinus in the fifth, and Secundus, who was driven out by the Vandals, in the sixth century.

Like most towns in the country, Thamugas has apparently suffered more from neglect and abandonment than from any other cause, although there are indications of attempts to destroy it by fire. It was built on a series of hills cut into broad terraces on the lower northern slopes of the Aurès, and was traversed by the high road from Theveste to Lambæsis. The forum and public buildings were on the higher ground, but the principal part of the town was at a lower level. The configuration of the ground was favourable to the distribution of water, which appears to have followed the lines of the main streets running northwards. Some of the walls which confined the watercourse still exist, and conduits still perform their original functions; but there are no remains of any aqueduct, or of bridges over the ravines. The north façade of the buildings forming one side of the forum had a colonnade in its entire length, intersected by a gateway of monumental character. A flight of ten steps within the gateway formed the principal approach to the forum, which measured 162 feet by 145 feet, entirely paved and surrounded by a broad colonnade of the

---

[1] An earthquake occurred in Africa during the reign of Gallienus, A.D. 267, and another of a more violent nature A.D. 560, during the Byzantine occupation.

Corinthian order, raised two steps above the general area. On the east side was the basilica, and on the south the theatre. On the west side was the *curia* or city hall, measuring about 50 feet by 32 feet, of which the substructure and parts of the walls are still standing. In front of the *curia*[1] and approached by nine steps, six of which still exist, is a platform about 40 feet long and 12 feet 6 inches wide, raised 6 feet 6 inches above the area of the forum. There was a balustrade or low wall in front of the platform. This platform was undoubtedly the tribunal,[2] which held so prominent a place in the public life of the Romans. Here, too, was the *sella curulis*, where the magistrate sat when transacting public business. The area of the forum is covered with pedestals and inscriptions which are quite legible, and there is reason to believe, from the fragments of statuary which have been discovered, as well as from the nature of the inscriptions, that the entire forum was embellished with statues and dedicatory pedestals to the glory of the emperors, or to perpetuate the good deeds of worthy citizens.

The principal building was the temple of Jupiter Capitolinus; in other words, the Capitol. It occupied a commanding position south-west of the city, and stood within a large walled enclosure. The floor of the temple was at a considerable altitude, as there was a stately flight of forty steps to the portico-entrance on the north-east side. The edifice itself was, to use architectural phraseology, hexastyle prostyle, having columns in front and at the sides only. They were of the Corinthian order, fluted, and about 45 feet in height. The proportions of the order are similar to those of the temple of Jupiter Tonans in Rome. When Bruce visited Timegad in December 1765, five of the great columns and a portion of the entablature were standing, but these have long since been overthrown. The capitals were beautifully carved, and the cornices and other parts were highly enriched. It is doubtful whether the inscrip-

---

[1] 'The chief place of meeting of the Roman Senate was called the *Curia*, from the thirty tribes or Curiæ into which Romulus was said to have divided the *Populus*, after an alliance had been made between the Latins and Sabines. The *Curia* was an inaugurated building, and therefore a *templum*, but not *sanctum*.' (J. H. Middleton, *Ancient Rome*, p. 149. *Vide* also Varro, *Ling. Lat.* vi. 10.)

[2] Few of these ancient *tribunalia* are remaining. The one at Thamugas deserves special notice, as all the parts are in fair preservation, although the forum was not large, nor remarkable for any display of architectural grandeur.

tion discovered here in four stones forming a panel, refers to one of the portico-entrances in the large walled enclosure, or to the great portico of the temple itself.[1] The date of the inscription would be A.D. 364–375. *Pro magnificentia sæculi dominorum nostrorum Valentiniani et Valentis semper Augustorum et perpetuorum, porticus Capitolii, seriæ vetustatis absumptus et usque ad ima fundamenta conlapsus, novo opere perfectus exornatusque dedicavit Publilius Cæionius Cæcina Albinus vir clarissimus, consularis, curantibus Ælio Juliano, iterum reipublicæ curatore, Flavio Aquilino flamine perpetuo, Antonio Petroniano flamine perpetuo, Antonio Januariano flamine perpetuo.* The magniloquence of the inscription prompts the supposition that it refers to the rebuilding of the front of the Capitol with the splendid shafts which adorned the portico.

Among other public buildings mention may be made of the Basilica, on the east side of the forum. It was about 92 feet long and 48 feet wide internally, without aisles, divided into eight bays, and roofed in one span with a flat trabeated ceiling. At the north end are three niches, in which are the remains of pedestals, but the statues have disappeared. In front of the *curia*, on the west side of the forum, are two inscribed pedestals undisturbed. One of them is dedicated to Trajan, designated as tribune for the twenty-third time, Emperor for the eighteenth year, Consul for the sixth time, and *Pater Patriæ*. The other refers to the decurions or senators of Thamugas, in commemoration of the unanimity which characterised their deliberations, and records the beneficence of C. Publius, son of Caius, of the tribe Papiria, who was raised to the high office of chief magistrate. But the most valuable of the inscriptions was one brought to light in the *curia*[2] many years ago by M. Masqueray. It gives the names and official titles of sixty-eight *duumvirs*, quæstors, priests, and other functionaries at Thamugas. The list was continued on another slab found some years afterwards, but the names are scarcely legible.

The plan and general arrangement of the Theatre on the

[1] *I.R.A.* No. 1520. Copied by Renier, De la Mare, and others.

[2] A *duumvir* literally means one of two men holding office as a magistrate or commissioner either in Rome or in a town ranked as a *colonia* or *municipium*. One inscription (*C.I.L.* vi. No. 3732) uses the expression *duo vir*; while another (*C.I.L.* vi. No. 1196) refers to *duo viri*. It is a question, therefore, whether the word admits of being used in the plural as *duumviri*. (Smith's *Dict.* vol. ii.)

south side of the forum, built into the side of the hill, and separated from the forum by a broad paved street, are now easily traced, although the enclosing walls of the superstructure have been overthrown. As usual in Roman theatres, the *cavea* was a complete semicircle, this one at Thamugas measuring in its extreme diameter 208 feet. A comparison of this dimension with those of the rather smaller theatres at Pompeii and Herculaneum, with that at Orange in France, and the still larger one in more perfect condition at Arles, is of some assistance in computing the average population of Thamugas in the days of its prosperity.[1] The wall of the *scena* or stage appears to have been embellished with columns and statuary, and lined with slabs of marble. Behind the *proscenium* was a broad loggia or colonnade about 130 feet in length, and here were found two inscriptions bearing dates A.D. 158 and A.D. 167, dedicatory to the Emperor Antoninus and his two successors, M. Aurelius and L. Aurelius Verus.

At the intersection of three main roads on the south side of the town, at a distance of about 500 feet from the forum, are the remains of the *Thermæ*, which have been recently unearthed. They are of considerable extent, covering an area of more than half an acre, and bear traces of work of a palatial character. The walls of the substructure, the mosaic floors of the principal apartments, the bases of numerous columns, and openings in the walls above the ground-floor level are sufficient to enable an expert to reconstruct on paper this fine edifice. These public baths appear to have been built in the reign of Trajan, and a magnificent inscription[2] informs us that they were enlarged A.D. 198, in the time of Septimius Severus, by order of the magistrates and at the expense of the State, Q. Amicius Faustus being the *legatus proprætor*.[3] Among other remains of public

---

[1]
Herculaneum	Italy	180 feet
Pompeii	Italy	197 ,,
Timegad	Africa	208 ,,
Dougga	Africa	246 ,,
Philippeville	Africa	270 ,,
Orange	France	301 ,,
Arles	France	332 ,,
Taormina	Sicily	354 ,,

extreme width externally.

[2] M. A. Ballu, *Les Ruines de Timgad*, p. 181.

[3] A *legatus* was sometimes an envoy or ambassador acting under the directions of

buildings worthy of passing mention are those of the *macellum* or general market. An inscription informs us that a certain wealthy citizen of Thamugas named Plotius Faustus Sertius, of knightly order and in command of the militia force in the district, settled in his native town on retirement from active service, and was honoured by his fellow-citizens with the distinction of *Flamen perpetuus*.[1] We are further told that this honour conferred on the Sertian family was followed by the erection and presentation of this palatial market, paid for by Plotius Faustus and his wife, Cornelia Valentina.

The ruined monuments of Thamugas form a pleasing study to the antiquary, and the large assortment of half-legible inscriptions are a constant delight to the epigraphist. But to the ordinary visitor they impart only a transient interest. A labyrinth of walls, an overthrown column, a fragment of sculptured ornament, or a few sharply incised initial letters have to him but little meaning. And yet from these isolated masses of stone and marble an expert can often reconstruct, stone upon stone, the work as originally designed, and a few scattered letters will become the basis of a well-worded inscription. Such is the case with the most interesting structure which time has spared in this ruined city. Although in a dilapidated condition, this venerable edifice, known as the Arch of Trajan, still stands erect in honour of the illustrious Emperor and founder of the city. Its battered face exposed to eighteen centuries of wind and weather, its broken shafts and fallen attic, its arches half filled up for the purposes of preservation, and its niches which

the Senate, and engaged on some diplomatic investigation, either in parts of Italy or in any of the Roman provinces. But the title was generally used (especially in these pages) to designate a lieutenant or deputy-governor attached to the governor of a province. Down to the time of Diocletian imperial provinces were governed by *legati* of consular or prætorian rank, commonly designated *legati Augusti pro prætore* (*vide* p. 32); *vide Roman System of Provincial Administration*, W. T. Arnold (Oxford, 1879). The only exception known is that of Pliny when he was sent to Bithynia as *legatus pro prætore consulari potestate* (*C.I.L.* vol. v. No. 5262). *Vide* Mommsen and Marquardt, *Manuel des Antiq. Rom.* vol. iii.

[1] A *flamen* was a priest of any particular deity. Such priests were attached to municipal towns, and an emperor had frequently a *flamen* assigned to him. With the exception of the elder Faustina, who had more than one *flaminica* during the lifetime of Antonine, no empress was allowed the privilege. The term *perpetuus* designated the appointment for life. *Flaminica* was the title originally given to the wife of a *flamen Dialis* (*Duovis*), said to have been established by Romulus, together with the flamen Martialis. (*Vide* Plutarch.)

ARCH OF TRAJAN AT THAMUGAS (TIMEGAD)
(Restored).

were once graced with statues or busts of departed emperors, give a piteous aspect to a noble structure. When Bruce visited Timegad in 1765 the Arch was half buried on its east side by an accumulation of fallen masonry and a heap of soil formed by the alteration of the surface of the ground during many centuries of neglect and abandonment. In 1884 it was in a more dilapidated state, and by this time would probably have been a mass of ruins if the Société des Monuments Historiques had not come to its rescue. Thoughtful care and patient labour have been eminently successful. The ruined monument is now in a stable condition, and the removal of the débris, together with the opening up of the old Roman highway and its paved surfaces, places before us a bit of the Roman world not surpassed by anything that is seen among the ruins of Pompeii. The architectural treatment of the monument is original. Over the side arches are square recesses flanked by small columns of the Corinthian order, supported on decorative corbels, and surmounted by a projecting entablature breaking all round. The principal cornice and the cornices of the segmental pediments over the side arches are broken in the same way, producing aitogether a very rich effect. Both façades are similar, but the capitals vary in detail, quaint eagles and other devices being still visible on two of them. The attic, intended to receive the dedicatory inscription, appears to have extended over the whole of the edifice. The original inscription,[1] found in a fragmentary state many years ago near the forum, may be read as follows:

> IMPERATOR CAESAR DIVI
> NERVAE FILIVS NERVAE TRAIANVS
> AVGVSTVS GERMANICVS PONTIFEX MAXIMVS
> IMPERATOR III TRIBVNICIA POTESTATE IV
>   CONSVL III PATER PATRIAE COLONIAM
> MARCIANVM TRAIANVM THA
> MVGADI PER LEGIONEM TERTIAM AVGVSTAM
> FECIT LVCIVS MVNATIVS GALLVS LEGATVS
> AVGVSTI PRO PRAETORE
> DEDICAVIT.

[1] *I.R.A.* No. 1479. The illustration, showing a restoration of this beautiful monument, was prepared in 1886. Since that time a large number of blocks of stone, then lying under the surface, have been brought to light, and placed, as far as possible, in the positions they originally occupied. This conjectural restoration may be regarded as correct, except in a few matters of detail.

The third consulate of Trajan fixes the date A.D. 100, being the year of the foundation of the city. The mass of the monument is sandstone, but the principal columns and other decorative features are of very fine white limestone, having all the appearance of marble. The small columns flanking the niches are of coloured marble. The weak point of the monument as an architectural composition is the lowness of the attic. In other respects the proportions are good, and the mouldings and decorative features of a high order. It appears to have been surrounded by statues and dedicatory pedestals, forming altogether a monumental group of which the citizens of Thamugas might well have been proud.

Those who desire to study in detail these monumental ruins, as well as the remains on other portions of the site, are referred to the works already mentioned, as the most recent contributions to our knowledge of Thamugas. The arrangements of private dwelling-houses of more or less pretensions, shops, paved streets, and passages can now be traced, and a general conception of the extent of the town obtained. And in an angle of the forum will be found, in fair condition, the public latrines, with portions of their fittings in excellent preservation.[1] One at least of the Emperors paid special attention to providing these sanitary conveniences, and regarded them as a source of revenue, much in the same way as our municipal authorities regard the underground arrangements of modern times, though of a more luxurious character. If we are to believe Suetonius, the idea of putting a tax upon urine originated with Vespasian at a time when the imperial treasury was running dry. Suetonius adds that 'Titus blamed his father for imposing such an objectionable tax. Whereupon Vespasian applied to his son's nose a piece of the money received in the first payment, and asked him if it smelt badly. "No!" said Titus. "And yet," said the Emperor, "it comes from urine."'

Judging from fragmentary remains scattered over the site, a variety of marbles appear to have been used for internal decoration. The building stone mostly in use was a sandstone from the adjacent hills. It was easily worked and well adapted for rubble walling. A blue limestone was also largely employed, especially for the paving of the principal streets, and for slabs

[1] *Vide* M. Albert Ballu, *Les Ruines de Timgad*, p. 112.

or panels that were to receive inscriptions. In addition a white limestone, in texture and appearance like white marble, was reserved for columns and decorative features of public and other buildings of an ornate character. This excellent material was quarried some twenty miles distant.

The inscriptions found at Timegad have an interest quite apart from the architectural remains. It seems to have been the custom here from the time of Trajan till the reign of Gordian III., A.D. 238-244, to record on marble or stone the names and titles of citizen benefactors, and consequently an unusually large number of dedicatory pedestals and slabs have been brought to light during the systematic exploration of the city. Here, for instance, is a dedication on a stone found in the forum to a citizen of renown, who had filled several offices of the highest distinction.[1]

P IULIO IVNIANO MARTIALINO C · V · COS · LEG · AVG · PR
· PR · PROVINCIAE
NVMIDIAE PROCOS PROVINCIAE MACEDONIAE PRAEF ·
AERARI . MI
LITARIS CVRATORI VIAE CLODIAE PRAETORIAE TRIBVNO
PLEBEI
QVAESTORI PROVINCIAE ASIAE PATRONO COLONIAE ET
MVNI
CIPI RESPVBLICA COLONIAE THAMVGADENSIVM DE
CRETO DECVRIONVM

It was also not unusual throughout the Empire to record the payments made by magistrates and others on their election to posts of distinction. The amounts of such payments were fixed beforehand by statute, but they were generally far exceeded by donations of various kinds, sometimes for the erection of some public work, at other times to defray the cost of a statue to be placed in the forum. For instance, a citizen named L. Germeus Silvanus, upon whom the dignity of *augur* had been conferred, paid to the municipality the sum of 21,200 sesterces (170*l*.), and, in addition, gave a statue of Mercury and defrayed the expenses of several performances at the theatre. Another inscription, still standing on the west side of the forum, narrates the dedication of a shrine to Fortuna Augusta costing 4,400 sesterces, by two women Annia Cara and Annia, the daughters of two

[1] *C.I.L.* No. 2392, *I.R.A.* 1505; copied and explained by De la Mare and Renier.

freedmen named Annius Hilarus and Annius Protus; and the placing therein a statue of the goddess, the cost of which was borne by the two parents, Annius Protus having bequeathed the sum of 22,000 sesterces for that purpose. To celebrate the inauguration, these two sisters paid for an entertainment at the town-hall. In removing the ground a short time ago round the Arch of Trajan,[1] an interesting inscription tells us that L. Licinius Optatianus, on being appointed *flamen* for life, had promised statues costing 20,000 sesterces, which was far in excess of the sum that could have been legally demanded; that he had added largely to the amount, and altogether had spent 35,000 sesterces. In addition, he had made presents to all the senators of Thamugas, had given an entertainment at the town-hall, and defrayed the cost of performances at the theatre. Another worthy Roman, named P. Julius Liberalis, chief magistrate of the town of Thysdrus (El-Djem), on being appointed *flamen* of Thamugas for life, during the seventeenth tribuneship of Caracalla, built for the use of the citizens one of two large reservoirs bearing the name of *Lacus*, to distinguish it from the adjoining one named *Fons*.[2] Among the inscriptions of special interest, one discovered in the forum many years ago is exceptional.[3] It is a list of the principal clerks employed in the legal department of the establishment of the commander of the province. There is the *Princeps*, who was a sort of general secretary of the provincial government, and was chief of the staff. The *Cornicularius* was a chief clerk, but with larger powers than are accorded to a similar functionary in modern times. He had control over the Court, both lawyers and suitors, and was the guardian of order; he wrote down all decisions and sentences, signed them, and was responsible for their execution. The *Commentariensis* had the control of the prisoners and kept a registry. It was his duty to transmit every month to the judge a list of persons arrested, giving their rank, age, and the particulars of the crime with which they were charged. The *Scholastici* were lawyers who assisted litigants in the Court. Their rapacity was well known. They plundered the suitors and did not hesitate to receive payment in kind as well as in money. The *Exceptores* assisted at hearings, took notes of

---

[1] *Les Ruines de Timgad*, p. 109. [2] *I.R.A.* No. 1527 and *C.I.L.* No. 2391.
[3] *Annuaire de Constantine*, 1883, xxii. 403. M. Poulle descrip.

what transpired, and kept the registers. The *Chartularii* had charge of the records, the library, and the written judicial ordinances. The *Libellensis* is supposed to have been a functionary who had charge of the chest containing papers, summonses, and other official documents (*scrinium libellorum*), and received appeals and addresses to the Emperor. He does not appear, from the position he occupies in the inscription, to have been an officer of importance, his duties being strictly clerical. No doubt he received 'tips' from persons who frequented the Court for general information. All these functionaries received allowances of food and wheat in accordance with their rank.

These few inscriptions, selected from a large number which are fortunately still legible, throw some light on the prosperous condition of this remote African city during the second and third centuries, and give some idea of the public spirit which animated its citizens. Thamugas was essentially a Roman city, founded by Roman colonists under the auspices of the greatest of Roman Emperors. The disposition of the city, the public buildings, the arrangements of dwelling-houses, and the municipal regulations were all based on the same methods which prevailed in the metropolis. Many thousands of names have been brought to light, and they are all Roman names.

Standing amidst this scene of desolation at the end of the nineteenth century—this wilderness of stone and marble—one is inclined to ask why such a city, with so large an accumulation of treasure attesting a high degree of prosperity, should have been erected in this wild and treeless region, where nature presents so many difficulties to overcome, and offers so little encouragement to the cultivation of those gentle arts whic must have flourished here for at least three centuries. You climb the hill above the forum, and, sitting upon the ruined wall of the old theatre, the problem is solved. Those ravines, east and west, where the mountain waters unchecked now rush wildly into the plains, were once water-conduits. You see how they were confined by stone walls, where they supplied the public baths, how they passed under the main streets, and then, descending into the plain, contributed by a proper system of irrigation to that fertility which, to the Roman husbandman, was only another word for abundance. You see the little forum at your feet, with its pretty colonnade, its ranges of pedestals of stone and marble and alabaster, its statues and busts of men and women honoured in their lives, its inscriptions recording the lives of its citizens clear and imperishable. On your right you see where the Roman multitude thronged the basilica. On your left stands pre-eminent the magnificent peristyle of the lordly Temple of Jupiter Capitolinus, and a little lower down the beautiful Arch with its attendant groups of pedestals and statuary, and the Lambæsis road winding gracefully through it up the hillside. These bare mountain slopes were once forests of oak and ash. Those spots on the adjacent hills were cultivated gardens, the delight of the magnates of Thamugas. Beyond were the olive woods covering the spurs of the mountain, and below was the great plain, a sea of fruitful verdure or abundant grain. Thamugas must have been a pleasant dwelling-place seventeen centuries ago.

No other city of equal importance in North Africa yet unearthed is so intimately associated with the name of Trajan. But the spade and the pickaxe are constantly at work; and persistent enthusiasm, which is the keynote of archæology, may one day bring to light his honoured name in many other parts of Roman Africa.

CHAPTER IV

AFRICA UNDER HADRIAN

A.D. 117-138

IT is not within the range of this outline of Romano-African history to comment upon the public or private career of any of the Emperors, except where they are intimately associated with or relevant to the present subject of inquiry. The Cæsars, up to the accession of Hadrian, had governed their African dominions with varying success, but with little personal knowledge of the country or the native races held in subjection.[1] Some of them entirely neglected this wealthy appendage to the Empire, while others gave it their fostering care, and encouraged the spread of colonisation by wise edicts and just administration. The active rule and firm policy adopted by Julius and Augustus were the prelude to the establishment of a system of government inaugurated by Vespasian, and continued with beneficial results under a long line of emperors. To Trajan's successful rule was due the era of prosperity which dawned upon Africa at the commencement of the second century, and it remained for Hadrian to follow in the steps of his wise predecessor. Historians and commentators upon the career of this remarkable ruler have often regretted that so little has been recorded of this stirring epoch in Roman history. Contemporary writers are conspicuous for their silence, but it is fair to assume that numerous treatises of the time emanating from Rome, or well-established schools of literature in Carthage or the chief cities of Africa, have been lost or thoughtlessly destroyed. Suetonius takes rank as an illustrious writer in the early part of the second century; but, with the exception of the lives of the twelve Cæsars and some fragments of other compositions of less interest, his works no longer exist. As the confidential friend and secretary of the Emperor Hadrian and

---

[1] Julius Cæsar was Consul only, but not *Imperator*, during his African campaign.

his companion on so many journeys, his writings would have thrown much light on this period of history. At a later date we have Dion Cassius, who devoted ten years to collecting materials for his history of Rome, written in Greek and published in eighty books. His scholarship was of high repute, and it is a matter of regret that fragments only of the last twenty books have been handed down to us, the remainder having been mutilated or lost. As governor of Roman Africa in the reign of Alexander Severus, A.D. 220–235, he had unusual opportunities of recording his impressions of the country and its inhabitants. Amongst later authors Ælius Spartianus and Julius Capitolinus, who flourished in the days of Diocletian, may be regarded as the most reliable authorities of their time, portions of their principal works being embodied in the volumes entitled *Scriptores Historiæ Augustæ*. The life of Hadrian, written by the former, covers, it should be observed, no more than a dozen pages, and cannot be definitely classed as either history or biography, but, as a study of character, throws considerable light upon the career of this very remarkable Emperor. These authors were followed by Aurelius Victor in the time of Constantius, and at a later period by Zosimus, a man of high distinction in the army of Theodosius, adding considerable lustre to a long line of Roman historians and commentators. The list may be closed with the name of Xiphilin, a learned monk of the eleventh century, who devoted some fifteen pages to a study of Hadrian's career in his compendium of the last forty-five books of Dion Cassius. Occasional notes by other authors of varying repute should also be acknowledged. Fortunately archæology comes to our aid where written records fail, and, with the further assistance rendered by inscriptions on the coins of his reign, we are able to obtain a fair idea of the intellectual as well as personal character of the renowned Hadrian. No less than fifty-three coins commemorative of his visits to the various provinces of the Empire were issued during the latter part of his reign. Those relating to his African visits are seven in number, with the following letters on the reverse: *Africa; Restitutori Africæ; Adventui Aug. Africæ; Mauretania S. C.; Adventui Aug. Mauretaniæ S. C.; Exercitus Mauretanicus S. C.; Restitutori Mauretaniæ S.C.*[1] They indicate the countries

[1] J. H. von Eckhel, *Traité élémentaire de Numismatique* (Paris, 1825), i. 486–501.

visited, but do not give the dates. Perhaps no historian of modern times has more fully realised the versatile character of this gifted Emperor, or has portrayed with more faithful colours the Hadrian we are familiar with in bronze and marble, than Merivale. As pictured by him, Hadrian stands before us 'in face and figure eminently handsome. He reminds us more than any Roman before him of what we proudly style the thorough English gentleman, with shapely limbs and well-set head. Refined, intelligent, an administrator rather than a statesman, a man of taste rather than a philosopher.'[1] For analytical studies of Hadrian's career, written from two different points of view, the more extensive work of Gregorovius[2] is full of interest, and the scholarly pages of Le Comte de Champagny[3] portray in vivid colouring the many distinct phases of a remarkable character. We learn from Dion,[4] who lived in the early part of the third century, that Hadrian 'visited more cities than any other ruler, and to all he was beneficent. He gave them harbours and aqueducts, corn and gold, buildings and honours of many kinds.'[5] It is not quite clear whether Hadrian made two separate journeys into the interior of Africa, but that he traversed the country A.D. 125 is quite certain, the first visit having been apparently to the coast towns three years previously.[6] He appears to have moved from town to town, grasping the most complicated matters of civil and military administration, paying a special regard to the habits and requirements of the native races, and adding to the number of *coloniæ* and *municipia*, in accordance with the needs of localities.[7] His artistic perception and cultured taste favoured the em-

---

[1] Merivale, *A History of the Romans under the Empire*, vii. 493.

[2] Ferd. Gregorovius, *The Emperor Hadrian*, translated by Mary Robinson (London, 1898).

[3] Le Comte de Champagny, *Les Antonins*, ii. 4 et seq.

[4] Dion Cassius, lxix. 5.

[5] Spartianus, c. 13. *In Africam transiit ac multum beneficiorum provinciis Africanis attribuit.*

[6] Orelli, *Inscript. Lat. Coll.* 3564.

[7] Conspicuous among the towns raised to a higher state was old Utica, henceforth designated Colonia Julia Ælia Hadriana Augusta Utika. According to Spartianus, c. 20, Thenæ and Zama were also raised to the dignity of *coloniæ*, and Carthage was renamed Hadrianopolis. There are many other towns mentioned as having been favoured by Hadrian, but many of the inscriptions are scarcely legible, and the dates uncertain.

bellishment of towns with noble edifices, and, like Trajan, he held that the promotion of Art in every form redounded to the glory of the Empire and the welfare of the State.

Roman Africa had enjoyed the blessings of peace for so long a period under the firm rule of Trajan that the colonists were little prepared for an uprising on the frontier soon after Hadrian had ascended the throne. The southern boundaries were well protected by military posts and large well-organised bodies of troops; but the western frontier, presenting a long tract of country without adequate defences and thinly peopled by Italian settlers, became the scene of an insurrection by Moors of western Mauritania. The suddenness of the disturbance may have been anticipated by the Emperor and the Senate in Rome, who were acquainted with the ambitious designs of some of Trajan's most trusted generals. Among them was Lusius Quietus, a Moorish chief, who had raised a band of mercenaries and assumed a Roman name. The sculptures on the column of Trajan show clearly enough the costume and general appearance of the Moorish cavalry under his command in the Dacian war. The troopers are mounted on little horses without bridles, and the costume consists of a short tunic gathered up at the shoulders and fastened by a brooch. A somewhat similar garment is still worn by Arabs. The hair is carefully curled and dressed round the head. Each trooper carries a small shield, and, from the bend of the arm and hand we may assume that he was armed with a lance or similar weapon, but this is now effaced. The military success which had attended Quietus had gained for him the appreciation of the Roman legions, and his services to Trajan in the Dacian and Parthian wars, as well as in suppressing a revolt of the Jews in Palestine, had made him the recipient of many honours. But he was over-ambitious and dreamt of sovereignty. As a military leader he may have had some claim to nomination as Trajan's successor, but as a statesman and ruler of mankind he had no qualifications. Fortunately for the Roman people, this cunning half-civilised Moor was not at headquarters when Trajan was lying on his death-bed, with scarcely strength enough to whisper the name of his immediate successor. When the intelligence reached Quietus that the lot had fallen upon Hadrian, his resolution was formed, and henceforth he bided his opportunity to throw off the Roman yoke. The Moor had not long to wait, for Hadrian removed him from command in Syria and appointed him governor of Mauritania. Here he instigated an uprising of the Moors with partial success, and, subsequently being accused of conspiring to assassinate the Emperor, was put to death by order of the Senate. This Moorish insurrection was of long duration, but was finally quelled by the military skill of Marcius Turbo, combined with the enthusiasm aroused in the Roman legions by the presence of the Emperor. This was Hadrian's first appearance in Africa, and it was natural that the Senate should attribute the suppression of the rebellion and the success of Roman arms to the skill of their distinguished ruler. Festivals were ordered, and coins were struck in his honour as Restorer of Mauritania, and in gratitude for a revival of security for the colonists of Roman Africa.

ADVENTVI · AVG · MAVRETANIAE · EXERCITVS · MAVRE-
TANICVS · RESTITVTORI · MAVRETANIAE[1]

There is no town of importance in Africa which is intimately associated with Hadrian as its founder; but the whole colony, even in the present day, bears numerous traces of works of utility and adornment carried out by his instructions for the benefit of the provinces. An inscription informs us that Hadrian visited the camp of the third Augustan legion, which constituted the main body of the African army, and that he put in order the military organisation of the country. The record of this visit has been preserved on two pedestals discovered at Lambessa many years ago. One inscription runs thus:[2]

IMP CAESA	*Imperatori Caesari, Traiano Hadriano*
TRAIANO	*Augusto, fortissimo liberalissimoque*
HADRIANO AVG	*dedicante Publio Cassio Secundo*
FORTISSIMO	*legato Augusti pro prætore Veterani*
LIBERALISSIMOQ	*legionis tertiæ Augustæ qui mili-*
DEDICANTE	*tare cœperunt.*
P · CASSIO SECVNDO	
LEG · AVG · PR · PR	
VETERANI	
LEG ✶ AVG	
QVI MILITAR	
COEPERVN	

On the faces of another pedestal bearing a monumental

---
[1] Eckhel, vi. 198; an inscription on a coin. [2] *I.R.A.* No. 1; copied by Renier.

column is inscribed the Emperor's address to the legion, covering no less than sixty-three lines. After reviewing the troops he alludes in eulogistic terms to the excellence of their manœuvres and the handling of their weapons, and praises the arrangements of the camp and the admirable construction of the entrenchments. Among the works of utility associated with his name, the maintenance and extension of the great highways deserve record. Upon a milliary column found in the neighbourhood of Carthage, we read that Hadrian ordered the soldiers of the third legion to pave the military road between Carthage and Theveste,[1] and to construct a road from Rusicada (Philippeville) to Cirta (Constantine).[2]

IMP CAESAR	EX AVCTORITATE
DIVI NERVAE NEPOS	IMP CAESARIS
DIVI TRAIANA PARTHICI F	TRAIANI HADRI
TRAIANVS HADRIANVS	AN AVG PONTES
AVG · PONT · MAX · TRIB	VIAE NOVAE RVSI
POT · VII COS · III	CADENSIS RP CIR
VIAM A CARTHAGINE	TENSIVM SVA PECV
THEVESTEN STRAVIT	NIA FECIT SEX IVLIO
PER LEG · III · AVG	MAIORE LEG AVG
P METILIO SECVNDO	LEG III AVG PR PR
LEG · AVG · PR · PR	

The latter inscription gives us to understand that the work was paid for out of the imperial treasury.

The one monumental work with which the name of Hadrian will be always associated is the great aqueduct which brought the waters of Mount Zaghouan and Mount Djougar to the cities of Carthage and Tunis.[3] It is a question whether there is any Roman structure now standing within the vast area of the Empire which bears in so high a degree the impress of imperial will, or attests so visibly the strength of Roman character, as this stately line of piers and arches. 'The waters flow to Carthage,' says

[1] Shaw's *Travels in Barbary*, p. 573.
[2] *I.R.A.* No. 2296, copied by Renier. *Vide* De la Mare, *Explor. de l'Algérie*. Also Letronne, *Journal des Savants* (1847), p. 624.
[3] According to Frontinus (*de Aquæd. Urb. Rom.*), who was for some years *curator aquarum* in the time of Vespasian, A.D. 74, the first aqueduct constructed by the Romans in Italy was B.C. 231. The *Aqua Trajana*, which supplied the Janiculum in the *Transtiberine* region, bears the dates A.D. 110 and 111 on coins of gold, silver, and bronze.
  The *curator aquarum* was an officer of great dignity and was appointed for life. The first was Marcus Agrippa (Front. 98-99), who held the office till his death, B.C. 12. (J. H. Middleton, *Ancient Rome in* 1885, p. 453.)

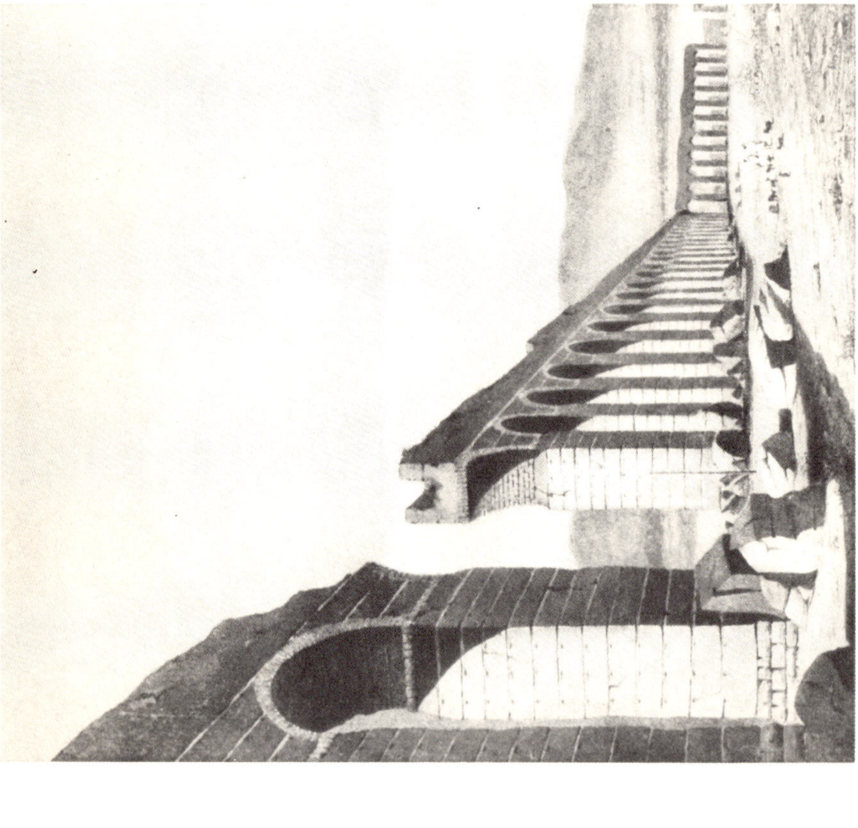

El-Bekri, 'on ranges of arches placed one above the other, reaching even to the clouds.' This stupendous work was conceived by Hadrian, and commenced, it is said, after his second visit to Africa. There is reason to believe that it was completed as far as Zaghouan during his reign, a length of about thirty-five miles, but the extension to Mount Djougar was not finished till the reign of Septimius Severus. A coin bearing his effigy was struck in the mint at Carthage, having on the reverse a figure of Astarte, as the tutelary genius of that city, seated on a lion in front of a spring of water issuing from a rock. The most gigantic portion of the aqueduct was that across the Oued Melian, mentioned by El-Bekri. It was in fair preservation some sixty years ago, but, a new bridge over the river being necessary in consequence of increasing traffic between Tunis and Zaghouan, the piers and superstructure were wantonly overthrown to provide materials for its foundation. The bridge might have been constructed a few hundred yards higher up, and this noble monument left intact. It need scarcely be stated that the modern bridge exhibits the usual combination of iron and stone, and has nothing in extenuation to recommend it.

The great aqueduct, we are told, was a work of necessity. A cry of distress from Carthage had reached Rome. For five consecutive years no rain had fallen in that part of Africa. The cisterns were empty, the land was parched, the harvest was failing, and the grainships for Rome were lying idle in the harbours. There was an abundance of corn in African granaries to meet the immediate demands of Roman colonists and the native population; but for years past Rome, as well as the chief towns in Italy, had looked to the other side of the Mediterranean for their principal supply, and, as the long wars under Trajan had withdrawn a large able-bodied population from agricultural pursuits, the failure of the crops became a matter of grave consideration by the Senate at Rome. There is no need, therefore, to be surprised at Hadrian's desire for a continuance of good harvests in the African provinces. The gods favoured him, for we are told by Spartian that on the day when the Emperor set foot in the country the clouds gathered, the rain fell in abundance, and men's hearts rejoiced.[1] Little wonder

[1] *Quando in Africam venit, ad adventum ejus, post quinquennium pluit, atque ideo ab Africanis dilectus est.* (Spart. *Had.* xxii.)

then that the peasantry regarded Hadrian as a deity, and that his sojourn in the land was marked by unusual gladness!

The system of rain-water storage, which the Carthaginians had inherited from the Phœnicians, and had brought to perfection, was continued by the Romans in rebuilding Carthage. The great reservoirs which El-Bekri calls 'the cisterns of the demons' were restored for the service of the great aqueduct; and another range of cisterns, called the smaller cisterns, of which there were eighteen, each measuring 93 feet by 19 feet 8 inches and 27 feet 6 inches to the crown of the vault, capable of holding upwards of four million gallons, were built for the storage of rain-water. These cisterns are built with rubble stone and remarkably hard mortar, and are coated internally with thin cement, apparently made with marble dust. Some of these cisterns are still in fair preservation and are used by the peasantry. The larger cisterns of the Carthaginians are in ruins. Shaw says 'there were twenty in his time, the dimensions being 350 feet by 25 feet. They were supplied by an aqueduct from Zaghouan, and the channel or duct was 3 feet wide.' At the angles, as well as in the centre of their length, there were circular filters domed over. Even in their present ruined condition the forms of these gigantic reservoirs are easily traced. For a long period the Romans adopted the methods of their predecessors, constructing their cisterns in long parallel basins with very thick rubble walls and rubble vaulting. According to M. Daux and other investigators, there were covered galleries more than six feet wide on each side for the purpose of protecting from the sun the inhabitants who came to draw water. In the plains the cisterns were frequently of polygonal form, built with rubble and strengthened by counterforts within and without. Those of a large size were not covered. In some cases a second basin of rectangular shape was added, vaulted over, but with a flat roof externally, and with openings at intervals to facilitate the lowering of pitchers into the water. A range of cisterns of this form may still be seen on the road between Susa and Kairouan. There is another, mentioned and illustrated by Daux, on the road to Aquæ Regiæ, the celebrated warm baths frequented by the kings of Numidia, at the junction of the road leading by Avidus and Sarsura to Thysdrus. A reproduction of the drawing will be found in MM. Perrot and

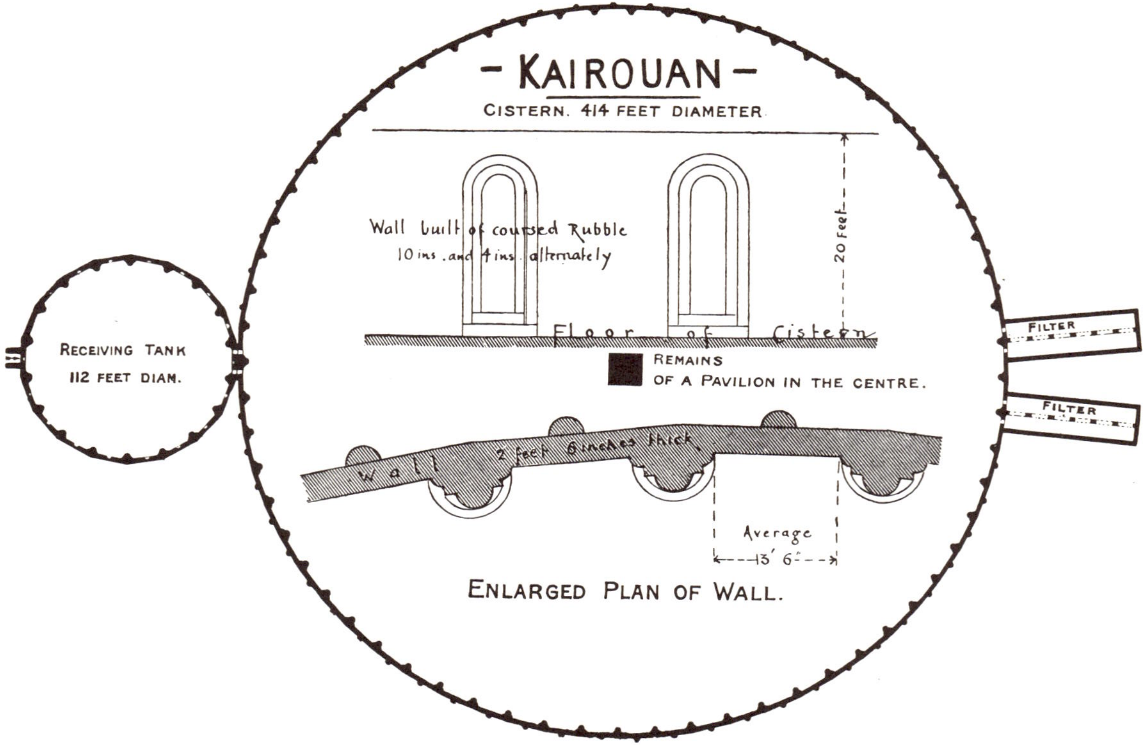

— KAIROUAN —
CISTERN. 414 FEET DIAMETER.

Wall built of coursed Rubble 10 ins. and 4 ins. alternately

20 feet

Floor of Cistern

REMAINS OF A PAVILION IN THE CENTRE.

Wall 2 feet 6 inches thick

Average 15′ 6″

ENLARGED PLAN OF WALL.

FILTER FILTER

RECEIVING TANK
112 FEET DIAM.

Chipiez's *History of Art in Phœnicia*. These authors ascribe the two circular basins to the Carthaginians, and the square filter to their conquerors.

The most remarkable reservoir in North Africa is outside the walls of Kairouan. Here are two large basins of polygonal shape, the larger being 414 feet in diameter and 20 feet deep, having in the centre the substructure of a pavilion, which was probably of an ornate character and enriched with sculpture. Around the smaller basin is a series of niches. Communicating with the larger reservoir are two parallel basins or filters, formerly covered by galleries or arcades. The walls of the great basin are constructed with rubble stones in alternate courses of ten inches and four inches, and strengthened on both sides by counterforts symmetrically placed at intervals, semi-circular on plan and at the top, like a niche reversed. The inner faces of the basins are coated with thin cement. This extraordinary work is attributed by the Arabs, on the sole authority of El-Bekri, to the Aghlabites, who ruled over North Africa at the commencement of the ninth century. In all probability these reservoirs were built during a late period of the Empire, and were subsequently restored by the Arabs. Shaw tells us that the cisterns built by Sultan ben Iglit in several parts of Tunisia are of equal solidity with the celebrated ones at Carthage, and continue firm to the present day. 'The plaster is made of the following proportions: one part of sand, two parts of wood-ashes, and three of lime; which, after being well mixed, is beaten incessantly for three days and three nights with wooden mallets, sprinkling a little oil and water alternately till the plaster becomes of equal consistency. This is chiefly used in making arches, cisterns, and the terraces or tops of houses. Their pipes were let into each other, and jointed with tow and lime beaten together with oil only and without water. Both these compositions quickly assume the hardness of stone, and are impervious to water.' There is little doubt that these constructive methods were traditional, and originated with the Phœnician settlers.[1]

---

[1] The Romans in the time of the elder Pliny knew that water found its own level (Pliny, iv. 11, xxxi. 57), and were acquainted with the principle of the siphon. Of these siphons one has been noted at Cirta (Constantine), others at Lyons and in Pamphylia. The finest and the most daring is at Alatri, B.C. 150, capable of supporting a

Cisterns and wells play an important part in Oriental life, especially in a dry and thirsty land, where the rainfall is less regular than in more temperate zones, where the river beds are bare the greater part of the year, and where the waters of the lakes are more or less impregnated with salt. The storage of water thus became a science at a remote period, and the paving of streets probably originated with the necessity of storing the rainfall in as pure a condition as possible. Cisterns were constructed with great care under every house, and public reservoirs, into which the street waters were conveyed, were built in every town and maintained by the municipalities. Under the Romans the reservoirs were kept free from impurities, and general regulations to ensure cleanliness were strictly enforced. In later times, under the irregular rule of both Moors and Arabs, these sanitary traditions were wholly neglected. The custom of building cisterns under ordinary dwelling-houses was still preserved, but public reservoirs, the pride of Carthaginian and Roman, were thoughtlessly abandoned. In their place we find throughout the country open ponds fouled by accumulation of mud, without any attempt at maintenance or purification. The Roman cisterns in North Africa are a remarkable feature. They are nearly all of the same type, consisting of a series of vaulted chambers side by side, the number of chambers varying with the sizes of the towns. Those at Sicca (El-Kef) are a good example of work of this kind, and, though used at present for other purposes, are fortunately in excellent preservation. There are no less than thirteen of these chambers, each about 90 feet long, 23 feet wide, and 20 feet high, and the original cement lining is in some parts quite smooth and perfect.

From an inscription on a marble altar discovered near Lambessa in 1866,[1] we have a graphic account of the difficulties experienced, A.D. 152, by the citizens of Saldæ (Bougie) in obtaining a supply of water from a spring some fourteen miles distant. We are introduced to the governor of the province, the hydraulic engineer, and the contractor for the work; and

---

pressure of 10 atmospheres. The Romans were unacquainted with cast iron, and no pipe, except of cast iron, could have supported the pressure of such volumes of water. (Sig. Lanciani, *Ancient Rome*, p. 59.)

[1] Translated by Signor Lanciani, *Ancient Rome*, p. 61.

Africa under Hadrian

we learn that an expert named Nonius Datus, attached to the third Augustan legion at Lambæsis, had visited Saldæ by the desire of Varius Clemens, governor of Mauritania, and had prepared the necessary plans for executing the work. We are further informed that the duct for conveying the water had to pass through an adjacent mountain by means of a tunnel. The contractor, it appears, commenced his borings at both ends, and, whether through carelessness or neglect to follow the lines and levels furnished by Nonius Datus, found that he was making two tunnels instead of one. The engineer was consequently sent for, and, on the fulfilment of his mission, presented the following Report to the magistrates of Saldæ: 'After leaving my quarters (at Lambæsis) I met with brigands on my way, who robbed me even of clothes and wounded me severely. I succeeded, however, in reaching Saldæ, where I was met by the governor, who, after allowing me some rest, took me to the tunnel. There I found everybody sad and despondent. They had given up all hopes that the two opposite sections of the tunnel would meet, because each section had already been excavated beyond the middle of the mountain, and a junction had not been effected. As always happens in these cases, the fault was attributed to the engineer for not having taken all precautions to secure the success of his work. What could I have done better? I began by surveying and taking the levels of the mountain. I marked most carefully the axis of the tunnel across the ridges; I drew plans and sections of the whole work, and handed them over to Petronius Celer, at that time governor of Mauritania. As an extra precaution, I summoned the contractor and his workmen, and began the excavations in their presence, with the help of two gangs of experienced veterans, viz. a detachment of marine infantry (*classicos milites*) and a detachment of Alpine troops (*gæsati*). What more could I have done? Well, during the four years I was absent at Lambæsis, expecting every day to hear the glad tidings of an abundant water supply at Saldæ, the contractor and his assistant had committed blunder after blunder. In each section of the tunnel they had diverged from the straight line, each towards the right, and had I waited a little longer before coming, Saldæ would have possessed two tunnels instead of one.' We learn that Nonius Datus, having discovered the mistake, caused the two diverging arms to be united by a transverse channel, and that the arrival of the waters of Ain-Seur was celebrated with extraordinary rejoicings, in the presence of the governor, Varius Clemens, and of the engineer. This little episode is of special interest in our own days, when the earth is being tunnelled in all directions for the service of mankind.

The total length of the aqueduct of Carthage has been estimated at 54 miles. The actual duct or channel is 3 feet wide and 6 feet high, arched over, and with openings at intervals for inspection and ventilation. The springs from the two mountains were (and are still, I believe) capable of supplying 81 gallons per second, or upwards of eight millions of gallons in twenty-four hours. The construction varies in different portions. That which was first commenced, nearest to Zaghouan, in the plains of the Oued-Melian, is beautifully built with courses of finely cut stone, each course being 20 inches high. The sizes of the piers average 12 feet wide and 15 feet thick, and the spans of the arches average 15 feet. A roll moulding 20 inches thick forms the impost. The voussoirs of the arches are carefully cut, and the actual duct above these is formed entirely with rubble. The most interesting portion of the aqueduct, as a building construction, is that across the Medjerda plain, within 10 miles of Tunis. It is made of what is known as *pisé*, being simply the clayey soil of the district, mixed with a certain portion of lime, and built up in sections, after the manner of modern concrete construction. This method of building is attributed to the Phœnicians. Hannibal, during his long sojourn in Spain, raised his fortifications in this way, wherever the material was available. Pliny speaks of *pisé* with rapture on account of its durability and the ease with which it can be put together, giving the name of *formacei* to walls of this kind, as made in a *forma* or frame.[1] It is quite possible that the Carthaginians found this mode of building prevalent among the earlier inhabitants of North Africa and transmitted it to their successors. The piers in this portion of the aqueduct

---

[1] *Quid? Non in Africa Hispaniaque ex terra parietes, quos appellant formaceos, quoniam in forma circumdatis utrimque duabus tabulis inferciuntur verius quam struuntur, ævis durant, incorrupti imbribus, ventis, ignibus, omnique cæmento firmiores? Spectat etiamnunc speculas Hannibalis Hispania terrenasque turres jugis montium impositas.* (Pliny, *Hist. Nat.* xxxv. 14.)

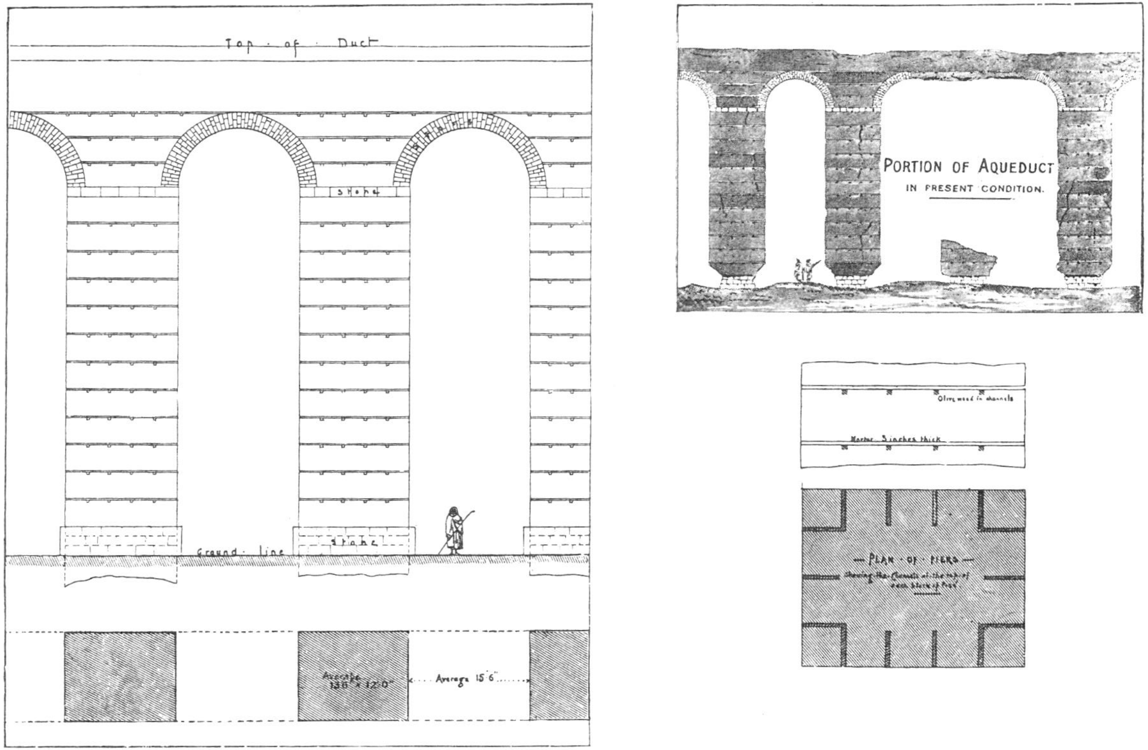

AQUEDUCT OF CARTHAGE IN THE MEDJERDA PLAIN, SHOWING CONSTRUCTION.

are 13 feet wide and nearly 15 feet thick, the spans of the arches being 15 feet. The foundations consist of several courses of cut stone, and the superstructure is built up in sections 3 feet 8 inches high. On the upper surface of each section, channels 6 inches square and 2 feet 3 inches long are left by the insertion of a mould. There were five such channels on the faces, and three generally in the thickness. In these were laid strips of olive-wood 1 inch or more thick and 6 inches wide. When the material was well consolidated and dry, strong mortar $2\frac{1}{2}$ inches thick, containing a large admixture of wood-ashes, was laid over the entire surface, filling up the channels. Wooden pegs were driven in at intervals in order to ascertain and secure a perfectly level bed for the next section, and so on up to the summit sixty or more feet from the ground. There is a course of cut stone at the springing of the arches, and the voussoirs are 2 feet on the face, but of two or more stones in depth.

The stability of this form of construction is shown by the excellent condition of portions of the aqueduct now standing, although they have been subjected to repeated earthquakes. In some parts the Arabs, with their usual destructiveness, have removed more than half the stones forming the bases of these gigantic piers without affecting the superstructure, and in others whole piers have fallen or been thrown down, leaving the duct poised in mid-air without apparent support.

In an article on *Pisé*,[1] written some years ago, it is stated that the walls of most of the houses on the banks of the Rhine were built of nothing but earth, with planks of wood laid at intervals in the body of the material, care being taken that the ends of the planks were not exposed to the air. In taking down old houses of *pisé* the wood has been found to be perfectly sound, and in some cases the original colour had been retained. The rich traders of Lyons, we are told, had no other way of building their country-houses.

The entire aqueduct of Carthage, as the work of the infidel, would have been destroyed by the Arabs centuries ago if some Eastern story-teller had not woven a legend in its favour, and attributed its construction to a true follower of the Prophet. The story says that, under the Carthaginian rule, a neighbouring king, who was a good Mohammedan, fell in love with the

[1] Rees's *Cyclopædia*, art. Pisé.

daughter of a Carthaginian senator and demanded her in marriage. Consent was given on the condition that he brought the waters of Zaghouan and Djougar to Carthage. The work was long and tedious, and at the moment of completion the girl died. A younger sister stepped forward to take her place. The work was finished and the marriage was celebrated.

The source of the main supply from Mount Zaghouan lies at a short distance from the modern town of Zaghouan, which replaced a Roman village or settlement probably called Zeugitanus. But this is purely conjectural, learned archæologists having given the name of Villa Magna to the old Roman town. There are the remains of a triumphal arch, which Shaw says was decorated with sculpture, but absence of inscriptions deprives this ruined monument of any interest. The name of this town may be synonymous with Zeugitania, the title by which *Africa Provincia* was known at the time of the Roman invasion. Shaw says that the boundary of the province was at the foot of the mountain now called Zaghouan, and adds that the Zygantes mentioned by Herodotus were the presumed inhabitants of this country. The waters of Zaghouan are not only renowned for their purity, but for certain properties useful in dyeing. At the present time a considerable industry has arisen in the dyeing of the red caps worn in Mohammedan countries, called *chachias*, in Egypt *tarboosh*, and in Turkey *fez*. But the special interest in the place, in connection with the reign of Hadrian, is centred in the monumental remains of a small temple constructed under the spur of the mountain, to mark the source of the water supply and to commemorate the achievement of a magnificent undertaking. The temple is on a small scale, and is placed in the centre of the arc of a semicircular colonnade, the entire composition bearing some resemblance to a Roman theatre as seen from the *proscenium*, or recalling, on a much smaller scale, the portico of St. Peter's at Rome with its colonnades. The width of this colonnade at Zaghouan is 15 feet; the columns in front were of the Corinthian order, the roof was vaulted, and the back wall resting against a lower slope of the mountain was built with finely cut blocks of stone. In each alternate intercolumniation was a niche for a statue. The total number of intercolumniations was twenty-four, twelve on each side the central temple. The entire area in front, 94 feet wide and

VIEW OF MOUNT ZAGHOUAN.

86 feet long, was paved with large flat stones. The spring flowed under this area, the water passing into a basin of the form of a double horseshoe, to which there was access by a flight of steps at each end. Here commenced the conduits which served to irrigate the adjacent land and to supply the great aqueduct. This ruined structure, originally designed with much care, has beauty of its own apart from its charming position, and, like many other monumental remains in North Africa, is a pleasant memorial of a great people long since passed away. The columns are overthrown, the niches are empty, and the carved capitals have been removed. They may be found, as usual in this country, in some neighbouring mosque, misapplied, wedged up to support a flimsy Arab roof and coated with inevitable whitewash. Modern Tunis, it may be observed, is still supplied with water from the same source, but through a more prosaic channel than the stately duct which once led to Roman Carthage.

Among other cities in North Africa favoured by the Emperor's notice was Leptis Magna. An inscription on a block of marble discovered by Hebenstreit in 1732 records his name in connection with an aqueduct to the city from the river Cinyphus, at the expense of Q. Servilius Candidus.[1] The date would be A.D. 119 or 121.

IMP · CAES · DIVI · TRAIANI
PARTHICI · FIL · DIVI · NERVAE . NEPOTE · TRAIANO
HADRIANO · AVG · PONT · MAX · TRIB · POT · · · COS III
Q · SERVILIVS · CANDIDVS · SVA
IMPENSA · AQVAM · QVAESITAM · ET · ELEVATAM
IN · COLONIAM · PERDVXIT

The comparative paucity of inscriptions in Roman Africa, bearing the name of Hadrian, is somewhat remarkable. With the exception of Septimius Severus, an African by birth, no emperor devoted so much personal attention to the needs of the Roman colonists, or strove by such peaceful methods to attract the native populations to the ways of civilisation, as Hadrian. And yet the records of his active career in Africa are few, and monumental remains bearing his name are not numerous. No period of the Empire was more favourable to

---

[1] *C.I.L.* No. 11.

the promotion of art or the encouragement of the adornment of cities than the later years of his reign. Since the time of Tiberius the arts, especially that of architecture, had been retrograding, and it remained for Trajan, as an imperial builder, to give an impetus to the erection of public works both in Rome and the provinces, which should express the magnificence of imperial rule. Trajan cannot be regarded as a lover of art, but rather as a believer in art as an instrument of power and as an expression of grandeur and nobility; and though he is credited with having rebuilt half the Roman world, he must yield the palm to his successor as the greatest of building emperors. The many-sided character of Hadrian's career has proved an interesting study to the commentators of his time. His success as a peaceful administrator was partly due to an inherent desire to govern by negotiation rather than by force; but it may be attributed in a great measure to his intimate acquaintance with the habits and wants of the various races he was called to rule over. This was especially the case with the natives of his African provinces, who enjoyed a continuance of the prosperity secured to them by Trajan. It is to Hadrian's credit that he lightened taxation, promoted education, maintained thirty legions in different parts of the Empire, and left to his successor a well-filled treasury. His career as an artist must be taken seriously, for he not only had artistic perception of a high order, but he made himself a master of the technicalities of the various forms of art. The indulgence of building propensities, which were displayed principally in Rome, in his country retreats, and on the outskirts of Athens, formed the chief enjoyment of his life. Wherever the Emperor went he left some conspicuous mark of his taste in architectural art, and, consequently, whenever the spade of the explorer has brought to light the name of Hadrian on some inscribed slab, we may expect to find some ruined monumental building that had been raised in his honour. There are many stories handed down to us of his controversies with Apollodorus, the great architect of his time, and the designer of the chief public buildings of his predecessor, but they should be accepted with reserve. That Hadrian was vain of his intellectual and artistic powers, and that Apollodorus was proud of his skill and of a long succession of imperial favours, is beyond controversy. But it is difficult to believe that blunt criticism of the Emperor's designs (probably justifiable from an architect's point of view) should be followed by an order of Hadrian to put Apollodorus to death, and that his instructions were carried out forthwith. This is the story as told by Dion, who gives no authority for the statement. Hadrian, we are told, submitted to Apollodorus his design for a Temple of Venus to be erected in Rome, and the architect sent word to the Emperor that the proposed edifice was not high enough 'nor large enough; that in height it was not important enough for such a thoroughfare as the Via Sacra. The proposed statues were too large and not proportioned to the height of the building, and if the goddesses should feel inclined to rise from their sitting posture, the roof would hinder them.' Spartian makes no mention of this tale, nor does it find a place in the works of other Latin authors who treat of this period of Roman history.[1] It is satisfactory to note that so many writers of repute give little credence to it, regarding the legend as having originated with some court gossip. Or it might have been the invention of Suetonius, the Emperor's secretary, who was dismissed from imperial service for disrespectful behaviour to the Empress Sabina.

Few empresses have left a slighter record than the wife of Hadrian. Her marriage was a matter of imperial policy, and does not appear to have been based on affection on either side. The little we know of Sabina's public and private life gives evidence of amiability and benevolence. From the day that she entered the palace of the Cæsars to her decease, some two years before the death of the Emperor, her time passed uneventfully, taking little interest in Hadrian's incessant travels, and bearing with equanimity a harshness of conduct to which she became accustomed with advancing years. Whether Sabina ever accompanied the Emperor in either of his journeys through the African provinces is doubtful, but an inscription found many years ago on a marble pedestal at Saldæ (Bougie) renders it probable. The dedication is to the Empress, and is thus interpreted by Hübner:[2]

*Divæ Sabinæ Augustæ coloni coloniæ Juliæ Salditanæ
decreto decurionum, pecunia publica posuerunt*

[1] *Vide* Ferd. Gregorovius, *The Emperor Hadrian*, b. ii. c. xxv. Duruy, *Histoire des Romains*, iv. 395.
[2] Acad. Berlin, *Societas Regia Scientiarum*, Æmilius Hübner, 1885.

CHAPTER V

AFRICA UNDER ANTONINUS PIUS

A.D. 138-161

GOOD fortune favoured Antoninus during an uninterrupted reign of twenty-three years. His correct name was Titus Aurelius Fulvus Boionius Arrius Antoninus, which was changed on his assuming the purple to Titus Ælius Hadrianus Antoninus Augustus.[1] Rome was then at peace with the rest of the world, and the provinces were reaping the benefits arising from forty years of wise and beneficent government under Trajan and his successor. Slight disturbances arose on the Moorish frontier at the commencement of Antonine's career, but they do not appear to have affected general prosperity, nor to have retarded the work of colonisation in that direction. At subsequent periods of Roman history the Moors caused an infinity of trouble, and, on one occasion, succeeded in evading the Roman army and encamping for a short time before the walls of Carthage. Pausanias, referring to this particular disturbance, says that 'the Moors form the largest population of the Libyans, who are nomads like the Scythians, and are very difficult to overcome. They travel about on horseback accompanied by their wives and families, and not in vehicles. Antoninus chased them from all parts of Africa held by the Romans and drove them back to the Atlas Mountains.'[2] The record of this Emperor's uneventful reign of twenty-three years is almost a blank. Dion's manuscript is unfortunately lost, and Capitolinus devotes only half a dozen pages to his career. Xiphilin, in his abridgment of Dion, has nothing but praise for this gentle peace-loving ruler, and Sextus Aurelius Victor, a reliable author of the fourth century, closes his brief memoir by telling us that

---

[1] *Vide* Guérin, *Voyage en Tunisie*, Paris, 1862, Inscript. No. 19, vol. i. p. 100, and No. 183, vol. i. p. 411.

[2] Pausanias, *Arcadia*, lib. viii.

Africa under Antoninus Pius

'without making any war at all Antoninus ruled the world for three-and-twenty years by his own authority, insomuch that all kings, nations, and people did stand in awe of him, loving him withal. They rather esteemed him to be their Father and Patron than their Lord and Emperor, and with one consent they all sought his decision in their controversies, looking on him as if he had slid down from heaven.'

Unlike Hadrian, whose life reads like one long day of incessant locomotion, Antonine scarcely travelled beyond the outskirts of Rome, dividing his time between duties in the Senate-house and homely pleasures at his country seat at Lorium, some ten miles distant from the capital on the Appian Way. It is true that such a career, undisturbed by wars abroad or the troubles of factious intrigues at home, has afforded few materials for biographers, but it has led historians to consider how far so uneventful a reign of three-and-twenty years contributed to the progress of the Empire in the provinces as well as in Italy. In Africa there is little to indicate the direct influence of Antonine's rule. Dedicatory inscriptions are not wanting, and, strange to say, the most remote towns, whose inhabitants were unacquainted with the Emperor's personality, bear testimony to the present day of their goodwill towards so benign a ruler. At Œa, for instance, the modern Tripoli, may still be seen on a ruined arch of great magnificence a much-worn inscription recording the commencement of this monumental edifice in the reign of Antonine, and of its dedication when completed to his joint successors M. Aurelius and L. Verus, during the consulate of Scipio Œfritus.[1] The grandeur of this arch, which is entirely of white marble and embellished with an unusual amount of sculpture, is specially noteworthy as indicating the high esteem in which the Emperor was held by his distant subjects. Such a work would occupy many years. It was evidently not completed at the time of Antonine's death, and there was nothing unreasonable in dedicating the monument at a later date to the succeeding Emperors. In one of the defiles of the Aurès mountains, known as Khanga-Tigaminin, may still be seen the old familiar lettering cut in the solid rock,

---

[1] Sir R. Lambert Playfair, *Travels in the Footsteps of Bruce*, p. 280. A drawing of this arch, as it appeared in 1766, gives a fair idea of its magnificence.

recording the completion of an important public road during his reign.[1]

IMP · CAES · T · AELIO	*Imperatore Cæsare Tito*
HADRIANO · ANTONINO	*Ælio Hadriano Antonino*
AVG · PIO · P · P ⅠⅠⅠⅠ · ET M	*Augusto, Pio, Pater patriæ*
AVRELIO · CAESARE · II	*quartum et Marco Aurelio*
COS · PER · · PRASTINA	*Cæsare secundum, consulibus*
MESSALINVM · LEG	*per Prastinam Messalinum*
AVG · PR · PR . VEXIL	*legatum Augusti, proprætore*
LEG · VI · FERR · VIA	*vexillatio legionis Sextæ Ferratæ*
FECIT	*viam fecit.*

It will be observed that the sixth legion Ferrata referred to was employed in opening up communication across the Aurès by means of a military road. This legion formed no part of the army of Africa, but was probably sent thither by the Emperor at a time when the third legion Augusta was engaged in defending the western frontiers against irruptions by the Moors. Some fifty years ago the late General St. Arnaud was conducting a column through this identical pass, and when he had reached the summit and looked down on the Great Desert stretched at his feet, he remarked in the enthusiasm of the moment, 'We may flatter ourselves we are the first soldiers to pass through this region.' Strange error! There by the mountain track, on the face of the imperishable rock, was the record of a nation long since passed away—a memorial of a Roman legion who had bivouacked on that very spot more than seventeen centuries ago.

Among other dedications to Antonine mention should be made of an inscription on the great gateway forming the approach to the principal temples at Sufetula in the far south, now known as Sbeitla. This remote town has played an important part in the making of Roman Africa, and was the scene of the great heroic struggle at a later date between Christian and Moslem for supremacy in that country. Its early history is veiled in obscurity, and its name is supposed by Bruce and other travellers to have been derived from the Sufetes, the title held by all magistrates in towns dependent upon Carthage.[2] The modern

---

[1] *I.R.A.* No. 4360. Henzen, *Orellianæ Collect.* vol. iii. No. 6621.

[2] The Roman *duumvirs* called themselves sufetes in Punic towns, the word appearing on several inscriptions. *Vide* Guérin, vol. i. p. 429; also *C.I.L.* No. 797.

ENTRANCE TO THE HIERON AT SUFETULA.

name of the place, Sbeitla, is an Arab corruption. We learn from the Itinerary of Antonine that it is twenty-five miles from Sufes, changed by the Arabs into Sbiba—a city of renown in pre-Roman times. 'We arrived at Sbiba,' says El-Bekri in the eleventh century, 'a town of great antiquity, built of stone, and containing a college and several baths. The whole country around is covered with gardens, and produces a saffron of the greatest excellence.' Sbiba is now a wilderness. The soil is covered with rough herbage, the once flourishing city is now the home of the jackal, and human habitations are not to be found within a radius of twenty miles. What a change from the lordly days when Sufes took high rank among the earlier Roman settlements, placed under the protection of Hercules, and described as *splendidissimus et felicissimus ordo Coloniæ Sufetanæ*! In the Epistles of St. Augustine we learn something of its later career, when Paganism and Christianity were striving for the mastery, and there is a record of sixty inhabitants of the town suffering martyrdom for having overthrown a statue of its protecting deity.[1] But Sufes has long since passed away, and the few travellers who explore this trackless region must build up from their imagination the stone-built city with its pleasant gardens, and the hillsides clothed with timber and perennial verdure. Sufetula, on the contrary, still exists as one of the most interesting places in old Byzacene —a city of ruins in a beautiful country, once remarkable for its abundant supply of water, the sweetness of its climate, and the wealth of its inhabitants. It was entirely surrounded by gardens and orchards, and the productiveness of the soil is apparent in the present day. Sufetula appears to have been in a flourishing condition during the reigns of Antonine and Marcus Aurelius, and, judging by inscriptions of a later date that are still legible, it must have enjoyed great prosperity long after the fall of the Roman Empire. Of its earlier career we have no record, but its last days, tinged with the romance so dear to Arab writers, have furnished abundant material for the exercise of the imagination. From Ibn Khaldoun we learn that in the year A.D. 647 the Khalif Othman determined to effect the conquest of Africa, and that, having raised a large army in Egypt, he despatched it to Tripoli under the command of his brother,

[1] This event is still recorded in the Romish calendar for the month of August.

Abdulla Ibn Saad. At that time Gregorius was governor of Africa, under the nominal suzerainty of the Emperor of the East; but, finding his popularity increasing among the native races, he threw off the Byzantine yoke and proclaimed himself an independent sovereign. His dominions, according to the same authority, extended from Tripoli to Tangier; and Sufetula, his capital, acquired increased renown from the presence of so powerful a ruler. It was not long before the Mohammedan general, with his well-trained army of some 40,000 men, roused to enthusiasm by victory after victory in their onward march from Cyrene and Tripoli, encamped in the near neighbourhood of Sufetula. The two armies met, and for two days were engaged in mortal combat. Such was the excitement in the Byzantine camp that the daughter of Gregorius, a maiden of rare beauty, did not hesitate to fight at her father's side, and to promise her hand and the sum of 100,000 dinars to any one who would slay Abdulla Ibn Saad. The challenge was taken up by the Arab leader, who offered the same money prize to any one who would slay the renowned Gregorius. We are told that the Byzantines were utterly defeated, that Gregorius was killed, and that the beautiful maid was handed over to Ibn ez-Zobeid, who had slain her father. Sufetula was then besieged, taken, and destroyed. The city was pillaged and the booty divided. So great, indeed, was the plunder, we are told, that every horseman of Othman's army received 3,000 dinars, and every foot soldier 1000! The records of Sufetula cease with this calamity, when one of the chief strongholds of the Christian creed was destroyed, and when Christianity in Africa may be said to have received its final blow. The factious spirit of many of the African bishops, their numerous heresies, and their sufferings at the time of the Vandal invasion and for a century afterwards, paved the way for the final overthrow of the Christian Church by the Arabs. And it was aptly remarked by Gibbon in the last century that 'the northern coast of Africa is the only land in which the light of the Gospel, after a long and perfect establishment, has been totally extinguished. The arts, which had been taught by Carthage and Rome, were involved in the cloud of ignorance, and the doctrines of Cyprian and St. Augustine ceased to be studied. Five hundred episcopal churches were overturned by the hostile fury of Donatists, Van-

Africa under Antoninus Pius

dals, and Moors. The zeal and number of the clergy declined, and the peoples, without discipline or knowledge or hope, submissively sank under the yoke of the Arabian prophet.'[1] In further testimony of the complete annihilation of Christianity in a land where its influence was paramount for so many generations, we may quote Victor Vitensis, the historian of the Vandal invasion of North Africa, more than two centuries before the fall of Sufetula. He tells us that during the persecution 4,976 bishops, priests, deacons, and other clerics were taken to Sicca Veneria (El-Kef) and Lares, and handed over to the Moors, who conducted them into the Desert![2]

To the architect the ruins of Sufetula are among the most valuable of the monumental remains in Tunisia. From their extent and variety, and the fair condition of many of the buildings, they take rank with those of Lambæsis and Thamugas, and offer to the student excellent examples of Roman architecture before its final decline.

The principal ruin consists of a rectangular walled enclosure, 238 feet by 198 feet, to which access is obtained through a monumental gateway, nearly in the centre of one side, and through smaller openings on the three others. This enclosure, commonly known as the *hieron*, is at present so encumbered with fallen masonry that accurate measurements are not easily taken. Moreover, a portion of the enclosure having evidently been rebuilt at a subsequent period (probably during the Byzantine occupation in the time of Gregorius), considerable study of the masonry is necessary to enable any one to give a reliable opinion upon the exact outline of the original walls, the height of the enclosure, and the general surroundings both within and without. The entrance gateway was dedicated to Antoninus Pius, as recorded in an inscription in the frieze, but the lettering, it will be observed, is very incomplete.[3]

```
. . . . . . IVI · HADRIANI · ANTONINI
. . . DIVI · · NERVAE · PRONEP  . . . . R
. . INO . . .  PONT · MAX · T . . II · P · P
```

[1] Gibbon, vol. vi. c. 51, p. 369.

[2] Victor Vitensis, as he is generally called—a bishop of Vita, a town in the province of Byzacene. (*The Memorable and Tragical History of the Persecutions in Africke under Gensericke and Hunericke, Arrian Kings of the Vandals*, London, 1605.)

[3] V. Guérin, vol. i. p. 381. Also Sir Grenville Temple, *Excursions in the Mediterranean, Algiers, and Tunis*, London, 1835, vol. ii. p. 339.

Facing the gateway and within the enclosure were three temples, side by side, the front and back walls of the *cellæ* being connected by open arches. The back wall of these temples formed one side of the enclosure, and behind ran one of the streets of the city. The central temple, which is of the Composite order, has a *cella* 44 feet long. The side temples, of the Corinthian order, are somewhat smaller. The porticoes of the temples were all tetrastyle prostyle, the centre one being higher, but in other respects the detached columns were of similar design. Taking the three porticoes together, there were eighteen shafts, the height of those of the central order being 29 feet, and those of the side temples 25 feet 3 inches. They all stood on lofty stylobates constructed with huge blocks of stone. The side and back walls of the central structure were ornamented with engaged shafts projecting a full half-diameter. The walls of the side structures were ornamented with pilasters. All the porticoes are entirely overthrown. The broken shafts, which were all monoliths, the capitals, the fragments of cornices and other enrichments lie piled up one above the other, forming a majestic and imposing mass. So much material lies buried beneath the surface that it is impossible to say whether the pediments were embellished with sculpture. The decorative character of the cornices and other parts lying broken on the ground favours the supposition that the central edifice, at least, was enriched with figure sculpture. The whole enclosure was paved with large stones, some of which are more than seven feet long. The entrance gateway, already referred to, consists of a large central arch and two side ones, and was decorated with four engaged Corinthian shafts on the outer face. Within the gateway was a portico communicating with a colonnade, which continued round the enclosure till it abutted against the walls of the side temples. A range of shops stood against one of the side-walls, but these were evidently of a later erection. There is, however, sufficient evidence, after an examination of the details of these monumental buildings, that the temples and the enclosure were of the same date, and may be attributed to the reign of Antonine. The custom of enclosing temples within walls of defence may have originated at a time when a city's treasures were deposited in sacred edifices, and as a means of affording sanctuary and shelter for women and children, like

THE BRIDGE AT SUFETULA (SBEITLA).

the citadels of primitive times. For instance, the temple of Æsculapius (the largest fane in Carthage) stood within the citadel, the Parthenon at Athens was within the walls of the Acropolis, and the Temple of Jupiter at Rome was at one time within the Capitol. There is another example at Baalbec, where the enclosure, or so-called *hieron*, bears some resemblance, though on a larger scale, to the one at Sufetula.

Among other remains scattered over the site a triumphal arch towards the south of the city deserves mention, although it does not exhibit any features of special merit. An inscription on the frieze tells us that it was dedicated to the Emperors Maximian and Constantine, and it appears to have been built A.D. 305–306 in memory of the latter.[1]

D D D . . . N . . . ER . . . VIS · IMP · PE . . . . .
INVICTIS · AVG · ITEMQVE · CONSTANTIO · MAXIMIANO . . .
LISSIMIS · CAESARIBVS · ON . . . AVGVSTO . . . . . .
ISTIC . . IN · PROVINCIA . . SVA . M . . TVTOS

The remote position of the city has certainly been the best protection of its monuments, and there is little doubt that if there had been any habitations within twenty miles, and ordinary facilities for transport over a country difficult of access, the few buildings still standing would long since have been overthrown. The situation is admirable, on elevated ground at the foot of a range of hills, and on the banks of a river bearing the same name, which has its source some few miles higher up. The water, always tepid, comes bubbling over the rocks, and, rushing towards the plain in whirling eddies, is soon lost in the region of sand.

In nearly all the inscriptions of this reign the appropriate words *Pater patriæ*, abbreviated to P. P., are introduced, for the first time, in conjunction with the more revered title of *Pius*. This word has a far-reaching significance. It may be said to comprise the higher moral qualities of manhood, and to bring within the range of its application a reverence for the gods as well as a faithful discharge of duty to the State and to every citizen of the Empire. The direct indications of Antonine's work in most parts of Africa are difficult to trace, but his name as the pious father of his country remained a pleasant memory

[1] Sir R. L. Playfair, *Travels*, p. 182.

for many succeeding generations. Capitolinus reckons that no less than eight emperors, however unworthy of the distinction, assumed the name of Antonine, and we find that Alexander Severus, who would have honoured the title, modestly refused it on the ground of personal unworthiness, although pressed by the Senate to assume the name. The indirect influence of Antonine's career may rather be sought for in the chief cities and towns of Roman Africa, which at this period had attained a high degree of civilisation, and took rank with Rome, Alexandria, and Antioch as centres of enlightenment and intellectual activity. A century and a half had elapsed since Juba II. had introduced into his remote capital at Cæsarea the elements of Hellenic culture, of which so many traces remain to the present day. During that long interval Carthage, rebuilt almost by enchantment at the will of Augustus, had gradually attained the position of metropolis of Roman Africa, and its schools, modelled after those at Athens and Corinth, never failed to attract ambitious youths from all parts of Mauritania and Numidia. Hadrumetum, Cirta, Theveste, and other towns had also well-established schools, whose reputation was celebrated throughout the Empire in the age of the Antonines; and though we have no actual record of the course of study prevailing at that period, the testimony of contemporary writers is indisputable as to the high esteem in which they were held, confirmed in later times by such reliable authorities as St. Augustine, Lactantius, and Salvian.[1] It is quite certain, however, that the *curriculum* included philosophy and rhetoric, law and medicine, mathematics and natural philosophy. Natural history was not forgotten, and painting and architecture were taught by distinguished professors.[2] From St. Augustine, who received his elementary education at Thagaste (Souk-Ahras),

[1] *Illic* (i.e. Carthage) *artium liberalium scholæ. Illic philosophorum officinæ, cuncta denique vel linguarum gymnasia vel morum.*—Salvian (5th century), *De Gub. Dei*, vii. 67.

[2] Inscriptions in honour of professors are not wanting. It may be said that in the African provinces were the elements of a great national university, where the higher branches of science were liberally taught, and where young men from all parts of the country obtained superior education. The university existed from the age of the Antonines to the time of the Vandal kings; and owing to the influence exercised by many of the teachers, and the abundance of students, the schools of Carthage scarcely yielded the palm to those of Athens or Rome. (Paul Monceaux, *Les Africains*, Paris, 1894, p. 61.)

VIEW OF SUFETULA (SBEITLA)

Africa under Antoninus Pius

we obtain a glimpse of the course of complete study desirable for youths who were natives of Africa. From Thagaste, he tells us, he was removed to Madaura in Numidia, where the schools at that time were in high repute, and afterwards to Carthage, where the collegiate system was in operation, and the teaching of the highest class. But in many instances education did not stop there. The Latin of Africa was not the Latin of Rome. It therefore became necessary for any one who was ambitious of high office in public or professional life to make himself acquainted with the Latin tongue as spoken by the educated classes in Rome. Apuleius tells us that when he left Carthage to study law in Rome he found himself quite out of his element, and, learned as he then was as a Greek scholar and a master of African Latin, had to devote himself to the study of Roman Latin.[1] African students in Rome were numerous, especially at a later period of the Empire, for we learn from an edict in the reign of Valentinian that, complaints having been lodged of their dissipated habits, they were ordered not to frequent theatres too often, nor indulge in festive entertainments at late hours. Failing obedience, they would be put on board ship and sent back home.

Numerous inscriptions in North Africa bear testimony to the eagerness displayed by scholars in the acquisition of knowledge, as well as in putting on record their proficiency in the higher branches of intellectual study.

```
     D · M · S                  D · M · S
    L · BALBIVS              M · DAMATIVS
     BARBARVS                   VRBANVS
   STVDENS KAR              SVMMARVM ARTI
   THAGINI DE               VM   LIBERALIVM
     FVNCTVS                LITTERARVM STVDIIS
 V . A . XX . M · VII       VTRIVSQ · LINGVAE
     H · S · E              PERFECTE ERVDITVS
                            OPTIMA FACVNDIA
                            PRAEDITVS V · A · XXII
                            D · VII · H S E · VIII K · OCTOBR
                                A · P CLXXXX
                            M. DAMAT · FELIX PATER PIVS
                                    FECIT
```

[1] Apuleius, *Metamorph.* I. i. Also *Codex Theod.* xiv. 9, 1.

The first inscription[1] simply records that the deceased was a foreigner and a student at Carthage. The second[2] is to the memory of a learned scholar at Cirta, a master of Greek and Latin (*utriusque linguæ*), and a renowned orator, aged twenty-two years seven days.

Fuit suorum amator et patriæ; læsit neminem; clarissimum virorum et equitum Romanorum propinquus; adfuit eloquentia et industria in agendo ornatus multis; dictamine facilis extemporali volumina(?) dialogorum et epistolarum et edyliorum conscripsit.

This last-mentioned inscription from Announa covers twenty-two lines, but eleven only are legible.[3] It tells us of an amiable student of high social position, noted for his eloquence as well as application to many branches of study, in all of which he was distinguished. With pardonable pride the family of this distinguished youth wish posterity to know that the deceased could compose dialogues, idylls, and epistles, and could extemporise on any given subject. The name, age, and parentage of this ill-fated scholar whose career was cut short are unfortunately lost.

D.M.S. Caledius Rufus Parcæ quos tribuerunt ter quinos bis singulos peregi annos; ingenio non humili quo gratus apud magistros fui; qui dixi scribi pincsi bene; puer doctrinæ æque dedidi mentem; nam bis septenos cum agerem annos, notas græcas quis in commatibus . . . .

Here we have a memorial by the deceased himself,[4] but the date of the drafting of this singular inscription is not given on the lines which have been preserved. There are eight additional lines, but they are not legible. In the above we are told that this youth was held in high esteem by his masters: that from childhood he had devoted himself to study: that he could speak well, write well, and paint well: and that when he was 14 years old he could write Greek shorthand — a useful accomplishment in those days. It was not unusual in this country for a man to write his own epitaph, nor was it regarded as a breach of good manners on the part of educated men to use self-laudatory expressions in regard to their own merits or

---

[1] *C.I.L.* No. 12,152.   [2] *C.I.L.* No. 8500.   *I.R.A.* No. 3338.
[3] *C.I.L.* No. 5530 (Wilmanns descrip.).
C.I.L. No. 724 (Wilmanns descrip. summo labore).

accomplishments. The memorial of the goldsmith of Cirta already referred to is a still more noteworthy example of this class of inscriptions.

Carthage held its own as the chief intellectual centre of Africa till the fatal invasion of the Vandals, and its renowned university, completed under the reign of Alexander Severus, A.D. 222–235, sent forth into the civilised world enlightened men, trained in the varied schools of literature, science, and art. Rhetoric or oratory appears to have been held in much esteem at Carthage and in other African cities, for Juvenal, who flourished in the time of Trajan, exhorts the Italian professors of the art, who are desirous of making a fortune, to cross the sea to Africa.[1] But all the higher branches of learning seem to have been equally encouraged, and their disciples held in honour by the citizens. An instance may be recorded in the case of Apuleius, whose services in the cause of literature and philosophy had reflected distinction upon the university of Carthage. It was resolved to erect a statue in the city to his honour. And this is an extract from the philosopher's reply to the official communication he received on the subject, sufficient to show the estimation in which the African metropolis was held at that period by the educated classes:—' The grandeur of Carthage is worthy that even a philosopher shall sue to it for honour, where all your citizens are learned: amongst whom boys learn all they know, adults display their knowledge, and old men teach it. Carthage, the venerable mistress of our Province: Carthage, the celestial Muse of Africa: Carthage, the *Camena* of those who wear the *toga*!'[2] The remarkable

---

[1] Juv. *Sat.* vii. 147, 148. Terence, a native of Carthage and of obscure parentage, is an exceptional instance. He appears to have been taken to Rome by a slave-dealer and freed by the senator Terentius Lucanus in the days of his youth. His introduction to Scipio Africanus and his colleague C. Laelius was the chief cause of his social success. There is little to indicate African life or manners in any of his writings.

[2] Apul. *Flor.* xx. The *toga* was of various kinds. Its assumption distinguished the civilian from the soldier. There was the *toga virilis* assumed by Roman youths on their coming of age, celebrated on the feast of the Liberalia, March 17. The *toga purpurea* or *picta* took the highest rank, being a purple mantle with gold embroidery. The *toga* alluded to by Apuleius was the *toga praetexta*, which was white with a purple hem, worn by magistrates in the coloniae and municipia, and was regarded as a robe of distinction. *Vide* Smith's *Dict. of Gr. and Rom. Antiq.*; also Livy, bk. xxxiv. c. 7.

career of this eminent though erratic philosopher and romancist, and the principal works associated with his name, throw a good deal of light on African social life in the age of the Antonines. In his *Metamorphoses* Apuleius intentionally introduces his own personality as the hero of his story, and, with a touch of pardonable vanity, represents himself as an elegant youth. 'Is it not permissible,' he said, ' even for a philosopher to be of graceful appearance? Was not Zeno, as Plato affirms, remarkable for the graces of his person, and was not Pythagoras the handsomest man of his time?'

Apuleius was born towards the close of Trajan's reign at Madaura in Numidia (now called by the Arabs Mdaourouch), near the southern frontier separating the Roman province from the land of the Getulians. He calls himself half Numidian, half Getulian, and proudly proclaims himself a native of Africa. Among the monumental remains of Madaura which lie scattered over the plain, indicated more by undulations of the ground than by connected masses of masonry, there is nothing left in the present day to attest the importance it held in the second century, but the inscriptions give sufficient evidence of the existence at one time of a large residential population, and of its having been essentially a Roman town. Among the votive tablets are many relating to priests and priestesses of the various temples, Saturn being held, as elsewhere in Roman Africa, in the highest veneration. As late as the time of Theodosius (A.D. 379-395), Madaura was known as a stronghold of paganism, but the part it played in the movements of Christianity was not conspicuous. The names of several martyrs are recorded, and mention is also made of bishops of Madaura. But Christianity evidently made little progress in this wild part of Numidia, for St. Augustine informs us that paganism predominated there in his time. Apuleius was fortunate in his parentage. His father was in affluent circumstances, and his position as one of the chief magistrates, *duumviri*, at Madaura enabled his son to pursue his studies at Carthage, and afterwards at Athens, with exceptional advantages. On the completion of his university career Apuleius went to Rome, where he studied law and Latin;[1] and then, after a brief sojourn at Carthage, indulged his erratic propensities by

[1] Apul. *Flor.* 16-18.

taking ship for Alexandria. Falling ill by the way, he landed at Œa (the modern Tripoli), where an old fellow-student lived with his widowed mother, named Pudentilla, who was destined to exercise so potent an influence on his career. This town, which became a *colonia* in the second century, is little mentioned by historians. It took rank with Leptis Magna and Sabrata, and the three together constituted a federal union under the name of Tripoli.[1] A long era of prosperity came suddenly to an end in the middle of the fourth century, when the territory of the union was invaded by the savages of Getulia. Leptis and Sabrata suffered from the corrupt and vicious rule of Romanus, the military governor of Africa, and subsequently from the Vandal invasion. Their fortifications were destroyed, and the citizens left unprotected against the incursions of the Moors. Procopius[2] tells us that Justinian rebuilt the walls of both cities, and that he succeeded in repeopling Leptis by inducing the inhabitants of the surrounding district to embrace Christianity and settle there. With the Mohammedan invasion the history of the federal union comes to a close, and now, after a lapse of 1,200 years, modern Tripoli, which has risen on the outskirts of ancient Œa, takes rank as a commercial port of great importance on the shores of the Mediterranean, and the capital of the pashalik of the same name.

After a residence of some months in Œa, Apuleius found favour with Pudentilla, a person of wealth, who had been attracted by the wit and elegance of the young philosopher. We are informed that their marriage took place at some distance from the town, with a view, perhaps, of avoiding the payment of a heavy *honorarium*, which was customary on such occasions when the principals were in affluent circumstances. The widow had experienced this form of expenditure a few years previously, for we are told that when her eldest son came of age she presented to the town the sum of 50,000 sesterces (400*l.*). The family approved of the match in spite of the difference of years between the bridegroom and bride. But, alas! family rejoicings came to an end when the heirs-at-law found that the husband's influence over his enamoured spouse

[1] For an account of the provinces and the city of Tripoli consult Leo Africanus, a Moor, *De totius Africæ Descriptione*, Leyden, 1682.
[2] Procopius, *De Ædific.* vi. c. 4.

extended to the transfer of her property in his favour. Apuleius had many admirers in the city of his adoption, but he had many enemies. His ready wit, his versatile talent and exceptional brilliancy as a public speaker, had secured for him a high reputation as a scholar and an orator, and his philosophic discourses had gained the approval of the disciples of the school of Plato. But, as a lover of occult science, deeply versed in the mysteries of various creeds, and fascinated by a study of things unseen and unknown, his practices aroused suspicion, and prompted his adversaries to charge him with the exercise of magic in gaining the affection of Pudentilla. The indictment was carefully drafted and comprised the following separate charges : [1]—

1. The defendant Apuleius purchased fish of very rare kinds. He cut them up in his laboratory and concocted a liquid by which he was enabled to cast a spell over a woman. A slave in his employ named Themison is to be questioned on this matter.

2. When Apuleius lived with Pontianus (the son of Pudentilla) he was in the habit of secreting himself in the library, where he kept, carefully hidden, a mysterious talisman in a handkerchief. There is an irreproachable witness of this in the person of the librarian himself, a freedman of Pontianus.

3. Apuleius had a little wood skeleton made, upon which he performed experiments in magic. The artist who received the instructions and executed the work is Saturninus of Œa. He is here now.

4. Apuleius was in the habit of offering up sacrifices at night-time in the lodgings occupied by his friend, Appius Quintianus. Shortly afterwards Quintianus left, and in one of the rooms, the walls of which were blackened by smoke, feathers of birds were found. Junius Crassus, the owner of the house, will give evidence on this matter.

5. Apuleius bewitched a young slave named Thallus in a lonely spot near a little altar under the glimmering light of a lantern. As soon as the words of incantation were pronounced the youth fell to the ground senseless. Then the operator

[1] This tabulated statement of charges brought against Apuleius is partly a translation from M. Paul Monceaux's *Les Africains*, pp. 292-293.

brought him back to life. Fourteen slaves in the service of Thallus will confirm this process, and among them Sicinius Pudens, who was an eye-witness. Moreover, several other young people have been similarly bewitched.

6. Apuleius undertook to heal a sick woman who was brought to his house by a doctor. As soon as the woman entered his room his first glance caused her to fall on the floor senseless. The doctor is to be questioned on this matter.

7. Apuleius forced Pudentilla by the exercise of magic to marry him. They were no sooner married than he made her assign to him a considerable part of her property. With his wife's money he purchased a splendid estate. Everybody in Œa knows this, and in a letter which we produce Pudentilla herself declares 'Apuleius is a magician and I have been bewitched by him.'

Such grave charges, apparently supported by facts, would have disconcerted an ordinary man, but Apuleius was cast in a different mould, and any one who reads between the lines of his remarkable defence will note the skilful way in which he fenced the main issues, and how he succeeded in turning the tables upon his calumniators, conciliating the judges, and eventually leaving the court as the hero of the hour. The trial took place at the end of Antonine's reign in the neighbouring city of Sabrata, where the Roman proconsul Claudius Maximus was holding the assizes: and if the whole proceedings were proportionate to the lengthy character of the defence, which has been handed down to us intact in the form of the *Apologia*, the trial must have occupied many days.

The practice of magic had long been under the ban of Roman law, and continued so till the fall of the Empire. Experts in occult science were regarded as a grave danger to the State, and as far back as the reign of Tiberius special laws were framed with a view to their suppression. But the severe penalties attached to the exercise of various forms of the sorcerer's art did not deter those who regarded sorcery as a means of livelihood, nor that class of enchanter or wizard who may still be found in North Africa, exercising the healing art by the aid of incantations, philters, or gesticulations. In the principal towns such men were to be found attracting the ignorant, exciting the curious, and amusing the mob by a display of homely wit, sometimes coarse, but always good-humoured, and rarely failing to promote merriment. But it was not the ignorant only who became the prey of the magician. Pliny the Elder tells us of the innate powers of some of the natives of Africa in casting a spell over children, as well as trees and herds of cattle. Wherever the charm took effect death or decay ensued.[1] And what is still more remarkable is Pliny's belief in the performance of miracles by human agency. 'I have seen a woman transformed into a man on her wedding-day. The name of the man is Lucius Cossitius, a native of Thysdrus, who was alive when I was telling the story.'[2] It is a pity that so enthusiastic a scholar as Pliny did not carry his researches a little further. An account of the experiences of this bisexous individual would have been entertaining as well as instructive to mankind. In the reign of Marcus Aurelius so distinguished a person as Septimius Severus, a native of Leptis Magna, was tried as a magician, and we learn from Spartian that when he was Emperor the proconsul Apronianus was tried for the same offence, condemned and put to death. Under Valentinian a proconsul of Carthage was put to torture for having consulted sorcerers;[3] and in the time of Constantine a philosopher named Sopater, a friend of the Emperor's, was actually condemned to death on the plea that he had cast a spell over the winds and prevented the grain-ships from reaching Byzantium.

There is no doubt that Apuleius was not only an ardent believer in occult science, but that he practised magic as a student, and not for personal gain. He admits as much in the *Apologia*. He was also acquainted with the methods and operations of the Christian Church, which afforded him a subject for raillery; and it may be reasonable to suppose that he attributed the miracles wrought by Divine power in a neighbouring land to the same human agency which formed the basis of his own philosophic teaching. At a later period, when Paganism and Christianity were striving for the mastery, the miracles wrought by Apuleius[4] were compared with those recorded in the New

---

[1] Pliny, *Hist. Nat.* vii. 2.
[2] Apuleius, *Metamorph.* ix. 14. Pliny, *Hist. Nat.* vii. 4.
[3] *Codex Theod.* ix. 16, 4-6; Ammianus Marcellinus, xxviii. 1, 17.
[4] Lactantius, *Inst. Divin.* v. 3, 7.

Testament, and Pagan and Christian were found fighting in opposite camps, both doing battle in the cause of the supernatural. Apuleius was fortunate in living under the rule of so amiable an Emperor as Antonine, when the conscience of every citizen was respected, and freedom of opinion in matters of religion was tolerated, as far as possible, in every part of the Empire. He was fortunate also in being on terms of intimacy with the proconsul who presided at the assizes. According to the account given in the *Apologia*, our philosopher entered the court with a light heart, and made merry of the whole proceedings. He tells us how he descanted upon natural philosophy, history, and medicine, as well as the mysteries of science; how he evaded every point which related to the exercise of his powers as a magician; how he aroused enthusiasm in the court, and even promoted merriment among the judges. As for the charges made against him, serious as they looked at first sight, they could easily be disposed of. The fish he had purchased from time to time were ordinary fish, for the purpose of experiments in anatomy. The talisman kept in his library was an emblem of religion, only to be shown to those who had been initiated into the mysteries of his faith. The skeleton referred to was a charming statuette of Mercury, modelled by Cornelius Saturninus, which he was delighted to bring into court and show to the judges. As for the alleged secret sacrifices at night, the evidence rested solely on the statement of a drunken man, who had been paid for bearing false witness against him. Then this man Thallus and his wife, who fell speechless in his presence, were unfortunate epileptics, upon whom it would have been ridiculous to practise magic. Then comes the grave charge of bewitching his wife Pudentilla. 'It may be called witchery,' said Apuleius, 'or anything you please, but what were the facts?' The gods had given him good looks, and bestowed on him great talents. He had been charged with undue regard for his personal appearance. 'It is true,' he added, 'that I have not been negligent of my person. I have used a mirror; I have combed my hair, and I have actually been guilty of cleaning my teeth!' What more natural than that a woman of homely features, not particularly beautiful, and certainly no longer young, should feel the power of such attractions as his, and seize the opportunity of obtaining a good husband! If it was magic, it was nothing more than the employment of gifts which the gods had bestowed on him. As for his wife's fortune, he had not touched it, and if he died without issue it would revert to her family. The estate in the country which had been talked about was only a small domain purchased in Pudentilla's name.

It was doubtful whether the citizens of Œa could regard with favour any one, however talented, who had been suspected of sorcery, and who had openly admitted an intimate acquaintance with the mysteries of magic. Apuleius thought so too. He quitted Œa at the close of the trial, and settled permanently in Carthage, where honours of many kinds were showered upon him, far more than on any other philosopher born in Africa.

However great the merits of this remarkable *Apologia*, the reputation of Apuleius as a scholar and romancist will always be associated with his better-known work entitled *The Metamorphoses, or the Golden Ass*. It appears, on good authority, to have been written during the latter portion of his career in Carthage, and, according to a recent writer on the subject, was first mentioned by Capitolinus in his life of Albinus at the time when Septimius Severus and Albinus, both natives of Carthage, were disputing the throne. Severus rallied his competitor for wasting his time in reading old women's tales, and getting old in the company of the Punic fables of Apuleius and literary diversions. The story, as narrated in the *Metamorphoses*, is a fanciful legend of Greek origin, and, in the words of its author, is made up of a series of fables after the manner of the Milesians.[1] These fabulous tales, so popular among the Romans, were distinguished both for humour and wantonness, and have formed the groundwork of many a fanciful story in more recent times. Lucius, the imaginary hero of the *Metamorphoses*, may be accepted as a portraiture of Apuleius himself, a student of magic and a diligent inquirer into the mysteries of occult science. Seeing a sorceress at work one day in her laboratory transforming herself into a bird with the aid of some mysterious ointment, Lucius at once resolved to imitate her. But by some mishap he took up the wrong mixture and was changed into an

---

[1] The raillery of the Emperor was thus expressed: *Quum ille næniis quibusdam anilibus occupatus inter Milesias Punicas Apuleii sui, et ludicra litteraria consenesceret.* (Capitolinus, *Clod. Albin.* 12.)

Africa under Antoninus Pius

ass, retaining the spirit of a man. The goddess, who wrought this direful spell, so far favoured the unfortunate ass as to inform it that, after munching some rose-leaves, transformation to human shape would immediately ensue. The adventures of the animal in search of flowers to break the spell form a large portion of the romance, and its experiences in the ways of mankind, sometimes humorous, sometimes doleful, read like a satire on the habits of certain classes of African society in the second century. But the patience of the ass was at last rewarded. The goddess Isis appeared at Corinth one night and announced the end of its troubles. In short, on the morrow a procession issued from the city on its way to the harbour at Cenchrea to inaugurate the launching of a new ship. At the head of the procession was a priest, who carried in his hand a chaplet of roses. Surreptitiously the ass approached and, munching a few leaves, resumed his human form.

Interspersed among the pages of this remarkable composition are a number of tales or episodes, as they are called, full of that species of humour which is so conspicuous in the writings of Cervantes, and, in a lesser degree, may be found in the spirited pages of 'Gil Blas.' The fifth episode, entitled 'Cupid and Psyche,' which may be classed as a philosophic allegory, stands pre-eminent, and has had the distinction of attracting more notice from literary disputants than any other of the works of this author. A correspondent of 'Notes and Queries' (ii. 429, first series), says: 'This is probably an old folk-tale originally, perhaps an antique philosophic temple-allegory. Apuleius appears only to have dressed it up in a new shape. The tale is still current, but in a form not derived from him, among Swedes, Norwegians, Danes, Scots, Germans, French, Wallachians, Hindoos, and Italians.' And another writer says: 'This fable is a representation of the destiny of the human soul. The soul, which is of divine origin, is here below subjected to error in its prison, the body. Hence trials and purifications are set before it, that it may become capable of a higher order of things, and of true desire. Two loves meet—the earthly a deceiver, who drags it down to earthly things; the heavenly, who directs its view to the originally fair and divine, and who, gaining the victory over his rival, leads off the soul as his bride.'

The position which Apuleius adorned as philosopher and romancist in the Antonine age, and the influence exercised by his genius and personality on African literature, both pagan and Christian, are universally recognised. Tertullian, a native of Carthage and an eminent Christian writer at the end of the second century, may be accepted as a representative of the style of Apuleius. In a later age St. Augustine, who had to combat with his doctrines as a professor of magic, was fain to acknowledge that Apuleius was the most popular of African writers; and Lactantius remarks that the early pagan controversialists used to rank Apuleius with Apollonius of Tyana as a thaumaturgist, citing various miracles performed by him as equal or superior to those of Christ.

Carthage was not the only city to send forth literary celebrities. Sicca Veneria (El-Kef) produced the grammarian Eutychius Proculus, one of the tutors of Marcus Aurelius, and renowned for his work entitled *De Regionibus*. Leptis Magna was the birthplace of Septimius Severus, grandfather of the Emperor of that name. He obtained repute at Rome as an orator, and his talents excited the admiration of Statius the poet. 'Who could ever believe,' he said, 'that a man gifted with such eloquence should come from such a place as Leptis, far away in the region of the Syrtes?' Hippone (Bone) was the native town of Servilius Silanus, and Cirta was the birthplace of Festus Postumius, both of whom achieved reputation by their writings. Carthage also produced the renowned grammarian Sulpicius Apollinaris, whose school attracted scholars from all parts of the country. Aulus Gellius, Celsinus, and Pertinax took rank among the most eminent of his pupils. Of the career of Celsinus we know little, but it is probable that he acquired renown as a schoolmaster and grammarian. Gellius, on the other hand, held so prominent a position as philosopher and rhetorician that he figures largely in the history of the Antonine age. There is good reason for supposing that he was a native of Africa, for his name appears on an inscription discovered at Cherchel a few years ago.[1] His lifelong attachment to his master Apollinaris, and his intimacy with Herodes Atticus, one of the tutors of Marcus Aurelius, and renowned for his munificence

---

[1] Waille, *Lettre sur les fouilles de Carthage* (*C. R. de l'Acad. des Inscript.* Jan. 1888).

to his adopted city, made him a conspicuous character in the chief cities and universities of the Empire. The publication of the *Noctes Africæ*, a series of notes jotted down from day to day on a variety of subjects and penned by a master hand, formed the climax of his popularity, and provided a fund of original material from which contemporary authors did not fail to borrow. Both Lactantius and St. Augustine did not hesitate to acknowledge their indebtedness to Aulus Gellius, whom the latter calls *vir elegantissimi eloquii et multæ ac facundæ scientiæ*.[1] But among the pupils of Apollinaris, Publius Helvius Pertinax achieved the highest honours, beginning life in his father's trade as a small dealer in charcoal, and terminating a remarkable career on the throne of the Cæsars. When Apollinaris gave up his school, Pertinax succeeded him for a short time, but, not finding it lucrative, abandoned teaching and followed the army in various campaigns. Step by step, in a civil as well as military capacity, he filled various offices, and became proconsul of Africa. Finally, on the death of Commodus, he was chosen Emperor by acclamation, and for the short period of eighty-seven days ruled his subjects with wisdom and benevolence. Patriotic administration and honesty in all his actions gained him the affection of every right-minded person in the Empire, and the hatred and distrust of those who were living on the plunder acquired during the reign of his contemptible predecessor. When Pertinax attempted to correct the grave abuses that had crept into the administration of the army, the Prætorian guard, always a powerful body, and occasionally overruling the decisions of the Senate, rose against him, and openly murdered him in the light of day. It was fortunate that the gentle schoolmaster of Carthage, who was proud of his distinguished pupil, was not present when this atrocious crime was perpetrated. Mention must also be made of P. Annæus Florus, whose birthplace is not known; but there is little doubt, from his frequent allusions to Africa and the knowledge he displayed in his descriptions of events that had occurred there, that he was a native of one of the African provinces. His epitome of Roman history, entitled *Epitomæ de T. Livio bellorum omnium annorum DCC. libri duo*, on which his reputation as a writer depends, has been described 'as rather a panegyric on the Romans than an accurate history

[1] St. Augustine, *De Civitate Dei*, ix. 4.

of their actions.' During his studies in Rome in the reign of Domitian, Florus was a competitor for a prize of distinction, and in the opinion of the public as well as of the judges was entitled to the first place. But the Emperor refused to accept their decision, on the ground that citizens of Rome should not be held inferior to provincials. Poor Florus was in despair at losing this coveted honour, and he tells us in his own words that he fled from the capital in horror, so crushed by resentment that he forgot the claims of his country and of his dear relatives at home, and like a madman rushed about the world from one place to another. He travelled about for many years, seeking rest and finding none, and at last, by accident rather than from any definite cause, he found himself at Tarraco in Spain. Here he settled, establishing a high reputation for rhetoric, and honoured by the patronage and friendship of the Emperor Hadrian.

On taking a general survey of the representatives of literature in Africa during the latter half of the second century, Apuleius of Madaura has to share the chief honours with M. Cornelius Fronto, a native of Cirta, the capital of Numidia. Dion Cassius says that Fronto was renowned as an orator in the time of Hadrian, and that, at the close of his reign, he was regarded as the first advocate and pleader of his time. Between this Emperor and the youthful orator there does not appear to have been any intimate friendship—respect for talent on the part of Hadrian and loyal veneration on the part of the scholar. Indeed, Fronto himself says of Hadrian that he 'was not at ease in his presence, but regarded him rather as a deity to be propitiated than a man to be loved.' It was not till Antonine had ascended the throne and had nominated the young princes Lucius Verus and Marcus Aurelius as his successors that we recognise the sweet and gentle nature of Fronto's disposition. The high esteem in which he was held by Antonine, as much for personal character and charm of manner as for literary attainments, caused his nomination as preceptor to the young princes. And this was the turning-point in Fronto's career, marred only by constant ill-health in advancing years, and the troubles and anxieties of a large family. None of his principal works have been handed down unmutilated, leaving us only fragments of history, treatises on various subjects, and voluminous correspondence with his pupils, either as princes or emperors. In the early part of this century, Monsignor Mai, librarian of the Vatican, had the good fortune to discover some of the lost correspondence on palimpsests stored in the Ambrosian Library, and after patient labour succeeded in deciphering them. The first edition was published in Milan in 1815, followed by others in 1823 and 1832, containing additional correspondence. Since then a critical edition, embracing all the discovered documents, was issued at Leipzig in 1867 by M. S. A. Naber. The letters comprised in this correspondence have no claim to literary merit, nor can they be regarded as compositions of a high order. And yet they have exceptional interest. No one can read those genial homely lines without feeling touched by the expressions of love and sympathy which knit together two such kindred spirits as Marcus Aurelius and his tutor, Cornelius Fronto. We get a glimpse of family life in the imperial circle, and a sketch of the sunny boyhood of a sedate and philosophic ruler. In nearly all the letters there is exaggeration of expression, and constant use of superlative epithets, which sound to us unnecessary and unfamiliar in these more prosaic days. But this was an age of exaggerated phraseology, pardonable as indicating in a measure the joyousness of a people who lived in the brightest epoch of Roman history. Dedicatory inscriptions and votive memorials of the time bear testimony to a free employment of high-sounding adjectives. When a *municipium* was raised to the rank of *colonia*, the title of *splendidissima* expressed the distinction conferred upon its citizens. When a parent lost a wife or daughter, *carissima*, *piissima*, *dulcissima*, were the epithets frequently used; the memory of students who had been cut off in their youth was preserved in such expressive words as *diligentissimus* or *rarissimus*; and a citizen of renown amongst his fellows bore the title of *obsequentissimus* or *honestissimus*, sometimes both. Such being the custom of the time, we read without surprise the conclusion of a letter from M. Aurelius, the prince (at that time about twenty years of age), to his dear master, Fronto.[1] 'Farewell, most eloquent, most learned, most dear, most sweet, most preferred preceptor, most desired friend.' A subsequent letter concludes thus: 'Farewell, my dearest master. My mother salutes you. I am so wearied that

---

[1] The following letters are taken from a selection of correspondence translated and edited by M. J. McQuige, Rome, 1824.

I hardly exist.' The prince went out hunting one morning with the Emperor, and on his return, he says in a letter to Fronto, 'I betook myself to my books. Therefore, having taken off my shoes and laid aside my clothes, I remained in bed for two hours. I read two orations of Cato. I think I have taken cold, perhaps because I walked in sandals this morning. Therefore, I will pour oil on my head and go to sleep. Farewell, my dearest and sweetest master, whom I love better than Rome itself.' On another occasion M. Aurelius attended the Emperor at a sacrifice, and in the evening wrote to Fronto as follows: 'Afterwards I went to take some refreshment. And what do you think I ate? A little morsel of bread, while I saw others devouring boiled beans, and onions, and pilchards. After that we went to the vineyard, where we laboured and amused ourselves. At the sixth hour we returned home. I studied a little, but without profit. Afterward, sitting with my dear mother on a couch, I prattled of many things. I said, "What do you think my Fronto is doing now?" She replied, "But what do you think my Gratia is doing?" Then I said, "No. What is our dear sweet little darling Gratia doing?" While we were talking and disputing which loved you most, the *discus* sounded. We supped. And now before I turn on my side and snore I give an account of the day to my dear master, whom I could not love more than I do.' Amongst the correspondence is a letter from Fronto to Lucius Verus, on his return from a successful campaign against the Parthians: 'Although illness has long made me weary of my life, yet I do not think that I have lived in vain, nor shall I continue to live with reluctance, since I have seen you return with so much glory obtained by your valour. Farewell, my dearest lord. Salute your mother-in-law and your children.'

But the day came when the favoured prince became Emperor and received by letter the congratulations of his old master. This is the reply of M. Aurelius: 'As I am convinced of the sincerity of your affection for me, my dearest Fronto, it is not difficult to persuade me that this day, on which it has pleased the gods to call me to this station, is by you above all others truly and religiously celebrated.'

Good fortune seems to have attended Fronto's career in everything except health and domestic anxieties. Antonine raised him to the dignity of Consul, and at a later period, when the proconsulships of Asia and Africa were vacant, the former was offered for his acceptance. These were the only provinces of the Empire having senatorial rank, both taking a position somewhat similar to that enjoyed by the Governor-General of India in our own days. But Fronto was dissatisfied. As a native of Africa he had been looking forward to holding high office in his own land and amongst his own people; but on hearing that the African appointment had been definitely settled with the approval of the Emperor, he declined the proconsulship of Asia on the ground of failing health. Amongst Africans Fronto was deservedly popular on account of his good name, recognised talents, and high social position. As an acknowledgment of the services he had rendered to his countrymen he was made patron of his native city, as well as of the rising town of Kalama (Guelma), on the highway between Hippone on the coast and Cirta, the capital of Numidia. He was also selected by the citizens of Carthage to write a congratulatory address to the Emperor for favours conferred upon their city. Among the vast number of inscriptions discovered at Cirta, there is not one relating to his name or his career, but there is a letter of his extant, addressed to the triumvirs and decurions of the city, acknowledging the benefits conceded to him.[1] On the wall of a house at Kalama (Guelma), built into the masonry, may still be read the official notification of Fronto as patron of Kalama, at a time when the town ranked only as a *municipium*.[2]

<pre>
            M · CORNELIO
            T · F · QUIR
              FRONTONI
           III VIR · CAPITAL
              Q. PROVINC
          SICIL · AEDIL · PL
              PRAETORI
              MVNICIPES
              KALAMENSI
              VM PATRONO
</pre>

[1] *Ad Amicos*, ii. 10, p. 200. Triumvirs were magistrates who acted as judges in the *coloniæ* and *municipia*. They were originally three in number, but were sometimes increased to four to meet the necessities of a town. Sometimes there were only two.

[2] *C.I.L.* No. 5350, copied by M. Aubin. *I.R.A.* No. 2717.

In a subsequent reign it bore the honoured designation of *ordo splendidissimus Colonia Kalamensium*, or, according to De la Mare, *civitas splendidissima Kalamensium*.

There was a group of towns and villages in the neighbourhood of Kalama which, at a later period of the Empire, became thickly populated, and, although of no political importance, they bear testimony to the success of Roman colonisation in the interior of the country towards the close of the second century. There is nothing remarkable about the monumental remains of Kalama, or of the neighbouring town of Tibilis, now known as Announa. They are not in the best style of Roman art, and are indicative of prosperity rather than culture among the inhabitants. In both cases they cover a large tract of land, and inscriptions, both dedicatory and votive, are numerous.[1] A healthy climate, fertile soil, charming scenery, and sheltered woods must have proved attractive to a good class of citizens. In addition, the proximity of the *Aquæ Tibilitanæ*, held in high repute for their healing powers in rheumatic affections and cutaneous complaints, may have induced many families to take up their residence in some neighbouring town. The appearance of these waters, heavily charged with carbonate of lime, is extraordinary. As they bubble up from the surface of the sloping rock in a well-wooded glen, they fall into a series of cascades and leave behind them in their flow a deposit of carbonate of lime, which soon hardens and assumes the appearance of white marble. The temperature of the water, never varying, is 203° Fahr., and if the elevation of the source above the sea-level be taken into account, it will be above the boiling-point of water. In some parts cones of deposit have been formed nearly forty feet high, and where the boiling stream has forced its way through crevices in the rock, small islands of evergreens and herbage stand out conspicuously in their cinctures of white. Some of the Roman baths cut out of the rock are still in use, while others have been partly or wholly submerged by an accumulated deposit of at least 1,500 years. The Arabs renamed these waters under the designation of Hammam Meskoutin, or the Accursed Baths, and, as usual, wove a legendary tale about

[1] Charles, Comte de Peysonnel, who visited Announa in 1724, says that 'the numerous ruins show that it must have been a large and beautiful city.' The monuments existing in the present day may be assigned to a late period of the Empire.

them, in order to account for this extraordinary natural phenomenon. According to M. Piesse it runs thus: 'An Arab, rich and powerful, had a sister whom he thought too beautiful to be married to any one but himself. He determined to marry her in spite of the prohibition of the Mohammedan law and the remonstrances and supplications of the elders of his tribe, whose heads he cut off in front of his tent. After the marriage ceremony, when the accursed couple were about to retire, the elements were set in motion. Fire came out of the earth, the water left its bed, and the thunder pealed forth in a fearful manner. When tranquillity was restored, the Arab and his sister and every one connected with the feast were found petrified, the white cone still representing the actors in this drama.'

Many other towns shared with Kalama the advantages of a long era of quietude, but their record is a blank. They rose gradually under the civilising rule of the Romans, attained a position in the commercial or agricultural life of the country, and when the Empire came to an end fell by degrees into a distressful condition, preluding their final extinction. Such, no doubt, was the fate of the ancient Verecunda, now known as Markouna. The site is about two miles from Lambessa, and it was probably a suburb of that city. An inscription on a pedestal found among the remains of the ancient *forum* relates to the water-supply in the reign of Antonine:[1]

DIVO	
ANTONN	*Divo Antonino Augusto, ex cujus in-*
AVG	*dulgentia aqua vici Augustorum*
EX CVI	*Verecundensis perducta est, dedicante*
AQVA VIC	*Decimo Fonteio Frontiniano, legato*
AVGVSTOR	*Augustorum pro prætore, decreto*
VERECVNDENS	*decurionum, pecunia publica.*
PERDVCTA EST	
DEDIC	
D · FONTEIO	
LEG · AVG · PR · PR	
D · D . P · P	

Inscriptions in all cases afford some clue to the period of greatest prosperity, the healthiness of the climate, and the domestic happiness of the inhabitants. Both at Kalama

[1] *I.R.A.* No. 1413.

(Guelma) and Tibilis (Announa), which may be regarded as representative towns inhabited by large middle-class populations, the words *beatissimis temporibus* are of frequent recurrence in the reigns of Valentinian and Valens, Theodosius the Great, and Theodosius the younger. The rule of these emperors extended from A.D. 363 to A.D. 450. Among the inscriptions at Kalama there are two relating to the erection and adornment of the theatre, the remains of which are still an attractive object on the outskirts of the pretty little town of Guelma.[1] The one relating to the embellishment of the building runs thus :[2]

ANNIAE AELI AE · L · FIL · RESTIT AE · FLAM · AVGG P · OB · EGREGIAM IN VOS CIVES LIBERA ITATEM THEATRO PECVNIA SVA EXOR NANDA . . . . RIAE SPONTE P . . . ESSO AD REFERENDAM GR TIAM ORDO VNIVER SVS STATV . . . QVINQ DE PVBL FACIEND DECREVIT	*Anniæ Æliæ L. fil. Restitutæ flaminicæ Augustorum perpetuæ, ob egregiam in suos cives liberalitatem, theatro pecunia sua exornando patriæ sponte permisso ad referendam gratiam, ordo universus statuas numero quinque de publico faciendas decrevit.*

It will be observed that the munificent donor was the daughter of a *flaminica*, but there is no date on the inscribed slab to enable us to state definitely under whose reign this public work, including the erection of the five statues, was carried out. It was probably much later than the time of Antonine. There are two other inscriptions at Kalama which have some little historic interest. One of them informs us that in the very happy times of Valentinian and Valens, A.D. 363–375, during the proconsulate of the most illustrious P. Ampelius, and by the foresight of the most illustrious Fabius Fabianus, the water-supply to the town, which had been very indifferent, was now abundant, rushing into the public reservoirs with great noise; and that Q. Basilius Flaccianus, perpetual flamen, augur, and controller, kept the reservoir in good condition. The other, equally profuse

---

[1] Restorations of the theatre and baths of Kalama are shown in an interesting work by M. Amable Ravoisié, *Explor. Scientif. de l'Algérie*, Paris, 1846.
[2] *I.R.A.* No. 2765. De la Mare, *Explor. d'Algérie, Archéolog.* pl. clxxxiii.

Africa under Antoninus Pius 149

in its wording, tells us that in the most happy reign (*beatissimis temporibus*) of Honorius and Theodosius the younger, who shared the throne A.D. 408-423, and with the approval of the two imperial functionaries, both described as *viri clarissimi*, and one of them *amplissimus* also, the town, which had been allowed for some time to get into a filthy state, was put into good condition and made pleasant for visitors at the expense of a worthy man named Valentinus, who had the management of the town revenues, and is appropriately styled *honestissimus*.[1]

> *Beatissimis temporibus dominorum nostrorum Honori et Theodosi semper et ubique vincentium administrante Pomp . . . viro clarissimo amplissimoque proconsule et Thersio Crispino Megethio viro clarissimo legato . . . . Valentinus vir honestissimus curator rei publicæ locum ruinis obsitum, qui antea squalore et sordibus fœdabatur, ad necessarium usum et ad peregrinorum hospitalitatem in meliorem statum ad usum et aspectum propria pecunia reformavit feliciter.*

The record of Antonine's career is one of almost unbroken peace at home and abroad. To defend the Empire as it was handed to him by his predecessor, and to avoid the sacrifice of a single life in extending its borders, was the political creed of this tranquil ruler of mankind. 'I would rather,' said the Emperor, 'save the life of a single citizen than slay a thousand enemies.' A tender regard for the welfare of his subjects showed itself at the close of Antonine's career. When the last hour had come and the officer on guard was waiting in the antechamber for the watchword of the day, the word *Æquanimitas* was muttered by the Emperor with his last breath; and so he passed away as he had lived, even-minded in all things, loving empire for the sake of doing good, and secure in the esteem and affections of his people.

This excessive amiability was severely strained on several occasions by the conduct of the Empress Annia Gallia Faustina, called Faustina the elder to distinguish her from her daughter Faustina, the wife of Marcus Aurelius. If we are to accept all the evil things said by Latin authors about the wife of Antonine, justice to her memory compels also the acceptance of the Emperor's testimony to her worth. 'I would rather,' said Anto-

---

[1] *C.I.L.* No. 5341.

nine, 'live with her in the island of Gyaris[1] than without her in the palace of the Cæsars.' Capitolinus at a later date attributed to Faustina a loose tongue and loose manners,[2] while more recent authors do not hesitate to accept the rumours current at the time, without troubling themselves to arrive at the truth. The influence exercised by women for good or evil in the imperial circle during the first two centuries of Empire was considerable, and court scandal and gossip were consequently notorious. Allowance should be made for looseness of anecdote at a period when intrigue and place-hunting found favour in the courts of the palace, and when the rivalry created bitterness of speech and suspicion of motive. When the founder of the Empire said that the wife of Cæsar should be above suspicion, the words may have been prompted by some idle tale of court intrigue that may have reached his ears unexpectedly. Few of the Empresses have left a record untarnished by suspicion; some of them have been charged with the most heinous offences, without corroborative evidence; while others, among whom Plotina, the noble wife of the Emperor Trajan, stands conspicuous for public benevolence and the exercise of private virtues, have not escaped the malevolence of idle tongues. Whatever may have been the faults of Faustina, it stands to the credit of Antonine that he declined to tarnish the character of his wife. He honoured her memory, in accordance with the superstition of the times, by ranking her among the deities, and associating her name with his own in an inscription on a temple still forming an attractive ruin in the *Via Sacra*. The name of Faustina does not appear in any inscription yet discovered in Roman Africa, nor is it mentioned by contemporary authors in connection with any public work or ceremonial.

But court intrigues in far-distant Rome and domestic differences in the imperial circle possessed little interest to peace-loving, contented citizens in the North African provinces, and

---

[1] Gyaris or Gyara is an island in the Archipelago, now known as Joura. Criminals were sent thither. (Tacit. *Ann.* iii. 68, 69.) Juvenal says:
> *Aude aliquid brevibus Gyaris et carcere dignum,*
> *Si vis esse aliquid.*

(Juv. *Sat.* 1.) According to Strabo, the resident population consisted of a few poor fishermen. (Strabo, x. v. 3.)

[2] *De hujus uxore multa dicta sunt ob nimiam libertatem et vivendi facilitatem, quæ iste cum animi dolore compressit.* (Capitolinus, *Anton.* c. 3.)

the daily life of an Empress, unknown to them in person except on the coins of the time, had nothing in common with the pursuits of a hard-working industrial population. The reign just drawn to a close, uneventful in comparison with the more stirring days of Trajan or the restless activity of Hadrian, has left its mark in the form of unnumbered memorials of private rather than of public life. These records of the time, either on stone or marble, bear ample testimony to a long period of ease and quietude enjoyed by loyal citizens in all parts of North Africa. They tell the old story of human affections, of undying love and tender regard, expressed in a tongue which modern languages fail to equal either in strength or terseness, and in brevity inimitable. What epitaph written in English could set forth in such simple words and in a few short lines the lovable qualities of Geminia Ingenua, so good a mother and so kind a friend, ready to assist any one in need; and when her last hour had come and her remains were laid to rest in the necropolis at Cirta, her sorrowing relatives placed on record that this worthy woman, who lived to the age of eighty-one, *tristem fecit neminem?* [1]

D · M	*Diis Manibus. Geminia Ingenua,*
GEMINIA · INGE	*univira, conservatrix, dulcissima*
NVA · VNIVIRA · CONSE	*mater, omnium hominum parens,*
RVATRIX · DVLCISSIM	*obnibus (sic) subveniens, innocens,*
MATER · OMNIVM	*carissima, præstans, rarissima,*
HOMINVM · PARENS · OBNI	*vixit annis o.taginta uno. Tris-*
BVS · SVBVENIENS · INNOCE	*tem fecit neminem.*
NS · CASTISSIM · PRAESTA	*Oro ut bene quiescat!*
NS · RARISSIMA · V · A · LXXXI	
TRISTEM · FECIT · NEMINE	
O · V · B · Q	

The wording of these simple epitaphs is very varied. At Cæsarea (Cherchel) we find the virtues of an excellent wife recorded in a different form of phraseology:[2] *cum quâ vita jucunda, conversatio religiosa, frugalitas honesta, fides cum disciplina exacta est.* Sometimes the memorial takes the form of an imaginary conversation between a deceased husband and wife, indicating that the epitaph was prepared during their lifetime and afterwards inscribed on the slab. The following example may still be studied in the museum at Tebessa:[3]

[1] *C.I.L.* No. 7384.   [2] *C.I.L.* No. 9520.   [3] *C.I.L.* No. 1954. Wilmanns.

D · M · S · IVLIA FORTVNATA PIE VIXIT ANNIS LXII
CASTA BONA INVIOLANS RARVM HOC
A CONIVGE MVNVS FORTVNATA TIBI SIC PLACET
HARDALIO NOMINE DIGNA MEO QVOD TU MIHI KARE
SVPERSTES NATORVM NATIS TE INCOLVMI VIGVI

>Loquitur Hardalius :
>>*Casta, bona, inviolans, rarum hoc a conjuge munus.*
>>*Fortunata, tibi ; sic placet Hardalio.*
>Respondet Fortunata :
>>*Nomine digna meo, quod tu mihi, care, superstes,*
>>*Natorum natis te incolumi vigui.*

At Sigus in Numidia, now known as Ziganiah, some twenty-four miles from Constantine, a man laments the loss of his wife in the following expressive words :[1] *conjux uno animo, uno consilio, semper fruita mecum.* So enviable a spouse is scarcely excelled in worth by the good woman of Madaura (Mdaourouch), who is described as a *conjux rarissima, omni pietate, innocentia, gravitate morum fecunda, tecusa, karissima.*[2] And at Capsa (Gafsa) in the far south, where the sites of old Roman towns are naught but oases in a region of sand, domestic happiness and filial affection have left a pleasant record on imperishable stone in the memorial of a woman of many virtues named Domitia Cæsia.[3]

>D · M · S
>DOMITIA · CAESIA · OPTIMA
>IN VITA . . . .
>PVDICISSIMA FEMINA
>RARISSIMAE · FRVGALITA
>TIS · ET · INDVLGENTISSIMA · MA
>TRONA · VIXIT · ANNIS · LXVIII
>MONVMENTVM · AGENDVM
>CVRAVIT · IVLIVS · SENTEANVS
>FILIVS · EIVS
>O · T · B · Q

---

[1] *C.I.L.* No. 5798.   [2] *C.I.L.* No. 4692 (*tecusa* rarely used, Wilmanns).

[3] *C.I.L.* No. 134. Capsa has had a long history and, according to Sallust, was a town of great importance at the termination of the Punic wars. Its remote position on the Desert border, forming an oasis of beauty and productiveness, did not prevent the army of Caius Marius from encamping under its walls and destroying the town. But, owing to the fertility of the soil, abundance of water, and direct communication with the coast, Capsa soon recovered its old position and continued in prosperity long after the Arabs had swept over the land. 'It is built almost entirely,' says El-Bekri, the Arab writer of the eleventh century, 'with galleries of marble ;' and he adds 'that the ramparts were constructed by Chentian, page to

The frequent repetition of superlative epithets becomes somewhat monotonous, and difficult to appreciate in our more prosaic times. But it must be remembered that these old-world citizens had no other means of giving public expression to their grief in the hour of bereavement, and that the wording of these homely memorials, sometimes extending to twenty lines, was often prompted by the hope that the *Dii Manes* would not forget the good deeds of those who had passed away from this world. As an example of a thoroughly homely epitaph, one noted by Orelli[1] is worthy of mention here, principally on account of the unusual epithets *lanifica* and *domiseda*. It speaks well for this beautiful lady Amymone that she was skilled at the spinning-wheel; but what shall we say of a remarkable qualification expressed in the last word—that she stopped at home and minded the affairs of the house?

HIC SITA EST AMYMONE MARCI OPTIMA ET PVLCHERRIMA
LANIFICA PIA PVDICA FRUG CASTA DOMISEDA

The private lives of good fathers and estimable sons have also their full share of imperishable record and of superlative epithets. An eminent citizen of Lambæsis is described as *omnibus virtutibus abundans vir*, and a resident of Ammædara (Hydra) is inscribed as *homo bonus rebus hominibusque pernecessarius, quem quærit patriæ maximus hic populus*. Another dedication on a stone found on the road between Theveste and Cirta is to an excellent father in the following simple words: *cujus eximiam bonitatem et prudentiam non solum parentes, verum etiam finitimi doluerunt, quam ob rem filii dulcissimi patri rarissimo sestertium nummum quinque millibus, incolumes parentes*. At Hippo Regius (Bone) is an inscription of nineteen lines[2] to Lucius Postumius Felix Celerinus, who was not only *pontifex* and *duumvir*, but was honoured with the distinction of *flamen Augusti perpetuus*. Further lines speak of his *innocentiam splendoremque et in patriam suam incomparabilem amorem*.

Nimrod, whose name is still preserved in an inscription that is quite legible.' It need scarcely be said that the walls are mostly destroyed, and that nothing remains of the grandeur of the ancient Capsa.

[1] *Inscript. Lat. Collectio*, J. Caspar von Orelli, 1828-56, Turici, No. 4639, vol. ii. p. 319.
[2] *I.R.A.* No. 2871.

Such epitaphs as these may be found in nearly all parts of Roman Africa, but any list would be incomplete without reference to a remarkable example of a compact inscription found by Dr. Leclerc on an altar on the site of the Roman station Tingurtia, now known as Tiaret (a modern town in Algeria, on the lower slopes of Djebel Guezzoul).[1]

```
DISMAN
IBVSTE
RRISQVI
CVMQVE
VIATOR
TRANSIE
RISET DI
XERIS✶VI
✶TVMVLO
RVIIII✶
VESITTI
BITERLE
VISETPOS
TOBITVM
ITETVVMSIT
TIBITERR
ALEVIS
VALXXII
```

Diis Manibus. Terris quicumque viator transieris et dixeris huic tumulo: Rufine, have, sit tibi terra levis, et post obitum item tuum sit tibi terra levis! Vixit annis septuaginta duobus.

The wording recalls the less gracious couplet attributed to Horace Walpole on the death of Sir John Vanbrugh:

> Lie heavy on him, earth, for he
> Laid many a heavy load on thee.

But here, in this gentle epitaph in memory of Rufinus, the appeal to the passer-by is accompanied by the hope that, when he too passes away, the earth may rest as lightly on his remains as on those of the lamented Rufinus.

[1] *I.R.A.* No. 3712. *Vide Rev. arch.* 1852, p. 442.

CHAPTER VI

AFRICA UNDER MARCUS AURELIUS

A.D. 161-180

No Emperor ever acceded to a throne under more favourable auspices than Marcus Aurelius. Adopted by Antonine at the age of seventeen, when he bore the name of Marcus Ælius Verus, and renamed (according to Capitolinus) Ælius Aurelius Antoninus Pius Cæsar in compliment to the Emperor, this fortunate prince enjoyed, till the age of forty, a sunny existence unruffled by political dissensions, the clash of arms, or domestic anxieties. Beloved by his adoptive father, surrounded by friends, with a wife whom he trusted and children whom he adored, Marcus Aurelius had everything which life could offer to make it one long day of reasonable enjoyment. His affectionate intimacy with the Emperor is amply attested by correspondence and the wording of inscriptions discovered intact in various parts of the Empire. So endearing an epithet as *Verissimus*, which Antonine added to his name when he was a mere child, conveys an idea of extreme sincerity of character and an earnest desire to probe the truth for truth's sake. His philosophic tendencies were conspicuous in his early years, due as much to temperament as to the guidance of his instructors, selected by Antonine himself. Rusticus and Apollonius the Stoic were his masters in rhetoric; Eutychius Proculus, a native of Cirta, and Frontinius Cornelius his tutors for Latin; while Cornelius Fronto and Herodes the munificent Athenian roused his enthusiasm for philosophy. All these men were his intimate friends as well as teachers, and to them we are indebted for having brought to light those gentle qualities which are so conspicuous in the correspondence between the young prince and his attached friend of African birth, Cornelius Fronto.

On the death of Antonine, A.D. 161, Marcus Aurelius was free to take undivided possession of the throne and to grasp the reins of empire, which had been within his reach for so many years. But the prince was cast in a different mould from other men, and the bare idea of depriving any one, whose claims to exercise imperial authority, however slight, were recognised by the Senate or the people, would have been distasteful to so just and thoughtful a man. In his earlier days he had adopted as his future colleague, at the express desire of Hadrian, a little boy named Lucius Ceionius Commodus, whose father had been similarly adopted by that Emperor. To make the connection still more binding, Marcus Aurelius gave him the name of Verus, and a few years afterwards made him his son-in-law. For eight years and a few months the Empire was ruled by these two men conjointly, the one judicious in all his actions, governing with wisdom and with the trained mind of a student and philosopher; the other, of depraved tastes and dissolute habits, effeminate and extravagant, passing away at the age of thirty-five, the victim of debauchery and riotous living. The name of Verus would long ago have been almost forgotten had it not been for inscriptions in which he figures as joint Emperor with Marcus Aurelius. The monumental remains in Africa, bearing so dishonoured a name, are fortunately few in number, the most remarkable being the ruined triumphal arch at Tripoli, referred to on page 121. The inscription, still unmutilated and easily legible, runs thus:[1]

IMP · CAES · AVRELIO · ANTONIN · AVG · P · P · ET · IMP · CAES
    L · AVRELIO · VERO · ARMENICO · AVG
SER · S · OEFRITVS · PROCOS · CVM · VTTEDIO · MARCELLO ·
    LEG · SVO · DEDICAVIT · C
CALPVRNIVS · CELSIVS · CVRATOR · MVNERIS · PVB · MVNE-
    RARIVS · II VIR Q · Q · FLAMEN
PERPETVVS · ARCVS · MARMORE · SOLIDO · FECIT.

This dedication to the two Emperors appears to have been about A.D. 163, at the close of a successful expedition against the Armenians under the conduct of Verus. A traveller who visited Tripoli more than two centuries ago was enraptured with the beauty of this monument and its sculptures. He says: 'There are four gates (referring to this quadrifrontal arch) upon which is a triumphal car with a figure of Alexander drawn by

[1] *Travels in the Footsteps of Bruce*, p. 281.

two sphinxes. Below are the heads of slaves. Over the gates are Latin inscriptions. The vaulting is in good condition, with very fine sculpture in high relief. It is all built without mortar or cement. The blocks of marble are from four to five feet thick, and are laid on sheets of lead and held together with cramps.' It is a matter of doubt whether Verus took any active part in securing a victory for the Roman arms. His pleasure was not in the battle-field, and his ambition was to obtain the honour of a warrior at the expense of such trusted generals as Avidius Cassius, a Syrian by birth, Statius Priscus, or Pontius Lælianus. The delights of Antioch as a city of revelry, and the voluptuous amusements in the far-famed laurel groves of Daphne, were more to the taste of such a dissolute and worthless ruler of mankind. And yet a triumph was awarded to him by the Senate in Rome for distinguished services! Similar expeditions to suppress disturbances in Media and Parthia were afterwards undertaken under his command, and with similar results. According to Fronto, Marcus Aurelius was invited by his colleague to share the honour of a triumph A.D. 166, but, as a conscientious man, he unhesitatingly declined to accept reward for services in which he had taken no personal part. The above inscription at Tripoli is of some interest. It clearly tells us that Marcus Aurelius was recognised as *Augustus* and *Pater patriæ*, and that Verus was *Augustus* also and honoured with the title of *Armeniacus*. The words *marmore solido* are unusual. They give indications of the magnificence of this quadrifrontal arch, commenced in the reign of Antonine, and intended as a perpetual memorial of his benign rule. According to Capitolinus, the title of *Pater patriæ* was refused by Marcus Aurelius till the return of Verus after his successful expedition against the Parthians, and on the death of Verus he assumed the title of *Armeniacus* as well as *Germanicus*. It is quite possible that the letters P. P. on the Tripoli arch were not cut till after the Parthian campaign. The omission of the last of these titles is shown on an inscription at Verecunda (Markouna) bearing the date A.D. 163, the second year of the joint rule of these two Emperors.[1]

[1] *I.R.A.* No. 1415.

```
IMP · CAES · M · AVRELIO · ANT . . . . . . .
TRIB · POT · XVIII · COS III · P · P · ET IMP . . .
ARMENIACO . AVG · IMP · II · TRIB · POT · IIII
    .   .   .   .   .   .   .   .   .   .   .   .
    .   .   .   .   .   .   .   .   .   .   .   .
```

Imperatori Cæsari Marco Aurelio Antonino Augusto, Pontifici Maximo, Imperatori II. tribunicia potestate XVIII. Consuli III. patri patriæ, et Imperatori Cæsari Lucio Aurelio Vero Armeniaco Augusto, Imperatori II., tribunicia potestate IIII., consuli II. Respublica Verecundensium decreto decurionum, pecunia publica.

Another inscription bearing the full title, but somewhat illegible, may be seen on the attic of a triumphal arch also at Verecunda, and runs as follows, according to Léon Renier's interpretation : [1]

```
. . . . . RELIO · ANTONINO · AVG . . . . .
. . . . . THIC · GERM · MAX · P · M · TRIB · POT · XXVI ·
    DIVO · VERO
ROCOS · DIVI · VERI · PART · MAX · FRATRI · AVG
AN · NEPOTI · DIVI · TRAIAN · PARTHIC · PRO · NEP · DIVI ·
    NERY · AB · NEP
MACER · SATVRNINVS · LEG · AVG · PR · PR · PATRON · DEDI-
    CAVIT · D · D · P · P.
```

Imperatori Cæsari Marco Aurelio Antonino Augusto Armeniaco, Parthico, Germanico, Maximo, Pontifici Maximo, tribunicia potestate XXVI. Imperatori VI., Consuli III., Proconsuli, divi Veri Parthici Maximi fratri, divi Antonini Pii filio, divi Hadriani nepoti, divi Traiani Parthici pronepoti, divi Nervæ abnepoti, Respublica Verecundensium, Marcus Æmilius Macer Saturninus, legatus Augusti pro prætore, patronus, dedicavit decreto decurionum, pecunia publica.

Among other inscriptions worthy of notice there is one still to be seen on the frieze stones of a temple at Lambæsis (Lambessa) dedicated to Æsculapius and Health. It runs thus :

```
              AESCVLAPIO ET SALVTI
IMP · CAES · M · AVRELIVS · ANTONINVS · AVG · PONT ·
    MAX · ET
IMP · CAES · L · AVRELIVS · VERVS · AVGVSTVS
```

This temple appears to have been commenced in the time of Hadrian, and was built, as another inscription informs us, by the third Augustan legion quartered in that town. It is fair

[1] *I.R.A.* No. 1419.

Africa under Marcus Aurelius 159

to assume, from the absence of titles, that the above inscription was added at the beginning of the joint reign of these two Emperors.[1] Fifty years ago this temple of the Doric order, with its lateral chapels and surroundings, formed an interesting group of monumental buildings. The four columns of the tetrastyle portico of the central edifice, sketched by De la Mare in 1846, have long since been overthrown, and now there is little remaining except the lower parts of the walls of the *cella*, and a confused mass of stone slabs, both moulded and plain. Fortunately, the inscriptions in the subsidiary chapels are still legible, that on the left being dedicated to *Jupiter Valens*, and the one on the right to *Silvanus*. In front of the buildings was a large paved court of semicircular form, which still remains in good condition. Each temple was approached by a flight of steps, and a curved colonnade bound together the side-chapels with the central sanctuary. The approach was by a broad avenue, bordered at a later date by a number of shrines dedicated to various deities, many of them being faced with slabs of marble and paved with mosaics. Some of the mosaic patterns are interesting, especially one seen and described by Léon Renier, bearing the following inscription:

BONVS · INTRA · MELIOR · EXI

Strange to say, the slab of mosaic bearing these words has been lost. The remains of other memorials are better studied on the spot, and the sculptures and other remains, including fine statues of Æsculapius and his daughter Hygeia, are attractive objects in the local museum. The worship of Æsculapius was very popular in North Africa, and, according to Pausanias, sick persons desirous of supplicating the deity or his daughter were required to spend one or more nights in his sanctuary for the purpose of observing certain rites ordained by the priests attached to the temple. The remedies were usually revealed to supplicants in a dream. At Lambæsis special provision appears to have been made for such visitors, there being clear indications of a series of buildings grouped round the temples

---

[1] M. R. Cagnat says that the date of this edifice is A.D. 162, and that the lateral chapels were added successively during the reigns of the Emperors M. Aurelius Commodus and Septimius Severus. Everything appears to have been completed A.D. 211.

and fitted with baths and hypocausts. Whether they formed parts of a large thermal establishment where bodily treatment was practised is not quite apparent. But it is reasonable to suppose that, with the decline of Paganism at a later period, such places were resorted to by wealthy colonists, who held the worship of Æsculapius as a matter of secondary importance. It is worthy of mention that, at a place now called El Gara in North Africa, within the old province of Mauritania Sitifensis, an inscription still exists bearing the dedication of a shrine to Fortune, Health, and Æsculapius.[1] Here, it will be observed, the old Pagan deity comes last, Fortune holding the first place in public estimation.

In some inscriptions we find the name of Verus appearing as sole Emperor. At a town called Uzappa, in the province of Byzacene, there is a dedication to Verus by the inhabitants, in gratitude for alleged services in suppressing the revolt in Armenia, the date being A.D. 163-165. The name of Avidius Cassius, whose generalship contributed so largely to the success of the Roman arms, has no place in this inscription, which is one long string of self-laudatory expressions in honour of a man utterly incapable of any generous act.[2]

```
        IMP · CAES · L · AVRELI
        O · VERO · AVG · ARME
        NIACO · DIVI · ANTO
        NINI · FIL · DIVI · HA
        DRIANI · NEP · DIVI
        TRAIANI · PARTHI
        CI · PRONEP · DIVI
        NERVAE · ABNEP
        P · M · TRIB · POT
        IMP · II · COS II
        P · P · D · D · P · P
```

The lettering in the last line may be read as a bit of irony. It accords the highest distinction of *Pater patriæ* to an Emperor in every way unworthy of the honour. Of Uzappa we know nothing, except that it was raised to the position of a *municipium* towards the end of the third century. It need scarcely

[1] *C.I.L.* No. 8782.
[2] *C.I.L.* No. 11927. Cagnat. *Vide* Espérandieu, *Comptes-rendus de l'Acad. d'Hipp.* a. 1883.

be said that the town has long since been swept away and its existence almost forgotten.

It is a matter of regret that the chief authorities for this period of African history, embracing the career of such a remarkable Emperor as Marcus Aurelius, should have written so little about his eventful reign. Capitolinus has placed much ill-assorted material at the disposal of biographers, and Dion Cassius has supplied some fragmentary notes, strung together without much forethought and with no attempt at methodical arrangement. Where written records fail, inscriptions and coins are the sure guide ; and whether they relate to the Emperor's achievements in the defence of a vast Empire, or are expressive of the good will shown to him by his subjects for wise administration and just rule, they are for all purposes to be depended upon as faithful memorials.

The earlier years of the reign of Marcus Aurelius were troubled by incessant wars, in which the Emperor took no active part. But on the death of Verus the philosopher turned warrior from duty rather than choice, and conducted various campaigns with considerable success. Like most of his predecessors, the thought of crossing the Mediterranean—the *mare sævum*, as the Romans called it—was distasteful, partly on account of a somewhat fragile constitution and susceptibility of taking cold after the slightest exposure. To Marcus Aurelius Africa was personally an unknown country, but his regard for this magnificent appendage of the Empire is attested by the vast number of dedicatory inscriptions throughout the provinces. At the time of his accession the turbulent disposition of the Moors in the extreme west, which had caused Antonine some little anxiety at the close of his reign, had been successfully checked, but had never been entirely repressed. With that spirit of impetuosity which characterises southern races, these restless inhabitants of Western Mauritania were not content with making continual raids into the less protected parts of Roman territory, but, taking advantage of disturbances in other parts of the Empire, crossed the Mediterranean with the intention of forcing the Romans to surrender their hard-won possessions in Southern Spain. But this adventurous expedition was not attended with success.

The rapid spread of colonisation westward in the African

provinces during the last three reigns demanded increased security and better military organisation. It was to these points that the Emperor directed his attention. Outposts were increased, and Lambæsis, the headquarters of a Roman legion established there by Hadrian, was no longer a mere entrenched camp, such as he had inaugurated, but was assuming the appearance of a permanently constructed and well-ordered town. The history of Lambæsis is the key to the history of the Roman army in Africa. In the third century, under the firm rule of Septimius Severus, it became one of the most attractive cities in the country; and even now, after the lapse of seventeen centuries, its monumental remains and the wealth of inscriptions discovered on the site bear ample testimony to its importance and prosperity, and to the loyal allegiance of a large population, both civil and military.

The Roman army, at the time of the accession of Marcus Aurelius, consisted of thirty legions, distributed in various parts of the Empire. A list is given by Marquardt, inscribed on a column of this period, now preserved in the Vatican Museum.[1]

Place.	Number.	Names of Legions.
Lower Mœsia and Dacia . . .	4	I. Italica, V. Macedonica, XI. Claudia, XII. Gemina.
Upper Pannonia .	3	I. Adjutrix, X. Gemina, XIV. Gemina.
Britain . . .	3	II. Augusta, VI. Victrix, XX. Valeria Victrix.
Upper Mœsia . .	2	IV. Flavia, VII. Claudia.
Cappadocia . .	2	XII. Fulminata, XV. Apollinaris.
Syria . . .	2	IV. Scythica, XVI. Flavia.
Upper Germany .	2	VIII. Augusta, XXII. Primigenia.
Lower Germany .	2	I Minerva, XXX. Ulpia Victrix.
Africa . . .	1	III. Augusta.
Egypt . . .	1	II. Trajana.
Hispania . . .	1	VII. Gemina.
Judæa . . .	2	VI. Ferrrata, X. Fretensis.
Phœnicia . .	1	III. Gallica.
Lower Pannonia .	1	II. Adjutrix.
Noricum . . .	1	II. Italica.
Rhætia . . .	1	III. Italica.
Arabia . . .	1	III. Cyrenaica.

[1] M. R. Cagnat, *L'Armée Romaine d'Afrique*, Paris, 1892. This is an exhaustive treatise on the whole subject of military administration in Africa under the Emperors. The author acknowledges his great indebtedness to M. Cagnat for much information on the subject.

Africa under Marcus Aurelius

'In the days of Augustus and his successor, the legion quartered in Africa, with the auxiliary troops employed to defend the frontiers of the provinces, was under the control of the proconsul. But Caligula, whose disposition was wild and uncertain, was led to suspect Marcus Silanus, at that time governor of Africa. To settle any doubts on the matter, the Emperor transferred the command of the legion to an imperial lieutenant, whom he despatched from Rome for that purpose. The result was that, the power of granting preferment being divided between them, dissension arose and a spirit of rivalry aggravated the evil.'[1] But the African legion was supplemented by many others drafted into the country in the time of need ; for, in the index to the volumes of the *Corpus Inscriptionum Latinarum* relating to the African provinces, Wilmanns and others mention the following legions noted in inscriptions as having served in different districts: Apollinaris, Claudia, Cyrenaica, Ferrata, Flavia, Fretensis, Fulminata, Gallica, Hispana, Italica, Macedonica, Parthica, Primigenia, Scythica, Severiana, Ulpia, Valeria, Victrix, besides various *vexillationes, alae*, and *cohortes auxiliariae*. Twenty-six of these legions were formed before the reign of Trajan, who added the II Trajana and the III Ulpia Victrix. Marcus Aurelius subsequently added the II Italica and the III Italica. In the time of Septimius Severus the list was increased by the addition of the I Parthica, II Parthica, and III Parthica. The names given to the legions originated from various sources, mostly from the countries or provinces where they were raised, or in honour of successful campaigns. For instance, Gemina appears to have been adopted where two bodies of troops levied in the same country formed one legion. The little Fulminata had its origin under peculiar circumstances, which have not been disputed. According to Capitolinus, the Roman army under Marcus Aurelius was sore pressed in the war against the Quadi,[2] on account of a long continuance of hot weather and scarcity of water arising from a long period of

---

[1] Tacitus, *Hist*. iv. 48.

[2] The Quadi were a powerful tribe located in the south-east of what is now known as Bohemia. (Tacit. *Hist*. iii. 5. 21.) They ceased to exist at the end of the fourth century. Ammianus Marcellinus (xvii. 12) refers to their methods of warfare, which bear a strong resemblance to the tactics of the Boers in the South African war. He says that they had generally three swift horses for every man, and that they were more skilled in skirmishing than at close quarters in a battlefield.

drought. It was represented to the Emperor that one of the legions had been formed at Maltha, where the population was mostly Christian, and that, such was the power of the gods they served, they could obtain by prayer and invocation anything they required from heaven. By imperial command prayers were offered by this legion on behalf of the distressed army, and immediately the clouds gathered, the thunder pealed forth, the lightning flashed, and the welcome rain not only gave life and strength to the parched troops, but contributed largely to subsequent victory and the successful termination of an anxious campaign. This view of the story is supported by Xiphilin the monk, but Dion Cassius has placed on record that the appeal was made, by order of the Emperor, to an Egyptian magician named Arnuphius, who was serving in the Roman army. ' Mercury and other demons that preside in the air ' were invoked, and the desired rain fell. The former version is probably the true one, as well as a further statement by Capitolinus that the Emperor, in gratitude for such remarkable services, issued an edict in favour of the Christians, and bestowed on their religion the title of *Fulminans.* After the time of Caracalla legions usually took their distinguishing names from that of the reigning Emperor, thus making it easy to fix the date of their formation. Augustus was the first Emperor to raise standing armies in Italy as well as in some of the provinces. Before his time bodies of troops were raised for each expedition, and were disbanded at the close of the campaign. This action by Augustus gave rise to an increased taxation, which pressed heavily on the people in the earlier days of the Empire, but the Emperor met the annual charge by an imposition of one-twentieth on all legacies and inheritances. This continued till the time of Trajan, who lightened the burden and paved the way for its entire removal in the reign of Antonine. The legion allotted for the defence of Numidia received the title of the third Augusta, and, after its permanent settlement at Lambæsis in the time of Hadrian, does not appear to have quitted Africa. It became the representative legion of the African army. As late as the accession of Diocletian, A.D. 283, when an entirely new system of military organisation was introduced and many of the old legions of the Empire ceased to exist, this time-honoured body continued undisturbed in its old headquarters. Its services

Africa under Marcus Aurelius

were only interrupted for a short period during the struggle for empire between Gordian and his brutal rival Maximinus. This legion paid the penalty of siding with the latter, and was disbanded by order of the former when he ascended the throne. After a lapse of fifteen years it was reconstituted by Valerian and re-established at Lambæsis.

No camp in any part of the world has left so many indications of its existence, or so many memorials of military life and administration, as the camp of this Numidian legion. The inscriptions already discovered and interpreted number more than 2,500, and continued systematic exploration is constantly bringing others to light of more or less value to the historian as well as to the epigraphist. They are in the form of memorials of soldiers of all ranks who have faithfully discharged their duty, of dedications to emperors for just and benevolent rule, and of acts of munificence by residents of wealth and renown. One and all they bear testimony to a long period of tranquil enjoyment of life in a pleasant and fertile country, to the prevalence of respect paid by soldiers to their superiors, and to loyal obedience to imperial authority.

The commander-in-chief of the army occupying Numidia, or rather Africa, was at first a proconsul called *proconsul provinciæ Numidiæ*. He was of senatorial rank, and was selected from among those who had done good service to the State. When Mauritania became a Roman province in the time of Caligula, A.D. 37, a change in military administration, consequent upon the acquisition of so large an increase of territory, became necessary. Supreme military control was then centred in the Emperor's selected legate, who in other respects was not independent of the proconsul, and whose title was *Legatus Augusti pro prætore*.[1] Towards the end of the second century, when the African legion had been established at Lambæsis, the military authority of this legate was restricted to that portion of Africa which was regarded as a military province, the title of this high functionary being *Legatus Augusti provinciæ Africæ dioceseos Numidiæ*. And towards the middle of the third century the title was again altered to *pro prætore provinciæ Numidiæ*, according to two inscriptions found on the sites of Thamugas and Lambæsis. The

[1] *Vide* Smith's *Dict. Class. Antiq.* vol. ii. p. 26. This subject is fully explained in an article by W. W. F.

former reads thus,[1] and may be assigned to the reign of Alexander Severus:

P · IVLIO IVNIANO MARTIALINO C · V · COS · LEG · AVG · PR · PR · PROVINCIAE
NVMIDIAE PROCOS PROVINCIAE MACEDONIAE PRAEF AERARI MI
LITARIS CVRATORI VIAE CLODIAE PRAETORIAE TRIBVNO PLEBEI
QVAESTORI PROVINCIAE ASIAE PATRONO COLONIAE ET MVNI
CIPI RESPVBLICA COLONIAE THAMVGADENSIVM DE CRETO DECVRIONVM

The only exception worth noting may be seen on an inscription on a stone slab found on the east side of the forum at Thamugas.[2] It is a dedication to a Roman of high distinction, who had served his country in many capacities, the exception appearing on the eighth line, where the words *pro prætore exercitus provinciæ Africæ* occur. The inscription is supposed to be of the time of Hadrian.

A · LARCIO · A · FILIO · QVIRINA · PRISCO · VI · VIR · EQVITVM
ROMANOR · X · VIR · STLITIB · IVDICAND · QVAESTOR
PROVINCIAE · ASIAE · LEG · AVG · LEG IIII SCYTHICAE
PED · LEG · CONSVLARE · PROVINCIAE · SYRIAE · TRIB · PLEB
PRAETORI · PRAEF · FRVMENTI · DANDI · EX · S · C · LEG · PRO
VINCIAE · BAETICAE · HISPANIAE · PROCOS · PROVIN
CIAE GALLIAE · NARBON · LEG · AVG · LEG II AVG · LEG
AVG · PR · PR · EXERCITVS · PROVINCIAE · AFRIC · VII · VIR
EPLONVM · COS · DESIG · PATRONO · COL · D · D · P · P

The Roman *castrum*, and its diminutive the *castellum*, or fortified post, played an important part in the subjugation of Africa by the Romans. The *castrum*, of which so notable an example exists at Lambessa to the present day, was formed in accordance with the traditional rules which had prevailed from an early period. Polybius,[3] the earliest and perhaps the only

[1] *C.I.L.* No. 2392. Descrip. Wilmanns, also De la Mare and Renier. *Vide I.R.A.* No. 1505.

[2] *C.I.L.* No. 17891. Dessau and Cagnat. *Vide* Poulle, *Rec. de Const.* xxii. p. 356. Pallu de Lessert, *Les Fastes de la Numidie*, 1888, p. 60.

[3] Polybius, the Greek historian, was a native of Megalopolis in Peloponnesus, and served his country during the war in Macedonia, which became a Roman province B.C. 148. He was taken to Rome as a prisoner of war, but his high attainments and amiable disposition gained him the friendship of Scipio and other distinguished

Greek historian who was intimately acquainted with the military operations of his time, and who was present at the fall of Carthage, has left us accurate information about the form and arrangements of a Roman camp. He says that it was an exact square, measuring 2,222 feet each way, and accommodated two legions. Hyginus, an equally reliable authority, describes the camp enclosure of the third century as of oblong form, measuring 2,320 feet by 1,620 feet. The *castrum* at Lambæsis may be estimated at 1,670 feet by 1,330 feet. It was fortified by a strong wall rounded at the angles and flanked by towers, but without a ditch. Some fifty years ago portions of this wall were standing to a considerable height, but they have since been entirely overthrown. The arrangements of the camp were similar to those described by Hyginus, and the form of the enclosing wall agrees with the particulars set forth in his work on the subject.[1] There was a gateway in or near the centre of each of the four sides, and broad roads ran across the enclosures from gate to gate. The principal gate, which was of ornate character, was called *Prætoria*, the one in the opposite wall being called *Decumana*, and those in the side-walls designated respectively as *Principia*, *dextra* and *sinistra*.[2] At the intersection of these four roads was a large open space where the headquarters of the legion, termed the *Prætorium*, was placed.

In permanent encampments, such as at Lambæsis, this edifice had considerable architectural pretensions. Facing the principal entrance was a large open space, commonly known as *Principia*, or headquarters, used by the commanding officer

---

Romans. He accompanied Scipio to Carthage, and subsequently retired to his native city, where he wrote a universal history, beginning with the first outbreak of hostilities between Carthage and Rome, and terminating with an account of the Macedonian war. Of the forty books comprising the entire work, the first five only are extant, and fragments only of the remainder have been preserved. The twelfth book, treating of the geography of Africa, is unfortunately lost. Polybius was the first author to mention the Moors as Μαυρούσιοι, this term being subsequently applied by the Romans to the inhabitants of the whole country first given to Juba II., extending from the river Ampsaga to the Atlantic Ocean.

[1] Hyginus was a land surveyor in the time of Trajan. He appears to have been expert in forming military camps, of which he had made special study. His work *De Castrametatione* has gone through several editions, but with different titles, such as *De Castris Romanis* and *De Munitionibus Castrorum*.

[2] *Ad quatuor portas exercitum instruxit, ut, signo dato, ex omnibus portubus eruptionem facerent.* (Livy, b. xl. c. 27.)

as the place for addressing the troops, corresponding to our parade-grounds.[1] It was also available for pitching tents for the general and his staff at certain seasons. Near the centre of this open space an altar was erected. The location of the various bodies of troops belonging to all branches of military service was in accordance with a recognised system, one *castrum* being almost the exact counterpart of another, although the dimensions may have varied.[2]

The *castellum* was a fortified and entrenched outpost, either for the defence of the mountain passes, or to preserve the line of communication with towns and villages in the interior of the country. The *castella* were generally rectangular enclosures with gates like those of the *castra*. The largest of these enclosures known in North Africa is at El-Kesbat, which measures 780 feet by 460 feet. There is another at Tamesida measuring 300 feet by 184 feet, while that at Ksar Rhelan is of moderate dimensions, being only 100 feet by 81 feet. These fortified strongholds served many purposes. They were not only permanent habitations for small bodies of troops, but they were used as military stores and, in times of disturbance caused by an uprising of any of the frontier tribes, became places of refuge for unprotected colonists and their families. It is not surprising to find that in nearly all the *castella* yet discovered in this country there are indications of water supply from wells sunk within the enclosures, showing the care and foresight of Roman generals in the selection of fortified posts. At intervals between the *castella* were small watch-towers for signalling in case of necessity. When any danger was apprehended a fire was lighted on the summit, the flame of which was visible by night and the smoke by day. In some cases beams of timber were employed, being raised or lowered in accordance with a pre-arranged system of signalling—a primitive form of aerial signalling probably as useful in those days as the highly scientific wireless telegraphy in our own times.[3]

---

[1] Tacitus, *Ann.* b. iv. c. 3. *Vide* also *L'Armée Romaine d'Afrique*, p. 675.

[2] Such was the value attached to obedience to authority in a Roman camp that altars have been found bearing this simple dedication: *Disciplinæ Militari*. (*C.I.L.* Nos. 9832 and 10657.)

[3] *Si divisæ sunt copiæ, per noctem flammis, per diem fumo significant sociis quod*

Another kind of fortification, which for a long period was a feature in Roman Africa, consisted of fortified farms. Remains of these buildings, as well as similar ones on a larger scale in connection with imperial estates which bore the title of *saltus*,[1] may still be studied in the less frequented parts of the country. Among the inscriptions relating to this class of building there is one at a farm about eleven miles from Setif, now known as Ain Mellul. It is dedicated to Diana, the date of its construction being, according to Wilmanns, A.D. 234, the last year of the reign of Alexander Severus.[2]

```
           IMP · CAES · M
         AVRELIVS SEVERVS
        ALEXANDER INVICTVS
        PIVS FELIX AVG MVROS
        KASTELLI DIANENSIS EX
     TRVXIT PER COLONOS EIVSDE
       . . . . . . . . M KASTELLI
              P CLXXXXV
```

It appears to have been built by the colonists for their own protection. Inscriptions relating to fortifications for the protection of larger holdings are not numerous, but the annexed dedication during the short rule of Pertinax, A.D. 192, gives some idea of the wording usually employed:[3]

```
              PRO SALVTE
             IMP CAESARIS
             P HEL PERTINA
           CIS TRIBVNICIE PO
          TESTATIS COS II P · P
             COLONI DOMINI N
            CAPVT SALTVS HOR
           REOR PARDALARI HA
           NC ARAM POSVERVNT
                ET D · D ·
```

aliter non potest nuntiari. Aliquanti in castellorum aut urbium turribus appendunt trabes, quibus aliquando erectis, aliquando depositis, indicant quæ geruntur. (Veg. iii. 5.) Flavius Vegetius Renatus dedicated his work on military institutions to Valentinian. It is best known as *De Re militari*, but it has other titles, *Epitoma Institutorum Rei militaris*, and *Epitoma Rei militaris*.

[1] For definition of *saltus*, vide p. 189.

[2] *C.I.L.* No. 8701. *Rec. de Const.* 1875, p. 338. Some travellers have noted that the name of the Emperor had been erased in the usual way.

[3] *C.I.L.* No. 8425. Poulle, *Rec. de Const.* 1873-74, p. 363.

There is another of the time of Aurelian, A.D. 213, which runs thus : *Coloni caput saltus horreorum et Kalefacelenses Pardalarienses aram pro salute eius consecraverunt et nomen castello quem constituerunt.*

A study of the vast number of inscriptions relating to the camp at Lambæsis and the town which sprang up in the immediate vicinity, bearing the title of *Respublica Lambæsitanorum* and made a *municipium* by Marcus Aurelius, aided by some valuable notes furnished by the authors of the *Corpus Inscriptionum Latinarum*, reveals the whole system of military administration by the Romans from the second to the fourth century. And further than this, we get an insight into the domestic life of the troops and their families, and a record of their work in a civil as well as military capacity.

In the earlier days of the Empire no encouragement was given to soldiers of the legions serving in the provinces to contract matrimony, and consequently a state of concubinage, tacitly approved by the Senate, was found to exist in the chief garrison towns. A married soldier could retain his wife, but he was not allowed to keep her in the camp. Similar restrictions were imposed upon magistrates and other high functionaries, who were not allowed to be accompanied by their wives whenever they accepted foreign appointments. Suetonius, however, in his life of Augustus, says that the Emperor very reluctantly permitted the legates to visit their wives and families during the winter months.[1] From Tacitus we have a graphic account of a heated debate in the Senate during the reign of Tiberius, when the question of removing such restrictions was proposed. He tells us that a senator named Cæcina Severus moved, as a counter proposition, that no magistrate holding office in any province should be accompanied by his wife.[2] 'A train of women,' he added, 'introduced habits of luxury in time of peace, and whenever war broke out or disturbances arose they retarded operations by their fears and expostulations, making a Roman army resemble in its march the motley assemblage of a barbarian horde. Such was the power of women that they ruled all things, not only their families but courts of justice, and ultimately they would even

---

[1] Suetonius, *Augustus*, c. 24.   [2] Tacitus, b. iii. c. 33.

THE CAPITOL AT THUGGA (DOUGGA)

control their armies.' But this senator was overruled, the restriction was withdrawn, and it was not long before minor functionaries, as well as officers, found themselves peacefully settled with their wives and families in some town or village close to the camp. At Lambæsis the immediate result was a considerable extension of the town *extra muros*, and the establishment of a large settled population enjoying a high degree of prosperity. Veterans of the third Augustan legion, as well as of the auxiliary forces under the command of Roman officers, became attached to the neighbourhood where they had happily passed so many years of active service, and never left it. In some instances, borne out by votive offerings scattered over the ground, they removed to the adjacent towns of Mascula, Verecunda, or Thamugas. All the inscriptions, as we read them in the present day, whether in the museum at Lambessa or some other local depository, or even in the galleries of the Louvre, may be regarded as faithful registers of daily life and daily work in the service of the Empire. The activity of the Roman soldier, wherever he was quartered, was unbounded. In times of peace he made those magnificent highways, portions of which still greet the traveller's eye and excite his admiration as he journeys across the silent plains of North Africa. He constructed fortifications which would have endured to the present day, if they could have escaped the ravages of the Vandals or the wanton neglect of the Arabs. He built bridges and aqueducts in a manner that no other nation has surpassed. Temples and triumphal arches, fountains and baths, theatres and colonnades arose at the bidding of an Emperor, while works of utility and adornment were raised by loyal citizens as enduring memorials of affection for their country. Inscriptions inform us that the building of the city of Thamugas was almost entirely the work of the third legion, and such was the skill of the designers and artificers in their ranks that we find their services employed elsewhere. Soldiers under the Empire, especially in the second and third centuries, appear to have been well cared for and well paid.[1] As a single man a soldier could live in the camp or in the neighbouring town. He could

---

[1] *Et non saxum erat ut antehac cubile, sed pluma et flexiles lectuli.* (Ammianus Marcellinus, b. xii. c. 4.) This indicates that soldiers were provided with pillows and mattresses, which they took with them in their campaigns.

save money and, on retirement, could live with ease and comfort. The pay varied at different periods, but it was more than sufficient for ordinary requirements. The allowances on retirement varied also, but it may be reckoned at a sum equivalent to 100*l*. Some of the soldiers were *duplicarii*, receiving double pay and exceptional privileges, while others were *sesquiplicarii*, receiving pay in the same proportion. No inscriptions have, I believe, yet been found in Africa relating to the latter, but there are several quite legible relating to the former, such as the annexed one found at Tipasa, extending to eighteen lines, now deposited in the museum at Algiers.

>   DVPLICARIVS
>   EX NVMERVM SINGULARI
>   VM QVI AT MONTE ZELEL
>   INTERCEPTVS EST VI ANS
>   XXXVI MIIII DIES X MA
>   TER DVLCISSIO FILIOMFE
>   CIT . . . .

It is the dedication by a mother to her very dear son, who was a *duplicarius* in a select body of troops, and was killed at Mount Zelel, aged 37 years. On the accession of an Emperor and on special occasions, when it was desirable to secure the good will of the legions in any imperial undertaking, a donative was presented to each soldier.[1] Suetonius says that Domitian limited the amount; but whatever was the sum granted to each man, the moiety was deposited in a savings bank under the control of the standard-bearers bearing the military title of *signiferi*, who were assisted by men in the ranks called *librarii depositorum*, in other words, savings-bank clerks. The money deposited was called *peculium castrense*.[2] The annexed inscription on a stone in the cemetery at Lambæsis is a record of filial affection for a *signifer* of the Augustan legion.[3]

[1] Capitolinus states that on the accession of Marcus Aurelius and Lucius Verus each soldier received 20,000 sesterces, equal to 156*l*. Lampridius mentions that Commodus on a like occasion gave large donatives to the army. And we learn from Herodian that Caracalla on ascending the throne gave every soldier 2500 Attic drachms, representing 78*l*. 2*s*. 6*d*. To use the words of Spartianus on one occasion, this Emperor *enormitate stipendii militibus, ut solet, placuit.*
[2] *Dig.* xlix. 17, 11.
[3] *C.I.L.* No. 18280.

D · M · S
L · AELIVS · VICT
OR · SIG · LEG · III · AVG
VIX · ANIS · XL . . . .
AELIVS FELIX PATRI
KARISSIM · FECIT

In the *Prætorium* was found a dedication to two *signiferi*, father and son, during the reign of Septimius Severus; and on an altar in the camp was a somewhat similar one, worth mentioning,[1] the two *signiferi* by whom the memorial was raised having charge of the public market.

I · O · M · DOL
P · P · FLAVI STVDI
OSI · SABINIVS
INGENVVS · ET
AVRELIVS · SED
ATVS · SIG · LEG
III · AVG · AGENTES
CVRA · MACELLI
V · L · A · S · CVM · A
ZVTORIBVS · SVIS

Publii Flavii Studiosi Sabinus Ingenuus et Aurelius Sedatus Signiferi leg. III Augusta agentes curam macelli votum libentes animis solverunt cum azutoribus suis.

Of higher rank than the standard-bearer was the eagle-bearer or *aquilifer*, one only being attached to each legion. The following memorial of an *aquilifer* who was buried in the cemetery at Lambæsis, and whose name was perpetuated by his uncle, is worth recording:[2]

D · M · S
ICTVRIO · FELICI
VIXIT ANOS XXV
MESSES II DIES XVI
DISCENS AQVILIFER
LEG III AVG MEMORIAE
EIVS POSVIT ISBON
CIVS SECVNDVS
AVVNCVLO

The keeping of slaves was not forbidden in any rank of Roman society, and from two inscriptions found near the camp it would seem that when soldiers were prosperous they had slaves or freedmen in their service. The wording of both of

[1] *C.I.L.* No. 18224. *Bull. du Com.* 1890, p. 455. (Masqueray descrip.)
[2] *C.I.L.* No. 18302. *Bull. du Com.* 1887, p. 74.

them is equally clear. *Victori Juli Marciani mil. frum. servo*, and *D. M. Victoris, natione Maurum, annorum XX, libertus Numeriani equitis ala I Asturium*.

There is no branch of military service that is not represented at Lambæsis and the neighbourhood. Hundreds of inscriptions attesting the labours of officers and soldiers of the legion, and auxiliaries raised in other countries, form an unerring record of more than two centuries of loyal attachment to the Empire. As the eye traces the long line of familiar lettering, imagination depicts a little world of contented Roman colonists in this far-off settlement, some engaged in the purely military duties of the camp, others actively employed on works of utility or adornment in the town or its vicinity, while not a few, exempt from services of every kind, tilled the soil or cultivated their gardens in the fertile plain or on the hillsides in the neighbourhood of the camp. So many of the memorial slabs have been removed from the spots where they were discovered that their exact location cannot be easily determined; but from the fact that the lettering *leg. III Aug.* occurs on most of them, there is no reason to doubt their genuineness as memorials of residents of old Lambæsis. The principal inscriptions of this nature may be studied in the local museum, while some few are imbedded in the walls of more recent structures. All ranks of military and civil life are fairly well represented. Among them are several relating to *speculatores* of the legion, corresponding to modern aides-de-camp or adjutants, of which the following[1] may be taken as an example:

```
        GENIO
     SCHOLAE SVAE
   P · AVREL · FELIX         Genio scholæ suæ, P. Aurelius Felix,
      SPECVLATOR             speculator, leg. III Augustæ domo
     LEG · III · AVG         Thamugada, donum dedit.
     DOMO THAMVGA
      DONVM DEDIT
```

Another found near the camp preserves the memory of the wife of an imperial legate, the monument having been raised by a number of *speculatores* and *beneficiarii* of the legion.[2] The latter were a class of soldiers exempted, by the favour of commanding officers, from the performance of heavy duties,

[1] *C.I.L.* No. 2603; *I.R.A.* No. 132.   [2] *I.R.A.* No. 44.

Africa under Marcus Aurelius

and are mentioned by Julius Cæsar as *beneficiarii superiorum exercituum*.

STATIAE · AGRIPPINAE
CONIVGIS · MODI · IVSTI
LEG · AVG · PR · PR. CONSVLIS
SPECVLATORES · ET · BENEFICIARI

Another class of soldiers were the *immunes*, who were apparently freed from all military services, and had settled down in the vicinity of the camp. A pleasing memorial in the following dedication to a wife, described as *conjugi rarissimæ*, may still be studied on the spot:[1]

D · M	*Diis Manibus. Flaviæ Victoriæ*
FLAVIAE · VICTORIAE · CONIVGI	*conjugi rarissimæ, vixit annis*
RARISSIMAE · VIXIT · AN · XXXIII	*XXXIII, Julius Extricatus,*
IVLIVS · EXTRICATVS · IMMVN · LEG	*immunis legionis III Augus-*
III · AVG · P · V · EX PRECEPTO PIVS	*tæ, Piæ vindicis, ex precepto*
PARENTIBVS FECIT	*ejus, parentibus fecit.*

A very similar dedication to a *matri carissimæ* by an *immunis* of the same legion was found in the necropolis at Lambæsis:[2]

D · M · S
RESTVTAE · DONATAE
V · A · LXXX HOMVLLIVS IANVARIVS
IMM LEG III AVG MATRI
CARISSIME · FECIT · H · S · E

Diis Manibus sacris, Restutæ Donatæ vixit annis octaginta, Homullius Januarius, immunis legionis tertiæ Augustæ, matri carissimæ fecit. Hic sita est.

Prominent among soldiers of the legion were the *cornicularii*, who took rank as assistant officers or subalterns. They were men who had received the adornment of a *corniculum* for military services, and were held in much esteem. This device was in the form of a little horn attached to the helmet. It was fastened on, but did not form part of the helmet. In the cemetery at Lambæsis a slab bearing the following dedication by a sorrowing stepson, and a centurion of the legion, is interesting, the deceased being a veteran of that class:[3]

---

[1] *I.R.A.* No. 743.   [2] *I.R.A.* No. 704.
[3] *I.R.A.* No. 771.

```
          D · M
       C · POMPONI
       O · MAXIMO
      VET · EX · COR
        NICVLARIO
     VIX · ANN · LXXXI
   IVL · LONGINIANVS> · LEG
      VITRICO · MAER
```

The *frumentarii*, too, were important functionaries in all provinces of the Empire. Although their duties were chiefly in connection with the supply and distribution of corn, they acted in other capacities, such as might be performed by letter-carriers; and, according to Spartian, they were occasionally employed as spies.[1] The principal inscriptions relating to these officials have been found in the Appian Way between Rome and the coast at Puteoli, where their headquarters were established. Their attachment to a legion does not appear to have entailed any military service, the duties being essentially of a civil kind. The following affectionate memorial to the wife of a *frumentarius* attached to the fifth Macedonian legion, and buried at Lambæsis, is clearly expressed:[2]

VLPIAE · PRIS	
CAE · HO · MVL · CON	*Ulpiæ Priscæ, honestæ mulieri*
IVGI · CARISSIME	*conjugi carissimæ, M. Flavius*
M · FLAVI · CAECI	*Cæcilius Telesphorianus, Fru-*
LIVS · TELESPHORI	*mentarius legionis quintæ*
ANVS FVM LEG	*Macedonicæ.*
V MACEDONIC	

Among soldiers of a lower rank the *tesserarii* held a conspicuous position, and as there was one in each company or century of one hundred men, according to a statement by Vegetius,[3] they formed a numerous body in so large a military establishment as that at Lambæsis. The origin of this system of communication by means of *tesseræ*—small tablets of wood bearing the watchword for the night throughout a Roman camp—is not traced by any ancient author. But we learn that the soldiers selected for their distribution repaired every evening at a fixed hour to the tent or headquarters of the military tribune, and received from him a *tessera* bearing some mark or inscrip-

---

[1] Spart. *Hadrian*, ii. 4.   [2] *I.R.A.* No. 622.   Also *C.I.L.* No. 2867.
[3] *Qui tesseras per contubernia militum nuntiarunt*, Vegetius, ii. 7.

tion which constituted the watchword for the night. This was passed on silently to each company or squadron in rotation, and was finally returned to the tribune. The *tesseræ* were then examined and counted, and if any of them failed to be presented an inquiry was made immediately, and punishment inflicted for the slightest breach of regulations. Frequent mention of *tesseræ* is made by Livy,[1] who speaks of the *tacitum signum* of a Roman camp. The following inscription relating to a *tesserarius* may be seen in the public prison close to the ruins of Lambæsis. The last lines are almost illegible, but there is sufficient to indicate that the memorial was dedicated by a *custos armorum*, whose military duties seem to be clearly defined by this title.[2]

```
            D · M · S
         C · TERENTIVS
        SECVND · OPITER
          TESSERARIVS
         LEG · III · AVG
           VIX · AN XLII
         L · FVRNASIDIVS
    AS  . . . . . ARMORVM
             H · E · P
```

Among the memorials at Lambæsis the following inscription has been found: *Caius Cornelius Pietas, armorum custos legionis tertiæ Augustæ, vixit annos quadraginta quinque. Pius frater fecit*.[3] Even the trumpeter is not forgotten, the following memorial to a *tubicen legionis* by his mother and his wife Rufina being as legible on the stone slab as though it had been the work of yesterday:[4]

```
            D · M · S
       C · IVLIVS · EMERITVS
     TVB · LEG · III · AVG · VIX
       AN · XXXV · M · VIII · MAT
    ET · RVFI · COIVX · FECERVNT
```

The civil staff attached to the legion preserve their names and their functions in a variety of inscriptions which may still

---

[1] Livy, xxvii. 46, xxxix. 30.   [2] *I.R.A.* No. 1213.
[3] *I.R.A.* No. 556.
[4] *I.R.A.* No. 737. A *tubicen* (*tuba-cano*) blew the straight trumpet, in contradistinction to a *liticen* (*lituus-cano*), who blew the curved trumpet or clarion. Then there was the *cornicen*, the horn-blower. *Vide* Livy, i. 64: *Cornicines tubicinesque canere jubet*.

be studied in the museum at Lambessa. Among these officials were the *mensores*, who may be regarded as land-surveyors, though the term is equally applicable to those who measured corn or other kinds of produce; and when written *mensores ædificiorum*, may designate a class of officials known in modern times as clerks of works. The memorial at Lambæsis to Modius Felix shows how the term was applied:[1]

    M · MODIVS · FELIX
    MENSOR LEG · III AVG
    VIX · AN · LX · ARRANI
    SATVRNIN · FE

Then there were the *dispensatores*, usually slaves, who had charge of accounts and made payments after the manner of a steward. Their opportunities of enriching themselves at the expense of others are attested by a statement made by Suetonius in his life of Otho, who obtained from a slave whom he had recommended to the Emperor Galba for the office of a *dispensator* the sum of one million sesterces (8,072*l.*).[2] The following dedicatory inscription to one who had been born in servitude and had faithfully served his master, a retired *dispensator* of the legion, is worth recording:[3]

  D · M · S
  HYGINO · SER
  FIDELISSIMO *Diis Manibus sacrum Hygino, servo fidelis-*
  V · A · XXIII *simo, vixit annis viginti tribus, Adventus*
  ADVENTVS · AVG *Augusti verna exdispensator legionis tertiæ*
  VERN · EX · DISP *Augustæ*
  LEG · III · AVG

A still more interesting one, and in perfect condition, on an altar in the plains of Batna, near Lambessa, was copied by Renier.[4] It is a dedication by an *arcarius* of the legion to his old friend the *dispensator*, who died in his 111th year.

    D · M · S
CASSIO AVGGG NNNVERN *Cassio Augustorum nostrorum triumvernæ,*
DISP LEG III AVG · P · V *dispensatori legionis tertiæ Augustæ Piæ*
QVI VIXIT ANN CX · MVII *Vindicis, qui vixit annis centum et decem,*
DXXI VRSINVS ARK LEG *mensibus septem, diebus viginti uno. Ur-*
 EIVSDEM FECIT *sinus, arcarius legionis ejusdem, fecit*
  B   M   *bene merenti.*

[1] *I.R.A.* No. 1003.   [2] Suetonius, *Otho*, c. 5.
[3] *C.I.L.* No. 3291.   [4] *I.R.A.* No. 493.

Africa under Marcus Aurelius

The loyal services of *liberti*, freedmen, are recorded on several memorial slabs found in the necropolis, such as the annexed dedication by a Roman lady, who laments the death of a freedman named Eutychianus.[1] Another of equal interest is a dedication to an excellent master by his two freedmen and heirs, Euhodus and Fortunatus.[2]

```
       D · M · S                   D · M
       EVTYCHIA                L · PVBLICIO
       NO LIBERTO                VICTORINO
     IVLIA CANDIDA                PATRONO
        PATRONA                    OPTVMO
     BENE MERENTI                 PVBLICII
         FECIT                    EVHODVS
                              ET FORTVNATVS
                               LIBERTI ET
                              HEREDES EIVS
```

The architect was an officer of high importance in the work of the legion. He was entrusted with designing military and civil buildings, bridges and aqueducts, and fulfilled such other duties as are now performed by military engineers. The annexed memorial of Cornelius Festus, who died at the age of thirty, is clearly expressed:[3]

```
           D · M · S
      M · CORNELIVS · FESTVS
        MIL · LEG · III · AVG
        ARCHITECTVS · VIC
         SIT · ANNIS · XXX
```

The *medici*, doctors, figure largely on memorial slabs. The following dedication *medico conjugi dignissimo* is rendered interesting from the fact that the deceased, who lived to the age of 85 years, 7 months, and 15 days, is styled *medicus ordinarius*:[4]

```
              D · M
       C · PAPIRIO · AELIAN
        O · MEDICO · ORDINA
       RIO · LEG · III · AVG VIX
       ANNIS · LXXXV · M . VII
        D · XV · PAPIRIA · VITAL
        IS · CONIVGI · DIGNISSIMO
```

---

[1] *C.I.L.* No. 3598; *I.R.A.* No. 851.   [2] *I.R.A.* No. 1115.
[3] De la Mare and Renier, *I.R.A.* No. 547; *C.I.L.* No. 2850.
[4] *C.I.L.* No. 18314. Poulle, *Rec. de Const.* xxii. 1882.

According to Mommsen, an *ordinarius* was attached to a *cohors* or company in contradistinction to a *medicus*, who was the medical officer of the legion. But Marquardt is of opinion that the *ordinarius* should be classed as an assistant physician. Inscriptions to *medici* are numerous at Lambæsis. The two following examples, one from the necropolis and the other now deposited in the Prætorium, are sufficient to indicate the phraseology usually adopted:[1]

```
        D · M                       D . M
  T · FLAVIVS · ITA           T · FL · ONE
  LVS · MED · LEG                SIPHORO
  III · AVG . . . . .        MED · LEG · III · AVG
  V · A · X . . . . .          AEMILIVS · FE
  . . . . . . . .              LIX . . . . SCRI
                                . . . . . . . .
```

Conjugal felicity is the subject of many touching memorials, bearing ample testimony to the existence of a contented, well-ordered community in this thickly populated region of North Africa. What can be more charmingly expressed in one short sentence than the following memorial found near Lambæsis on the road to Diana Veteranorum?[2] It is a dedication by Julia Ziora, widow of a centurion of the third legion, and her son, Rufinus Vitalis. The words *conjugi incomparabili* and *patri dulcissimo* need no translation. And the last line expresses the last wish of many sorrowing relatives:

```
      D · M · S
    RVFI RVFI
   NI>LEG III
   AVG IVLIA ZI          Diis Manibus sacrum Rufi Rufini,
   ORA COIVGI            centurioni legionis tertiæ Augustæ,
   INCOMPARABILI         Julia Ziora conjugi incomparabili, et
   ET RVFINVS VI         Rufinus Vitalis patri dulcissimo,
TALIS PATRI DVLCISSI     fecerunt. Vixit annis quinquaginta
   MO FECERVNT VI        quinque. Qui legis dic: sit tibi
  XITANNISLV QVILE       terra levis!
  GIS DIC SITTIBITER
      RA LVIS
```

Not less interesting is another inscription found, north of the forum, in honour of an illustrious wife of an illustrious governor.[3]

---

[1] *I.R.A.* Nos. 637 and 641. [2] *I.R.A.* No. 1130.
[3] *I.R.A.* No. 49. Also De la Mare.

Africa under Marcus Aurelius

It will be noted that the epithets in both cases are represented by initials, and that the memorial was raised during the short rule of the two Augusti, Caracalla and Geta, sons of Septimius Severus, A.D. 211-212.

AELIAE
PROSPERAE · C · F
CONIVGI · C
POMPONII · MAGN
LEG · AVGG · PRPR
C · V · PRAESIDIS
STRATORES

Æliæ Prosperæ, clarissimæ feminæ, conjugi Caii Pomponii Magni, legati Augustorum duorum proprætore clarissimi viri, præsidis, stratores.

This brief notice of the long array of memorial slabs brought to light in the neighbourhood of Lambæsis may be fitly concluded by the following inscription built into the ruined wall of a Byzantine edifice near the city. Imagination depicts the loving care of this soldier of the Empire, who traversed land and sea with the mortal remains of his beloved wife, and raised this stone to her memory in the pleasant land of his adoption:[1]

D · M · S · FLAVIAE · IVLIOSAE CONIVGI VIX AN XXVII
M SERVILIVS FORTVNATVS A MILITIIS QVI PER
MARIA ET TERRAS RETVLIT RELIQVIAS CONIVGIS EX
PROVINCIA DACIA

The custom of recording on stone or marble the completion of any public work, whether executed by imperial command, or by the exercise of municipal authority, or, as it so frequently happened, through the munificence of private individuals, extended to bridges, aqueducts, reservoirs, public roads, and other works of utility. These were undoubtedly the work of the legions. The construction and maintenance of *viæ publicæ* was always a marked feature of Roman civilisation, and created an amount of interest and enthusiasm that would be difficult to arouse in our more prosaic age. In all the provinces of the Empire may be found innumerable inscriptions relating to the care of highways, and nowhere are they more abundant than in North Africa. Many are mutilated or destroyed, while others, lettered in imperishable limestone, are as legible as on the day when the simple abbreviated words were traced by the

[1] *C.I.L.* No. 2772. Renier and De la Mare descrip.

mason's chisel. Those which have been preserved relate to the following : [1]

Theveste to Tacape, *temp.* Tiberius, A.D. 14.	*vide* C.I.L. 10,023
Theveste to Hippo Regius, *temp.* Titus, A.D. 75 .	C.I.L. 10,119
Theveste to Leptis Magna, *temp.* Nerva (*restit.*) .	C.I.L. 10,016
Theveste to Thamugas, *temp.* Trajan, A.D. 100 .	C.I.L. 10,186
Ad Piscinam to Ad Majores, *temp.* Trajan, A.D. 104–5	I.R.A. 178
Rusicada to Cirta, *temp.* Hadrian . . .	I.R.A. 2,296
Theveste to Carthage, *temp.* Hadrian . . .	C.I.L. 10,048
Sitifis to Auzia, *temp.* Hadrian and Sept. Severus	C.I.L. 10,363
Lambæsis to Ad Piscinam, *temp.* Antonine .	C.I.L. 10,230
Auzia to Rapidi and further, *temp.* Antonine, A.D. 155	C.I.L. 10,439
Lambæsis to Ad Piscinam per El-Kantara, Pertinax *restit.* A.D. 193	C.I.L. 10,238
Usinaz to Temet-el-Had, *temp.* Sept. Severus .	*Eph. Epig.* vii. 66
Sitifis to Mons, *temp.* Sept. Severus, *reficit* A.D. 195	C.I.L. 10,351
Sitifis to Zarai, *temp.* Sept. Severus, *reficit* A.D. 195	C.I.L. 10,361
Numerus Syrorum to Altava and further, *temp.* Alex. Severus	C.I.L. 10,470

The importance of the road between Theveste and Carthage is borne out by many inscriptions relating to it, one of which has already been given on p. 108. They mostly bear the date A.D. 123. The extension of this great military highway to Thamugas and Lambæsis was probably honoured in a similar way. So general, indeed, was the sustom of placing on record any operations connected with road construction that even works of repair were not left unnoticed. On a stone pillar about eight feet high, brought to light many years ago by Duveyrier, near the track between the old towns of Tacape and Capsa, an inscription records the construction and maintenance of a road by the third legion in this far-off corner of Roman Africa. And another inscription mentioned by several travellers tells us that they restored *viam a Karthagine usque ad fines Numidiæ provinciæ longa incuria corruptam atque dilapsam.*[2]

Mention has already been made of the mountain road across the Aurès, constructed by the sixth legion Ferrata. There is reason to believe that similar work was performed by other

[1] This list of roads is mostly borrowed from M. Cagnat, *L'Armée Romaine d'Afrique* : *vide* p. 687 *et seq.*   [2] C.I.L. No. 10047. Renier, Temple, and others.

Africa under Marcus Aurelius

legions temporarily stationed in the same locality. An inscription informs us that the legion raised in Palmyra—a city which attained notoriety during the reign of Aurelian—was located here for a considerable period. Among several memorials of this legion encamped at that delightful spot called Calceus Herculis, now known as El-Kantara, the following is the best preserved,[1] and as a dedication in honour of Caracalla may be noticed here:

MERCVRIO · AVG · SACR
PRO · SALVTE · IMP · CAESARIS · M · AVRE
LI · ANTONIN · AVG · PII · M · ANNIVS
VALENS · LEG · III · AVG . . . .
N · PALMYRENORVM · PRO · SALVTE
SVA · ET · SVORVM · V · S · L · A

MALAGBELO
AVG
SANCTO SACR
T · FL · MANSVE
TVS · LEG · III · AVG
V · S · L · L · M

A stone panel close by records the dedication of a temple or altar to Malagbelus, who was one of the deities worshipped at Palmyra.[2] The toleration granted at this period of Roman history to the creeds of other countries included in the Empire is indicated by a few dedicatory inscriptions, more especially at Lambæsis, which became the permanent home of soldiers recruited from all parts of the Empire. The following memorial found near the temple of Æsculapius in that city, is somewhat remarkable, being the dedication of a temple to Isis and Serapis by a *legatus proprætor* and his wife and daughter. It appears to have been embellished by a portico with columns, the gift of the soldiers of the third Augustan legion, in A.D. 158, towards the close of Antonine's reign:[3]

ISIDI · ET · SERAPI
L · MATVCCIVS · FVSCINVS · LEG · AVG
PR · PR · AEDEM · CVM · VOLTEIA · CORNIFICIA · VXORE
ET · MATVCCIA · FVSCINA · FILIA · AB · ANTECESSORIBVS
SVIS · INSTITVTAM · EXVLTATAM · ET · ADIECTO
PRONAO · PER · LEG · III · AVG
COLVMNIS · SVA · PECVNIA POSITIS · EXORNAVIT

[1] *C.I.L.* No. 2486. Between Biskra and Hammam. *Rec. de Const.* 1871-72, p. 425.
[2] *C.I.L.* No. 2497. *I.R.A.* No. 1634.   [3] *I.R.A.* No. 23

Auxiliary troops doing duty in Africa were mostly from other provinces of the Empire. In the early days of Roman colonisation the enrolment of natives of Africa for service in their own country was regarded as a source of danger, mainly on account of the frequent uprising of tribes on the frontier. But, with the spread of civilisation, order and good government were secured, and at the commencement of the third century no danger was apprehended from the enrolment of natives both as cavalry and infantry. There appears, however, to be a record of only three bodies of native troops in any of the African provinces. These were designated respectively as the *cohors Maurorum*, the *ala Numidarum*, and the *cohors Musulamiorum*.[1] The last are mentioned on a slab found by M. Tissot at Ksar Gurai, in the neighbourhood of Theveste. The reading of the four last words, according to Wilmanns, is *privilegii vetustatis sectam abolevisse*.

>   EX AVCTORITATE
>   IMP CAES TRAIANI
>   AVG GER DACICI
>   MVNATIVS GALLVS
>   LEG PRO PR
> . . . . FINIBVS MVSVLAMIOR
> . . . . LEG II VETVSTATIS
> . . . . TAM ABOLEVIT ·

Of the foreign auxiliary troops, such as the legions *Gemina, Cyrenaica, Italica*, and others, two inscriptions will suffice as memorials of their presence in Africa during some period or other of the Roman occupation. The first relates to a distinguished Roman, who had served his country in many capacities, and was lieutenant-general of the third legion Gemina.[2] As this slab was discovered in a house in a modern village, which has replaced the once important town of Milevum, it is probable that he was a native of that place.

>   Q CAECILIO C V QVIR
>   C V PROCOS PROVINCIAE BAE
>   TICAE SODALI AVGVSTALI LEG
>   LEG III GEMINAE CVRATORI
>   COL PISAVRENTIVM CVRATO
>   RI COL FORMIANORVM PRAE

---

[1] *C.I.L.* No. 10667. The Musulami occupied land in the vicinity of *Saltus Beguensis*, between Sufetula and Ammædara. *Vide* Guérin, i. p. 391.

[2] *C.I.L.* No. 8207. Ravoisié, *Explor.* tab. 27. Also Wilmanns.

Africa under Marcus Aurelius

Quinto Cæcilio, Caii filio, Quirina tribu, clarissimo viro, proconsuli provinciæ Bæticæ, sodali Augustali, legato legionis tertiæ decimæ Geminæ, curatori coloniæ Pisaurensium, curatori coloniæ Formianorum, prætori . . . .

The other, found at Lambessa, is a memorial of a soldier of the second legion *Parthica*, which was formed in the time of Septimius Severus. According to the inscription this Aurelius Victorinus was a centurion of the fourth *pilus posterior*,[1] and a soldier of merit.

        D · M
AVRELIO VICTO
RINO MILLEG
II PARTH SEVE
RIANAE P FI AE
TERNAE >IIII PIL
POST QVI BIXIT (*sic*)
ANNOS XXX MIL
ANNOS VIII. . . .

Diis Manibus, Aurelio Victorino, militi legionis secundæ Parthicæ Severianæ piæ, fidelis, æternæ, centurioni quarto pilo posteriori, qui vixit annos XXX, militavit annos VIII . . . . .

The name of a *primus pilus* is preserved in an inscription discovered near Lambessa on the road to Diana Veteranorum. It is a dedication, by a soldier of that rank serving in the third Augustan legion, to a freedman named Zosimus, whose good memory he desired to perpetuate.[2]

        D · M
ZOSIMO LIBERTO
MATIVS QVARTVS P P
LEG III AVG BENE
MERENTI FECIT

Diis Manibus, Zosimo, liberto Matius Quartus, primus pilus legionis tertiæ Augustæ, bene merenti fecit.

The monumental remains of Lambæsis as a permanent military establishment, and of the town which sprang up in the immediate vicinity, are not conspicuous for architectural merit, and give little evidence of magnificence of conception or prevalence of good taste in general design. It must be borne in mind that they were mostly constructed at a late period of the Empire, when Roman art was rapidly declining, and that the

---

[1] *De Urbe Lambæse et de Legione tertia Augusta*, p. 49. G. Boisssière, Paris, 1877. A *pilus* was a company of *Triarii*, so called because they took the third place in any formation, the first or front company being termed *hastati*, the second being composed of *principes*. There was a *primus pilus*, sometimes written *primipilus*. The *primipilarii*, sometimes called *pilani*, were the first centurions of each legion.

[2] *C.I.L.* No. 2768. *Vide* Renier, No. 983.

requirements of a garrison town were easily satisfied by the erection of buildings of an ordinary kind. Lambæsis was never a fashionable resort, nor did it attract to its suburbs the magnates and colonists of influence whose memorials abound in the more attractive city of Thamugas. The whole place in its ruined condition has now been exposed, after diligent, thoughtful labour, to public gaze, exhibiting to the artist little deserving his study, but providing for the archæologist and the historian a wealth of materials which has already contributed largely to our knowledge of North Africa during the Roman occupation. Conspicuous among the ruined remains and towering high above other fallen monuments in the plain of Lambessa, are the external walls of the Prætorium,[1] forming the headquarters of the third Augustan legion. This building is of rectangular form, measuring externally about 92 feet by 65 feet. The extreme height may be estimated at 50 feet. Within the walls is a large court, around which were the offices and apartments of the general, and several rooms which may have been occupied by the staff, or served as chapels or shrines for tutelary deities as protectors of the army. The original Prætorium erected by Marcus Aurelius on this site was overthrown by an earthquake and reinstated during the last year of the reign of Gallienus, A.D. 268. An inscription on the face of the present edifice confirms this, and on the keystone of one of the gateways on the east side a standard is carved bearing the words *Legio tertia Augusta*. The walls of the great court are strengthened with engaged columns, but there are no indications of their having supported the timbers of a roof. In all probability the court was open, a *velarium* being spread over it for protection against the sun or during inclement weather. Around and attached to the edifice were apparently a number of smaller buildings, but these have

---

[1] Tacitus (*Ann.* i. 7) says that the general's tent or pavilion in a Roman camp was called the *Prætorium*, because the ancient Latins styled their commanders Prætors. Scipio Africanus raised a prætorian cohort to serve near his pavilion as a bodyguard. They formed a select company, and were to hold themselves in readiness to accompany the general in all sudden emergencies. In the time of Augustus the Emperor's tent was called *Prætorium Augustale*. This name was continued by his successors, who gave the title of Præfectus Prætorii to the officer in command. The soldiers were for some time quartered in Rome, but were moved by Ælius Sejanus, their commander in the time of Tiberius, to a short distance from the city, in order to favour his seditious designs against the Emperor.

THE PRÆTORIUM AT LAMBÆSIS (LAMBESSA).

long since been overthrown and most of the materials removed.

The joint rule of Marcus Aurelius and his unworthy son and successor, Commodus, has furnished numerous inscriptions in North Africa bearing the names of these two Cæsars. Although neither of them ever visited this populous and thriving colony, dedications in their honour are not wanting in any of the African provinces ; and it is somewhat gratifying to find that attempts were made in succeeding generations to erase from marble and stone the name of Commodus as a contemptible character in public and private life, and an infamous ruler. As an example of a spoilt child with natural depraved tastes, Commodus stands pre-eminent. To be saluted as Augustus at the age of five, to be conveyed in triumph as *imperator* through the streets of Rome when he had scarcely turned his sixteenth year, and to take part in the government of a great Empire at the age of nineteen, were sufficient to turn the head of a less giddy and depraved youth. But Marcus Aurelius was either neglectful or over-indulgent, and, with his philosophic training, austere habits of life, and stoical methods of thought, had nothing in common with a youth who regarded life as the arena for incessant folly and unchecked dissipation In the many inscriptions bearing the name of Commodus, there is nothing to indicate that this prince was favoured by the goodwill or respect of the subjects of the Empire, and the presence of chiselled marks against his name in several inscriptions, or total erasure, testifies to the contempt in which his memory was held when a tyrannical rule of twelve years came to an end. What good could be expected from an Emperor whose vanity and arrogance were only exceeded by his depravity? In addressing the Senate, says Dion Cassius in his brief memoir of Marcus Aurelius, Commodus glorifies his own personality in the following terms as joint Emperor : —'The Emperor Cæsar, Lucius Ælius Aurelius Commodus, Augustus, Pius, Felix, Sarmaticus, Germanicus, Britannicus, the Great Controller of the World, Invincible, the Roman Hercules, High Priest, eighteen times Tribune, eight times Emperor, seven times Consul, Pater Patriæ, to the Consuls, Prætors, Tribunes of the People, and to the Commodian happy Senate ; Greeting.'

Among the dedicatory inscriptions, in which an attempt has been made to erase the name of Commodus in a somewhat unusual form, mention may be made of a large panel discovered at El Outhaia,[1] in a mass of ruins that are probably the remains of the amphitheatre referred to.

> IMP CAESARES M AVRELIVS ANTONINVS ET
> L AVRELIVS COMMODVS AVG GERMANICI
> SARMATICI FORTISSIMI AMPHITHEATRVM
> VETVSTAE CORRVPTVM A SOLO RESTI
> TVERVNT PER ▒▒▒▒▒ COH VI COMMAG
> A IVLIO POMPILIO PISONE LAEVILLO LEG
> AVG PR PR CVRANTE AELIO SERENO PRAEF

From this we learn that the joint Emperors rebuilt the amphitheatre, and that the work was done by the sixth cohort of the Commageni,[2] an auxiliary force quartered in that locality. The usual form of erasure, similar to the method adopted with the third legion during the period of its disgrace, may be exemplified in the two following inscriptions. The first was discovered at Henchir Ain Zaga,[3] and the other at Vallis,[4] both in the proconsular province.

IMP · CAES · M · AVRELIVS	SERAPI AVG SACR
[COMMODVS x x x x x x x	PRO SALVTE IMP CAES
ANTONINVS AVG SARMATI	M · AVRELI [COMMODI] ANTO
CVS GERMANICVS MAXIMVS	NINI PII x x x x x x x x x
x x x x x x x x x x x x x x	x x x x x x x x x x x x x

Some years ago an interesting inscription bearing the name

---

[1] *C.I.L.* No. 2488. El Outhaia, as it is now called, is an Arab village on the site of the Roman town of Mesarfalta, lying on the highway between El-Kantara and Biskra. At a late period of the Empire it must have been a place of some importance, and is mentioned as the seat of a Christian bishopric.

[2] The word *Commageni* frequently occurs in Roman military history, and refers to the auxiliary troops raised in Commagena, a district in Syria lying between Mt. Taurus and the Euphrates, and forming part of the kingdom of Antiochus. The last of that name was deposed by Pompey, B.C. 69, Syria becoming a Roman province, and the name of Antiochus, which had been associated with the rulers of Syria for about 250 years, becoming extinct. According to Tacitus (*Hist.* b. ii. c. 81), Antiochus IV. of Commagena was the richest of all the kings who submitted to the authority of Rome. There were no less than thirteen successive kings bearing that name, the last of them alluded to by Tacitus being sometimes called king of Commagena, and not of Syria. His career was an eventful one. Dethroned by Caligula and reinstated by Claudius, he was ultimately deposed by Titus, after a reign of thirty-four years, for alleged conspiracy against the Romans. His army rendered great service to its new masters, especially during the reign of Vespasian. At a later period detachments were quartered in North Africa.

[3] *C.I.L.* No. 14451.   [4] *C.I.L.* No. 14792.

Africa under Marcus Aurelius 189

of Commodus was unearthed at a place called Souk-el-Kmis, east of Bulla Regia, and described by M. Tissot. There are four columns of letters, each of thirty lines, the first column being unfortunately broken and the words illegible. An interpretation of the three legible columns has been given by Mommsen, from which it appears that the colonists on a certain estate named *Saltus Buritanus*, had cause to complain to the Emperor of the exorbitant demands of a Roman tax-collector named Ælius Maximus. In accordance with a written law, the colonists were bound to provide six days' labour per head of the male population in the course of the year:—two for ordinary labour, two for weeding and cleaning the land, and two in time of harvest. The demands of the government agent being in excess of this stipulation, the colonists petitioned the Emperor Commodus for redress. According to the inscription this petition was favourably considered, with the result that the agent and his subordinate officers were restrained from demanding more than the law permitted. There is a tone of piteousness in the wording of the memorial which is very touching. 'We are only poor peasants,' say the petitioners in their address to the Emperor. 'We earn our living by the sweat of our brows. Have pity on us poor sons of the soil, and let us not be molested by the tax-gatherers on the estate.'[1] Whether this petition ever reached the Emperor in person is doubtful. From his general line of conduct, utter indifference to the wants and aspirations of the people in Rome, and total neglect of his enterprising colonists in all parts of the Empire, we may assume that this grievance was redressed by the governor of the province in the Emperor's name.

The word *saltus* as applied to a large domain or estate, such as the *Saltus Buritanus* above mentioned, is of frequent occurrence in inscriptions in North Africa. In its restricted sense the word means a large tract of grazing land for cattle, combined with ranges of woodland for shelter. In course of time, when pastoral life gave place to the permanent settlement of colonists on estates possessing these combined advantages, village communities sprang up, and in some instances small towns were included in any tract of land that had been recognised as a *saltus*. The history of some of these estates has a special

[1] C. Tissot, *Le Bassin du Bagrada*.

interest in our own times; one of them, known as the Enfida estate or *saltus*, in the beylik of Tunisia, having been the subject of a dispute which contributed more than anything else to the French protectorate of that country and its ultimate submission to the rule of France. The causes of this long-pending controversy between Kheir-el-Din, the prime minister of Tunis in 1879, and the Bey, are too well known to need repetition. After much litigation and a round of diplomatic correspondence, this magnificent estate, comprising more than 300,000 acres, and with a population of about 7,000 settled occupants, was finally handed over in perpetuity to the Société Franco-Africaine. The traveller going south from Tunis passes through the middle of this domain, which in form may roughly be described as a parallelogram, lying between the towns of Susa and Hammamet on the coast, and Kairouan and Zaghouan in the interior.

The origin of these vast estates may be traced to the earlier days of Roman colonisation, when successful settlers found themselves involved in dispute with exacting governors or tyrannical emperors. The result was that confiscation ensued, and territory after territory became the private property of the Emperor himself, or of some member of the imperial family. Nero stands conspicuous for his arbitrary conduct and cruel exactions of lands and herds, merely to gratify the whim of a passing hour or the rapacity of some greedy court official. Such was the growth of these estates that, in the time of Trajan, one half of Roman Africa, according to Pliny, was in the hands of six proprietors, the Emperor being by inheritance the largest owner. Fronto, in one of his letters to Marcus Aurelius, refers to the great African domain held by Matidia, niece of Trajan, known as the *saltus Matidia*, and tells us that the Emperor, prompted by delicacy of feeling, refused to accept it at her decease, but was afterwards forced to do so at the instigation of his wife Faustina, whose personal influence over this philosophic ruler of mankind is generally acknowledged. An interesting inscription relating to this estate was brought to light nearly forty years ago in the district of Bou-Areridj in that portion of the Medjerda plains which lies in the province of of Mauritania Sitifensis.[1] Some dispute appears to have arisen during the

[1] *C.I.L.* No. 8812. *Vide Rec. de Const.* 1864, p. 101. Payen and Renier descrip.

Africa under Marcus Aurelius

reign of Alexander Severus as to the boundaries of this property, and we learn from the wording of the inscription that Axius Ælianus, the steward of the estate, engaged the services of Cælius Martialis, a land measurer, to make a survey of the property and define the boundaries. The words *rationis privatæ* seem to indicate that the steward had his own reasons for ascertaining the exact area of the property committed to his charge, but this is conjectural, and the dedication to the Emperor by the inhabitants of Kasturrensis was a fitting conclusion to the whole matter.

D · M
IMP C M AV
RELIO SEVERO ALE   *Domino nostro Imperatori Cæsare*
XANDRO PIO FELICE   *M. Aurelio Severo Alexandro*
AVG TERMINAC . .   *Pio Felice Augusto terminationes*
GRORVM DEFE . . . .   *agrorum definitionis Matidiæ ad-*
CIONIS MATIDIAE A .   *signantur colonis Kasturrensibus*
SIGNATVR COLO . .   *jussu viri egregii Axi Æliani*
NIS KASTVRRE . . .   *procuratoris Augusti rationis*
IVSSV VE AXI AEL .   *privatæ per Cælium Martialem*
ANI PROC AVG . . .   *agrimesorem.*
PER CAE MARTIA .
AGRIMES . . . . .

Another inscription realating to a *saltus* was discovered by Pellissier at a place now called Henchir-el-Hammam, near the western frontier of Tunisia.[1] The name *Saltus Massipianus* has been preserved on the frieze of a ruined triumphal arch, and if we may judge from the use still made of the hot and cold springs by native Arabs, we may reasonably assume that this spot was resorted to in Roman times as a thermal establishment. The wording of the inscription, deciphered by Pellissier, is sufficiently clear, being a dedication to Caracalla by the inhabitants on the estate, on the occasion of a reinstatement of several public buildings that had become dilapidated.

PRO · SALVTE · IMP · CAES · M · AVRELI · ANTONINI · LI
BERORVMQ · EIVS · COLONI · SALTVS · MASSIPIANI
                AEDIFICIA VETVSTATE
CONLAPSA · S · P · R · ITEM ARCVVS · DVOS · A · S · F
                IVBENTE PROVIN
CIALE · AVG · LIB · PROC · EODEMQVE · DEDICANTE

[1] Pellissier, *Description de la Tunisie*, p. 294. Guérin, vol. i. p. 344.

The public influence of women in imperial circles, so conspicuous in the reign of Antonine, asserted itself in an equal degree under the rule of Marcus Aurelius. The Empress, commonly known as Annia Faustina the younger, to distinguish her from Annia Galeria Faustina the elder, figures prominently in African inscriptions. It has been remarked on a previous page that the name of the latter does not appear in a single inscription on stone or marble yet brought to light in the country, although medals and coins bearing her effigy abound in a variety of types. The daughter's career, as a leader of imperial society and a prime mover in the court intrigues of the period, differs little from that of her mother, except that love of movement and interest in the conduct of military campaigns prompted her to accompany the Emperor Marcus Aurelius in his various expeditions. Latin historians make little mention of the virtues or vices of this remarkable woman, who was honoured during life by the proud title of 'Mother of the Army,' and whose memory was long preserved by statues and dedicatory inscriptions in many towns of the Empire. There is nothing remarkable in the wording of any of these memorials, of which the following, found on the site of Colonia Bisica Lucana, is an example : [1]

<pre>
          FAVSTINAE
             AVG
    IMP · CAES · M · AVRELI
         ANTONI · AVG
       PONT · MAX · TRIB
       POT · XV · COS · III
           D · D · P · P
</pre>

If we are to credit the statements of Dion Cassius, Marcus Aurelius declined to make strict inquiry into the conduct of his wife, nor did he act harshly towards those who were said to

[1] Bisica Lucana has been identified with the modern town of Testour, situated on the right bank of the Medjerda, and on the old highway between Carthage and Sicca Veneria. Two milliary columns of the time of Marcus Aurelius were discovered here many years ago; and an inscription relating to Colonia Bisica Lucana commemorates the successful campaigns of the Emperor Licinius in the earlier portion of his divided rule. (*Vide* Shaw, vol. i. p. 215; also Guérin, vol. ii. p. 165.) The town of Bisica is supposed to have been the *Visica* referred to at a later period as the seat of a bishopric, mentioned by Morcelli, *Africa Christiana*, vol. i. p. 357, in reference to an *episcopus Visicensis*. Of the Roman town of Bisica Lucana there is no record.

have been associated with the Empress in attempts at usurpation. But he tells us that on her death the Senate was ordered to set up two statues of silver within the temple of Venus in Rome, one in honour of Marcus Aurelius and the other of Faustina. And as a further mark of honour to the memory of that princess it was ordained that, whenever the Emperor went to the theatre, the golden statue of Faustina was to be set up in the place where she had been wont to sit when alive, and that the ladies of the court should reverence the effigy as though it were the living princess. As marks of personal honour, Marcus Aurelius erected a column in the village of Hallala at the foot of Mount Taurus, where Faustina died, and augmented by a large subsidy the endowment of a charitable institution, founded in honour of her mother, and known as the *puellæ Faustinianæ*.

The name of the mother of Marcus Aurelius does not appear on any slab or stone or marble yet discovered in North Africa, but it is recorded on a piece of broken pottery brought to light at Hadrumetum (Susa).[1] It is inscribed in full, *Domitia Lucilla*.

Of the family of the Emperor and his wife Faustina we have scant record, but two memorials of their daughter, Vibia Aurelia, were found at Kalama, and may be seen in the museum in the modern town of Guelma. One of them is here given.[2]

```
        VIBIAE AV
        RELIAE DI
        VI M F DIVI
        SEVERI SOR
         SABINAE
        PATRONAE
        MVNICIPII
        DECVRIO . .
        . . . . . . .
```

With the close of this reign terminates one of the leading chapters in Roman history, marking an era in the development of North Africa. The old order of things was passing away, and unconsciously the seeds of decline were being imperceptibly sown. The great Latin families, tracing their descent far back

[1] *C.I.L.* No. 10475.
[2] *C.I.L.* No. 5328. *Ann. de Const.* 1854-55, p. 163.

into the glorious days of the Republic, and furnishing emperors for a period of more than two centuries, had ceased to exist. The Julian line became extinct with the death of Nero. The Flavian family, which had contributed so largely to the extension of empire, had lost its authority, and the Antonines came to an end when the wretched Commodus fell by the hands of an assassin. The accession of Marcus Aurelius, whose early career as a prince of the Empire had been conspicuous for popularity, was thought to presage a long run of peace and prosperity. His eleven successful years of independent rule had encouraged the notion that a form of government, based on the creed of some ancient school of philosophy, was preferable to the stirring administration favoured by more active emperors. The world was henceforth to be governed in accordance with the principles enunciated in the groves of Athens; and the dictum of Plato, that an era of happiness for mankind would be the immediate result, seemed likely to ensue when the Emperor assumed the rôle of a disciple of the school of Zeno. To his credit it may be said that he loyally fulfilled his mission, upheld the doctrines of his youth, and passed away unconscious of the coming storm which taxed the energy and resources of later emperors to dispel. Any further notice of his depraved son and successor Commodus is unnecessary, nor would it throw any light on African history. Everything in connection with this Emperor appears to have been treated with contempt by a later generation, and his name erased from public memorials. But his wife, Brutia Crispina, daughter of Brutus Præsens, was happily saved from the same indignity, clearly indicated on the annexed inscription at Thamugas, found nearly fifty years ago between the Byzantine fort and the remains of the Roman theatre:[1]

CRISPINAE
AVG
IMP · CAES
L · AELI AV
RELI · COM
MODI · AVG
CONIVGI
D · D P · P

[1] *I.R.A.* No. 1496, noted by De la Mare and Creully.

Africa under Marcus Aurelius

The fall of Commodus was followed by the short rule of his two successors, Julian and Pertinax, whose place in African history is almost a blank. The name of the former is not recorded in a single inscription, although he had rendered himself conspicuous for an active career of about seven months. But Pertinax occupies a position of high distinction, and, notwithstanding his short rule of scarcely three months, adorned the throne of the Cæsars with the nobility of a true Roman. An African by birth, a native of Hadrumetum, but probably of Latin descent, he was deservedly honoured by his countrymen for patriotic conduct and a blameless career, and, as Dion Cassius informs us, his statue of gold was set up in the Circus Maximus as a permanent testimony of public esteem. Among the inscriptions in North Africa in which the name of Pertinax appears, there is one on a *milliarium* at Sba-Meghata, on the banks of the river El-Kantara, and on the high road from Lambæsis.[1] The other, bearing the same date, A.D. 192, is the dedication of an altar to the Emperor by the colonists on one of the African estates.[2]

	PRO SALVTE
IMP CAES P HE	IMP CAESARIS
LVIO PERTINA	P HEL PERTINA
CE AVG P P TRIB P	CIS TRIBVNICIE PO
COS II L NAEVIO	TESTATIS COS II PP
QVADRATIAN	COLONI DOMINI N
O LEG AVG P·R	CAPVT SALTVS HOR
PR A LAMBESE	REOR PARDALARI HA
M P LVIIII	NC ARAM POSVERVNT
	ET D · D

[1] *I.R.A.* No. 4305. L. Renier, *Archives des Missions*, v. 11, p. 446.
[2] *C.I.L.* No. 8425. Poulle, *Rec. de Const.* 1873-74, p. 363.

CHAPTER VII

AFRICA UNDER SEPTIMIUS SEVERUS

A.D. 193-211

THE Roman world had hitherto been governed by Emperors of European descent. Some were military commanders, others were statesmen or administrators of the highest rank, while not a few were invested with the purple at the bidding of a turbulent populace or to meet the exacting demands of a dissatisfied soldiery. There had been a time when the watchword *Senatus populusque Romanus* represented in all its potency the revered authority of the Senate in Rome and the will and determination of the Roman people. But the spell was broken. The rank and authority of the Senators so distinguished in the brighter days of the Republic, and once described by the minister of a foreign potentate as a venerable assembly of kings, ceased to exist under the despotic rule of the Emperors. As a matter of courtesy the Senate was appealed to whenever the throne of the Cæsars became vacant, but it was powerless to take independent action, and ultimately became subservient to the will of the army established in various parts of the Empire. It was this assertion of military authority which altered the character of imperial government, and was the chief cause of the internal troubles and dissensions which threatened to destroy the Empire towards the close of the third century.

On the death of Pertinax there were four claimants to the throne: Didius Julianus, Pescennius Niger, Clodius Albinus, and Septimius Severus. The first, whose mother was a native of Africa and of good family, was brought up under the care of Domitia Lucilla, mother of Marcus Aurelius. He was nominated by the Senate, and had purchased the support of the Prætorian guard by offers of large gifts of money. Julianus plays no part in African history. His assumption of the purple was followed by a refusal to pay the promised donatives, and after

an uneventful reign of about seven months he was put to death
by his own soldiers. Of Pescennius Niger we have no record,
and his place in Africa is a blank. But of the two remaining
claimants, Albinus and Severus, both of them natives of Africa,
there is abundant evidence of their struggle for supremacy
in the records of contemporary writers. Albinus, we know,
was born at Hadrumetum (Susa), his father's name being
Cejonius Postumius. The extreme whiteness of his skin pro-
cured for him the name by which he is generally known. Military success in early life during the reign of Commodus entitled
him to high rank in the Roman army, and consequently, when
the governorship of Great Britain was vacant, the Emperor
nominated him to this distinguished appointment. It is said
that when the title of Cæsar was offered to him by Commodus
he refused, but that subsequently, on the death of Pertinax, being
pressed by the Senate and with the concurrence of Septimius
Severus, he acquiesced. The pretended friendship of Severus
for his powerful rival is clearly expressed in a letter written by
Severus A.D. 197, and quoted by Capitolinus. It ran thus:
'The Emperor Severus Augustus to Clodius Albinus Cæsar,
his dearly beloved and most valued brother, Greeting. After
our conquest of Pescennius we sent a letter to the Senate at
Rome, which, full of good will towards us, was graciously received.
I beg you will display towards the government the same temper
of mind which makes you the dear brother of my heart, the
brother of the Empire. Bassianus and Geta (his two sons) salute
you. Our dear Julia (Julia Domna, wife of Severus) salutes
you and your sister. We send to your little boy Pescennius
Prineus some presents worthy of his rank and yours.' This
letter was confided by Severus to a few trusted companions, who
were instructed to induce Albinus to leave the palace, with a
view to his being murdered in some little-frequented spot.
Albinus suspected that a snare was being laid for him, and,
having put the messengers to torture, learnt the truth. He
then assembled a big army and met his antagonist in the plains
of Gaul. The following year Albinus was defeated and his head
carried in triumph through the streets of Rome. His name
appears on a broken slab found at Agbia (Ain Hedjah) [1] bearing
the date A.D. 194, and is also recorded on a stone near Khen-

[1] *C.I.L.* No. 1549. Temple, ii. p. 308.

chela, where some Roman baths named Aquæ Flavianæ had been established.

CLODI · SEPTIMI · ALBINI · CAES

The date is also A.D. 194, but the chief interest attached to this dedication is the recognition of these joint Emperors, one as Augustus, and the other as Cæsar.[1] The name of the latter has been subject to the usual erasure, probably by the order of Severus.

PRO SALVTE · ET VICTORIA · DOMINI · N ·
IMP L · SEPTIMI SEVERI PERTINACIS AVG ET
CLODI ALBINI CAES AESCVLAPEM . ET · HYGIAM
DEDICANTE LEPIDO TERTVLLO · LEG · AVG
PR · PR · C · V · M · OPPIVS · ANTIOCHIANVS ...
LEG III AVG II ... E VINDICIS POSVIT ET V · S

For the first time in Roman history an Emperor of foreign extraction was to take high rank in the long line of Cæsars, and the obscure town of Leptis in Africa was to become prominent as the birthplace of that remarkable ruler of men, Lucius Septimius Severus. His association with the progress and development of North Africa, second to none other at that period of the possessions of the Empire, is marked by innumerable inscriptions in most parts of the country. During his reign of eighteen years colonisation spread to the extreme west bordering on the Atlantic; villages became towns, protection was afforded to settlers on the Desert frontier, and the uprising of turbulent native tribes was almost unknown. This was the climax of Roman Africa. The patronage of the Court was extended to its citizens, and for the first time the African and the Italian shared alike the patronage of the Palace and the favours of the Emperor. The stern rule of Severus and his activity as a soldier had nothing in common with the gentle sway of Antonine or the calm dignity of Aurelius. Tranquillity of life and the pleasures of the metropolis had no charms for his restless intriguing disposition. We hear of him everywhere. From the banks of the Euphrates to the borders of Scotland there was scarcely a province of the great Empire which had not shared the favour of his presence, or participated in the benefits of his strong personality. Of distinguished parentage, attaining success early in life in various branches of literature and philosophy, and exhibiting

[1] *C.I.L.* No. 17726. *Comptes rendus de l'Académie d'Hippo*, a. 1888, pp. 7-64.

in manhood a high military capacity, there is little wonder that his countrymen should have honoured the name Severus in most parts of his African possessions. It must be admitted, on the authority of so reliable an authority as Justinus, that Severus was cruel by nature and despotic in administration. And even later writers such as Spartianus and Capitolinus hesitate to attribute to the Emperor one single incident in his career which bears the stamp of clemency or magnanimity. The facts that he caused divine honours to be bestowed on the wretched Commodus, and that a revengeful spirit prompted him to expose in the streets of Rome the heads of his rivals, Niger and Albinus, are sufficient testimony to a savage disposition. But to his credit it may be said that strength of will and force of character secured the regard of his subjects, and gave him the command of the world during the greater part of his imperial career. The increasing power of the army, which had been gradually asserting itself, from the time of the accession of Marcus Aurelius, as a great political factor in Rome and the garrison towns, was not lost on so astute a ruler as Severus. He purchased their goodwill and adhesion to his cause by large annual donations, and on his deathbed is alleged to have said to his sons, ' Live peaceably together, enrich the soldiers, and take no account of the rest of your subjects.' And we are told, on the authority of Justinus, that when he entered Rome in triumph after the final defeat of Albinus, his first public act gave indications of a determination to be ruler of the army as well as of the Senate and people. Summoning the all-powerful Prætorian guard to appear unarmed outside the city walls, he encompassed them with troops upon whom he could rely. Then, reproaching them for their treachery to his predecessor Pertinax, he disbanded them and forbade their settling within a hundred miles of Rome.[1]

The large number of dedicatory inscriptions in honour of Severus are in many ways remarkable. In most of them the name of the Emperor is associated with his two sons, Caracalla and Geta, invariably termed the Augusti, and in many instances with Julia Domna, his second wife, bearing the proud title of *Mater Castrorum*. The political influence exercised by women

[1] Gibbon, vol. i. chap. v. The subject is referred to by Herodian, Dion Cassius, and other Latin authors. The dismissal of the Guard was probably witnessed by Dion himself.

of family at this period is attested by numerous writers, and no name appears more frequently in the inscriptions handed down to us than that of this celebrated Empress. Of the mother of Severus there is nothing to record, but it is reasonable to assume that, like her husband, she was an African and a native of Leptis. Her memory, as the mother of an Emperor and bearing the title of Augusta, is preserved on a slab of stone built into a wall at Constantine.[1]

    IVLIAE · VICTOR
     MATRI IMP
    CAES · L · SEPTI
     MI · SEV · VII
     PERTINACI
     AVGG ET
     . . . . .
     . . . . .
     . . . . .
      TOTIVS
    QVE DOMVS
    SEVERIANAE
     D · D · P

Concerning Marciana, the first wife of Severus, whom he married at Leptis in his early youth and deserted in later years, there is no record; for, in all probability, she took no part in public life and was content to pass her days in retirement. Fortunately her name may still be read in an inscription in the public gardens at Constantine.[2] The word *quondam* seems to indicate that the tablet was erected during her lifetime when Julia Domna had been declared Empress. There is a touch of sympathy in the wording of this simple memorial to a deserted princess, whom the inhabitants of the renowned city of Cirta desired to honour.

     PACCIAE MAR
     CIANAE QVON
     DAM CONIVGI
     IMP SEVERIAVG
     PIISSIMI MAXI
     MI PRINCIPIS
     RES PVBL IIII COL
     CIRTA DD PP

---

[1] *C.I.L.* No. 10868.   [2] *C.I.L.* No. 19494.

Female influence in public affairs was developed during the career of the two Faustinas, but it reached its climax when Julia Domna was raised to the throne. The prominent part played in political life by this remarkable personage is almost unique. A Phœnician by birth and daughter of a priest of the temple of the Sun at Emesa in Syria, she emerged from comparative obscurity in a remote town to become the most conspicuous figure of her time. Her mental powers were only excelled by personal charms, and her influence in imperial matters was second only to that of the Emperor himself. But her conduct in private life was notorious and can only be measured by the loose tone of morality which then prevailed in court society. The reins of government appear to have been so essential to her existence that, on the death of Severus, Julia Domna did not hesitate to marry his son and successor Caracalla, although he was her stepson. There is much conflicting evidence as to the truth of this statement. Dion Cassius, a person in high authority during this reign, is silent on this subject, but Justinus, who was also a contemporary, endorses the statement, and Spartianus, Aurelius Victor, and others give it their support. The words used by Spartianus are: *quemadmodum novercam suam Juliam uxorem duxisse dicatur*; and in his account of her marriage with Caracalla he says, in words that will scarcely bear translation: *Quæ quum esset pulcherrima, et quasi per negligentiam se maxima corporis parte nudasset, dixissetque Antoninus ' Vellem, si liceret;' respondisse fertur, ' Si libet, licet. An nescis te imperatorem esse, et leges dare, non accipere?'*

The name of Domna is peculiar. According to Suidas it was a Syrian proper name, but some commentators regard the word as an abbreviation of domina *nostra*, the Emperor Severus being dominus *noster*. Among the numerous dedications to the Empress, one at Castellum near Sicca Veneria (El-Kef) possesses some interest, clearly indicating the unusual titles of distinction accorded to her as Mother of the Army, the Senate, and the country.[1] And another found at Thagaste (Souk-Ahras) gives the name of the Empress followed by that of the Emperor, as though Septimius Severus were a secondary person in public estimation.[2] The date of this inscription is A.D. 198, the year

[1] *C.I.L.* No. 15722.   [2] *C.I.L.* No. 17214.

of his defeat of Albinus and the undisputed assumption of imperial power.

IVLIAE · AVG
PIAE · FELICI
MATRI · AVGVS
TI · ET CASTRO
RVM · ET · SENA
TVS · ET · PATRIAE
SENIORES · KAST
POS · ET · DEDIC

IVLIAE DOMNAE
AVGVSTAE
MATRI CASTRO
RVM
IMP · CAES · E · SEPTI
MI · SEVERI · PII · PER
TINACIS · AVG · ARA
BICI · ADIABENICI
PART · MAX · TRIB
POT · VI · IMP · XI · COS
II · PROCOS · P · P · PACIS
PVBL · RESTITVTORIS · D · D

As an example of a fine inscription of the time, mention should be made of one discovered on a magnificent slab of stone in the temple of Æsculapius at Lambæsis, being a dedication to the Emperor Severus and his family by thirty-six *cornicines* of the third Augustan legion, all the names being given in full. The interpretation by Renier is as follows:[1]

Pro felicitate et incolumitate sæculi dominorum nostrorum Augustorum trium, Lucii Septimii Severi Pii Pertinacis Augusti, et Marci Aurelii Antonini Augusti, et Lucii Septimii Getæ Cæsaris Augusti, et Juliæ Augustæ matris Augustorum duorum et castrorum, et Fulviæ Plautillæ Augustæ, Antonini Augusti nostri conjugis. Cornicines legionis tertiæ Augustæ Piæ Vindicis.

The names of the Emperor, his two sons and his wife are followed, it will be observed, by that of Plautilla, the unfortunate wife of Caracalla. So numerous are inscriptions bearing the name of Julia Domna that its omission in imperial dedications is exceptional. The few relating to the Emperor alone are conspicuous for their length, and for the long array of ancestors whom Severus pompously associated with himself in the line of Cæsars, as far back as a fourth generation. Throughout his reign he never seems to have forgotten that he was an African: and we are told by Spartianus that, though the Emperor was *græcis litteris eruditissimus*, he spoke with a native accent till the later years of his life. His regard for his countrymen is shown in the arrangements of his magnificent palace in Rome, a part of which called the *Septizonium* was distinguished for its grandeur and is

---

[1] *C.I.L.* No. 2557; *I.R.A.* No. 70. Renier and De la Mare.

Africa under Septimius Severus

alleged to have been seven stories in height.[1] It was placed as a conspicuous object near the road by which travellers from Africa approached the city, and was intended by the Emperor to impress his countrymen with the magnificence of their ruler. The monumental remains in the African provinces, which may be assigned to his reign, are not remarkable for grandeur of conception, with the exception of a triumphal arch at Zanfour, the ancient Assuras. When Bruce visited this spot in 1765 the monument was in fair condition, but since that time the Corinthian columns which adorned the archway have been overthrown, and the structure generally has a ruinous aspect. It had only one arch, the width being 17 feet 5 inches. The height of the edifice, which was surmounted by an attic bearing an inscription, may be estimated at 41 feet. According to Guérin the dedicatory inscription reads thus:[2]

DIVO OPTIMO ... SEVERO PIO AVG · ARAB .. IAB · PART · MAX ·
ET IMP · CAES · M · AVRELIO ANTONINO PIO · AVG · FELICI
    PART · MAX
BRIT · MAX · GERM · MAX · PONT · MAX · FIL · TRIB · $\overline{XVIII}$
    IMP $\overline{III}$
COS · $\overline{IIII}$ P · P · PROCOS · OPTIMO MAXIMOQVE PRINCIPI ET
IVLIAE DOMNAE PIAE FELICI AVG · MATRI AVG · ET
    CASTRORVM
ET SENATVS ET PATRIAE VXORI DIVI SEVERI AVG · PII
    COL · IVL
ASSVRAS DEVOTA NVMINI EORVM D · D P · P

    The records of Assuras, *Colonia Julia Assuras*, are very scanty. It is mentioned by Pliny as *Oppidum Azuritanum*, and is noted in the Itinerary of Antoninus as well as by Ptolemy. For many generations it was a stronghold of Christianity, and was the seat of a bishopric mentioned by St. Cyprian, who addressed one of his epistles to the *episcopum et plebem Assuritanorum*. The situation of Assuras had much to commend it as a residential town, favoured by charming scenery, surrounded by country of great fertility, and with a river of pure water that never failed.

---

[1] A view of the remains of the Septizonium, as they appeared in the sixteenth century, is reproduced by Signor Lanciani, *Ancient Rome*, p. 126, from a drawing in the Uffizi Palace, Florence.

[2] Playfair, *Travels in the Footsteps of Bruce*, p. 208. A drawing is given of this arch as it appeared in Bruce's time. The inscription has been noted by Bruce; Temple, ii. p. 266; and Guérin, ii. p. 90.

It was girt by a wall of defence of which the foundations remain to the present day, and was approached by two bridges which crossed the river at considerable altitude.

Conspicuous among the very few good qualities which history has associated with Septimius Severus was a studious regard for an abundant supply of corn and oil. And so largely did he value the African supply that, when his great rival Pescennius Niger, the governor of Syria, contemplated the invasion of Africa by transporting his army through Egypt and Libya, the Emperor despatched his legions across the Mediterranean to guard the grain stores and prevent their falling into the hands of his enemy. On his death he left corn enough to last seven years, and oil in abundance. As a working Emperor, Severus held his own against any of his predecessors, and when he felt that his last hour had come, he gave as the watchword of the day '*Laboremus*.' Associated with him during his latter days were his two sons, Caracalla and Geta, the elder created Augustus by the army, and the younger at the instigation of his mother Julia Domna. The following inscription from Gigthis, an almost forgotten town in the province of Tripoli, mentions the three Augusti in connection with the conquest of Britain, but there is no clue to the date nor any special mention of Severus, who commanded in person this ill-fated expedition.[1] It may be assigned to A.D. 212, the year after the death of the Emperor at Eboracum (York).

VICTORIAE BRITANNICAE IMPP · L · SEPTIMI · SEVRI · PII PERTINACIS ET M · AVRELII ANTONIN ET P · SEPTIMI GETAE AVGGG · GIGTHENSES · PVBLICE

Inscriptions relating to Geta alone, who was murdered by his brother A.D. 212, within twelve months after the death of Severus, are few in number, but his memory is preserved on a slab in the museum at Aumale (the ancient Auzia) bearing the date A.D. 205, when this prince had attained his sixteenth year. The dedication is to *L. Septimio Getæ, Pontifici maximo, nobilissimo Cæsari Principi juventutis*, sufficiently indicating his popularity in his father's lifetime, and the ground for the animosity of his elder brother. So far was Caracalla impressed with the necessity of his removal that, on his assumption of

[1] *C.I.L.* No. 11018. *Bull. du Comité*, 1886, p. 46.

Africa under Septimius Severus

supreme authority, Geta was declared a public enemy, or, as Spartianus says, *Geta hostis est adjudicatus*; and, with a view to allaying the anxiety of the Empress mother for his safety, it was arranged to divide the Empire between the two Augusti. Geta was to take up his residence either at Alexandria or Antioch, both of them being great cities scarcely yielding to Rome in magnificence, and was to govern all Africa and Asia east of Libya, while Caracalla was to reside in Rome and take over the remainder, including all the African provinces.

The name of Caracalla (as this Emperor was commonly called) figures largely in African inscriptions during the six years of an unusually active reign, and the long array of titles and distinctions which he assumed were not exceeded by those of any other Emperor. The cruelty inherent in his native race, combined with an utter disregard for human sufferings, seems to have reached its limits in the person of this depraved ruler. No contemporary writer, nor any of the few reliable authorities of a later age, place to his credit a single redeeming quality. And yet the inscriptions (if we are governed by mere words) bear testimony to a magnificence of rule and the apparent respect of Roman citizens of wealth and renown who had settled permanently in the African provinces. Take, for instance, a dedication to the Emperor by a family named Granius, preserved on a slab of white marble which may still be studied in the museum at Philippeville.[1] No less than nineteen lines set forth the praises of Caracalla, as though he were an Augustus or a Trajan. To the *invictissimo Augusto* the inhabitants of Rusicada are called upon to bow the knee. And at Constantine may be read another equally long inscription in which the Emperor is described as *maximus, invictissimus, sanctissimus, fortissimus, felicissimus, et super omnes principes indulgentissimus*. The date of this rhapsodic memorial is, according to Wilmanns, A.D. 216.[2] There is also a *milliarium*, which formerly stood on one of the highways out of Cirta, giving Caracalla the distinguishing titles of *nobilissimus omnium* and *felicissimus principum*. Perhaps the earliest inscription bearing his name was discovered a few years ago in the forum at Thamugas, the date being A.D. 197, according to Wilmanns.[3] Its value lies in the exceptional

[1] *C.I.L.* No. 7973. *Vide* Cherbonneau, *Ann. de Constantine*, 1860-61, p. 334.
[2] *C.I.L.* No. 10305. *Ann. de Const.* 1858-59, p. 121.   [3] *C.I.L.* No. 17870.

wording of the first line, where Caracalla figures as *Imperator destinatus*, the dedicator being Q. Anicius Faustus, *legatus Augustorum proprætor*. And there is no mention of his younger brother Geta, who had not then acquired any distinctive titles.

    M · AVRELIO · ANTONINO · CAESARI IMPERATORI · DESTINATO · IMPERATORIS · CAES
    L · SEPTIMI · SEVERI · PII · PERTINACIS · AVG · ARABICI · ADIABENCI · VINDICIS ET CONDITORIS ROMANAE · DISCIPLINAE · FILIO · DIVI · M · ANTO-NINI · PII · GERM · SARM · NEPOTI
DIVI · ANTONINI · PII · PRONEPOTI · DIVI · HADRIANI · ABNEPOTI · DIVI · TRAIANI · PAR THICI · ET · DIVI · NERVAE · ABNEPOT · DECRETO · DECVRIONVM · PECVNIA · PVBLICA
Q · ANICIVS · FAVSTVS · LEG · AVGVSTORVM · PRO · PRAETORE · PATR · COL · DEDICAVIT

Prominent among other inscriptions is one on a milliary column near the well-known tomb of Flavius outside the walls of Lambæsis.[1] The date is A.D. 215. In this instance the name of Julia Domna is associated with that of the Emperor, but on another military column of the same date, at a place now called Henchir-el-Bidr, the name of the Emperor stands alone.[2]

IMP · CAES · M · AVREL SEV · ANTON · AVG · PL FEL · PARTH · MAX · BRI MAX · GER · MAX PONT · MAX · TRIB · POT XVIII · IMP · IIII COS IV · P · P · PROCOS · ET IVL · AVG · MAT · AVG ET · CAS · ET · SEN · AC PATRI A E M · P · III	IMP · CAES · M AVRELIO SE VERO ANTO NINO PIO FE LICI AVG PAR TICO MAXIMO BRITANICO MA XIMO PONTIFI CI MAXIMO TRIB POT XVIII IMP III COS IIII PR OCOS · P · P · AL AMBAESE · MI LIA · XIIII

The similarity of wording in these two inscriptions is noticeable, with the exception of the omission of the name of the Empress-Mother in the latter. Among the dedications

[1] *C.I.L.* No. 10263. Wilmanns.
[2] *C.I.L.* No. 10236. Also De la Mare and Foy, and *I.R.A.* No. 4303.

Africa under Septimius Severus

conspicuous for a self-laudatory array of titles and a reference to a line of ancestral Cæsars extending to the fifth generation, an inscription discovered at Siaga, near the modern town of Hammamet in Tunisia, and taking rank as a *civitas* in the time of Caracalla, is very complete :[1]

<pre>
         IMP · CAES · DIVI SEPTIMI SEVERI
         PARTH · ARABICI · ADIABENICI
         MAX · BRIT · MAX · FIL · DIVI
         M · ANTONINI · PII · GERMANICI
         SARMAT · NEPOT · DIVI · ANTONINI
         PRO · NEPOTI · DIVI · AELI · HADRIANI
         ABNEPOT · DIVI · TRAIANI · PAR · ET
              DIVI · NERVAE · ADNEPOTI
         M · AVRELIO · ANTONINO · PIO · FEL
         PAR · MAX · BRIT · MAX · GERM
         MAX · IMP · III · COS · III · P · P
         CIVITAS · SIAGITANORVM · D · D · P · P ·
</pre>

And this was the Emperor who formed the monstrous project of killing his own father, who murdered his brother, married his stepmother, forced his lawful wife into obscurity, and terminated an infamous career by murdering both wife and father-in-law for the sole reason that they stood in the way of his ambitious projects!

The word Caracalla does not appear on any inscriptions or coins. This word or nickname signifies, according to Aurelius Victor in his short history of the Emperor, a large flowing garment hanging down to the ankles, worn by the people of *Gallia Lugdunensis* (Lyons) where this prince was born and passed the earlier years of his life. His proper surname was Bassianus, after his grandfather, but on assuming the title of Augustus he became henceforth known as Marcus Aurelius Antoninus Severus Augustus. All the inscriptions of his time confirm this.

The exceptional influence exercised by Julia Domna in all imperial matters was shared towards the latter days of Caracalla's reign by her younger sister Julia Mæsa. The career of these two daughters of Phœnicia, whose father Bassianus was an obscure priest at Emesa, and without any claim to nobility or hereditary rank, is truly remarkable; and it is not surprising to

[1] Shaw, *Travels in Barbary*.

learn from contemporary writers that they contributed in a large measure to lower the tone of public morality, and to promote a system of corruption baneful to the Empire. The little we learn from the pages of Herodian about the younger sister, who took up her quarters in the Imperial Court by the favour of the Emperor Septimius Severus, portrays a strong-minded, self-willed, unscrupulous woman, tactful in her operations, and seizing her opportunities of acquiring wealth or power without regard for the interests of others. Such was the weight of her authority that Severus gave her the distinguished title of Augusta, and when she died peacefully in old age and one of the wealthiest women of her time, the Senate bestowed on her memory divine honours. The name of Julia Mæsa appears in a few inscriptions in North Africa. At the camp at Lambæsis she is described as *Augusta avia domini nostri* and *Mater Castrorum et Senatus*. This dedication may be assigned to the reign of her grandson Elagabalus, A.D. 218-222. Her daughter, Julia Soæmias, sometimes written Sœmis according to Dion Cassius, was another Empress conspicuous for activity and intrigue during the last days of the reign of her husband Caracalla and their son Elagabalus. But her record in Africa is restricted to one inscription found at Lambæsis, where she is styled *Julia Soæmias Augusta mater Augusti nostri*. Far more noteworthy and deserving honourable recognition was the career of Julia Mammæa, the younger sister of Soæmias, and the distinguished mother of the renowned Emperor Alexander Severus. The story of her life, handed down to us by Herodian and other writers, reveals a woman of indomitable will, ambitious of supreme power, and of unbounded avarice. For a space of five-and-twenty years these four women, in their relations as grandmothers, aunts, or mothers of Emperors, may be said to have ruled the world. In the Senate-house, the camp, or public ceremonials, they were present to share the honours and privileges of empire. In the palace their authority was paramount, and the will of a woman became the will of a submissive Emperor. Julia Domna did not hesitate to take a seat in the Senate-house at Rome, and her niece Soæmias founded and presided over a female parliament in the Quirinal, to regulate what we should call in modern life the social and moral habits of a female aristocracy.

CHAPTER VIII

AFRICA UNDER ALEXANDER SEVERUS

A.D. 222–235

WHEN Caracalla, the legitimate son of Septimius Severus, succeeded his father as joint Emperor with his brother Geta, there was every prospect of a continuance of an African dynasty bearing the title of Bassianus, and of giving increased notoriety to the name of an obscure priest of a Syrian temple of the Sun, as father and grandfather of two generations of Emperors. The Julian and Flavian dynasties had passed away with the efflux of time; the Ulpian family, so called, which had exhausted its energies under the magnificent reign of Trajan, and had contributed so largely to the extension and consolidation of the Empire, had almost been lost sight of; and the families which, for the sake of abbreviation, are commonly known as the Antonines, came to an end when the wretched Commodus fell by the hands of an assassin. Hereditary succession had long since been disregarded. For more than two centuries Rome had looked to Italy and Spain to fill the imperial throne, and the approval of the subjects of the Empire had followed the will of the Senate in Rome. But with the fall of the last of the Antonines a new order of things had been established. The will of the people was no longer to be regarded as a factor in political life, but the will of the army was to be paramount, and the Cæsar of the future was to be any ambitious adventurer who bid high for their services. The power of the soldiery openly asserted itself when Pertinax fell a victim to the greed of the Prætorian guards, followed a few years later by their deliberate murder of the Emperor Julianus. But their assumption of supreme power reached its climax when it added to the death-roll the name of so estimable a ruler as Alexander Severus. The fall of Caracalla was an opportunity for military adventurers. Wherever the Roman legions were

P

encamped in any part of the wide-spread Empire, a successful general with daring equal to the occasion, and with a promise of large donatives to the soldiers, might claim the right of succession without consulting the wishes of the Senate. Such a man, distinguished for his prowess in many a field of battle, was Marcus Opilius Severus Macrinus (as he is commonly called), a native of *Julia Cæsarea*, the old capital of Juba II. This ambitious soldier was a Moor by birth as well as in habit, for, in common with the fashion of his race, he had an ear pierced to mark his nationality. He had risen from obscurity till he had attained the high distinction of prefect of the Prætorian guard. His short rule of only two months and three days is marked in North Africa by several inscriptions, showing that his son Diadumenianus shared with him the title of Cæsar. Like their predecessors, Pertinax and Julianus, these two African Emperors paid the penalty of purchasing imperial power at the hands of a grasping and corrupt army. According to Justinus, both father and son were disposed of, as soon as it was discovered that Macrinus endeavoured to reduce their pay and attempted to suppress the luxurious habits which prevailed in the Prætorian camp. The following dedication by the citizens of Diana is recorded on a ruined triumphal arch, and was first deciphered by Peysonnel. It is also noted by Shaw, as well as by Renier and Wilmanns.[1]

IMP · CAES · M · OPELLIO · SEVERO · MACRINO · PIO ·
FELICI · AVG · PONT · MAX · TRIB · POTEST
COS · DESIG · P · P · PROCOS · PROVIDENTISSIMO ·
ET · SANCTISSIMO · PRINCIPI
ET · M · OPELLIO · ANTONINO · DIADVMENIANO ·
NOBILISSIMO · CAESARI
PRINCIPI · IVVENTVTIS · RESPVBLICA · DIANEN-
SIVM · DEC · EX · DEC ·

The epithet *providentissimus* is unusual, and combined with *sanctissimus* is difficult to comprehend. It is fair to assume that this monumental arch was erected by the citizens of Diana at the commencement of the Emperor's reign, which was marked at first by toleration, and by the abolition of several taxes that had been imposed by Septimius Severus and his successor. But such epithets were wholly inapplicable to the

[1] *I.R.A.* No. 1731. Renier, *Mélanges d'Épigraphie*, p. 198.

Africa under Alexander Severus

rule of Macrinus, which was conspicuous for many acts of cruelty and an utter disregard for the value of human life. Another inscription found on a *milliarium* discovered at Turris (Telmina) mentions both father and son in connection with a new highway.[1] But their record is very slight, the name of Macrinus not being associated with any movement that had the slightest influence on the progress and civilisation of North Africa.

```
       IMP · CAES · M · OPEL
       LIVS · SEVERVS · MACRI
       NVS · PIVS · FELIX · AVG
       COS · ET · M · OPELLIVS
       ANTONINVS · DIADVME
       NIANVS · NOS · CAES · VIA
       M · STRATAM · NOV
       INSTITVERVNT ·
                IIIIX
```

Of their successor Aurelius Antoninus Varius, commonly known as Heliogabalus,[2] the less said the better about a loathsome career that did not betray one single quality commendable in mankind. As a link in the chain of African history, apart from the disgusting personality of this half-African youth who disgraced the Empire for a space of nearly four years, it brings into unusual prominence the extraordinary influence exercised by his mother Soæmias and his grandmother Julia Mæsa. Both these women were ambitious and greedy of power. By the intrigues of the former and the wealth of the latter Macrinus and his son were got rid of, and this stripling just entering his fourteenth year, a legitimate son of Soæmias by her first husband, Varius Marcellus, was declared to be the legitimate son of Caracalla by Soæmias, and consequently the rightful heir to the throne.[3] Historians of this period have dealt leniently with this depraved ill-trained youth, and contemporary records on stone or marble are almost a blank. It is some satisfaction to find, in turning over the long pages of published inscriptions which have been brought to light in

---

[1] *C.I.L.* No. 10056. Tissot descrip.

[2] The name is written in various ways. Lampridius writes it Heliogabalus, which is the direct pronunciation of the Greek word employed by Herodian. On coins it is spelt Elagabalus. English writers usually accept the authority of Lampridius.

[3] Justinus, in his life of this Emperor, says that he was the son of Caracalla by his cousin-german Soæmias, and that he was privately begotten in adultery.

North Africa, that the name of Aurelius Antoninus Varius rarely appears, and that the few tablets referring to him are in a more or less fragmentary condition. Among them is one found many years ago in a ruined Byzantine fortress at Lambessa, much defaced and almost illegible, but with the aid of so expert an epigraphist as Léon Renier the stones were put together and the record made complete. It is a dedication to the Emperor by the duplarii of the third legion Augusta on the occasion of the return of the African army to headquarters after a successful expedition in the East. The chief value of the inscription lies in the inclusion of the two Empresses, grandmother and mother of Heliogabalus, thus perpetuating the career of these two women as sharing imperial power with Cæsar himself. The wording as interpreted by Renier runs thus:[1]

Pro salute domini nostri Imperatoris Cæsaris, Marci Aurelii Antonini, Pii Felicis Augusti, pontificis maximi, patris patriæ, tribunicia potestate, consulis, proconsulis, divi Magni Antonini filii, Divi Pii Severi nepotis, et Juliæ Mæsæ Augustæ, aviæ Augusti nostri, matris castrorum et Senatus, et Juliæ Soæmiadis Bassianæ Augustæ, matris Augusti nostri.

It may be observed that the name of the Emperor's reputed father Caracalla is not mentioned. This omission is noteworthy and helps to bear testimony to the statements of most writers that Heliogabalus had no hereditary claim to the throne. The suppression may be reasonably attributed to the two intriguing Empresses, who virtually ruled the Empire during his reign. The very few other inscriptions are open to doubt, inasmuch as they are equally applicable to Caracalla and to Alexander Severus, who was recognised by the Senate as his successor on the throne.

The career of Alexander Severus is a pleasant chapter of African history, recalling the brightest days of the Empire under Augustus, Trajan, and Antoninus Pius. His father's name, Genesius Marcianus (supposed to have been a native of Phœnicia), has been almost forgotten, but the memory of his mother, Julia Mammæa, the sister of Julia Soæmias and the granddaughter of Bassianus, will be retained to all time. No one can read the biographical notices of the two Emperors

[1] *I.R.A.* No. 90.

Heliogabalus and Alexander Severus without being struck with the extraordinary difference in their mental and moral qualities. Both of them were of African descent, with little trace of Italian blood, and both of them passed their early youth as priests in the gorgeous temple of the Sun at Emesa in Syria,[1] where their great-grandfather Bassianus had ministered during a long life. It has been said that Soæmias and her son represented the genius of evil, while Julia Mammæa and her son impersonated the genius of good.[2] This is scarcely borne out by contemporary writers, and although neither of these remarkable women stands forth as an exponent of those higher qualities which command the respect of mankind in our more civilised times, yet the name of Alexander Severus is as conspicuous for everything that was good as that of his predecessor is for all that was bad. His reign of fourteen years was marked by justice to all subjects of the Empire, honesty in all his transactions, and such regard for the welfare of his people that not one single life was sacrificed by his orders in any part of his dominions. Mother and son, sharing the burdens of state and the desire to ameliorate the condition of the people in the provinces as well as in Rome, participated also in the honour of numerous dedicatory inscriptions which time has fortunately preserved. More than sixty already discovered in North Africa bear ample testimony to the work of this amiable ruler, whose merits entitle him to the long array of superlative epithets attached to his name. The full title of Marcus Aurelius Severus Alexander Pius Felix Augustus is sometimes accompanied by *dominus noster*, and such terms as *sanctissimus, fortissimus*, and *super omnes indulgentissimus* may still be read on several slabs in the local museums of North Africa.[3] According to Lampridius, in his

[1] Emesa was a city in Syria, renowned for its magnificent temple of the Sun. According to Ptolemy the geographer, it stood on the eastern bank of the river Orontes. Not far from here the memorable battle took place when the army of Zenobia, Queen of Palmyra, was completely routed by the Emperor Aurelian. Emesa was made a *colonia* by Caracalla in honour of his mother's family, and at a later date became the capital of Phœnicia Libanesia. *Vide* Eckhel for coins of Caracalla, with the temple on the reverse.

[2] *Les Antonins*, vol. iii. liv. 7, p. 342.

[3] Herodian says that Alexander Severus was named Alexianus, afterwards changed to Alexander. Lampridius calls this Emperor Aurelius Alexander, and adds that he was a native of Arka in Phœnicia, and called Alexander because he was

life of this Emperor, the modesty and unassuming character of Alexander Severus were never more apparent than on the occasion when the Senate offered to confer upon him the title of Antonine in memory of his great predecessor. In declining the proposed honour the Emperor, according to the account given in the pages of Lampridius, is stated to have said : 'If I accept the title of Antonine, why not those of Trajan, of Titus, and of Vespasian?' And the conscript fathers answered : 'In our eyes the name of Antonine is equal to that of Augustus.' On another occasion the Senate expressed a desire that Alexander should accept the title of Magnus, but once again the Emperor declined. The ordinary wording of a large number of simple inscriptions may be illustrated by the accompanying dedication on a milliary column, the name of the Emperor having the usual wording, Marcus Aurelius Severus Alexander Pius Felix Augustus.

```
         IMP · CAE
         SAR · M · AV
         RELIVS · SEVE
         RVS · ALEXAN
         DER-PIVS · FEL
         DIVI · SEVERI · NEP
         PONT · MAXIM
         TRIB · POT · COS
         P · RESTITVIT
               XVI
```

A far more interesting inscription is one discovered at Lambessa many years ago on the *Via Septimiana*[1] not far from the amphitheatre. It is a dedication of an altar to Jupiter, as the preserver of the Emperor, and his mother Julia Mammæa and their family, by a chief magistrate named Lucius Marius Crescentianus. This tablet, which is in good condition, may still be seen in the prætorium at Lambessa, which has become a local museum of considerable interest.[2] Renier's interpretation, which varies slightly from the text, is also given.

born either in a temple sacred to Alexander the Great, or perhaps on the birthday of the great Macedonian.

[1] The *Via Septimiana* at Lambæsis was the principal road between the camp and the town. According to an inscription (*C.I.L.* No. 2705) it was made by the soldiers of the third legion Augusta in the time of Septimius Severus. Some of the paving slabs are still in existence; *vide* Renier, *Arch. des Missions Scient.* 1851, p. 173.

[2] *C.I.L.* No. 2620. *I.R.A.* No. 1406.

Africa under Alexander Severus

I · O · M
CONSERVATORI
IMP · CAES · M · AVRELI · SE
VERI · ALEXANDRI · INVIC
TI · PII · FELICIS · AVG · ET · IVLIAE
MAMEAE · MATRIS · D · N
AVG · TOTIVSQ · DOMVS · DIVINAE
L · MARIVS · CRESCENTI
ANVS · Q · AEDIL · II · VIRA
DEVOT · NVMINI · EORVM · A
RAM · QVAM · DEVOVIT · SVA
PECVNIA · POSVIT.

Iovi optimo maximo, conservatori imperatoris Cæsaris Marci Aureli Severi Alexandri Invicti, Pii, Felicis Augusti, et Juliæ Mammææ Augustæ, matris Augusti, totiusque domus divinæ.

Lucius Marius Crescentianus, quæstorius, ædilicius, duumviralicius, devotus numini eorum, aram, quam devovit, suâ pecuniâ posuit.

At Ain Tunga, formerly known as *Thignica*,[1] an important town in Africa Provincia and marked at the present day by extensive ruins, there is a dedication to the Emperor and his mother in which the latter is styled as *Augusta* and *mater Augusti et castrorum et senatus et patriæ*. The inscription is on six stones in a fragmentary condition, recording the reconstruction of the market A.D. 229.[2] This date may be assigned as the climax of his estimable reign, when he had attained his 21st year.

Imperatori Cæsari divi magni Antonini, pii, felici, divi Severi pii nepoti, Marco Aurelio Severo Alexandro, pio, felici Augusto, pontifici maximo, tribunicia potestate VIII, consuli III, pater patriæ, et Juliæ Mammææ augustæ matri Augusti et castrorum et senatus et patriæ, macellum vetustate collapsum municipium Septimium Aurelium Antoninianum Alexandrianum Herculeum frugiferum Thignica devotum numini majestatique eorum pecunia publica a solo refecit, itemque dedicavit.

Although this Emperor was acclaimed Cæsar in the fourteenth year of his age and terminated his career before he had reached his twenty-eighth birthday, yet he was married, we are told, three times. There are no inscriptions relating to one of his wives named Sulpicia Memmia, daughter of Sulpicius, a man of consular rank. Unlike her mother-in-law, Julia Mam-

---

[1] The four towns, Thignica, Thugga, Agbia, and Thubursicum, were in the same district, and in the third and fourth centuries were in a flourishing condition.

[2] *C.I.L.* No. 1406. *Vide* Guérin, vol. ii. p. 152.

mæa, whose activity and intrigue were unbounded, this quiet-going princess appears to have taken no part in public life, nor to have exhibited any interest in proceedings outside the court circle. Her career is therefore a blank. And little more is known of another of the Emperor's wives named *Sallustia Barbia Orbiana*, whose memory has been preserved in an inscription at Cæsarea, which may still be seen in the little museum at Cherchel.[1] As the wife of the Emperor she was bound, in accordance with custom, to assume the title of Empress, and probably did so. But Herodian informs us that Julia Mammæa raised her objections to this assumption mainly on the ground that she alone, as Empress-Mother, wished to be called Empress. The same author adds that, in spite of Alexander's resistance to his mother's wishes, Orbiana was banished from Rome and ordered to pass the rest of her days in obscurity in a city in North Africa.

   GNEAE · SEIAE · HIERENNIAE · SALLVSTIAE
  BARBIAE · ORBIANAE · SANCTISSIMAE · AVGVSTAE
      CONIVGI · AVG · NOSTRI
    EQQ · SINGVLARES · DEVOTI
  NVMINI · MAIESTATIQVE · EIVS · CVRANTE
  LICINIO · HIEROCLETE · PROC · AVG
      PRAESIDE · PROVINCIAE

Orbiana, it will be noted, is proclaimed to be *sanctissima* and *augusta*, but the name of the Emperor is not mentioned. As a simple record of one who might, under other circumstances, have played an important part in imperial matters, this dedication by the *equites singulares* is of value. It is a memorial of an ill-starred princess, whom destiny removed from the gaieties of Rome to gratify the ambition and avarice of the Emperor's mother. Perhaps the quieter delights of a provincial city like Julia Cæsarea were more to her taste than the intrigue and corruption then prevailing in the metropolis, and daily life was attended by untold pleasures in so sweet a spot. There is no more enticing locality in North Africa than the surroundings of this ruined capital of the enlightened Juba II. The air is sweet and invigorating, the hills are clothed with timber, and the blue waters of the Mediterranean break lightly on its

---

[1] *C.I.L.* No. 9355. *Revue Africaine*, 1860, p. 156.

picturesque headland. In the third century Cæsarea contained a large population of wealthy citizens, descendants of Roman families who had settled there in the days of Claudius to do honour to so kingly a dependent as Juba II. Every traveller who has visited Cherchel can bear testimony to the extent of the ruins of the ancient city and its extensive suburbs. The undulations on the hillsides mark the sites of Roman villas, and it is within the range of probability that the lordly dwelling which became the home of the banished princess may some day be unearthed, and some memorials of her career brought to light. The fate of Orbiana as a dweller in such a spot as Cherchel needs little commiseration.

It is a reproach against Alexander Severus that excessive amiability often caused much injury to others, and that abject deference to his mother's will was a blot in a career which, in other respects, was almost blameless. Like so many of his predecessors, who had attempted to correct long-standing abuses in the army and to restore discipline in the garrison towns, his career also was terminated by the hands of a soldier assassin. The decree of the Prætorian guard was omnipotent, and the rule of the sword irresistible. Alexander, as a reforming Emperor, was condemned, and, almost simultaneously, mother and son fell together. If we are to credit Herodian, who shows no favour to Julia Mammæa, Alexander was a victim to the greed and sordid avarice of his mother. To gratify her desire for wealth she forced the Emperor to reduce the pay of the soldiers for the sole purpose of personal aggrandisement.

In testimony of inherent vitality in the Roman people, the progress of colonisation in the African provinces was not materially affected by these frequent attempts to undermine the constitution and place the Empire at the mercy of the sword. The reign of Alexander, which happily lasted for nearly fourteen years, had been specially favourable to an increase of population in the towns of North Africa, to the advance of agriculture in the interior of the country, and to the establishment of numerous *castella* and other works of defence for the protection of the frontiers from tribal attacks. For instance, a stone found on the plains of Setif bears an inscription relating to the construction of a *castellum Dianense* during his reign.[1]

[1] *C.I.L.* No. 8701. *Rec. de Const.* 1875, p. 338.

IMP · CAESAR · M ·
AVRELIVS · SEVERVS
ALEXANDER · INVICTVS
PIVS · FELIX · AVG · MVROS
KASTELLI · DIANESIS · EX
TRVXIT · PER · COLONOS · EIVSDE
M · KASTELLI
P · CLXXXXV

And in the extreme west two other slabs record the presence of a body of troops designated as *Numerus Alexandrianus Severianus Syrorum*,[1] the last word indicating a tribe of that name referred to in the Geography of Ptolemy.

M. Edouard Cat, in his notice of these two inscriptions in his erudite treatise on the Roman province of *Mauritania Cæsariensis*,[2] suggests that the original title was abbreviated into *Castra Severiana* at some later date, partly on the ground that there was a bishop residing there in the fifth century (according to Victor de Vite), who bore the title of *Castraseberianensis*. The just government of Alexander throughout the African provinces, and a sense of security against disturbances, had attracted citizens from various parts of the Empire. We hear of no political agitation since the fall of Macrinus the Moor; and inscriptions, which form the best testimony to the general condition of the people, evince a spirit of contentment, respect for imperial authority, and undisguised reverence for an amiable Emperor. It would have been well for the Roman world if Alexander had been permitted to reign for the full term of his natural life and to continue his popular and beneficent rule. Excessive goodwill towards his subjects may be ascribed as one of the causes of his untimely end, together with a spirit of forbearance rarely to be met with in potentates of Syrian origin. We are told by Lampridius, his biographer, that on one occasion both his mother Julia Mammæa and his third wife Memmia upbraided him for his actions in the following words: *Molliorem tibi potestatem et contemptibiliorem imperii fecisti*. A slight study of the career of Alexander Severus confirms the opinion

[1] *C.I.L.* No. 10469. *Rev. Afr.* 1, p. 103. Macarthy descrip.

[2] This military post occupied an important position west of Pomaria (Tlemcen), and is now represented by extensive ruins, upon which the Arab town of Lalla Maghnia has been built. (Edouard Cat, *Essai sur la Province Romaine de Mauretanie Césarienne*, Paris, 1891.)

aptly expressed by Gibbon, that 'this amiable prince was hardly equal to the difficulties of his situation, and the firmness of his conduct was inferior to the purity of his intentions.'

The period of nearly fifty years which followed the death of Alexander is marked by constantly recurring internal strife and conspicuous action by the legions in Africa in the cause of order and good government. From A.D. 235 to A.D. 284 no fewer than sixteen emperors ascended the throne in rapid succession, six of them reigning for a few months, the three generations of Gordians for eight years, and Aurelian and Probus being allowed, by favour of the army, to rule respectively for the unusually long periods of five and eight years. With the exception of the Gordians, who made Africa the battle-field of the Empire and contributed largely towards the close of their career to promote the welfare of its citizens, no one of these emperors appears to have taken an active part in any great movement in that country, nor, if we are to judge from the numerous inscriptions which have been fortunately preserved, to have aroused the enthusiasm which characterised the rule of Trajan and the Antonines, and, in a lesser degree, of Alexander Severus. That the Roman world should have been governed for a period of thirty-eight years by a Syro-Phœnician dynasty, and that the names of five emperors and four empresses, some of them born on African soil, should have left their mark in the history of the Empire, are facts worth recording in treating of the Roman occupation of North Africa. This dynasty may be briefly tabulated in the manner set forth in Smith's *Dictionary of Gr. and Rom. Biog. and Mythol.*, art. 'Caracalla.'

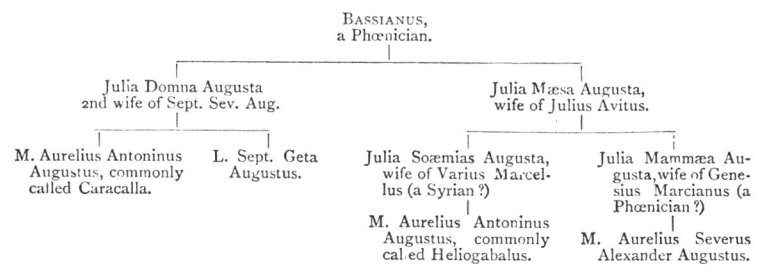

BASSIANUS, a Phœnician.

Julia Domna Augusta, 2nd wife of Sept. Sev. Aug.

Julia Mæsa Augusta, wife of Julius Avitus.

M. Aurelius Antoninus Augustus, commonly called Caracalla.

L. Sept. Geta Augustus.

Julia Soæmias Augusta, wife of Varius Marcellus (a Syrian ?)

Julia Mammæa Augusta, wife of Genesius Marcianus (a Phœnician ?)

M. Aurelius Antoninus Augustus, commonly called Heliogabalus.

M. Aurelius Severus Alexander Augustus.

The name of Bassianus was specially honoured by his descendants, for we find it on a dedicatory inscription to his granddaughter Julia Soæmias, found at Velitræ, a city of Latium, on the Alban Hills, in 1765.

CHAPTER IX

AFRICA UNDER THE GORDIANS

A.D. 236—244

THE termination of the Syro-Phœnician dynasty (as it may be termed) by the death of Alexander Severus, who had no issue, left the Empire at the mercy of any unscrupulous adventurer with a reputation for success in the field of battle. A few years previously Macrinus the Moor had ascended the throne for a brief period by the aid of a liberal display of these qualities combined with the cruelty and cunning of his native race. It was now the turn of Maximinus, a Goth, a man of low extraction, to play a similar part in the drama of imperial progress. A shepherd in his earlier days, he had learnt the rude art of attack and defence in protecting sheep and cattle on his native plains from the hands of the marauder. A soldier in middle life, he rose, step by step, till he obtained the command of a legion; and then, by the promise of large donatives and the employment of various forms of corruption, gained the adherence of his troops in his daring bid for the throne of the Cæsars. When the opportune moment arrived for declaring himself *Imperator*, he unfurled the standard of revolt, in defiance of the will of the Senate, and announced his intention of marching to Rome to claim imperial power. Success, though sometimes temporary in its achievements, invariably follows daring and promptitude, independently of the justice or iniquity of a cause. Maximinus had little else to depend upon. With a dash of heroism about him, he led his troops undaunted in the direction of the capital, and with the assistance of Capellianus, governor of Mauritania, in stirring up the native races of North Africa against the Roman legions established in the country, seemed to be on the point of attaining the full measure of his ambition. Cruelty and extortion marked his footsteps, and the destructive qualities of a barbarian unaccustomed to civilised

Africa under the Gordians

life showed themselves by his utter contempt for the monumental buildings of the great Empire. Whatever may have been his real name, we only know him as Caius Julius Verus Maximinus; and his son, whom he created Cæsar simultaneously with his assumption of the purple, bears the same name as the father. A few inscriptions in North Africa designate Maximinus *Imperator Cæsar Julius Verus Maximinus Pius Felix Augustus*, and his son Maximinus as *Caius Julius Verus Maximus Nobilissimus Cæsar*. The most complete and legible record of their joint names may be read on a milliary column near the entrance to an old mosque in Tunis, bearing the date A.D. 237.[1]

```
       IMP · CAES · ⎡C · IVLIVS⎤
      ⎣VERVS· MAXIMINVS · PIVS⎦
       FELIX · AVG · GERM · MAX · SAR
       MAT · MAX · DACICVS · PONT
       MAX · TRIB · POTEST · III · IMP · VI
      ⎡L · IVLIVS · VERVS · MAXIMUS · NO⎤
      ⎣BILISSIMVS CAES ·⎦ PRINCEPS
       IVVENTVTIS · GERM · MAX · SAR
       MAT · MAX · DACICVS · MAX
       VIAM · A · CARTHAGINE · VS
       QVE · AD · FINES · NVMIDIAE
       PROVINCIAE · LONGA · INCVRIA
       CORRVPTAM · ADQVE · DILAP
       SAM · RESTITVERVNT
                    LXX
```

In this inscription the names of both these Cæsars are erased in the usual way by marginal lines. Somewhat similar ones of the same year may be seen on two milliary columns in the neighbourhood of Agbia, one on the road to *Thubursicum*, and the other to *Musti*. All of them seem to indicate that Maximinus was engaged in repairing the principal highways in Africa, in order to facilitate military operations for a revolt in the spring of the following year. One other inscription worth noting was found at *Gales* in the proconsular province of Africa, and is a dedication to Maximinus only *et divinæ domus ejus*. This had been erased by Gordian I., but was afterwards restored.

Three years' rule under such an Emperor, who remained a

[1] *C.I.L.* No. 10047. *Vide* Guérin, vol. i. p. 27.

barbarian to the end of his career, and whose motto was *Nisi crudelitate imperium non teneri*, was productive of infinite harm, and contributed more to promote the decline of the Empire than the infamous conduct of Caracalla and Heliogabalus. Like so many of their predecessors, Maximinus and his son became the victims of the same men who had raised them to power. The dagger of the soldier said the last word, and, after a short interval of a few weeks, the statues raised in honour of these two Augusti were overthrown and the names of both father and son held in contempt. Their record in North Africa is a blank; for, with the exception of the milliary stones above referred to, there are no inscriptions indicating one single act of munificence or thought for the welfare of the vast population of this great colony. No words can better express the growth of decay at this period of the Roman Empire than the following paragraph penned by our great historian.[1] 'In the decline of Empire, A.D. 200-250, the form was still the same, but the animating vigour and health were fled. The industry of the people was discouraged and exhausted by a long period of oppression. The discipline of the legions, which alone, after the extinction of every other virtue, had propped the greatness of the State, was corrupted by the ambition, or relaxed by the weakness, of the Emperors. The strength of the frontiers, which had always consisted in arms rather than in fortifications, was insensibly undermined; and the fairest provinces were left exposed to the rapaciousness or ambition of the barbarians, who soon discovered the decline of the Roman Empire.'

There are few names more intimately associated with the history of Roman Africa than those of the three Gordian Emperors, whose figures pass too rapidly across the stage at this period; and there is no one in the long roll of Emperors whose actions were so repulsive to the citizens of Rome and the provinces as those of the savage Maximinus. With a rabble army he was spreading devastation everywhere in his course, and seemed to be on the point of assured success when the legions of Africa declared against him. At that time the proconsul of Africa was a noble Roman of distinguished family, a man of high attainments and commanding universal respect. It was during the reign of Septimius Severus that the Senate

[1] Gibbon, vol. i. p. 329.

conferred upon Antoninus Gordianus this coveted distinction, and we are told by Capitolinus that as soon as the Emperor heard of the appointment he wrote to the conscript fathers, 'You could not do anything more agreeable or more pleasant to me than to send to Africa as proconsul so good a man, noble, just, enlightened, and temperate in all things.' Such was the reputation of the man who saved the Empire in a day of peril, and, with some little hesitation excusable in a veteran then entering upon his eightieth year, gave up the quiet enjoyments of provincial life at the call of his country. It appears that Gordian was residing at some country retreat near Thysdrus in Africa Provincia at the time when Capellianus, as the ally of Maximinus, was inciting the native races to revolt, and we learn from contemporary writers that Gordian was proclaimed Cæsar Imperator by the army of Africa in that remote town.[1] Gordian then proceeded to Carthage in state to receive the congratulations of its citizens, and from thence despatched messengers to Rome announcing his acceptance of imperial power. But the joy of the Senate at the prospect of relief from the cruelties of Maximinus was short-lived, for the troops of Gordian were vanquished by the irregular army under Capellianus, and the eldest son of the Emperor, associated with him as Cæsar, was killed. The shock was greater than the aged Gordian could endure. His brain became affected, and in a fit of despair he committed suicide. Great was the consternation of the Senate, presided over by Flavius Valens, who was subsequently created Emperor with his brother Valentinian. Maximinus was at that time encamped at Aquileia with a large army, making preparations for a triumphal entry into Rome, and in a few weeks the fate of the Empire might be sealed, and a reign of military despotism begun. To meet the urgency of the situation, two senators of consular rank and mature years were selected to guard the national interests. One of them, named Marcus Clodius Pupienus Maximus, who had considerable military experience, was sent to Aquileia to give battle to Maximinus; the other, named Decimus Cælius Calvinus Balbinus, a man of noble birth and of tried capacity in administrative affairs, was to remain in Rome as the guardian of the

[1] Gordian I. received the title of Africanus when he was saluted as Emperor at Thysdrus and taken in triumph to Carthage to be formally proclaimed.

people. And with a view to securing a continuance of the Gordian dynasty, a grandson of the elder Gordian, at that time a youth about twelve years old, was to be associated with both of them as the Cæsar Imperator of the future. An interesting inscription on a milliary stone found nearly a mile from Bouhira, in the province of Mauritania Sitifensis, on the slope of a hill covered with ruins, records the names of all three Cæsars.[1]

```
           IMP CAES M CLODIO PVPIENI
             O MAXIMO PIO FELICI AVG
              PONT MAX TRIB POT COS
                 II PROCOS P P ET
            IMP CAES D CAELIO CALVINO
              BALBINO PIO FELICI AVG
              PONT MAX TRIB POT COS
                 II PROCOS P P ET
             M ANTONIO GORDIANO NO
               BILISSIMO CAES PI AVG
              NEPOTI DIVORVM GOR
              DIANORVM RES P COL
                  NERV AVG SITIF
                       MVIIII
```

It will be observed that the citizens of Sitifis, in their dedication to the two Emperors and the youthful Gordian, designate each of the former as *pontifex maximus*. This was a departure from an ancient rule of the constitution, which made the high office of chief pontiff indivisible, and thus established a precedent which ultimately tended to bring the title into disfavour.[2] In

[1] *C.I.L.* No. 10365. *Vide* Poulle, *Rec. de Const.* 1873-4, p. 366.

[2] The origin of so distinguished a title as *Pontifex maximus* is veiled in considerable obscurity, and has been the subject of a variety of statements, which may be classed as conjectural. Among ancient authors who have assisted in throwing light on the matter, Zosimus the historian, during the reign of Theodosius, may claim a hearing. He tells us that 'the origin of Pontifices may be traced to a remote period when mankind was unacquainted with the mode of worshipping gods in the form of statues. Images of the deities were first made in Thessaly. As there were no temples in those days (for the use of such edifices was unknown), they set up figures of their gods on a bridge over the river Peneus, and called those who sacrificed to these images *Gephyræi*, Priests of the Bridge (Gr. γέφυρα, a bridge). Hence the Romans, deriving it from the Greeks, called their own priests *Pontifices*, and enacted a law that kings, for the sake of dignity, should be considered of the number. The first king to enjoy this distinction was Numa Pompilius. After him it was conferred not only on kings, but on Augustus and his successors in the Roman Empire. Upon the elevation of any one to the imperial dignity, the *Pontifices* brought him the priestly habit, and he was immediately styled *Pontifex*

the earlier days of the Republic a *pontifex maximus*, as head of the college of priests, was not permitted to set foot out of Italy, but as soon as the Emperors assumed a right to the title this restriction was withdrawn. Julius Cæsar set the example by making an expedition into the province of Gaul after his acceptance from the Senate of this high office. It may be observed that Valentinian II., at the close of the fourth century, was the last of the Emperors to retain the dignity of chief pontiff, and that it remained in abeyance till its assumption by the Christian Bishops of Rome.

The few months' rule of these two high-minded senators, who succeeded in ridding the world of the tyrant Maximinus and securing tranquil succession to the youthful Gordian, is marked by several incidents affecting the interests of Roman Africa. Fortune for the moment favoured the army despatched from Rome to arrest the progress of the usurping Emperor in his march towards the capital. Maximinus was slain by his own rebellious soldiers, and the troubles of the Empire seem to have terminated. Had Maximinus been successful in his campaign, all Africa would have been in arms, subjecting the country to a long course of barbarity and the many evils inseparable from irregular warfare. In the days of the great Republic, and under the Cæsars till the time of Septimius Severus, the authority of the Senate representing the interests of the Empire would have asserted itself whenever dissensions at home or abroad endangered the State. But the old order of things had passed away. The army was no longer the loyal servant of the Senate, but its exacting master; and the will of the Prætorians, prepared for any emergency, was irresistible. The citizens of Rome disputed their authority, troubles ensued, and ultimately Pupienus and Balbinus were sacrificed to the fury of the soldiers. The names of both these Emperors are now almost forgotten in the long array of Cæsars of the third century; but the part they played in the Gordian drama, and their loyalty to their country in the hour of distress, entitled them to a more honourable place than time has accorded them.

Such was the state of affairs when Gordian III., at the age of sixteen, was raised to the purple. Possessing all the charms

maximus. According to Orelli, Gratian was the last of the Emperors to use this title.

of youth, an amiable disposition, and an honoured name, he soon endeared himself to his subjects in all parts of the Empire. For a time the Prætorians were quiet, waiting their opportunity to test the military capacity and moral courage of the youthful Cæsar. Scarcely had Gordian been seated on the throne when insurrection broke out in Africa. But the Emperor was equal to the occasion. The military qualities he had exhibited in early days, aided by the loyalty of his supporters, nipped the rebellion in the bud, and peace and prosperity blossomed once more under his amiable rule. Numerous inscriptions in North Africa, bearing his honoured name, during this brief period, attest a well-merited popularity. In nearly all parts of the Empire dedications were made expressing satisfaction and contentment, many of them referring to acts of munificence and to encouragement given to the arts of peace in Rome as well as in the provinces. In North Africa the titles of the Emperor vary considerably. At Verecunda, for instance, there is a dedication in which he is styled *Gordiani nepoti et divi Gordiani sororis filio*.[1] At Lambæsis we find that the soldiers of Julia Cæsarea were not unmindful of their Emperor;[2] and on the road between Mostaganem and Mascara a milliarium was found on which the full titles are briefly given.[3] The date will be A.D. 239.

IMP · CAES · M	
ANTONIO GORDI	DOMINO
ANO PIO FELICI IN	IMP · CAES · M
VICTO AVG VEXIL	ANTONIO · GOR
LATIO MILITVM	DINO · INVIC
MAVRORVM	TO · PIO · FELICI
CAESARIENS	AVG · PONT · MAXI
IVM GORDIA	MO · TRIB · POT · BIS
NORVM DEVO	P · P · COS · PRO · CON
TORVM NVM	SVLI · NEPOTI · DI
INI MAIEST	VORVM · GORDIA
ATIQVE	NORVM · M · P
EIVS	

But the most interesting inscriptions are those bearing the name of his wife Sabinia Tranquillina conjointly with his own,

---

[1] *I.R.A.* No. 1431.   [2] *I.R.A.* No. 99, copied by Renier and De la Mare.
[2] *C.I.L.* No. 10460. *Rec. de Const.* 1875, p. 438.

Africa under the Gordians

of which the following, found at a place now called Henchir Adjedj in the neighbourhood of Theveste, is a fair example:[1]

```
         IMP CAES
         M ANTONIO
         GORDIANO PIO
         FEL AVG ET
         TRANQVILLI
         NAE SABINAE
         AVG EIVS
```

A far more important dedication is on a slab discovered at Bir Haddada, the site of a Roman *castellum* in the province of *Mauritania Sitifensis*:

```
              I · O · M
         CETERISQ · DIS
         DEABVSQ · PRO · SA
         LVTE · ADQ · INCO
         LVMITATE · VIC
         TORIISQ · D N · SAN
         CTISSIMI · IMP · M
         ANTONI · GORDIA
         NI · INVICTI · PII · FE
         LICIS · AVG · ET · SABI
         NIAE · TRANQVILL
         INAE · AVG · CON
         IVGI · EIVS · AVG · N · TO
         TAQVE · DOMO · DIVINA EO
         RVM · K · B · D · D · S · P
```

Here we have in a few lines an invocation to Jupiter and all the gods to protect the Emperor and Empress and their divine family.[2] In some instances the dedications are to the Empress only, as in the following at Sigus in Numidia, the date being A.D. 242.[3] We know little of the career of Sabinia, except that she was the daughter of a noble Roman named Misitheus (sometimes called Timesicles on account of his Greek extraction), or Timasitheus, who was entrusted by her youthful son-in-law with the highest duties of the State, and as prefect of the Prætorians endeavoured to effect much-needed reforms in that powerful body.

---

[1] *C.I.L.* No. 10695. *Rec. de Const.* 1878, p. 32.
[2] *C.I.L.* No. 8710. *Rev. Afriq.* 1861, p. 448.
[3] *C.I.L.* No. 5701. De la Mare, *Explor.*, tab. 53, n. 3. *I.R.A.* No. 2467.

SABINIAE TRANQVIL
LINAE AVG CONIVGI
DOMINI NOSTRI
IMP CAES M ANTONI
GORDIANI PII FELICIS
INVICTI AVG PONT
MAX TRIB POT V
IMP VI COS II P P
PROCOS RESPVBLI
CA SIGVITANORVM

But honourable conduct seems to have been little valued in that corrupt age, and reform in any branch of military service was resisted to the utmost. Misitheus was succeeded in the prefecture by Philip the Arab, and ultimately was sacrificed to make way for his ambitious projects. Although the name of Sabinia has been almost forgotten, it is pleasant to find so many dedications in her honour in remote places in North Africa. It is, therefore, reasonable to assume that this Empress had established a good reputation and a degree of popularity among Roman citizens.

Capitolinus, in his lives of the Gordians, tells us that Gordian III. did much to promote art, and mentions as an instance of his regard for beautiful surroundings that he adorned the peristyle of the family villa in the Prenestine Way with 200 columns of marble—50 of marble of Carystea, 50 of Claudian, 50 of Synnada, and 50 of marble from Numidia— the last probably coming from the quarries at Simittu already referred to. But the name of this Emperor, linked with those of his grandfather and his uncle, will be for ever associated with the remote town of Thysdrus, where Gordian I. was drawn from a peaceful life to raise the standard of resistance against Maximinus the tyrant, and where a monument was raised in their honour, whose magnificent remains still excite the wonder and admiration of every traveller in modern Tunisia. The name of Thysdrus sounds unfamiliar in speaking of the present Arab village of El-Djem and the colossal amphitheatre there bearing the same title. Indeed, were it not for the presence of this structure, the site of the Roman town of Thysdrus would have been difficult to identify; and, owing to the absence of inscriptions and records of any kind relating to the amphitheatre, its ruined surroundings might have remained an un-

AMPHITHEATRE AT THYSDRUS (EL-DJEM).

Africa under the Gordians

solved problem. As to the town itself, we know from the writings of Hirtius that Julius Caesar levied a fine on its inhabitants after the battle of Thapsus, a coast town some twenty miles distant, where the issue proved fatal to the party of Scipio. Thysdrus cannot be said to exist at the present day, but the site is clearly indicated by the disturbed surface of the ground near the amphitheatre, and by the discovery in recent years of a number of tombstones. It could not have been a town of great size or importance at the commencement of the Christian era, for Hirtius tells us that Caesar mitigated the fine on account of the wretched condition of the inhabitants: *propter humilitatem civitatis certo numero frumenti multat.* The exact date of the erection of the amphitheatre is a matter of conjecture, and is likely to remain so. It is scarcely possible that so gigantic a structure, demanding considerable forethought in design and beset with many difficulties in its execution, could have been planned and commenced during the six weeks' reign of the first of the Gordians. Rather let us assume that when the third of the Gordians found himself securely seated on the throne, with every prospect of enjoying a peaceful reign, his thoughts may have reverted to the little town in Africa where his distinguished grandfather had been raised to the purple. It was the custom to mark the accession of an Emperor in the principal towns by a course of several weeks' festivities, defrayed by the imperial treasury. Perhaps the cost of the amphitheatre, needful for repeated exhibitions of the games of the arena, was defrayed from the same source on the accession of Gordian III. But this is a matter of conjecture, and the whole subject is involved in mystery. Capitolinus, writing in the reigns of Diocletian and Constantine, makes no mention of the amphitheatre. He alludes to the proclamation at Thysdrus of the first Gordian, and adds in a subsequent paragraph that great festivities were in preparation by Gordian III. for celebrating the thousandth anniversary of the foundation of Rome, commemorated a few years later by Philip his successor. It seems strange that such a monumental edifice of architectural pretensions, covering 4½ acres of ground, rising to a height of about 120 feet, and capable of seating more than 30,000 persons, should have been passed over without comment by so careful a biographer as Capitolinus. The coins struck in the reigns of the Gordians throw little light on the subject. According to Shaw there is one giving a representation of an amphitheatre not hitherto accounted for by medallists. But there is another well-known coin of this era with a somewhat similar representation of an amphitheatre, which undoubtedly refers to the repairing or completing the Flavian amphitheatre at Rome during the reign of Gordian III. The inscription *Munificentia Gordiani Aug.* is conclusive. In both coins the amphitheatre is shown with three stories of arcades surmounted by an attic, a colossus on one side and a portico on the other. It is quite possible that one coin was struck at Rome, and the other in the mint at Carthage, but they both refer to the edifice at Rome, and the colossus represented is none other than the so-called Colossus of Nero. The comparative silence of Latin authors, and of Arab writers of the eleventh and twelfth centuries, such as El-Bekri and Edrisi, on any matter relating to Thysdrus, renders a solution of this question somewhat difficult. Justus Lipsius, the author of *Admiranda, sive de Magnitudine Romana*, written in 1630, gives a list of all the known amphitheatres, but makes no mention of the one at Thysdrus. The Jesuit father, Josephe Gius, who wrote an elaborate description of Arles and other similar edifices, is quite silent on the point, and the Marquis Scipio Maffei,[1] when comparing the amphitheatre at Verona with those at Rome and Capua, boldly asserts that these were the only amphitheatres ever built by the Romans. The rest, including those whose remains may still be seen at Arles, Nîmes, Pompeii, and Pola (not mentioning Thysdrus), he describes as theatres, and not intended for gladiatorial exhibitions. Shaw, who travelled through Barbary 1730–38,[2] was the first to draw attention to this great monument at *Thysdrus*, and Bruce, some thirty years later, was probably the first traveller who made a drawing of it. Gibbon the historian gives no clue as to its origin, and accepts the statements of Capitolinus as the groundwork for this period of Roman history. Our own encyclopædias are also silent, and

---

[1] Marquis Francesco Scipione Maffei, *A compleat History of the Ancient Amphitheatres*. London : 1730. 8vo. Another writer on the subject was Justus Lipsius, *Admiranda, sive de Magnitudine Romana*, Lib. IV. Editio ultima, Antverpiæ. MDCXXX. No mention is made of Thysdrus.

[2] Shaw, p. 206.

THE AMPHITHEATRE AT THYSDRUS (EL-DJEM).

some of them ignore the monument altogether. There is little doubt, however, that many inscribed stones, removed from the amphitheatre from time to time, are built into the walls of Arab huts in the adjacent village of El-Djem, and that a systematic exploration of the site of the ancient town would bring to light some record of the building of this gigantic structure. For the present we must be content with traditional history, and assume (there is reasonable ground for the assumption) that the building was planned and nearly completed under the Gordian dynasty. The coming celebration of the tenth centenary of the foundation of Rome, for which the Gordians were preparing, would promote the building of amphitheatres and the completion of those that were in progress, not only in Rome, but in every province of the Empire. Capitolinus tells us plainly that the preparations of Gordian III. were on the most extensive scale, and that his munificence in encouraging the games of the arena was not surpassed by any one of the Roman Emperors.

Like the aqueduct of Carthage, this monument at *Thysdrus* is a standing testimony to the force of imperial will, and to the strength and determination so conspicuous in the Roman character. It mattered little to the Emperor whether stone or marble were at hand or transport of materials difficult. In the quarries at *Sullectum*, some twenty miles distant, stone of excellent quality was abundant, and to all appearances this stone and no other was used. What were the appliances for conveying tens of thousands of huge blocks of chiselled stone so long a distance, or how many thousands of forced labourers were employed on the work, we have no means of knowing. It is sufficient for us to regard with amazement the audacity of an undertaking which, in the present day and in the actual condition of the country, would be stamped with impossibility Like all the other great amphitheatres of the Empire, the divisions and arrangements of the one at *Thysdrus* present no distinctive features, having externally the usual open arcades, each presenting a complete Order. In this one the first and third are of Corinthian Order, and the second Composite. Whether the attic was Corinthian or not we have no means of judging, as only a portion of the inner wall of the top story remains. There were two principal entrances, one of which is entirely destroyed. The interior has suffered more than the exterior, owing partly to its having been used as a fortress, but principally to the wantonness of Arabs, who have been accustomed for centuries to regard the entire edifice as a very cheap and convenient stone quarry. When El-Bekri saw the amphitheatre in the eleventh century, he described the interior as being arranged in steps from top to bottom, and as late as Bruce's visit some portions of the seats and inclines must have been intact. There is every reason to suppose that the structure was never completed. The short rule of the Gordians, scarcely extending over six years, with whose memory it was intimately associated, was followed by a line of Emperors who had no interest in this obscure town in Africa, so far from the coast. This fact might help to account for so great a monument having been left unfinished. As for the structure itself, there are many indications that it was built with great rapidity with a view to its being used for some special occasion. Nearly every stone has a triangular-shaped lewis-hole on the external face, showing that the raising of the blocks into position was of more consideration than the appearance of the work. Again, the archstones are not all carefully cut to suit the extrados of the arches, and several of the modillions which adorn the cornices of the three stories are left uncut. There are indications of an intention to carve the keystones of the bottom arcade, but only two of them have been worked (perhaps by way of experiment), one representing the head of a lion and the other the bust of a female, the dressing of the head being in the fashion of the period. The three tiers of arcades appear to have been completed, with the exception perhaps of the cornice, but there is no indication whatever of any of the facing blocks of the attic story having been fixed in position. There is one peculiarity about the structure which is very noticeable. Nearly every course of masonry is of the same height, being within a fraction of 20 inches, the length of the stones averaging 38 inches. In each Order the entablatures are similar, the architrave, frieze, and cornice being each one stone in height. The bases of the engaged columns are in one stone, and the surbases also. The superficial area of this amphitheatre is almost identical with that of the incomplete amphitheatre at Verona, which ranks with that at Capua as one of the largest of provincial edifices

THE COLOSSEUM AT ROME.
(Major axis, 616 feet; minor axis, 512 feet.)

AMPHITHEATRE AT VERONA.
(Major axis, 508 feet; minor axis, 404 feet.)

AMPHITHEATRE AT THYSDRUS.
(Major axis, 489 feet; minor axis, 403 feet.)

AMPHITHEATRE AT ARLES.
Major axis, 452 feet; minor axis, 350 feet.

Africa under the Gordians

of this description. Comparing it with the Colosseum at Rome, there is marked variation in the dimensions of repeated features, especially in the proportions of wall spaces and the open arches of the arcades. The extreme major axis may be estimated at 489 feet, and the minor axis at 403 feet. The height of the first Order is 26 feet 6 inches, of the second Order 32 feet 10 inches, and of the third Order 29 feet 8 inches. Assuming that the attic was intended to be of the same proportionate height as its prototype in Rome, the total height of the external wall, measured from the ground, would have been 124 feet 6 inches. The construction itself possesses considerable merit. The stone, a shelly limestone, quite white when quarried, but after long exposure presenting a golden hue, is very beautiful when the sun is low on the horizon, but it did not admit of very fine workmanship. The surface of the stone is excellent, and the vaulting throughout, which is in smaller blocks, is well worthy of study. The stones have not in all cases been well fitted, owing probably to the rapid execution of the work, and consequently the mortar joints, especially in the corridors, are thicker than one generally meets with in the best class of Roman masonry. The proportions of the openings and wall spaces are very pleasing, and the mouldings generally, though simple and frequently repeated, have been well considered.

The history of this amphitheatre has been a stirring one in later times. Its form and solidity made it useful as a fortress, and we learn that, at the time of the Arab invasion of North Africa, a female chieftain named El-Kahina resisted their approach, taking shelter within the building and sustaining a long siege. In 1697 the tribes of the district refused payment of the annual tribute to the Bey and sought refuge within its walls. Artillery was brought to bear upon the edifice, and a breach equal to one-fourth of the perimeter prevented its ever being used again for a similar purpose. Since that time many of the dislodged blocks of stone have been carried off and the breach made larger. The miserable dwellings of Arabs now clustered round the walls, and even within the lower arcades, present a striking and piteous contrast to the noble workmanship of their predecessors.

The whole subject of amphitheatres forms an important chapter in Roman history. They are a type of public buildings essentially Roman, and are unknown in any country unsubdued by Roman arms. They may be divided into three classes. Those at Capua, El-Djem, Verona, Arles, Nîmes, and Pola, all modelled after the Colosseum at Rome, may represent the first class; those of which we have examples at Pæstum, Pompeii, Italica, Caerleon, as well as at Bou-Chater, Oudena, and numerous other towns in North Africa, partly excavated and partly embellished with masonry, may be assigned to the second class; and others still traceable, of which the one at Dorchester may be recognised as a typical example, being excavations of elliptical form with cut benches of turf, belong to the third class. These are rightly called *Castrensian* amphitheatres, and probably no Roman *castrum* in any province, however remote, was unprovided with one of these rough constructions. Montfaucon says that every Roman city had its amphitheatre, and certainly in North Africa there is scarcely a town where the lines of one cannot be traced.

Gordian III., the last survivor of a short-lived dynasty, shares with Alexander Severus the sympathetic regard of all law-abiding citizens of every age. Like so many of his predecessors, he paid the penalty for honourable conduct. The Prætorians, at the instigation of their prefect, demanded his removal. The youthful Emperor, just entering his twentieth year, was murdered, and Philip the Arab reigned in his stead. The name of Gordian must have continued a pleasant memory in after generations, for we are told by Capitolinus that, by a decree of the Senate, their descendants were to be free for ever, as citizens of Rome, from all the heavy taxes and burdens of the State. It is to be regretted that no Latin inscriptions have been brought to light in North Africa bearing the names of Gordian I. and his son. At Djemila (the ancient Cuiculum) a fragmentary slab has been found somewhat difficult to decipher, but the characters are Greek,[1] and the few words that are legible do not convey information of any value.

---

[1] *C.I.L.* No. 10895.

AMPHITHEATRE AT UTHINA (OUDENA)

CHAPTER X

AFRICA UNDER THE LATER EMPERORS

A.D. 244-254

IN the long list of Emperors who crossed the stage in rapid succession towards the decline of the Empire, many may be regarded as puppets in the hands of a faction; others were invested with the purple by accident rather than by the deliberate will of the people, while a few were mere implements at the disposal of a corrupt and undisciplined army. The short rule of a few months accorded to many of them prevented their taking an active part in administrative affairs outside the walls of Rome, or finding opportunities for visiting any of the great provinces of the Empire. Although Africa was an unknown country to some, yet their names, honoured or dishonoured, may be found recorded on stone or marble in nearly every part of this great colony. To some of the Emperors are accorded a long array of superlative epithets, which the greatest of the Cæsars in the better days of the Empire would have hesitated to accept; while to others are given the customary titles that tradition had assigned to the Cæsar of the day. In testimony of the change which had taken place since the days of Augustus, a comparison may be made between the titles accorded to that great Emperor and those adopted by such an unworthy representative of the line of Cæsars as Philip the Arab, who treacherously murdered Gordian III., and ruled for five years more as a military adventurer than as guardian of the interests of a great Empire. But fortune favoured his career far beyond his deserts. The thousandth anniversary of the foundation of Rome A.C. 753 was commemorated shortly after he came to the throne, and consequently festivities on an unusual scale were held in every city and town of the Empire. This is partly shown by the large number of inscriptions of that period dedicated to the Emperor and his wife, as well as to his son

Philip, who shared the imperial dignities, although he was only a child of eight years. Among those brought to light on African soil, the following, selected from a large number, will serve to indicate the tone of national feeling which prevailed on such a memorable occasion. In this instance the immediate cause of rejoicing was the reconstruction of the waterworks at a remote place in Mauritania Sitifensis, now known as Kharbet Zembia, but the dedication is complete, even to the bestowal of *invictus* on the little boy Cæsar.[1]

FELICISSIMIS · TEMPORIBVS · D · D · N · N · IMP · ·
CAES · M · IVLI · PHILIPPI · INVICTI · PII FELICIS · ET
· IMP · CAES · M · IVLI · PHILIPPI · INVICTI PII · FELI-
CIS · AVG ET MARCIAE · OTACILIAE SEVERAE · AVG ·
AQVAE · FONTIS · QVAE · MVLTO · TEMPORE DEPERIERAT ·
ET · CIVES · INOPIA · AQVAE LABORABANT · INSTANTIA ·
M · AVRELII · ATHONIS · MARCELLI · V · E · PROC · AVGG
· RARISSIMI · PRAESIDIS N PATRONI · MVNCIPII ·
INNOVATO · OPERE · AQVAE · DVCTVS · ABVNDANS ·
IN · FONTE EST PERDVCTA.

Sometimes the dedication was to the Empress, shown in an interesting inscription found at Djemila, the ancient Cuiculum, where the designations of wife and mother are clearly expressed, and the full titles of Roman Empresses at this period are set forth.[2]

MARCIAE OTACILIAE SEVERAE
AVG CONIVGI D N IMP CAES
M IVLI PHILIPPI PII FELIC AVG
PONT MAX TRIB POT V COS III
PROCOS P P MAT IMP CAES M IVLI
PHILIPPI AVG F PII FELICIS
PONT MAX TRIB POT II COS
II PROCOS P P PRINCIPIS IV
VENTVTIS AVG ET CASTRO
RVM ET SENATVS ET PATRIAE
RES P CVICVLITANOR DEVOTA
NVMINI MAIESTATIQ EORVM
D D   P P

The prominence given to her name leads one to suppose that Marcia played a conspicuous part in public affairs. Of

---

[1] *C.I.L.* No. 8809. Some attempts at erasure are apparent; *vide Ann. de Const.* 1860-61, p. 226. [2] *C.I.L.* No. 20139.

Philip's career we know but little. As an African he might have been expected to associate his name with some city in his native country, or with some great movement affecting the welfare of his African subjects. But the habits of his youth, trained in the rough ways of the Desert, did not lend themselves to any of the gentler arts of civilisation. During the five years of his reign the excitements of the battle-field and the pleasures of the camp proved more congenial to his tastes than the discharge of civil and administrative duties. Like his immediate predecessors, he shared a similar fate at the hands of his own soldiers, and the favourite of the hour reigned in his stead.

Little information can be gathered from contemporary historians about the progress of civilisation in North Africa during the reigns of the short-lived Emperors in the latter half of the third century. Flavius Vopiscus, as a writer, may be regarded as the most reliable, but he is almost silent on the subject. Inscriptions also give little aid, though the wording of a large number of votive memorials and dedications to honoured citizens is sufficient evidence of a spread of contentment and prosperity, of municipalities increasing in influence and population, and of citizens in the full enjoyment of national security. There were no disturbances to cause disquietude, frontier towns were well protected by numerous *castella*, and the great central garrison at *Lambæsis* was strengthened from time to time by the addition of troops drawn from other parts of the Empire.

The accession of Decius, a native of Bubalia in Lower Pannonia, after the murder of Philip, was favoured by the army and approved by the Senate. His reign for about two years was marked by an incident which affected the welfare of North Africa for at least a generation. Prompted by Pagan fanatics, this Emperor was induced to issue an edict encouraging persecution of Christians in every part of the Empire, with the result that the lives of numerous citizens settled in Africa were sacrificed, and the progress of flourishing law-abiding communities was checked in their civilising career. Beyond this we know little of Decius, but from Aurelius Victor, who wrote about a century later, we learn that this Emperor was highly educated, well trained in all the arts, addicted to virtue, and a brave soldier ; and from the pages of Vopiscus we gather some insight into the character of Decius from the following expression, referring to the Emperors generally and to the few who could be called good princes: *Quam pauci sint principes boni.* And then, in his mention of Decius, he says *Decium excerpere debeam, cujus et vita et mors veteribus comparanda est.* The following inscription on a *milliarium* found between the modern villages of Gastonville and Robertville gives the full titles of this Emperor,[1] the date being A.D. 250:

  IMP CAES C MESSIVS
  QVINTVS TRAIANVS
  DECIVS INICTVS PIVS F
  ELIX AVG PONTIFEX MA
  XIMVS TRIBVNICIAE PO
  TESTATIS CONSVL II PA
  TER PATRIAE PROCONSVL
  VIAM IMBRIBVS ET VETVS
  TATE CONLABSAM CVM
  PONTIBVS RESTITVIT

Another interesting inscription on a *milliarium* discovered in North Africa, bearing the same date, includes the name of his son Herennius, as well as of Hostilianus, both of whom were associated with him in imperial dignity.[2] Neither of these Cæsars acceded to the throne. In this latter inscription the name of Decius is misspelt, a common failing in Roman lettering. There are about seven inscriptions in North Africa bearing the name of Decius. Decius *filius* is mentioned in two of them, and Hostilianus in one only, as above recorded.

  IMP · CAES · C · MESSIVS
  Q · TRAIANVS · DECCIVS
  INVICTVS · PIVS · FELIX · AVG
  P · M · TRIB · P · COS · II · P · P · PROCOS
  ET · Q · HERENNIVS · ETRVSCVS
  MESSIVS · DECCIVS · CAESAR
  ET · C · VALENS · HOSTILIANVS
  MESSIVS QVINTVS. . . . . .

There is little need to make more than passing mention of the Emperors between the death of Decius, A.D. 251, and the accession of Diocletian, A.D. 283. Although their names inscribed in marble or stone have been found in so many parts

---

[1] *C.I.L.* No. 10318. *Arch. des Miss. Scient.* 1875, p. 412.
[2] *C.I.L.* No. 10051. A *milliarium* formerly to be seen in the ducal palace at Florence, but now lost. *Vide* Orelli, No. 992.

Africa under the later Emperors

of North Africa, the wording of most of the memorials throws little light on contemporary history. In nearly all cases we are confronted with the usual magniloquent titles peculiar to the Emperors of the third century, lacking that dignity of expression and pride of lineage which graced the names of the Cæsars till the time of Septimius Severus. Gallus, the successor of Decius, and his rival Æmilianus the Moor, who aspired to the purple, might be passed by without comment, were it not for several dedications in their honour on milliary columns. With Gallus was associated his son Volussianus, who shared with his father, after a reign of about two years, the usual fate reserved for Emperors of this period. A column recording their joint names was found at a place called Ngaous in the Hodna, but is now serving as a pillar in a neighbouring mosque. The lettering was copied by MM. De la Mare and Collineau, and is thus rendered by these experts : [1]

| IMPP |
| DD NN |
| CVIBIO TR |
| EBONIO GA |
| LLO ET C VIBI |
| O A FINIO G |
| ALLO VALD |
| VMIAN VOL |
| VSSIANO INVI |
| CTISSIMIS PR |
| CIPIB PP MA |
| AVGG NN II |
| COSS PP |

Imperatoribus dominis nostris Caio Vibio Trebonio Gallo et Caio Vibio Afinio Gallo Valdumiano Volussiano, invictissimis principibus, pontificibus maximis, Augustis nostris, bis consulibus, patribus patriæ.

Of Æmilianus, their successor, we only know that his claim was acknowledged by the Senate, and that he fell a victim to his soldiers after an imaginary reign of a few months. In North Africa the name of this almost forgotten Cæsar is recorded on a milliary stone found on the road between Lambæsis and Diana.[2]

IMP CAES
M AEMI
LIVS AE
MILIANV
S PIVS FE
LIX AVG

[1] *I.R.A.* No. 1672. [2] *I.R.A.* No. 4338.

The reign of Gallus had no influence on African progress, nor is there a single monument in that country associated with his name. We are told by Aurelius Victor that he was raised to the purple in the island of Meninx, immortalised by Homer as the island of the Lotophagi,[1] but better known in modern times by the name of Djerba. The quotation from this author, *Creati in insula Meninge, quæ nunc Girba dicitur*, implies that both Gallus and his son attained imperial dignity at the same time. Archæological research has not hitherto been successful in bringing to light the remains of any monumental edifices or other memorial of their reign in that far-off island. There is little in the present day to indicate the character of the buildings which once covered a large area at El-Kantara overlooking the straits which separate Djerba from the mainland, but the wealth of marble and sculptured stones scattered over the surface bears testimony to the existence, at that period of Roman history, of a city of renown, probably the capital of the island, and bearing the name of Meninx.

The short rule of Gallus, conspicuous for cruelty and indifference to the welfare of the State, was followed by the comparatively long and active reign of Valerianus and his son Gallienus. Inscriptions relating to these Emperors are numerous enough in all parts of the Empire, and in no country are the dedications more clearly worded than in North Africa.

Sometimes the names of father and son appear together, as in the following inscription of eight lines on a column at Cirta, now built into the wall of a house at Constantine:[2]

IMP · CAES · P · LICINIO   *Imperatori Cæsari Publio Licinio*
VALERIANO INVICTO   *Valeriano invicto pio felici Augusto*
PIO FEL AVG PONT MAX   *pontifici maximo tribuniciæ potestatis,*

---

[1] It seems strange that the lotus referred to in the *Odyssey* has not been satisfactorily identified. Shaw speaks of the seedra or lotus, in appearance not unlike a blackthorn. This has been recognised as the *zizyphus* lotus or jujube tree, which bears a fruit hardly eatable in its wild state, but when cultivated is somewhat better. But how does this agree with the passage in Homer? 'Whosoever did eat the honey-sweet fruit of the lotus had no longer any desire to bring tidings nor to return, but to abide with the lotus-eating men, ever feeding on the lotus and forgetful of the homeward way.' Rather let us search for this delectable food, observed the late Sir R. Lambert Playfair, in the island of Djerba of our own times, and claim as the lotus of the ancient world the most beneficent fruit which Providence ever bestowed on man—the honey-sweet date of the modern Arab.

[2] *I.R.A.* No. 1842.

Africa under the later Emperors 241

TRB PPPPROC ET
IMP CAES P LICINIO
GALLIENO INVICTO
PIO FELICE AVG PONT
MAX TRB P P P

patri patriæ, proconsuli, et imperatori Cæsari Publio Licinio Gallieno invicto pio felici Augusto pontifici maximo, tribuniciæ potestatis, patri patriæ.

Another interesting inscription, in which many of the words are linked together, may still be seen in the public gardens at Setif. It is a dedication by the veterans residing at Sitifis· to the family of Valerian, and bears the names of his son Gallienus, and of his two grandsons Valerianus and Saloninus. This inscription has attracted the attention of several epigraphists, and has been deciphered by Wilmanns, Berbrugger, Creully, and others:[1]

Divo Cæsari Publio Cornelio Licinio Valeriano, nepoti imperatoris Cæsaris Publii Licinii Valeriani Augusti, filio imperatoris Cæsaris Publii Licinii Gallieni Augusti, fratri Publii Cornelii Licinii Salonini nobilissimi Cæsaris Augusti, colonia Nerviana Augusta Martialis veteranorum Sitifensium, decreto decurionum, pecunia publica.

Of still greater interest is the inscription on a broken milliary column found near Khenschela (the ancient Mascula), being a dedication by its citizens to the three Emperors, father, son, and grandson, coupling with their names Cornelia Salonina, the illustrious wife of Gallienus:[2]

IMPPP DDD NNN
P LICINIO VALERIANO
ET P LICINIO EGNATIO
GALLIENO PIIS FELI AV (*sic*)
GVSTIS ET P CORNELIO
LICINIO VALERIANO NO
BILISSIMO CAESARI
ET CORNELIAE SALO
NINAE AVG
R · P · M · M

The last line may be read, according to Wilmanns, *Respublica municipii Masculatani.* It is gratifying to find the name of this excellent princess, who was distinguished for her virtues, her tender regard for the welfare of the people, and her liberal patronage of the arts of peace, recorded on a pedestal in a remote corner of the proconsular province of Africa, not far from the city of Tunis. This stone was unearthed about forty

[1] *I.R.A.* No. 3282. [2] *C.I.L.* No. 17680.

years ago by M. Guérin, and, according to his interpretation, is clearly worded.[1]

> CORNELIAE SALONINAE
> PIAE CONIVGI · D · N
> IMP · CAES · P · LICINI
> EGNATI GALLIENI PII
> FEL · AVG · MVNIC · AVREL
> VINA · DEVOT · NVMINI
> MAIESTATIQVE EIVS

A special value is attached to this discovery, for it proves that the scattered remains where this slab was found, at a place now called Henchir-el-Khanga, are those of the old *Municipium Aurelia Vina*, the existence of which had hitherto been unknown. It is probable that the inhabitants of this *municipium* had good cause for raising this memorial to so worthy an Empress as Cornelia Salonina.

It was during the reigns of Valerianus and Gallienus that the edict issued by their predecessor Decius for the suppression of Christianity throughout the Empire came into full operation, and was followed by such lamentable results in the chief cities of North Africa. The progress of the Christian Church in any of the Roman provinces is too large a subject to be dealt with in this slight outline of the history of the Roman occupation of this country, but it is so intimately interwoven with the life of the people that it merits more than passing mention. From the time of Nero, whose memory is associated with the first imperial persecution of Christians in Rome, down to the proclamation of the edict of Decius, the Church had been subject at intervals to the attacks of Pagan fanatics, and had more than recovered its ground on each occasion. But its existence as a Church, or organised form of a distinct religion, had not been regarded as illegal till Trajan found himself forced to issue an edict for its suppression in order to soothe the growing animosity between votaries of the old and the new cult. During his reign Christian communities were becoming a source of disquietude to provincial governors on account of their extended operations and the social position of many Roman citizens who had embraced the new creed. From Pliny, the governor of Bithynia and friendly correspondent of the Emperor Trajan, we gather

[1] *Vide* Guérin, *Voyage en Tunisie*, vol. ii. p. 264.

some idea of the anxiety which troubled him in dealing with recalcitrants in his far-distant province. So rapidly, he tells us, was Christianity spreading that the ancient temples were being deserted, and votive offerings to the gods he was taught to reverence were daily becoming matters of indifference. If such a state of things prevailed in a country of such secondary importance, how much more potent in its results would be the working of a similar movement in so renowned a centre of intellectual thought, and the home of so vast a population, as the city of Carthage! The schools of rhetoric and philosophy, which had been firmly established there during the rule of the Antonines, had attracted men of eminence from all parts of the Empire, and had made Carthage inferior only to Rome as a seat of learning in the second century. As a stronghold of Christianity it had asserted its authority in the time of Septimius Severus, when Tertullian, a native of that city and the first in point of date of the Latin Fathers, stands forth pre-eminently as the pioneer of the Church in Africa. The gentle rule of the Antonines had been tolerant of all forms of religion, and had given more tacit encouragement to freedom of thought than was accorded at any later period of the Empire. For more than eighty years, dating from the accession of Hadrian to the firm establishment of imperial government under Septimius Severus, Christian communities had enjoyed almost unrestrained liberty of action, and had extended the sphere of their operations into remote parts of the Empire. But their labours received a severe check when Tertullian of Carthage, a master of rhetoric, openly preached the new doctrine to not unwilling ears, and helped to provoke an edict by Severus for the suppression of all forms of Christian worship. Some thirty years later Alexander Severus, instigated by his ministers rather than from personal inclination, issued a similar proclamation; but it was not till the reign of Decius, A.D. 249–251, that Pagan zealots found in the African Church a field for systematic persecution, and invoked the Senate at Rome and the governors of provinces to refuse protection to any followers of the new creed. It is in this stage of the history of the Church that we are brought face to face with the fact that 'it was through Africa that Christianity became the religion of the world. Tertullian and Cyprian were from Carthage, Arnobius from Sicca Veneria, Lactantius and probably in like manner Minucius Felix were, in spite of their Latin names, natives of Africa, and not less so Augustine. In Africa the Church found its most zealous confessors of the faith and its most gifted defenders.'[1] Cyprian, too, passes across the stage at a period when Carthage was at the height of its renown. It was within the city walls that he pleaded the cause of Christianity, and it was on the summit of the citadel hill, where now stands the cathedral of St. Louis, that Cyprian convened a great Council of the Church, when no less than eighty-seven bishops from the provinces of Africa, Numidia, and Mauritania obeyed his summons. We may pass over the minor persecutions suffered by Christians in Africa during the latter half of the third century, for they all pale in their cruelty before the forcible edict of Diocletian, A.D. 303, which was nothing less than a determination on the part of that powerful Emperor to extirpate the Church for ever from his dominions. For ten years the battle of rival religions raged with terrible severity, and the slumbering passions of Pagan fanatics awoke to deeds of tyranny in every part of the Empire. But the violence of the movement, encouraged at a time when Christianity in Africa was a factor in national life, too deeply rooted to be overthrown by the force of an imperial edict, was the cause of its ill-success. Like all revolutionary measures, animated by the uncontrolled passions of a people, it caused a reaction which, in this case, culminated in the overthrow of the temples of the gods, and the unfurling the banner of the Cross in Italy and the provinces. The rising generation of citizens, who witnessed the cruelty and destruction of life resulting from the edict of Decius, lived to see some thirty years later the religion of Christ preached in basilica and forum in every city and town in the Empire. Nowhere in Africa was this reactionary movement more conspicuous than in Carthage, the metropolis of Africa, and Cirta, the capital of old Numidia. Unnumbered inscriptions brought to light in the latter city and its neighbourhood testify to the weight of authority exercised there by Christian writers in the time of Constantine, and to the affectionate regard in which the first of the Christian Emperors was held by citizens in every rank of life. With the fall of Paganism Cirta ceased

---

[1] T. Mommsen, *The African Provinces*, vol. ii. p. 345.

to exist, and the city of Constantine as a stronghold of Christianity rose triumphantly in its place.

The activity of the Church in Africa may be said to have come to a close with the Vandal invasion of the country under Genseric A.D. 429, and its last days may truly be associated with the undying memory of the venerable St. Augustine and his revered mother, the saintly Monnica. There are few spots in North Africa more reverenced by travellers, or more endeared to students of history, than the site of *Hippo Regius*, the *Ubba* of the Carthaginians, the *Hippone* of the Romans, and the scene of the lifelong labours of St. Augustine. What the Vandals did not reduce to ashes in the fifth century the Arabs did two centuries later, and with the stones of the Roman city the modern town of Bone, one mile and a half distant, was constructed. Nature has dealt very kindly with this hallowed spot. The hills where Roman citizens were wont to throng are now clothed with perennial verdure, while above the soft covering, grey fragments of Roman wall still rear their heads into the blue air sweet with perfume, for nowhere in all Algeria do the trees put forth their leaves in wilder luxuriance, the olive and the aloe, the acanthus and the pomegranate. And this peaceful shaded spot was once the capital of Eastern Numidia, a seat of commerce and prosperity, and the home of the chief Father of the Church in Africa. This is nature's memorial to one who combined the courage of the Roman with the devotional spirit of a true Christian.

Among the leading incidents affecting the African provinces during the reigns of Valerianus and Gallienus, mention should be made of the rising of the Quinquegentians, or, as it is commonly called, the Feud of the Five Peoples.[1] These five tribes are said to have occupied the region between Saldæ and Cissi, and to have had great reputation for their warlike qualities. (1) The *Masinissenses* were evidently the descendants

[1] This invasion of Numidia by the Quinquegentians taxed to the utmost the military skill of Maximianus, and his success was the cause of unusual rejoicing. At the close of the campaign Mamertinus (*Paneg. Vet.* vi. 18) addressed the conqueror in the following words: *Tu ferocissimos Mauretaniæ populos, inaccessis montium jugis et naturali munitione fidentes, expugnasti, recepisti, transtulisti!* One of these five tribes, called the *Fraxinenses*, were the ancestors, according to M. Berbrugger, of that branch of the Kabyles now known as the Beni-Fraoucen. (*Bull. de Corr. Afric.* i. p. 257.)

of followers of the hero of Numidia, and are still to be traced on the right bank of the Oued Sahel. (2) The *Jubaleni* may be claimed as descendants of the scattered army of the unfortunate Juba I. (3) The *Isaflenses*, now known as the Flissa. (4) The *Tyndenses*, still occupying passes of the Djurdjura under another name. And (5) the *Fraxinenses*, probably named after their chief Faraxen. The origin of the rising of certain tribes is not stated either by Eutropius or Aurelius Victor, but it is on record that it was not easily suppressed, and that some twenty years later the Emperor Maximianus went personally to Africa for the purpose of quelling the insurrection. Fortunately an inscription found in the temple of Æsculapius at Lambessa comes to our aid, and throws considerable light on a subject about which contemporary authors are almost silent.[1] The date, according to Wilmanns, is A.D. 260.

I · O · M
CETERISQ DIIS DEABVSQVE IMMORTALIB
C MACRINIVS DECIANVS V C LEG
AVGG PR PR PROV NVMIDIAE ET NO
RICI BAVARIBVS QVI ADVNATIS IIII
REGIBVS IN PROV NVMIDIAM IN
RVPERANT PRIMVM IN REGIONE
MILLEVITANA ITERATO IN CONFI
NIO MAVRETANIAE ET NVMIDI
AE TERTIO QVINQVEGENTANEIS
GENTILIBVS MAVRETANIAE CAE
SARIENSIS ITEM GENTILIBVS FRA
XINENSIBVS QVI PROVINCIAM
NVMIDIAM VASTABANT CAP
TO FAMOSISSIMO DVCE EORVM
CAESIS FVGATISQVE

Jovi Optimo maximo ceterisque diis deabusque immortalibus, C. Macrinius Decianus, vir clarissimus, legatus Augustorum duorum, pro prætore provinciarum Numidiæ et Norici, Bavaribus, qui adunatis IIII regibus in provinciam Numidiam inruperant, primum in regione Millevitana, iterato in confinio Mauretaniæ et Numidiæ, tertio Quinquegentaneis gentilibus Mauretaniæ Cæsariensis, item gentilibus Fraxinensibus, qui provinciam Numidiam vastabant, capto famosissimo duce eorum, cæsis fugatisque.

The two Augusti referred to are Valerianus and Gallienus, and the *dux famosissimus eorum* appears to have been, according

[1] *C.I.L.* No. 2615. *Rev. arch.* 1861, p. 55.

to Wilmanns's interpretation of the inscription, Faraxen, who may have given his name to the tribe of Fraxinenses. There are three other inscriptions in North Africa relating to this disturbance, but none of them throw any additional light on the subject.

Whatever may have been the merits attributed to Claudius the Dalmatian, who succeeded Gallienus on the throne of the Cæsars, there is nothing to indicate that he took any part in African affairs during a short reign of two years. Undaunted bravery combined with administrative ability and great benevolence of character secured the affection of his subjects, and prompted the Senate on one special occasion to address him as *Claudi Auguste, tu frater, tu pater, tu amicus, tu bonus senator, tu vere princeps*. His successful campaign against the Goths justified his acceptance of the new title of Gothicus, and it was probably on his return from this expedition that the citizens of *Thubursicum Numidarum*, now known as Khamisa, raised a statue or other memorial in his honour with the following inscription :[1]

IMP · CAES · M · AVRELIO · CLAVDIO
PIO · FELICI · AVG · P · M · GOTHICO · M
PARTHICO · M · TRIB · P · III · COS · II · P · P
PROCOS · RESPVB · COLONIAE
THVBVRS · NVMIDARVM

The mention of the city itself happens to be of considerable value, because it settles the site of the ancient *Thubursicum*, which up till that time had been a matter of doubt. Although only partly explored, there is ample evidence, from the extent of the remains, of the existence of a city of great importance and the seat of a large population. The ruined theatre at Thubursicum, for instance, among other monumental ruins, may still be seen, with its stone seats sparsely covered with vegetation, its entrances clearly defined, and a series of rooms grouped around, indicating by its dimensions and arrangements that it was designed to meet the requirements of a populous city.

In the short space of eleven years following the death of Claudian, no fewer than eight emperors ascended the throne,

[1] *C.I.L.* No. 4876. *Rec. de Const.* 1866, p. 134.

two of them only, Aurelian and Probus, reigning for a comparatively long period of five and six years respectively. Florian, a name almost forgotten, had a career of sixty days, and Tacitus, who merited a long run of imperial power as a reward for his excellent rule, fell a victim to disease or the dagger after a reign of two hundred days. With the exception of Florus their names are all faithfully recorded on column or pedestal in many parts of North Africa, in some instances being simply dedications to the Emperor of the day, while in others the wording employed is of more laudatory character. Aurelian appears to have taken no personal interest in his African possessions, but his brilliant successes in other parts of the world, notably his expedition against the celebrated Zenòbia, made his name an honoured one. As an example of a dedication, which may be assigned to A.D. 274, the following, in the form of a milliary column, found near Thamugas, gives the usual titles linked with his name:[1]

> PERPETVO VICTORI
> OSISSIMO INDVL
> GENTISSIMO IMP
> RESTITVTORI OR
> BIS · L · DOMITIO
> AVRELIANO PIO
> FELICI AVG · PONT
> MAX · TRIB · POT · V
> COS II · P · P · PROCOS
> RES · P · COL · THA
> MVG
> _____
> VIIII

Aurelian may fairly lay claim to the title *restitutor orbis*, for during his active career he is said to have delivered the Empire from all her enemies. It is also stated that, on the occasion of one of his triumphal entries into Rome, he exhibited in his train the people of no less than fifteen different nations whom he had subdued. The name of his successor, Tacitus, is recorded on several *milliaria* in the following words;[2] and we learn from Vopiscus that, during his short reign, the Senate recovered its ancient dignity and long-lost privileges:

[1] *C.I.L.* No. 10217. [2] *C.I.L.* No. 10072.

                FORTISSI
                MO IMPET
                PACATORI
                ORBIS M CLA
                VDIO TACI
                TO PIO FEL
                  AVG

In testimony of this beneficial change in the administration of the affairs of the Empire, both civil and military, the same author quotes a circular letter on the subject which was addressed to the *Curia* at Carthage, similar letters being subsequently sent to Alexandria, Antioch, Corinth, Milan, Athens, Thessalonica, and to the *Curia Trevirorum*. It ran thus: 'The right of bestowing the Empire and of nominating the rulers of the State has returned to the Senate. This precious right should contribute to the glory, the permanency, and the security of the Empire and the world. It is to us, then, you must refer on all matters of importance. It is to the prefect at Rome that all appeals must come—those at least which emanate from the proconsuls and the ordinary tribunals. In taking this step we anticipate for you also a return to your ancient dignity; for, in recovering its old supremacy, the Senate can guarantee the rights of every one.' It is interesting to note that Tacitus, in his desire to beautify the city of Ostia, which had been ennobled by Trajan and other emperors, despatched from the Numidian quarries no less than 100 marble columns 23 feet high for the adornment of its porticoes; and, learning that the roofs of the Capitol at Rome were in bad condition, this beneficent Emperor sold his estates in Mauritania to provide the funds necessary for the purpose.

So little is known of the other Cæsars prior to the accession of Diocletian, that their names might be passed by without comment. Inscriptions in Africa are not numerous, and their wording throws little light on the history of this period. Even Probus, whose career between A.D. 276 and 282 was conspicuous for unvarying success, has left few memorials of his activity. From Vopiscus we learn that this Emperor carried his arms into the remote region of Marmarica, lying between Cyrene and Egypt, and stretching far into the great Libyan Desert. Having subdued the tribes which harassed the Roman frontiers of Tripoli, he passed on to Carthage and successfully quelled a disturbance which had broken out among the native population. We then find him doing battle with Aradion, an African chief, who had rebelled against Roman authority. To mark his appreciation of the daring of his rival, who was slain in the fight, the Emperor raised a lordly monument in his honour, which Vopiscus describes as being nearly 200 feet in height. From the brief mention of this tomb, which existed as a mound for a long period, it was probably of the same type as the Medrassen, and the tomb of Juba II. already referred to. For all these achievements on African soil only six inscriptions bearing the name of Probus have as yet been discovered. None of them have any special character, either in the form of dedication or the titles of the Emperor. The following memorial on a *milliarium* at Ain-Hedjah, the ancient *Agbia*, is worth noting : [1]

IMP · CAESARI
M · AVRELIO
PROBO · PIO
FELICI · AVG
PONTIF · MA
XIMO · TRIB

The only variation noticeable in other inscriptions is the addition of the words *et tota divina domus*.

The career of Probus's successor, Carus, was too brief to exercise any influence on Roman progress either in Italy or in the provinces, but it proved attractive to Roman citizens in North Africa, in spite of the Emperor's unpopularity with the Senate. There are many dedications in his honour, the inscriptions generally bearing the names of his two sons, Carinus and Numerianus, who were conjointly created Caesars. The following inscription on a column at Ain-Amara, near *Tibilis*, is a fair example.[2] Carinus, his successor, a man devoid of all the qualities which should adorn an Emperor, appears to have been held in honour by African citizens.

[1] *C.I.L.* No. 10085. For a description of Agbia or *municipium Agbiensium*, *vide* Guérin, vol. ii. p. 144. An inscription at Chidibbia, *C.I.L.* No. 1329, and another at Testour, *C.I.L.* No. 1358, are dedications to Probus *et tota divina domus*.
[2] *C.I.L.* No. 10157. *Vide* Poulle, *Rec. de Const.* 1876-7, p. 538.

Africa under the later Emperors

<pre>
        IMP · CAES · M
        AVRELIO · CARO · IN
        VICTO · PIO · FELICI
        AVG · ET · M · AVREL
        IO CARINO · ET · M · AV
        RELIO NVMERIA
        NO NOBILISSIMIS CAE
        SARIBVS · S · S
</pre>

The following interpretation of an inscription on a pedestal at Guelma, the ancient *Kalama*, would have been applicable to a Trajan or an Alexander Severus rather than to so base and worthless a ruler.[1] Thus say the citizens of *Kalama*: *Marco Aurelio Carino, nobilissimo Cæsari Augusto, principi juventutis, consuli, filii Imperatoris Cæsaris Marci Aurelii Cari, Invicti, Pii Felicis Augusti, patris patriæ, tribuniciæ potestatis II. pontificis maximi, consulis, proconsulis, fratri Marci Aurelii Numeriani, nobilissimi Cæsaris Augusti, principis juventutis. Respublica coloniæ Kalamensium, curante Macrinio Sossiano, clarissimo viro, curatore reipublicæ.* The name of the Empress Urbica, wife of Carinus, is wellnigh forgotten, but here on the outskirts of the ruined city of Thamugas, on an octagonal pedestal now built into the enclosing wall of a sewer, a record of her existence may still be read in imperishable lettering.[2]

<pre>
        MAGNIAE
        VRBICAE
        AVG · MA
        TRI CAS
        TRORVM   Magniæ Urbicæ Augustæ, matri castro-
        SENATVS   rum, senatus ac patriæ, conjugi domini
        AC PATRI   nostri Carini invicti Augusti.
        AE CONIV
        GI D N CA
        RINI IN
        VICTI
        AVG
</pre>

The names of Carinus and Numerianus occur on an inscribed slab found on the north side of the necropolis at Marcouna, the ancient Verecunda. It is a dedication by Marcus Aurelius

---

[1] *I.R.A.* No. 2726, copied by Gen. Creully.
[2] *I.R.A.* No. 1512.

Decimus, *vir perfectissimus, præses provinciæ Numidiæ*. The date is A.D. 284, the year of their accession.[1]

PRO SALVTE IMPP FF DD NN CARINI ET NVMERIANI
DIVI CARI GENITORIS EORVM TEMPLVM A FVNDA
MENTIS R P MVN VERECVNDENSIVM CONSTITVIT DEDI-
CANTE
M AVRELIO DECIMO VPPPN

A very similar inscription of the same date was discovered in another part of the ancient Verecunda, but the dedication is to these joint Emperors as *pontificibus maximis*. In one instance, a *milliarium* at Ksar Kalaba, the ancient Gibba, the name of Numerian stands alone.[2]

IMP D NOSTR
O M AVRELIO N
VMERIO NVM
ERIANO NOB
ILISSIMO CAESA
RI CONSVLI DE
SIG

The history of all nations is marked by certain epochs, establishing periods of either rise or decline. The great Latin families, who had stocked the throne of the Cæsars for more than two centuries, had long since ceased to assert their claim to power through any collateral branches. For more than a hundred years after the death of the contemptible Commodus the throne was open to any one who combined military experience with the daring of an adventurer. Rank and fortune were totally disregarded by the Senate as well as by the army; and, in many instances, the man of the hour who seized his opportunities when a vacancy was declared or expected was considered equal to the task of ruling over the then known world. It is a far step from Julius and Augustus, Trajan and Antonine, to Philip the obscure, or Probus the gardener's son. And yet the successor of Carinus, a man sprung from the labouring classes, and commencing life in the lower ranks of the army, succeeded by the mere force of genius in creating an epoch in Roman history conspicuous for the display of some of

[1] *I.R.A.* 1433, copied and deciphered by Renier.
[2] *C.I.L.* No. 10283. *Vide* Payen, *Ann. de Const.* 1860-61, p. 125.

Africa under the later Emperors 253

the highest qualities of statesmanship. The reign of Diocletian, extending over a period of twenty-one years, is remarkable for an entire change in the administration of the Empire, and for a movement which, in the succeeding century, hastened its collapse. Attempts had been made by previous emperors, notably Marcus Aurelius with Verus as joint Cæsar, and still more so in the case of the Gordians, to divide imperial authority. It cannot be said that this initiatory movement was attended with success. But Diocletian was a man of broad views and great determination. He found the Empire to which he succeeded too vast in extent and peopled by too many nationalities, many of them still on the verge of barbarism, to be controlled by a single ruler. Grasping the situation with a more enlarged mind than most of his predecessors, he determined, as a preliminary step, to create two divisions of the Empire, the ruler of each division being clothed with absolute authority over the provinces committed to his charge. To Maximian, a man of obscure origin, sprung from the peasant class, who had been his loyal colleague in many campaigns, he ceded the command of Italy, Spain, Africa, and the western dominions, reserving for himself the rest of the Empire. Their joint rule is recorded on a slab at Lambæsis dedicated to Jupiter and Hercules as guardians of the two Emperors who are *pontifices maximi*, to which are added the names of Constantius Chlorus and Galerius Valerius Maximianus, who were acclaimed Cæsars at the same time : [1]

> IOVI ET HERCVLI
> COMITIBVS IMPPM
> DIOCLETIANI ET
> MAXIMIANI AVGG
> CONSTANTI ET
> MAXIMIANI

In less than four years after his accession Diocletian again divided the Empire, giving Maximian rule over Spain, Africa, and Italy, ceding Pannonia and Mœsia to Galerius, Gaul and Britain to Constantius, the eastern part of the Empire, including Egypt, being reserved for himself. There are several inscriptions in North Africa recording the names of these four Augusti, the words *pontifices maximi* being in all cases omitted. The following inscription, brought to light some years ago in the city

[1] *C.I.L.* No. 18230.

of Kairouan, when some repairs were in progress outside the Great Mosque, is an example of a dedication to the four Emperors on the occasion of the reconstruction of a temple sacred to Pluto :

 DEO · PLVTONI · SACR · PRO · SALV
 TE · DDDD · NNNN · DIOCLETIA
 NI · ET · MAXIMIANI · ET · CONSTANTI · ET
 MAXIMIANI · NOBILISSIMI · CAESSSS · CO
 TEMPLVM · PLVTONIS · LABSVM · ET
 DEDICATVM · PER · INSTANTIA · FELICI
 C · AELI · FORTVNATI · ET · L · C · ANTONI · NARSVA
 TIS · MAGG · FD · IVB · L · ET · FORTVNATVS ALIQVA
 TIS · ARCARIVS · ET · IV · HIN · POET · MAIEST · CVRA

The rendering of the concluding words in the last line, which is not very legible, is, according to Mommsen, *etiam hi numinis potestatem et majestatem curantes*.[1]

A subdivision of the great provinces of the Empire was one of Diocletian's early undertakings. Africa comprised seven sections, one only, (1) Mauritania Tingitana, being attached to the province of Spain, the others being (2) Zeugitania and (3) Byzacena, which had proconsular rank ; (4) Numidia Cirtensis, governed by a consul ; and (5) Numidia Militiana, (6) Mauritania Sitifensis, and (7) Mauritania Cæsariensis, under the control of a præses. Among the dedicatory inscriptions to Diocletian alone, there is one in the public gardens at Setif which may be assigned to A.D. 288 :

 D · N · IMP CAES
 C VALERIO AVRE
 LIO DIOCLETIANO
 INVIC PIO FEL AVG
 PONTIF MAX TRIB
 P V CONS III P P
 PROCOS
 FLAVIVS PECV
 ARIVS V P PRAE
 SES PROV MAVR
 CAES DEVOTVS
 NVMINI MAIES
 TATIQVE EIVS

[1] *C.I.L.* No. 11217. Descr. Broadley, *Tunis, Past and Present*, vol. ii. p. 164. Another dedication to the four Emperors was found at Tipasa (about sixty miles west of Algiers), *vide* S. Gsell, *De Tipasa, Mauretaniæ Cæsariensis urbe*, p. 102, Algerii, 1894 ; and a third between Macomades and Sigus in the province of Numidia, *Rec. de Const.* 1867, p. 238.

Africa under the later Emperors 255

According to Wilmanns, the name of the Emperor in the third line has been erased in the usual way, but the interest lies in the recognition of the title *præses* as president or governor of the province of *Mauritania Cæsariensis*.[1]

It is generally assumed that this title originated with Diocletian in connection with his new system of provincial administration, and that a separation of the civil from the military authority necessitated the use of a distinct title for the representative of civil government. But inscriptions fortunately come to our aid, and give clear indication that the word had long been in common use without any express definition of its meaning. So far back as the joint reign of Marcus Aurelius and Lucius Verus we find this word *præses* on a memorial slab, which may still be studied in the museum at Algiers. It is a dedication to the wife of a *legatus Augustorum duorum proprætor, clarissimus vir, præses* :

AELIAE
PROSPERAE · C · F
CONIVGI · C
POMPONI · MAGNI
LEG · AVGG · PR · PR
STRATORES

the term *vir clarissimus* indicating, as usual, that the *legatus* was of senatorial rank. At a still earlier period the word *præses* had a significance not easy to define, for we find in the time of Vespasian a *procurator et præses provinciæ Sardiniæ*, and a *præses provinciæ Tingitanæ*. The exact meaning has been well expressed by a recent author in the following words:[2] 'The word *præses*, as a technical and legal term, designates a governor of equestrian rank. The title of *præses*, in its proper sense, signifies a governor who is not a senator, *i.e.* a procurator, and is the sole title of a knight, as a procurator of a province, who is qualified to govern. *Præses*, in short, is sometimes invested with supreme civil authority in the government of a province. But it is also a general term, and, like the Greek word ἡγεμών, may be applicable to magistrates of the first rank.' In its more extended use the title may even be given to governors of senatorial rank. *Præsidis nomen*, says Macer (Dig. i. 18, 1), *generale est, eoque et*

---

[1] *C.I.L.* No. 8474. *Vide* De la Mare, *Explor.* tab. 87, also *Ann. de Const.* 1862, p. 173.

[2] Gustave Boissière, *Esquisse d'une Histoire de la Conquête et de l'Administration Romaines dans le Nord de l'Afrique*, p. 293. Paris, 1878.

proconsules, et legati Cæsaris, et omnes provincias regentes, licet senatores sint, præsides appellantur. From this we may infer that the meaning was not strictly defined till the time of Carinus, exemplified in the inscription (p. 252) where Marcus Aurelius Decimus, governor of Numidia, A.D. 283-285, is designated as V. P. P. P. N. And as one of the last discovered inscriptions relating to a governor of Numidia, who bore the title of *legatus* and *vir clarissimus*, the one given by Renier, attributed to the reign of Gallienus, A.D. 260, is the most notable.[1] The division of Numidia into two parts, Numidia Cirtensis and Numidia Militiana, appears to have been of short duration. In the camp at Lambessa an inscription, A.D. 286 or 287, records the name of M. Aurelius Diogenes, who was at that time governor of the undivided province of Numidia, and in the citadel at Constantine another inscription, probably A.D. 313, is of a similar character. It is during this interval of about twenty-seven years that may be found on some of the monumental remains the letters V. P. P. P. N. M., *vir perfectissimus præses provinciæ Numidiæ Militianæ;* and on others a reference to the existence of the two Numidias under the government of one *præses*.

> AELIVS AELIA
> NVS V P P NVMI
> DIARVM
> RET

Several instances have been furnished by M. Poulle, but in all cases the inscriptions are fragmentary. It is sufficient to state that for a short period there was a Numidia Cirtensis with Cirta for its capital, and Numidia Militiana with Lambæsis for its headquarters, deriving its title from the military character of its population and as the acknowledged centre of military activity in North Africa. Inscriptions relating to the divisions of Mauritania as African provinces are numerous enough, some of them indicating divided control, while others bear record to the appointment of one governor or *præses* for the two divisions. An inscription at Bougie, the ancient Saldæ, is a good example, being a dedication by a *præses* of the two divisions in honour of the Emperor Constantius II.;[2] while another found by Feraud

---

[1] *C.I.L.* No. 2615. A long inscription of sixteen lines on the base of an altar found in the temple of Æsculapius at Lambæsis, already referred to on p. 246.

[2] *C.I.L.* No. 8932. *Ann. de Const.* 1858-59, p. 120.

Africa under the later Emperors

at a place called Bou Grara, in the province of Tripoli, is worthy of mention on account of the letters P · T in the ninth line, clearly meaning *provinciæ Tripolitanæ*.

FELICISSIMO AC
BEATISSIMO PRIN
CIPI D N FLAVIO
IVLIO CONSTANTINO NOBI
LISSIMO CAESARI
FLAVIVS TERENTIA
NVS VP PRAESES PROV
MAVR CAE ET SITIFENSIS
DEVOTVS NVMINI
MAIESTATIQVE
EIVS

DIVINA STIRPE
PROGENITO
D N VALENTINIA
NO AVG
FORTISSIMO
PRINCIPI FL
VIVIVS BENE
DICTVS VP
PRAESES P · T NV
MINI MAIESTA
TIQ EIVS SEM
PER DEVOTVS

The dedication is to Valentinian I. and his heirs, and was probably made, like others of his reign, at the close of a successful campaign for the suppression of the Quadi. A somewhat similar inscription was found at Leptis Magna, the words *provinciæ Tripolitanæ* appearing in full :[1]

DIVINA STIRPE PROGENITO D · N · FORTISSIMO
PRINCIPI VALENTIANI VICTORI PIO FELICI A
TRIVMFATORE SEMPER AVGVSTO FLAVIVS
BENEDICTVS V P PRAESES PROVINCIAE TRIPO
LITANAE NVMINI MAIESTATIQVE EIVS
SEMPER DEVOTVS

The joint rule of Diocletian and Maximian, the one possessing extraordinary qualities as a statesman, the other an unlettered soldier and coarse in habit, was not only conspicuous for great changes in administration, but for marked activity in protecting the frontiers of the Empire from tribal invasions. As governor of Africa, and invested with absolute power, Maximian found ample opportunities for the exercise of his military qualities on the frontier of Mauritania. The rising of the Quinquegentians, which originated in the reign of Gallienus, when C. Macrinius Decianus was governor of Numidia, A.D. 260, had not yet been suppressed. A new leader named Aurelius Julianus headed the revolt and proclaimed himself Emperor. After several desperate engagements he was defeated by Maximian, who personally

[1] *C.I.L.* No. 12.

commanded the Roman legions. So decisive was the victory that it gave rise to general rejoicing and the dedication of statues and altars to both Emperors. At Lambessa, for instance, an inscription found in the camp behind the Prætorium refers to Maximian alone,[1] and close by was discovered another somewhat similar dedication to this Emperor.

PIISSIMO IMP
MAXIMIANO
INVICTO AVG
AC SVPER OMNES
RETRO PRINCIPES
FORTISSIMO PRIN
CIPI SVO AVRELIVS
DIOGENES VPPPN
NVMINI EIVS DI
CATISSIMVS

Piissimo Imperatori Maximiano, invicto, Augusto, ac super omnes retro principes fortissimo, principi suo, Aurelius Diogenes, vir perfectissimus, præses provinciæ Numidiæ numini eius dicatissimus.

The date of this memorial is probably before the joint abdication of these two Emperors.

The settlement of these frontier troubles and the restoration of peace throughout North Africa involved a readjustment of control over this vast additional territory acquired by Roman arms. With this end in view, Diocletian subdivided the provinces, making many of them much smaller and consequently more numerous; and as a further step he divided the whole Empire into *dioceses*,[2] each diocese comprising several provinces. To ensure more direct personal control, the Emperor created a new order of state officials, called *vicarii* or *vice agentes*.[3] These functionaries were to act directly under the Emperor, and were placed in authority over provincial governors of all grades. The whole Empire was divided into twelve dioceses, the largest, *Oriens*, comprising sixteen provinces, and the smallest, *Britannia*, with four provinces. Altogether there were, during his reign, 101 provinces of different grades throughout the Empire. A glance at the map of Africa in the year 297, clearly indicated by M. Champlouis in his excellent chart, shows how the country was divided into dioceses. Commencing at the eastern boundary we

[1] *I.R.A.* No. 110.
[2] The word 'diocese,' now applied to a bishop's province, was used in reference to a number of provinces forming a diocese. For instance, in the diocese of Egypt there were ten provinces.
[3] *Vicarius* may be accepted in its literal meaning, a deputy acting directly between the Emperor and the provincial governors.

find Cyrene, divided into Upper and Lower Libya, attached to the diocese of Oriens. Then we come to the six provinces which constituted the diocese of Africa proper: Tripoli, Byzacene, Zeugitania, Numidia, and the two Mauritanias. Westward was Mauritania Tingitana, which was attached to Spain, as heretofore. These subdivisions of North Africa were undoubtedly attended with beneficial results under the autocratic rule of so great a potentate as Diocletian, and it is reasonable to suppose that, after the restoration of peace from one end of the country to the other consequent upon the defeat of Julian, the citizens of the great towns and the Roman colonists, forming a vast agricultural and industrial population, delighted to do honour to so successful an Emperor. This is attested by a large number of dedicatory inscriptions. But the day was not far distant when the hand of the master was to be withdrawn, and the throne of the Cæsars was to be once more at the mercy of the army and military adventurers. In the revolutionary scheme of administration affecting every branch of national service, nothing tended more to weaken the Empire than the establishment of four Cæsars in different centres. The Senate, as a controlling authority in Rome, ceased to exist, except in name, and Rome was no longer regarded as the metropolis of the Roman world. The Prætorian guard, which had made and unmade Cæsars for so many generations, was reconstituted, without authority or the means of exercising it. It had had its day—a long day of luxury and corruption, of authority abused and discipline neglected. And the prefect of that powerful body, hitherto chosen from senatorial ranks, became an ordinary functionary with very limited authority. On the accession of Constantine the Great the Prætorian guard became little more than a police force, exercising its functions as a body-guard at the different centres of government. The *præfectus prætorio* was not abolished, for we find this official referred to in an inscription found by M. Tissot at a spot near Carthage, now known as Henchir Ain-Fournu. Its ancient name was Furnitanum, evidently a town of some importance, as one of the gates of Carthage was named after it. The date of the inscription is A.D. 366, during the reign of Valentinian. The interpretation is by M. Tissot.[1]

[1] *C.I.L.* No. 10609. Furnis or Furnitanum was situated on the slopes of a hill. At a later date it became the seat of a bishop, and was included in the list of towns

CLEMENTISSIMO
PRINCIPI AC TO
TIVS . . . . .
. . VALENTINI
-NO PRO CONS
FESTI VC SE
CVM ANTONIO DRA
CONTIO VC AGVPP
ORDO FVRNITA
NVS CONSECRAVIT

Clementissimo principi ac totius orbis restitutori domini nostri Valentiniano proconsulatu Festi viri clarissimi, secum Antonio Dracontio viro clarissimo agente vices præfectorium prætorio, ordo Furnitanus consecravit.

Additional interest is attached to this dedication in the use of the words *vice agentes*, implying that Antonius Dracontius was exercising the duties of *vicarius*.

In looking back at this period of Roman history, eventful for the provinces as well as for Rome, one cannot help acknowledging, in the words of a recent writer, that ' Diocletian accomplished a great social change on principles not before recognised in the Western world, and which, to this day, exercise no small influence upon the political condition of Europe.'[1] What Diocletian undertook, and what he succeeded in accomplishing during his reign of twenty-one years, as ruler of the Empire, has commanded the admiration of statesmen in more recent times, but his failure to establish a permanent form of government that would be acceptable to so many nationalities may be attributed to a variety of circumstances far beyond the grasp of human agency. Mr. Arnold has referred to the difficulties under which Diocletian and his successors laboured, and adds that ' Rome had undertaken an impossible task, that of ruling an immense Empire without federation and without a representative system, when the only sources of her power were the supreme central government and the army. It would be puerile, however, to blame her for not having grasped and applied ideas which were foreign to antiquity, and which have only been worked out by the slow experience of centuries. We should rather wonder at what Rome achieved.'[2] With the retirement of Diocletian into private life, A.D. 305, and the simultaneous forced abdication of

---

mentioned by Victor Vitensis as having sent a representative to the Council at Carthage, A.D. 411. The Festus referred to in the inscription was proconsul of Africa A.D. 366.

[1] Smith's *Class. Dict.*, art. 'Diocletian.'
[2] W. T. Arnold, *Roman System of Provincial Administration*, Oxford, 1879.

Africa under the later Emperors

his colleague Maximian, commenced once again the struggle for supremacy, and for a period of seven years battle after battle was fought without decisive issue, till Constantine the Great brought back peace on earth and goodwill amongst men of all countries and all religions.

In a division of the Empire between the two Augusti nominated by Diocletian—Flavius Valerius Constantius (or Constantius Chlorus, as he is commonly called), and Galerius Armentarius—the provinces of Africa were allotted to the former. The following inscription from Tibilis, the modern Announa, seems to testify to the supremacy of Constantius,[1] A.D. 306.

Imperatori Cæsari Flavio Valerio Constantio. invicto, pio, felici Augusto, pontifici maximo, tribuniciæ potestatis XIIII., Imperatori II., Consuli VI., patri patriæ —— P. Valerius Antoninus præses provinciæ Numidiæ Cirtensis, numini majestatique ejus devotus, pecunia publica posuit.

There is another inscription on a milliary stone found at Muzaiaville, supposed to have been the *Tanaramusa* of the Romans, where the two names are associated as Cæsars and not as Augusti.[2] The former of these two dedications was probably to honour the memory of Constantius immediately after his decease, A.D. 306, and the latter records the simple title of these two subordinate Emperors prior to the abdication of Diocletian, A.D. 304.

```
       FLAVIVS VALERI
         VS CONSTAN
        TIVS ET GALE
        RIVS VALERIVS
         MAXIMIANVS
           NOBILISS
            CAESS
             MP
            XVIII
```

The short rule of fifteen months enjoyed by Constantius as joint Emperor with Galerius, and his earlier career under the sway of Diocletian, were conspicuous for benevolence and humanity. As the husband of the saintly Helena and the father of Constantine the Great, Constantius merits a high place among the later Emperors, but he was unfortunate in his colleague. As

---

[1] *C.I.L.* No. 5526. [2] *C.I.L.* No. 10445. *Rev. Afr.* x. p. 359.

a man of good breeding and liberal education, as well as trained to the exercise of authority, he could have had little in common with so rough and unpolished a man as Galerius. It was equally unfortunate that, on his elevation to the dignity of Cæsar, he was compelled, for political reasons, to renounce his wife Helena, and to accept in her place a spouse nominated by Diocletian. But his happy relationship with the former appears to have governed his actions in later life, and the teachings of a woman, who passed all the days of a long career in endeavours to ameliorate the condition of the Christian populations of the Empire and to further the cause of Christianity, were not lost upon so benevolent and thoughtful an Emperor. Inscriptions relating to Helena are rarely met with. It is therefore gratifying to find her name recorded on a pedestal of white marble found at El-Kef, the ancient Sicca Veneria, at one period renowned for its Pagan ceremonials, and in later years the adopted home of some of the early fathers of the Christian Church. The dedication is probably the date of her decease, A.D. 326, and is in other respects interesting on account of the unusual wording of the eighth line, *curator reipublicæ et duovir*.[1]

        DOMINAE
        NOSTRAE
        FLAVIAE
        HELENAE
          AVG
        M · VALER
        GVPASIVS · V · C
        CVR · REIP · ET · D · V · DE
        VOT · NVMINI · MA
        IESTATIQVE EIVS

    Both in Gaul and Britain, which also fell to the share of Constantius, the Christians suffered neither harm nor persecution, although the edict issued by Diocletian for the suppression of Christianity applied equally to all the provinces of the Empire. It has been stated, but needs more confirmation, that the violent action of Diocletian towards anti-paganism was due to the mother of Galerius, who was known as a rabid supporter of some of the strangest and most revolting rites of Eastern worship. Whether this victim of superstition lived through the

[1] *C.I.L.* No. 1633. *Vide* V. Guérin, vol. ii. p. 65.

Africa under the later Emperors

age of Constantine is not recorded, nor do contemporary historians tell us whether this upholder of Paganism survived her imperial son to witness the temples of her gods overthrown and the symbols of a despised creed carved on post and lintel in most parts of the Empire.

There is considerable doubt whether Diocletian personally approved of the persecution of the adherents to the new creed. He was no ardent believer in the gods of any section of Pagan worshippers, nor was he addicted during a long reign to the shedding of blood. It has been stated that his wife Prisca respected the creed of the Christians, and not only worshipped secretly at their gatherings, but encouraged her daughter Valeria, the wife of Galerius, to uphold the new faith by disseminating its doctrines. As a matter of justice to Diocletian, it may fairly be presumed that his edict of repression was a political necessity and not the outcome of personal animosity. His revolutionary changes in administration had spread discontent throughout his dominions, and more especially in Italy. Rome had ceased to be the capital of the world, and the Senate, no longer able to exercise authority as a political body or to assert its rights, as of old, in the selection of an emperor, had become little more than an assemblage of citizens discharging the ordinary municipal functions. Diocletian, moreover, had no personal interest in the welfare of Rome, but regarded Nicomedia, his newly chosen capital in Bithynia, and Milan, the selected residence of his colleague Maximinian, as better located for a dual form of imperial government. His Oriental tastes and sumptuous surroundings gave encouragement to ways of extravagance hitherto unknown in provincial life; and the burden of taxation, essential to the support of a large army of court officials, pressed heavily upon all classes of citizens. Local resources were drained to fill the coffers of the imperial treasury; agriculture, unequal to the demands of pitiless collectors, was neglected; and industrial arts, fostered by Trajan and his successors, received a check from which they never recovered. This assumption of monarchical authority, so little in harmony with the traditions associated with the Empire of the Cæsars, proved a death-blow to municipal life, and henceforth the vitality which was so conspicuous in the remote towns of Northern Africa imperceptibly dwindled away into nothingness.

Face to face with this decay of national life was the progress of Christianity. Lactantius and Eusebius, both of them Africans, and the latter as bishop of Cæsarea (Cherchel) on terms of intimacy with the succeeding Emperor Constantius, have much to say on these eventful times. It may be that some of their statements present a one-sided view of the many problems which were then exciting the minds of men, both Pagan and Christian; but there is little doubt that such thoughtful men anticipated the fall of the great Empire, when the gods who had protected Rome and its dependencies for nigh a thousand years were being deserted, their effigies overthrown, and their temples becoming the home of a new creed.

The short reign of Constantius is not associated with administrative changes, nor with any memorable events in the progress of Roman Africa, but the close of his career at *Eboracum* (York), on an expedition against the Picts, gives him especial interest to all Englishmen. And to all students of Roman history Constantius is a pleasant memory, although his short-lived labours in the cause of humanity were cast into the shade by the magnificent rule of his son and successor, Constantine the Great.

During the six years that intervened between the death of Constantius and the enthronement of Constantine the Great as sole Emperor, a number of Cæsars pass across the stage whose names are now almost forgotten. Their record is little more than a series of struggles for supremacy, sometimes successful, but ultimately terminating in defeat on the field of battle or abject submission to an all-conquering rival. Contemporary historians pass by these minor Cæsars without comment, and inscriptions unfortunately render little assistance in elucidating an obscure chapter in Roman history. But their names are there, as usual, on imperishable stone, sufficient to indicate that citizens in the provinces were not unmindful of benefits conferred upon them by an aspiring Cæsar at the head of a legion. Among them may be noted Flavius Severus, who was associated with Galerius for a few months. Their joint names are recorded on two milliary stones in North Africa. The reading of the eighth line, according to Wilmanns, is *Respublica Romanis restituta*.[1]

[1] *C.I.L.* No. 10293. *Vide* Cherbonneau, *Ann. de Const.* 1860-61, p. 148.

Africa under the later Emperors

```
       D D  N N
         CAESS
       FLAVIO VA
       LERIO SEVE
       RO ET GALERI
       O VALERIO
         MAXIMINO
       R · PB · RS · RTA
            VIII
```

Another *milliarium* on the road from Thamugas to Theveste records the name of Severus only, the reading of the last two lines being *Pius Felix Augustus, Respublica coloniæ Lambæsitanæ*.[1]

```
       IMP CAES
       FL · VAL
        SEVERO
        PF AVG
         RPCL
```

Another claimant to imperial power was a Phrygian named Lucius Domitius Alexander, who was at one time governor of Africa, but fearing destruction at the hands of Maxentius, son of Maximianus, raised the standard of revolt at Carthage, and proclaimed himself Emperor of Rome. His brief uneventful career merits passing notice on account of an interesting inscription found at Cirta, which may still be seen in the museum of the new city named after Constantine the Great. The date of the inscription is A.D. 308–310, the governor of Numidia at that period being Scironius Pasicrates, whose name and office are clearly defined.[2]

```
   RESTITVTORI
  PVBLICAE LIBER
  TATIS AC PROPA
   GATORI TOTIVS        Restitutori publicæ libertatis ac propagatori totius
  GENERIS HVMANI        generis humani nominisque Romani, Domino
     NOMINISQVE         nostro L. Domitio Alexandro pio felici invicto
  ROMANI DNL DO         Augusto, Scironius Pasicrates, vir perfectissimus,
   MITIO ALEXAN         præses provinciæ Numidiæ.
  DRO PF INV AVG
   SCIRONIVS PA
   SICRATES VP
   P P NVMIDIAE
```

[1] *I.R.A.* No. 4368.
[2] *C.I.L.* No. 7004, now in the museum at Constantine. *Vide* Poulle, *Rec. de*

The partition of the Empire into four divisions by Diocletian, proclaiming himself and his colleague Maximianus as Augusti, and bestowing upon the two subordinate Emperors the title of Cæsar, was not favoured by later rulers, nor was any attempt made by his immediate successor (till forced to do so as matter of policy) to divide imperial authority. Constantine, as the eldest son of Constantius by his divorced wife Helena, became the rightful Emperor on the death of his father, but his claims were disputed by the three most prominent and successful men of the time. In order to assert his supremacy he had a more difficult task to accomplish than had befallen any previous Emperor. For a period of eighteen years Licinius, his brother-in-law and an acclaimed Emperor, was regarded as a sworn enemy, although his services in war were utilised by Constantine for the attainment of his own ends. For more than four years Maximianus, his father-in-law and a retired Emperor, was carrying fire and destruction into distant parts of the Empire; and for a period of eleven years Maxentius, his brother-in-law and son of Maximianus, was raising the standard of revolt in Africa and other provinces of the Empire. There are no inscriptions, yet discovered in North Africa, bearing the joint names of these four Cæsars, nor of any two of them, and those which have been brought to light give little information about an obscure period of Roman history. Party spirit must have run high in those turbulent times, when all these four determined men were striving for the mastery, and employing the legions under their command in their several spheres of action to gain the ascendency by some decisive engagement.

The favour shown to Christian communities by Constantine in the earlier days of his rule, long before his public acknowledgment of Christianity, stirred the antagonism of a rough unpolished man like Licinius, who was a stern upholder of Pagan rites. But personal animosity was compelled to yield to the necessities of the hour, and these two strong men, watching each other's movements in the senate-house and the battle-field, were linked together by a bond of mutual interest to rid themselves of Maximianus and his brutal son Maxentius. Success attended their arms. The former came to a miserable end,

Const. 1876-77, p. 464. '*Alexander vicarius præfecti prætorio in Africa*, A.D. 308, *a Maxentio descivit et Carthagine purpuram sumpsit.*' (Wilmanns.)

Africa under the later Emperors

A.D. 310, and two years later the son was drowned in the Tiber in a hurried retreat before the victorious Constantine. A duel for supremacy between two such ambitious and successful rivals was unavoidable, and for twelve years the struggle was continued, resulting in the overthrow of Licinius and the establishment of undivided empire under Constantine the Great. Among the dedications in North Africa to the Emperor Licinius, one found at Testour, the ancient Bisica Lucana, is the most complete, the date probably being A.D. 316, three years after his marriage with Constantia, the sister of Constantine.

```
           D · N · IMP · VALERIO · LICINI
          ANO · LICINIO · AVG . . . . MAX
          SARMATICO  ·  MAX  ·  GERMA
          NICO · MAX · TRIBVNICIA · POTES
 TATE · X · CONS · V · IMP · X · PATER · PATRIAE · PRO
 CONS · COL · BISICA · LVCANA · DEVOTA · NVMEN
                MAIESTATIQVE EIVS
```

Various readings of this inscription have been given by experts, but the controversy has turned rather upon the deciphering of certain letters than the direct meaning of the dedication.[1] The family of Licinius was involved in his ruin. An only son by Constantia, and bearing the same name, was put out of the way by order of his uncle Constantine, for fear that he might cause trouble hereafter. This unfortunate little boy, who was honoured with the title of Cæsar when scarcely twenty months old was not forgotten by his father's friends in Africa. A *milliarium* found at Equizetum, about a mile east of Bordj Medjana, records his existence as *nobilissimus Cæsar*.[2]

```
              VALERIO LICI
                NIANO LI
               CINIO IVN
              NOBILISSIMO
                  CAES
                  M XII
```

It could scarcely be expected that the re-assumption of imperial dignity by Maximianus, after he had only a few years previously solemnly renounced all claims to power, would be regarded either by Constantine or Licinius as anything more

[1] *C.I.L.* No. 1357. *Vide* Shaw, p. 169. Ximenez, *Hist. de Carth.* p. 260.
[2] *C.I.L.* No. 10429. *Rec. de Const.* 1876-77, p. 629.

than the action of a usurper. His treacherous conduct towards the former, who had married his daughter Fausta, and his ungrateful treatment of his son Maxentius, brought him to an untimely end. With the abdication of Diocletian the career of Maximianus had virtually closed. This seems to be borne out by inscriptions. As usurping Emperor in his later life, the name of Maximianus is not recorded in any part of North Africa, the only known inscription bearing his name as *Imperator*, given on page 258, being probably a dedication prior to his abdication, A.D. 305. So long as the master spirit of Diocletian controlled the army and the Senate, this turbulent colleague of his was held in restraint, and his passing into forced retirement was a mere cloak for more ambitious projects. In these he was aided by an uprising in favour of his son Maxentius, and by the revolt of L. Domitius Alexander already referred to. Seizing his opportunities Maximianus passed into Africa, subdued the pretender Alexander, and, giving free play to his pitiless propensities, subjected the beautiful city of Carthage to fire and rapine. It may be said that Roman Carthage, second only to Rome at the commencement of the fourth century in its splendour and importance, never recovered from the havoc perpetrated during this merciless war.

The six years' nominal rule in Africa and Italy by Maxentius, known as Marcus Aurelius Valerius Maxentius, scarcely merits notice. His claim to the throne rested on his connection with the Emperor Galerius, whose daughter he married, rather than as the son of an unpopular Emperor like Maximianus. Like other ambitious adventurers, he took every advantage of his opportunities, and finding a spread of discontent with the new system of administration inaugurated by Diocletian, he placed himself at the head of a movement, with a view to a restitution of the old order of imperial government. The favours he showered upon the legions attached to his standard gave him the command of a considerable army, and it required all the strategy of Constantine and his generals to destroy the power of such a formidable foe. The decisive battle on the banks of the Cremera, when the retreating forces of Maxentius were drowned through the failure of the Milvian bridge, takes rank with other memorable engagements in the world's history, and has afforded both poet and painter a fitting subject for the

Africa under the later Emperors 269

exercise of their imaginative powers. The record of Maxentius is a long array of evil-doings, without one single public act of benevolence or humanity. In Africa, where his military expedition was for some time crowned with success, his name is handed down to us in only one inscription on a milliary stone found between Diana and Seriana, now known as Kherbet-Taga.[1] It adds nothing to our scant information about his career, but the lettering clearly indicates that Maxentius was acknowledged as *Augustus* only, not as *Imperator*.

DMINOS
TRO MAX
ENTIO AV
GVSTO NO
BILISSIM
O VIRO
CONSVLI

When Constantine was proclaimed Emperor on the death of his father he was then nearly forty years of age, and when the followers of Licinius, the last of the rival claimants, were finally subdued, A.D. 324, Constantius had attained the age of fifty-seven. The last thirteen years of his career as sole Imperator were the most eventful for mankind, and were marked by the greatest administrative change that had occurred since the time of Augustus. It was during these peaceful years that Constantine conceived the idea of founding a second metropolis of the Roman Empire, making Rome the capital of the Western dominions, and Byzantium, the capital of Thrace, the reconstructed capital of the Eastern dominions, bearing the name of Constantinopolis. The Emperor had the gratification, during the last six years of his life, of watching the growth and magnificence of this rival Rome of the East, and of leaving to his sons and successors an Empire at peace within itself, both at home and abroad. So numerous are the dedications in honour of this great monarch that it is difficult to make a selection, even from those recorded in North Africa. It may suffice to state that the gratitude of the citizens for his magnificent rule found expression in the employment of words and phrases hitherto unknown in dedicatory memorials, and that provincial towns seem to have vied with each other in the free use of terms

[1] *C.I.L.* No. 10382.

of the most flattering kind. The following inscription from Ain-Rûa, near Setif, bearing the date A.D. 319, at a period of his reign when the Emperor was publicly recognising Christianity with favour, gives a full list of his achievements. The dedication, on behalf of the province of *Mauritania Sitifensis*, bears the name of the *præses*, *Flavius Terentianus, vir perfectissimus*.[1]

```
IMP · CAES · FLAVI
O · CONSTANTINO
MAXIMO · PIO · FELICI · IN
VICTO · AVG · PONT · MAX · GER
MAXIMO · III · SARM · MAX
BRIT · MAX · CARP · MAX · ARAB
MAX · MED · MAX · ARMEN
MAX · GOTH · MAX · TRIB · PO
TEST · XVIII · IMP · XIII · CON
SVL · IIII · PATRI · PATRIAE
FLAVIVS · TERENTIA
NVS · V · P · PRAESES
PROVINCIAE · MAV
RETANIAE · SITIF
NVMINI · MAIES
TATIQVE · EIVS · SEM
PER · DICATISSI
MVS
```

Another interesting inscription discovered at Cirta, which may be seen in the museum at Constantine, probably records the gratitude of the citizens after the fall of Maxentius, the words *tenebris servitutis oppressam* clearly indicating relief from the oppression of a tyrannical ruler. The dedication is by the præses of the province of Numidia, but the name of this high functionary is illegible. The wording, according to Renier, runs thus :[2]—

Triumphatori omnium gentium ac domitori universarum factionum qui libertatem, tenebris servitutis oppressam, sua felici victoria nova luce illuminavit et revocavit, domino nostro Flavio Valerio Constantino Maximo, Pio, Felici, Invicto, Augusto.

Another inscription found at Utica on a slab of marble, that appears to have been attached to a wall or pedestal by bronze pins, eulogises Constantine as *conditor adque amplificator totius*

[1] *C.I.L.* No. 8412. *Vide* Leclerc, *Rev. arch.* vii. 1850, p. 310.
[2] *I.R.A.* No. 1846.

Africa under the later Emperors

orbis, and in a dedication found at Thamugas the Emperor is spoken of as *pietate præcipuus, semper et ubique victor*. Another variation in wording appears in an inscription which may be studied in the museum at Constantine, the expression being equally significant, *fundator pacis, virtute felicitate pietate præstans, dominus noster*. The great military colony of Lambæsis showed their esteem for such a magnificent ruler in the following inscription, copied many years ago by Renier, and interpreted by him : [1]

    PROVIDEN
    TISSIMO ET
    CVM ORBE   *Providentissimo et cum orbe suo reddita*
    SVO REDDI   *libertate triumphanti domino nostro per-*
    TA LIBERTA   *petuo imperatori Flavio Valerio Con-*
    TE TRIVMFANT   *stantino, invicto pio felici Augusto, victori.*
    DN PERP IMP FL VAL   *Respublica coloniæ Lambæsitanorum*
    CONSTANTINO   *fecit.*
    INVIC P F AVG
      VICTORI
    RES · P . C · L · F

It will be observed that the honourable distinction *pater patriæ* is omitted, and *dominus noster* is substituted. This variation is very noticeable during the reign of Constantine. As an example of an abbreviated inscription the following dedication to the Emperor has proved attractive to students of epigraphy. This is probably another memorial of the defeat of Maxentius, A.D. 312, the date of the inscription being the following year.[2]

    IMP CAESARI
    FLAVIO VALERIO
    CONSTANTINO
    INVICTO PIO FELICI
    AVG · P · M · T P VIII CONS
    III IMP VII PPP
    VAL PAVLVS VPPPN
    DNMQ EORVM D
      D PPP

It was found at Announa, the ancient Tibilis, which was at that period a town of considerable pretensions, of great commercial importance, and the resort of a large population attracted by

---

[1] *I.R.A.* No. 218.
[2] *C.I.L.* No. 18905. *Vide* Poulle, *Rec. de Const.* xxvi. p. 334.

the marvellous hot springs in the neighbourhood. These have been already referred to as Hammam Meskoutin, or the Accursed Baths, but known to the Romans as Aquæ Tibilitanæ. The reading of this inscription, according to Wilmanns, is as follows :—

Imperatori Cæsari Flavio Valerio Constantino, invicto pio felici Augusto, pontifici maximo, tribuniciæ potestatis VIII., consuli III., Imperatori VII., patri patriæ, proconsuli, Valerius Paulus, vir perfectissimus, præses provinciæ Numidiæ, devotus numini majestatique eorum, decurionum decreto, pecunia publica posuit.

One other dedication to the Emperor deserves notice, as it is the only one in North Africa referring in direct words to the Milvian bridge, which proved fatal to Maxentius and his retreating army. The slab of marble bearing the inscription was found at Cæsarea, but unfortunately a portion only of the lettering has been preserved.[1]

PONS MVLVI
EXPEDITIO
IMPERATORIS
CONSTANTINI

We are told by Aurelius Victor that Constantine made his son Crispus by his concubine Minervina, and his son Constantine the younger, born about the same time, Cæsars, adding a third in the person of the infant Licinius, already mentioned, son of his old colleague and rival. Of Crispus we only know that his existence could not be tolerated by Fausta, the wife of Constantine and mother of Constantine the younger, Constantius, and Constans. Pressure was brought to bear upon the Emperor to put the unfortunate Crispus out of the way, with the result that he was murdered. This is another instance of the cruel abuse of power exercised by Roman Empresses in furtherance of ambitious views for themselves and their families. There are two imperfect inscriptions in North Africa, which may possibly be intended to preserve the name of this ill-begotten Cæsar, but neither Renier nor other experts have decided whether they refer to Crispus or his half-brother Constantius. Coins of the period are, however, explicit on this point, as there are many extant bearing the name of Crispus. His removal led to the

[1] *C.I.L.* No. 9356. *Rev. Afr.* iv. p. 221.

Africa under the later Emperors

absolute recognition of Fausta's sons as Cæsars A.D. 333-337, clearly indicated in the following inscription found at Cirta, which has an imperial ring about it harmonising with the close of the Great Constantine's splendid reign.[1]

PERPETVAE VICTORIAE	
DDD NNN CONSTANTINI	
MAXIMI TRIVMPHATORIS	*Perpetuæ Victoriæ trium dominorum*
SEMPER AVG ET CONSTANTI	*nostrorum Constantini Maximi, tri-*
ET CONSTANTI . . . ET	*umphatoris semper Augusti, et Con-*
CONSTANTIS NOBILISSI	*stantini, et Constantii, et Constantis,*
MORVM AC FLORENTISSI	*nobilissimorum ac florentissimorum*
MORVM CAESARVM	*Cæsarum, Clodius Celsinus, vir cla-*
CLODIVS CELSINVS V·C CONS	*rissimus, consularis provinciæ Nu-*
P N DEVOTVS SEMPER	*midiæ, devotus semper numini majes-*
NVMINI MAIESTATI	*tatique eorum.*
QVE EORVM	

In the division of the Empire among these three Cæsars, the countries of Spain, Gaul, and Britain were allotted to Constantine the younger; Italy, Africa, and Illyria fell to the share of Constans; and the rest of the dominions came under the rule of Constantius. The career of Constantine the younger came to an end before he had reigned three years, owing to an unfortunate dispute which had arisen between two of the brothers on the subject of limitations of boundaries, especially in the African provinces. One can easily understand how so trivial a matter may have roused the passions of these hot-headed, inexperienced youths, bearing in mind that from the time of Diocletian the country known as Bætica, comprising nearly half the Spanish peninsula, had always been incorporated with *Mauritania Tingitana*, comprising the western half of Mauritania. The boundaries had not been clearly defined even in the time of Constantine, and it is doubtful whether, even in the present day, the boundaries of Morocco and Algeria, which represented the two divisions of Mauritania in Roman times, have been definitely fixed. Still these two youthful Cæsars were foolish enough to dispute over a question of boundaries, their armies met to settle the matter, and Constantine the younger was defeated and slain. There are several inscriptions in North Africa recording the names of the two surviving Cæsars, many of them remarkable for the

[1] *C.I.L.* No. 7011. *I.R.A.* No. 1848. *Ann. de Const.* 1853, p. 62.

introduction of words and phrases not previously employed, flattering to the Emperors and to the distinguished functionaries to whom they were dedicated. The following inscription, found at Cirta, is a fair example of the wording of the time. It is a dedication by the citizens of Cirta, styled *colonia Constantinæ*, and the inhabitants of the province of Numidia to their excellent governor Cæionius Italicus, who appears to have been endowed with all the virtues that should adorn the holder of high office.[1]

Largitate Dominorum nostrorum piorum Augustorum duorum Constantii et Constantis, Ceionio Italico clarissimo atque consulari viro eximio ac singulari virtutum omnium, ob merita erga se et provinciam continentiæ, patientiæ, fortitudinis, liberalitatis et amoris in omnes precipui. Ordo felicis coloniæ Constantinæ et provincia Numidia patrono posuit.

Constans survived his brother Constantine ten years, ruling over Africa with justice and moderation, and promoting the prosperity of the country. The following dedication in an inscription at Cirta bears testimony to the gratitude of his subjects :[2]

Beatitudine domini nostri Constantis victoris ac triumphatoris semper Augusti, provisa copia quæ horreis deerat posteaquam condendis horrea deesse cœperunt, hæc Vulcacius Rufinus, vir clarissimus, præfectus prætorio, per se cæpta in securitatem perpetuam annonariæ dedicavit.

His career came to a close by the hand of an assassin named Magnentius, whose ambition prompted him to assume the purple and claim joint rights of empire with the last surviving brother, Constantius II. This occurred A.D. 350. For about three years this despicable Roman governed Africa, more in the capacity of a military adventurer than as an administrator. As a follower of Christianity Magnentius has the unenviable notoriety of being the first Christian to kill an Emperor. But his very name is now wellnigh forgotten, kept alive by a few inscriptions that may still be seen bearing his name. At Tipasa, for instance, in Mauritania Cæsariensis, a *colonia* of wealth and renown till a late period of the Empire, and whose monumental remains are scattered over a large extent of ground, there is an

[1] *C.I.L.* No. 7012. *Rev. Afr.* 1859, p. 135.
[2] *C.I.L.* No. 4180. Vol. v. *Les Fastes de la Numidie*, par M. Pallu de Lessert, 1888, p. 199.

imperfect inscription recording the names of three Augusti, the third being that of Magnentius.[1]

> . . . .
> CONSTANTINO
> CONSTANTIO
> A MAGNENTI
> INVICTIS SEMPER
> AVGVSTIS

But there is little doubt that the name of Constans had been erased, and that of his murderer substituted. Tipasa was one of the strongholds of Christianity in the time of Constantine the Great, and continued to be so, if one may judge from the large number of Christian memorials that may still be studied on the spot. There are other inscriptions bearing the name of this man Magnentius as Augustus, but they shed no light on the history or progress of North Africa.

By the death of his two brothers Constantius II. became sole Emperor, ruling for ten years without distinction. An inscription at Lambæsis implies that he was brought into the world for the benefit of mankind,[2] and another at Cæsarea refers to Constantine as *Restitutor libertatis ac triumphator orbis.*

> BONO GENERIS
> HVMANI PROGE
> NITO D N FLAV
> IO CONSTAN
> TIO NOB AC
> FLORENTIS
> SIMO CAES
> ORDO COL
> LAMB FECIT

Beyond these and other similar dedications there is nothing to indicate any marked activity in the African provinces during his reign. Indeed, it may be said that there is no monumental edifice existing in North Africa, whether a triumphal arch or a work of public utility, associated with the names of these three sons of Constantine the Great, nor is there any evidence of material progress during the twenty-three years of joint and separate rule.

[1] *De Tipasa*, par M. Stephanus Gsell, Algiers, 1894, p. 106. This work contains an interesting account of the remains of Tipasa, and is fully illustrated.
[2] *C.I.L.* No. 2720, copied by De la Mare and Renier.

The Age of Constantine, as it may be termed, comprising a period of about sixty years, received additional lustre from the exemplary high-minded conduct of Helena, the wife of Constantius I., and mother of Constantine the Great. She was born A.D. 248, and, we are told, favoured Christianity from her early youth. In the course of a long life Helena suffered many vicissitudes, but strength of will, coupled with devotion to the cause she advocated, enabled her to overcome the difficulties attendant upon her peculiar position as the divorced wife of an Emperor. Through all the troublous times which preceded the fall of Licentius, this saintly woman fearlessly pleaded the cause of Christ, and when Constantine ascended the throne she beheld the triumphant acknowledgment of the new creed under the auspices of an all-powerful ruler. Although Helena did not live to see the dedication by a Christian Emperor of the new metropolis of the East on the shores of the Bosphorus, yet her last years must have been sweetened by daily thoughts of the success which had attended her lifelong efforts. The features of Helena are familiar to us through coins struck in her honour, but inscriptions bearing her name are not numerous. In reference to the one discovered at Sicca Veneria, already mentioned, it seems opportune to record that there are few places in North Africa of greater interest than the site of this ancient stronghold, whose history dates back to pre-Roman times when an important Phœnician colony settled here. It acquired notoriety at a remote period from the performances of obscene rites in honour of Venus Astarte as the goddess of voluptuousness. This is proved by a passage in the writings of Valerius Maximus, who lived in the time of Tiberius: *Siccæ enim fanum est Veneris, in quo se matronæ conferebant atque inde procedentes ad quæstum, dotes corporis injuria contrahebant, honesta nimirum tam inhonesto vinculo conjugia juncturæ.* Of the temple dedicated to Venus there are no traces, nor is there a single inscription referring to it. Hercules appears also to have had many votaries here, judging from the remains of a temple of that deity of large proportions. But the construction of this building may be assigned, like many others in this ruined city, to the time of Diocletian, certain architectural features peculiar to that period being plainly discernible. Outside the walls once stood a Christian basilica of considerable pretensions.

The foundations of the external walls, a portion of the substructure of the apse, and fragments of marble shafts constitute the sole remains of a monumental edifice which was probably erected in the time of Constantine. It is a matter of regret that we know so little of Sicca, which had a history of its own long before the Roman occupation, and obtained notoriety in the Jugurthine war as one of the last of Numidian strongholds. Under its Roman name *Colonia Julia Cirta Nova*, or, according to some inscriptions, *Cirtha Sicca*, it grew into a large residential city, and received favours and benefactions from successive Cæsars.[1] Under Diocletian Sicca became a centre of religious controversy and the home of the distinguished philosopher Arnobius. It was within its walls that he wrote his celebrated treatise in favour of Christianity, treating the gods of his ancestors with ridicule, and pioneering a movement which placed Sicca among the leading centres of Christianity in Africa till the time of the Arab invasion. Whatever may have been the link of attachment between the divorced Empress Helena and the citizens of Sicca, there is little doubt that the bond of union was strengthened by the teaching of Arnobius. Her quiet unobtrusive life was no less remarkable for mental activity in every part of the Empire where Christianity was publicly preached.

The successor of Constantius II., Flavius Claudius Julianus, better known as Julian the Apostate, was a nephew of Constantine the Great, and grandson of Constantius I. This Emperor, clothed with full honours as *Imperator* and *Dominus noster* at the age of thirty, has received a larger share of attention than his achievements merited, on account of his secession from the Christian Church. But, apart from his predilections for the gods of his ancestors, there is nothing in his short rule of three years, marked by unusual activity, that does not commend itself to the respect of mankind. He was merciful in war, temperate in habits, and amiable in disposition. He may be blamed for his apostasy, but as a ruler of men, both in camp and court, his name has been held in honour. Among the dedications in North Africa there is one at Thamugas on an altar of octagonal form,

---

[1] *C.I.L.* No. 1632. Sicca is here called *Colonia Juliæ Veneriæ Cirtæ Novæ Siccæ. Vide Rev. arch.* 1857, p. 129.

which gives the full titles of the Emperor, commencing with *domitor hostium*, and omitting the time-honoured distinction of *pater patriæ*, which no longer appears in imperial memorials.[1] There is no clue to the date of this inscription, but it may be assigned to A.D. 360, the year when Julian received the purple at the hands of the army.

> DOMITORI HOSTI
> VM · INVICTO
> IMP · INDVLGEN
> TISSIMO · PRINCIPI
> D · N · FL · CL · IVLIANO
> INVICTO · PIO · FE
> LICI · SEMPER · AVG
> RESP · ET · ORDO · CO
> LONIAE · THAMVG
> CVRANTE · FL . . . .
> AQVILINO FL · P . . .
> CVRATORE · REI
> PVB · POSVIT · DEDI
> CAVITQVE

Another inscription at Cæsarea is worth recording, on account of its direct allusion to this Emperor as the 'restorer of the religion of the Romans.'[2] The lettering is incomplete and not very legible, but was deciphered and described by M. Poulle many years ago.

> D N FLV CLAV
> DIO IVLIANO
> PIO FELICI . . . .
> OMN . . . . FE
> . . IE . . . POLLE
> NTI VIRTV
> TVM INVICTO
> PRINCIPI RES
> TITVTORI LI
> BERTATIS ET RO
> MANAE RE
> LIGIONIS AC TRI
> VMFATORI OR
> BIS

Domino nostro Flavio Claudio Juliano, Pio, Felici, Augusto, omnium perfectione pollente virtutum, invicto principi, restitutori libertatis et Romanæ religionis ac triumphatori orbis.

---

[1] *C.I.L.* No. 1519.
[2] *C.I.L.* No. 4326. *Vide* Poulle, *Rec. de Const.* 1869, p. 652.

But beyond these and a few other similar dedications Julian has no record in North Africa. With him the rule of the Constantine family came to an end. Of his successor Jovian, who reigned for about seven months and was a true supporter of Christianity, we know very little. The few inscriptions in Africa bearing his name refer to this Emperor as *Domino nostro Joviano triumphatori semper Augusto.*

The tract of country in Eastern Europe called Pannonia, divided into Upper and Lower, furnished many Emperors. Decius, Probus, and Jovian were all natives of that province, and Gratian, the father of Valentinian I., was born, it is said, at Sirmium, the capital of Pannonia. Of Gratian and his achievements we have little knowledge, but his memory is pleasantly preserved in several inscriptions. On a milliarium at Cirta we find the following: *Memoriæ felicissimæ vir adque per omnia sæcula celebrandus Gratius pater . . . Valentiniani et Valentis*; and a stone built into the wall of the Kasbah in the same city records the dedication of a statue to the respected father of the two ruling Emperors.[1] *Atque per omnia sæcula celebrando Gratiano, patri dominorum principumque nostrorum Valentiniani et Valentis, nobilium ac triumphatorum semper Augustorum, juxta c . . . statuam dedicavit . . . Dracontius, vir clarissimus, vicarius præfecti per Africanas provincias, curante Valerio . . . viro egregio, sacerdotale.* The inscription is somewhat imperfect, but it tells us that Dracontius, a man of senatorial rank, was the *vicarius præfecti* of the African provinces under the regulations introduced A.D. 297 for the division of the whole country into dioceses controlled by *vicarii.*

When Valentinian I. was proclaimed Emperor at the age of 43, on the ground of long and distinguished services both as a soldier and a statesman, he took his younger brother Valens as his colleague on the throne, and a few years later caused his infant son Gratian to be acknowledged as Cæsar. In the division of the Empire the provinces of Africa were retained by Valentinian, probably in consequence of rumours of a tribal rising that would need suppression by a strong and experienced hand. The insurrection, however, did not take place till the close of his reign, but it taxed the skill of Valentinian and his

[1] *I.R.A.* No. 1851. *Vide* De la Mare, *Explor. de l'Algérie.* Also *Annuaire,* 1853.

generals to cope with one of the most formidable disturbances that had occurred since the Roman occupation. The frequency of these frontier uprisings, dating back from the earlier days of the Cæsars, had rendered the establishment of a long line of military outposts an absolute necessity. The ruins of these little forts still await the traveller as he wends his way along the Desert fringe, or essays some of the little-frequented passes of the Aurès mountains. The disturbances were mostly tribal, arising out of some petty feud between natives and colonists, and took little trouble to suppress. But such a rising as that of Tacfarinas in the reign of Tiberius, and the revolt of Firmus, when Valentinian was firmly established on the throne, were too formidable to be quelled by the ordinary troops stationed at the various outposts. We know that it took Tiberius and his legions seven long years to subdue so formidable a leader as Tacfarinas, and now Valentinian found himself, at the close of a successful career, face to face with a foe as determined and even more powerful. Between these two native leaders there was a marked difference. Tacfarinas was essentially an African, skilled in the art of war after the manner of the Numidians, an intrepid warrior, fearless in battle, and the recognised figure-head of the tribes of the Desert and the mountain fastnesses of Mauritania. Tacfarinas, we know, was subdued by the more scientific strategy of the Romans and fittingly closed his career on the battle-field. Firmus, the antagonist of Valentinian, was a different type of warrior. Although a native of Mauritania, his name betrays Roman descent. Moreover, he lived after the manner of the Romans and adopted their military tactics; and at the commencement of his revolutionary campaign assumed the purple with all the attributes of a Cæsar. The movement was initiated by Firmus with the sole object of wresting Numidia and Mauritania from the Romans and proclaiming himself sole Emperor of those countries. With a large army, supplemented by well-disciplined and experienced mercenaries, Firmus had fair prospect of success, but fortune favoured the legions of Valentinian. The bold adventurer fell by his own hand, his army was dispersed, and the land of Africa entered upon a career of peace which continued for nearly fifty years.

The campaigns undertaken by Valentinian in Gaul and

Britain, as well as in Africa, were the outcome of necessity as defensive measures rather than as attempts to extend the frontiers of the huge Empire committed to his charge. Anyhow they proved a useful field for the display of military skill, and brought into prominence several men of distinction who contributed largely to the Emperor's unvarying success. Conspicuous among them was Theodosius, the most distinguished general of his time, though his name and achievements were overshadowed by those of his more eminent son Theodosius the Great. But to his skill may be attributed the defeat of Firmus and the signal overthrow of the usurper's army. Strange to say, this great revolutionary movement, which had aroused a spirit of independence among native tribes, was held in remembrance for many a long day after. The idea of uprooting the Roman power, especially in the western provinces, passed on through succeeding generations, resulting in the formation of several petty kingdoms which combined subsequent to the Vandal invasion of Africa and were not finally suppressed till the Arab occupation. The most noticeable of these small independent kings was a Moor named Masuna, whose memory is preserved in an inscription discovered at Altava, in the province of Mauritania Cæsariensis, and bearing the date A.D. 468–9.[1]

PRO · SAL · ET · INCOL · REG · MASVNAE · GENT
MAVR · ET · ROMANOR · CASTRVM · EDIFIC · A · MAS
GIVINI · PREF · DE · SAFAR · . IIDIR · PROC · CAST
RA · SEVERIN · QVEM · MASVNA · ALTAVA · POSVIT
ET · MAXIM · PR · C · ALT · PERFEC · P · P · CCCCLXVIIII

Pro salute et incolumitate regis Masunæ gentium Maurorum et Romanorum castrum ædificatum a Masgivini præfecto de Safari idir (?) procuratore castra Severiana, quem Masuna Altava posuit, et Maximus procurator Altavæ perfecit. Positum (?) provinciæ cccclxviiii.

Procopius mentions a king named Masuna who, in conjunction with Ortaia, incited Solomon, the Byzantine general, to go to war with the King of the Moors A.D. 534. This Masuna may have been a descendant of the one mentioned in the inscription.

[1] *C.I.L.* No. 9835, deciphered by Wilmanns. *Rev. Afr.* 1878, p. 355.

If the wording of inscriptions offers fair evidence of the popularity of an Emperor, the claims of Valentinian cannot be disregarded. We gather from Marcellinus, the most reliable authority of this period, that this successful ruler of mankind was not of a lovable disposition, and that he was hot-tempered and impetuous. And we may infer that his success during a very active career of twelve years was due to strength of will and conspicuous ability in the conduct of military affairs. From the time Valentinian ascended the throne till the close of his life he had to contend with insurrections in various parts of his dominions, and nowhere did he achieve greater success than in North Africa. The troubles that arose from the rising of Firmus in Mauritania were preceded by a state of affairs in Tripoli which was gradually reducing that province to a condition of anarchy. The governor of Africa at that time was Romanus, a man of feeble disposition, inert and rapacious. Taking advantage of his incapacity, the Asturians, who were settled on the frontiers, laid siege to the walled city of Leptis, ravaged the surrounding country, and murdered the agricultural population. The citizens in their distress appealed to Carthage for assistance. Romanus declined, unless the people of Leptis sent him food for his army and 4,000 camels for transport. Such a demand could not be complied with by a starving population undergoing a state of siege. Romanus, comfortably quartered in Carthage, did nothing. As a last resource two ambassadors named Severus and Flaccianus were despatched to the Emperor, taking with them golden images of Victory in honour of Valentinian's recent accession to the throne. Their petition was heard, and Palladius was sent to Africa to redress the grievance and restore order on the frontiers of Tripoli. But the troubles of the citizens of Leptis were not over. Palladius conspired with Romanus to deceive the Emperor and to report that the Roman population had no cause for complaint. Two more ambassadors were accordingly sent by the disheartened citizens, and at last the truth came out. The Roman legions were ordered to Tripoli, the siege was raised, Romanus was cast into prison and Palladius put to death. Gratitude for abundant relief is shown in several inscriptions bearing the name of Valentinian alone, or associated with his younger brother Valens. The dedication to the former and his heirs on

Africa under the later Emperors 283

a slab discovered at Bou Grara[1] (given on p. 257) may be quoted as an example and may be read as follows:

> *Divina stirpe progenito domino nostro Valentiniano, Augusto, fortissimo principi, Flavius Vivius Benedictus vir perfectissimus, præses provinciæ Tripolitanæ, numini majestatique ejus semper devotus.*

Valens, the coadjutor and survivor of Valentinian, has no place in African history. As ruler of the eastern division of the Empire, his headquarters were at Constantinople, and consequently he had no special claim for recognition by the citizens of Roman Africa. His name, however, appears on a slab discovered at Apisa Maius, now known as Henchir Ain Tarf, in the proconsular province.[2]

> D · N
> IMP · AVG
> EL · VALENTI · PIO
> FELICI VICTORI AC
> TRIVMFATORI PER
> PETVO DEVOTVS
> ORDO MCP APISEN
> SIVM MAIORVM
> CVM VALERIO MARINO
> CVR · RP

The chief value of the inscription lies in the identification of the site of the *municipium Apisensiorum majorum*, but nothing is known of the *curator reipublicæ* named Valerius Marinus. The names of the joint Emperors are found in numerous inscriptions, all varying in their expressions of gratitude for benefits received. The wording on one stone is *Domini nostri invictissimi, et fortissimi, et gloriosissimi*, and on another, *toto orbe victores*.[3] Perhaps the following from Rusicada, which may be still studied in the museum at Philippeville, is the most complete:[4]

---

[1] *C.I.L.* No. 10489. *Vide Rev. Afr.* xx. 1876, p. 508.
[2] *C.I.L.* No. 780. Wilmanns descrip.
[3] *C.I.L.* No. 2722. *I.R.A.* No. 119, copied by Renier and De la Mare.
[4] *C.I.L.* No. 19852, descrip. Villefosse. *Vide Bull. Epigr. de la Gaule*, 1881, p. 167 *et seq.*

PRO MAGNIFICENTIA TEMPORVM
PRINCIPVM MAXIMORVM DOMI
NORVM ORBIS VALENTINIANI ET
VALENTIS SEMPER AVGG HORREA
AD SECVRITATEM POPVLI ROMANI
PARITER AC PROVINCIALIVM CON
STRVCTA OMNI MATVRITATE
DEDICAVIT PVBLILIVS CAEIONIVS
CAECINA ALBINVS V · C CONS
SEXF · P · N · CONS

There is another at Thamugas relating to the rebuilding of the portico of the Capitol, fully described on p. 93. And at Cuiculum was found an inscription referring to the dedication of a *basilica vestiarium* to Valentinian and Valens by P. Cæionius Cæcina Albinus. No further explanation is given, although some doubt has been expressed about the correctness of the reading of the letters *basili*. Whether the edifice was a *basilica* or an *apotheca* is of little consequence. It was certainly a public building of some importance, and, to adopt the explanation offered by Wilmanns, was *negotiatoribus vestiariis maxime destinatam*. Partial explorations of the site of *Cuiculum*, now known as Djemila, in the old province of Mauritania Sitifensis, have revealed the existence of a city of undoubted magnificence. Of its history and of the part it played in the progress of Roman colonisation we have no record, but the principal inscriptions scattered among the monumental remains being dedicatory to Marcus Aurelius and Caracalla, there is ample evidence that Cuiculum was a city of wealth and renown at the commencement of the third century. It is within the range of possibility that the remains of the stately edifice where clothes merchants were wont to congregate in the days of Valentinian may some day be identified.

In most of the dedicatory inscriptions yet discovered in the newly named province of *Numidia Constantiniana*, bearing the names of this Emperor and his brother Valens, we are made familiar with the name of the governor of that province, A.D. 364–367, Publilius Cæionius Cæcina Albinus. He was of senatorial rank and bore the distinguishing title of *sexfascalis*,[1]

[1] *C.I.L.* No. 7975. *Ann. de Const.* 1862, p. 144. This title of distinction seems to have been first bestowed on Ulpius Mariscianus in the reign of Julian, A.D. 361, who was *Consularis Sexfascalis provinciæ Numidiæ*. (*Dig.* l. 16.) It was conferred only on governors of *senatorial* provinces. (*Les Fastes de la Numidie*, p. 204.)

as will be observed in the last-quoted inscription. His munificence is attested by a lavish expenditure on public buildings or the restoration of monumental edifices that had fallen into decay. Whether Valentinian had issued an edict drawing attention to the necessity of repairing ancient monuments in different parts of the Empire we have no means of ascertaining. But the wholesale restoration of public buildings during his reign and those of his immediate successors seems to indicate that many of the edifices erected by the great building Emperors, Trajan and Hadrian, needed thorough repair after a lapse of nearly 250 years. It is possible, also, that in this part of the world, where slight earthquakes were not unknown, some disturbance may have affected public edifices; and although there is no record of any violent earthquake in North Africa at this period, we have ample evidence of a terrific disturbance in Eastern Europe only two years before Valentinian ascended the throne. From Marcellinus we learn that it spread through Asia Minor, Pontus, and Macedonia, and that Nicomedia, the capital of Bithynia, was entirely ruined.

The names of the three Emperors Valentinian, Valens, and Gratian, who reigned conjointly from A.D. 367 till the close of 375, when Valentinian died, are recorded in many parts of the country. Gratian, the son of Valentinian, was created Cæsar at the age of eight, and eight years after was proclaimed *Imperator*. His elevation to the throne was evidently the cause of great rejoicing, and of many congratulatory dedications. The following jubilant inscription at Constantine may be assigned to that date, when the popularity of Valentinian as a ruler was everywhere acknowledged: [1]

Aureo sæculo trium dominorum nostrorum invictissimorum principum Valentiniani, Valentis et Gratiani, porticum a fundamentis cœptam et constructam, Annius . . . minus, vir clarissimus, consularis sexfascalis provinciæ Numidiæ Constantinæ dedicavit et domini nostri Gratiani principis nomine nuncupavit, curante ac sua pecunia perficiente Nevio Numidiano. . . . .

Annius was governor of the province at some date between A.D. 367–375, and it may be assumed that his acceptance of the high office seemed a fitting occasion for dedicating a public

[1] *C.I.L.* No. 7015. *Vide* De la Mare, *Explor.* tab. 125. Also given by Renier, *I.R.A.* No. 1852.

edifice to the youthful Cæsar. Another very similar inscription of the same reign was found among the ruins of Cuiculum, the modern Djemila, and may still be read on a slab doing duty as a lintel in the construction of a modern fountain.[1]

PRO BEATVDINE PRINCIPVM MAXIMORVM
DDD NNN VALENTINIANI VALENTIS ADQ GRATIANI PERPETV
SEMPER AVGGG FL SIMPLICIVS VC CONSVLARIS SEXFASCALIS PN
CONSTANTINAE NVMINI MAIESTATIQ EORVM SEM-
PER DICATVS BASI
LICAM DEDICAVIT RVTILIVS VERO SATVRNINVS VC PRO EDITIONE MV
NERIS DEBITI A SOLO FACIENDAM EXAEDIFICAN-
DAM Q CVRAVIT

The exact date is a matter of conjecture, but it is possibly of the year 375, when the elevation of Gratian to the throne at the age of sixteen was the cause of general rejoicing. A dedication of a basilica in honour of the three Emperors on such an occasion was, therefore, extremely probable. On the death of his father, Gratian became sole Emperor of the West, and three years later, when Valens came to an untimely end, found himself in sole possession of the Empire. In the short interval between the death of Valentinian and of his brother Valens, A.D. 375-378, another infant Cæsar appears on the stage in the person of Valentinian II., the son of Valentinian I., thus sharing the throne with his uncle and brother. In testimony of their joint rule we have an interesting inscription at Cella, south of Sitifis and in the province of Mauritania Sitifensis:[2]

SALVIS DDD NNN IMPERATORIBVS INVICTIS PRINCIBVS
VALENTE GRATIANO ET VALENTINIANO PERPETVIS MAXI-
MIS
VICTORIBVS AC TRIVMFATORIBVS SEMPER AVGVSTIS
FLA VICTORIANVS VC PRIM ORDINIS COMES AFRICAE
SEMPER VESTRO NVMINI DEVOTVS CASTRAM DEDICAVIT

The date is probably A.D. 378, in honour of Valentinian II., who was raised to the purple a few days after the death of his

[1] *C.I.L.* No. 8324. This inscription is in excellent condition.
[2] *C.I.L.* No. 10937. Seen and translated by Villefosse.

Africa under the later Emperors

father. The words *primi ordinis comes Africæ* should be noted as an early example of a new form of title.

The merits of Gratian as a soldier and an administrator claim little notice—a learned man but a bad ruler, says Aurelius Victor. An inscription at Carpis, near Carthage, records his name as *pacificus dominus noster*, but this epithet *pacificus* is little in accord with the general tenour of his career. His violent antagonism to the revival of Pagan worship, even in those parts of his dominions where Christianity had hitherto made little progress, roused the animosity of many of his subjects, and led to the desertion of his soldiers during his last campaign against the Goths. Strong nations need strong rulers. This is clearly shown in many instances in this later period when the Roman Empire was tottering to its fall and was saved for a time by the accidental accession of a statesman or soldier of mark called suddenly to exercise supreme power. This was the case during the last four troubled years of Gratian's career, when necessity enforced the co-operation of the most distinguished soldier of his time, and the son of Valentinian's most successful general. It was A.D. 379, one year after the death of Valens, that Gratian raised to the purple this Spanish warrior, whose Byzantine name of Theodosius seems to indicate Greek parentage. Four years later another Spaniard named Maximus, of whose ancestry we have no knowledge, raised the standard of revolt in Spain and Africa and besought Theodosius to recognise his claim to the western dominions of the Empire. The situation was a critical one, as Maximus, the upholder of Paganism, had the support of many of the provinces and the command of a trained army. With the adroitness of a true statesman Theodosius lured the impatient Maximus to act on the offensive. The rivals met at Aquileia. Maximus was defeated and his army dispersed. Although this usurping Emperor has little place in Roman history, he appears to have secured the regard of his subjects in Africa as well as in Spain. This is attested by an interesting inscription found at Gigthis, in the province of Tripoli, where his name is associated with that of Valentinian II., Theodosius the Great, and Arcadius, the infant son of Theodosius.[1] The date of the inscription is A.D. 383–388, and the dedication is in commemoration of an

[1] *C.I.L.* No. 27. *Vide* Guérin, vol. i. p. 228.

embassy to that distant province. It will be observed that the name of Maximus has been erased in the usual way.

```
            QVINTO · FL · P · SAC · PROV
        SALVIS AC TOTO ORBE VINTIBVS
        DDDD NNNN FFFF LLLL
        VALENTINIANO THEODOSIO
        ARCADIO ET MAXIMO SEMP AVGVST
        OB MERITVM MAGNIFICE LEGATI
        ONIS QVAM PRO VOTO TOTIVS
        PROVINCIAE EXECVTVS EST ET . . .
        . . . . . IT QVINTVS VIR LAVDABILIS
        SACERDOTALIS HVIC CVPIENS
        COMPETENTIBVS MERITIS
        RESPONDERE TOTIVS PRO
        VINCIAE CONSILIO AD
        DECRETO ORDI
        NIS . . . . . . . .
```

Of the town of Gigthis we have little record. As a seaport it probably existed in Phœnician times. Under the Romans it maintained its position as a thriving *municipium* till the close of the Empire, and when Christianity flourished in this remote corner Gigthis became the seat of a bishop. The Vandal invasion in the fifth century does not seem to have affected its prosperity, nor did the Byzantine occupation at a later date. It was not till the Arabs swept over the land from east to west that the fate of this old-world town was sealed.

The death of Valentinian II., A.D. 392, placed the Empire in the hands of Theodosius and his son, and in the following year a younger son named Honorius was raised to full honours, although he had only attained his ninth year. It is strange to find a scarcity of memorials in North Africa relating to so distinguished a ruler as Theodosius, whose exploits fully justified the surname of Magnus. The only explanation that can be offered is that Theodosius was probably unknown personally to his African subjects.

An inscription at Kalama, in the form of a dedication by the citizens of this prosperous *colonia*, bears his honoured name.[1] And another found at a place called Henchir-el-Chrib, not far from Bizerta, may fairly be ascribed to his reign, the Emperor being called Theodosius *perpetuus Augustus Cæsar*.

[1] *C.I.L.* No. 5340. *I.R.A.* No. 2735. *Vide* De la Mare, *Explor. de l'Algérie*.

```
D · N · FL · THEODOSIO PER
PETVO AC VICTO
RI SEMPER AVG ORDO
SPLENDIDISSIMVS
COL · KALAMENSIVM
LOCAVIT DEDICAVIT
```

According to a statement by Aurelius Victor, this distinguished prince was blessed with many virtues and debased by no vicious propensities. He died at Milan at the close of an eventful reign of sixteen years—a good ruler, a tender father, a loving husband.

In the division of the Empire between Arcadius and Honorius, the elder brother acquired the Eastern dominions and the younger the Western. This was in accordance with the policy initiated by Diocletian and accepted by Constantine the Great and his successors. The capital of Arcadius was the newly erected city of Constantine, now rising in all its splendour, and destined to play a larger part in the drama of national life than its great founder ever contemplated. The capital of Honorius was to be once again the Roman metropolis, which Diocletian and his successors had neglected in favour of Milan as a more convenient military centre. Italy, Spain, Africa, and Gaul were thus placed under the rule of Honorius. Britain, hitherto regarded as an important appendage of the Empire of the West, played no part in its history at the close of the fourth century. Its remoteness by land and sea had checked the enthusiasm which prompted so many Emperors, from Julius Cæsar to Constantius, to convert the island into a Roman province. Under Honorius Roman Britain almost ceased to exist, and the last of the legions which had preserved England from the barbarism of the northern tribes was preparing to cross the Channel into the fair land of the Gauls. The history of Africa during the twenty-seven years' effeminate rule of Honorius is almost a blank, relieved only by an insurrection which caused great anxiety to so timid a potentate. Gildon, a Moor of distinction and a brother of Firmus, raised the standard of revolt soon after the Emperor ascended the throne, and with an army of 70,000 men was making preparations for a decisive encounter with the Roman legions. But ill-success attended his efforts. His troops were routed, and

Gildon, finding his cause was lost, made away with himself at the coast town of Tabarca. Africa then had peace for twenty-five years, and during that long interval reaped the benefits arising from undisturbed interchange of commercial products. The lull preceded the storm. The semi-barbarous nations of the North, Goths, Vandals, and Huns, were preparing for a trial of strength with the masters of the world, and lay waiting on the frontiers of Southern Europe ready to swoop down upon Rome and the sunny lands of Italy and Spain ; and then, gathering into their ranks irregular troops in their onward march, to cross the seas to spread havoc and desolation among the peace-loving citizens of Roman Africa. So inert a ruler as Honorius, thoughtful only of his own personal safety and regardless of the gathering clouds on the political horizon, has little place in the records of the country. One inscription only, at Altava in Mauritania Cæsariensis, a simple complimentary memorial by a citizen of that town, bears his name. Although imperfect and not very easy to decipher, Wilmanns has succeeded in shaping the letters into legible form.[1]

> PRO SALVTE CIVI
> TATIS ALTAVAE
> ET INCOLVMITATE
> AVG HONORIO FECER
> CREP VICTORIVS VE (?)
> RVS ET CIVES ALTAV (?)

The names of the joint Emperors appear in only one inscription yet discovered in North Africa, but they are recorded on a slab found in Rome in the form of a congratulatory dedication to the two brothers for the suppression of a revolt in Africa. No explanation of this inscription has been given by expert epigraphists, but it is sufficiently noteworthy to find a place here.[2]

IMPERATORIBVS INVICTISSIMIS FELICISSIMISQVE
DD . NN · ARCADIO ET HONORIO FRATRIBVS
SENATVS POPVLVSQVE ROMANVS VINDICATA REBELLIONE
ET AFRICAE RESTITVTIONE LAETVS

[1] *C.I.L.* No. 9834. Wilmanns.
[2] Orelli, *Inscript. Lat Coll.* No. 1132. Gruter, 287, 3. This dedication was probably A.D. 398, when Gildon the Moor was defeated in a pitched battle near Theveste and the insurrection brought to a close.

Africa under the later Emperors

The single inscription in Africa bearing the joint names was found on a pedestal at Nebeul, a small Arab town on the coast, not far from Hammamet in Africa Provincia, constructed with the materials of the old Roman town of Neapolis. There are no records of this ruined settlement, which appears to have been in existence long before the Roman occupation, and to have established in primitive times a reputation for its pottery. Fragments of earthenware, red, yellow, and green, turned up by the plough from year to year, give a colouring to the landscape, and the enduring glazes used by these old-world potters flash in the sunlight and illuminate the surface in all directions. It is gratifying to know that the industry which prospered more than two thousand years ago is still the staple manufacture of the modern town. The date of the inscription is A.D. 400-401, and the rendering by Wilmanns is as follows:[1]

```
SALVIS DD NN
ARCADIO ET HONORIO
INCLYTIS SEMPER AVGG
ADMINISTRANTE DM
GABINIO BARBARO
POMPEIANO VC PROC
P · A · V · S · I · COELIVS TITIANVS
VH · EX · T · ET · NAV · EX · MVN
ET EXCVRATORE R · P
CVM COELIO RES
TITVTO VH FILIO SVO
SVMPTV PROPRIO
INSTANTIA SVA
          DEDICAVIT
          ADMINISTRANTE
PVBLIANO · V · H · F · P · CVRAT · R · P
```

Salvis dominis nostris Arcadio et Honorio inclytis semper Augustis, administrante divino mandatu (?) Gabinio Barbaro Pompeiano viro clarissimo proconsuli provinciæ Africæ vice sacra judicante. Cœlius Titianus vir honestus ex transvecturario et naviculario, ex munerario, et ex curatore reipublicæ, cum Cœlio Restituto, viro honesto, filio suo sumptu proprio instantia sua dedicavit, administrante Publiano, viro honesto, flamine perpetuo, curatore reipublicæ.

The chief point of interest in this lengthy inscription will be found in the fifth and sixth lines, recording the name of G. Barbarus Pompeianus, the governor of Africa, A.D. 400-401.

[1] *C.I.L.* No. 969. *Vide* Guérin, vol. ii. p. 249.

This distinguished Roman has been identified, in recent years, with the owner of a princely establishment the remains of which were brought to light in 1878 by some chance excavations that were being made near the village of Oued-Atmenia, on the old Roman road between Setif and Constantine.[1] At a depth of between five and seven feet from the surface, the walls of an extensive range of buildings, with detached pavilions and numerous enclosures, were revealed. So clearly were the buildings defined, and so perfect was the mosaic flooring, that M. Martin, an architect, was deputed to measure the ruins and prepare drawings of the mosaics. After careful examination it was found that these were the remains of the Baths attached to the country seat of Pompeianus, whose official residence was at Carthage. The arrangement of the Baths does not need any special description. The apartments were not large, but the fittings were of a sumptuous character, coloured marbles and mosaics being freely used. The mosaic floors deserve special notice on account of their pictorial character, two of them representing the stables and racehorses of this princely governor, while others depict in a realistic manner the daily life and amusements of their owner and the costume of the period. The position of the stables represented in mosaic has been ascertained at a distance of 130 yards from the Baths.

The breeding and training of Numidian horses were much encouraged by the Emperors, perhaps in painful recognition of the wonderful exploits of the wild cavalry, unbridled and unsaddled, that more than once secured victory to Hannibal during the second Punic war. To the Carthaginians, or rather to her Numidian mercenaries, Rome was indebted for all her knowledge of the horse and its rider; and the institution of various kinds of chariot races, not only in Rome but in every large town of the Empire, drew the attention of such wealthy men as Pompeianus to the pecuniary and other advantages of a breeding establishment. Some thirty years ago an inscribed stone bearing on this subject was unearthed in Rome. It was deciphered by M. Renan, and was the subject of a paper read

---

[1] *Ann. de Const.* 1878-80 for a graphic description of these remarkable mosaics by M. A. Poulle. The four drawings, prepared under the direction of M. Martin, have been admirably reproduced in chromolithography. These can be purchased in Paris and are well worthy of study.

by him in Rome before the Société des Inscriptions et Belles-Lettres in November 1878. It commemorates the victories in the hippodrome at Rome, A D. 115-124, of one Crescens, a Moor aged twenty-two, and how during a period of ten years he succeeded, with four horses named *Circus*, *Acceptus*, *Delicatus*, and *Cotynus*, in gaining prizes of the value of 1,556,346 sesterces, equal to 12,500*l*. Crescens, the charioteer, was evidently the favourite of the day, occupying a position in the racing world similar to that acquired by so many successful jockeys of our own time, and running the horses of some great proprietor like Pompeianus of Oued-Atmenia. Were it not for the date of the inscription, one might be tempted to suggest that the charioteer referred to on the inscribed stone was identical with the personage represented in the pictorial mosaic. We have in the latter one Cresconius as the chief charioteer, and we have also the horse *Delicatus* tethered by himself as a favourite animal. The mosaic in the *Calidarium* is divided into four parts representing the horses and stables. In the first there is a pavilion within an enclosure ; there are the stables and apartments for grooms and charioteers, the name of the proprietor being written above the central edifice ; and below, in two divisions, are six horses covered with horsecloths and attached to four separate mangers. *Altus*, unequalled for strength, who can leap as high as the mountains, is tethered to the same manger as *Pullentianus*, the stallion ; then comes *Delicatus*, the elegant one ; and below are *Polydoxus*, the glorious one, who, whether he wins or loses, is still beloved, tethered with *Titas*, the giant ; and in the corner stands *Scholasticus*, the learned one, apart and by himself as a philosopher should be. In the doorway leading to the *Sudatorium* is an inscription which is difficult to translate : *Incredula Venila Benefica*. In this latter chamber is a mosaic in two compartments. In the upper one three pavilions are represented, and in the foreground a lady is seated in a high-backed chair under a palm-tree, a fan in her right hand and a pet dog beside her, in charge of a servant who protects his mistress from the rays of the sun by an umbrella in his left hand. Above is written *Filoso Filolocus*, probably from *filum*, a thread, this part of the garden being reserved for ladies as a place for sewing. In the lower compartment is a representation of a park enclosed with a hedge and a fence supported by strong stakes. This is the *Septum Venationis*, as it is written, and, consequently, two hounds are represented giving chase to three gazelles. In the angles are circular basins in which are fish and aquatic plants, and in a corner appears the word *Pecuarilocus*, showing that Pompeianus, much as he loved horses and hunting, had tastes also for cattle and the products of the soil. The mosaic on the floor of the *atrium* is divided into three compartments by a rich framework of flowers, the central one giving a view of the house, having several stories and numerous windows. Attached to the house is a tower surmounted by a balcony or awning, designated in the mosaic as *Saltuarii Janus*. The roofs of the buildings are covered with square red tiles in patterns, and chimneys or pipes appear above the ridge There are indications also of chimneys above the parapet of the principal pavilion. In the lower divisions Pompeianus himself is depicted as directing a stag-hunt, and the huntsmen, Cresconius, Argentium, Cessonius, and Neambas—the first mounted on the horse *Vernacel*—with lances in hand, are in full pursuit, preceded by the dogs *Fidelis* and *Castus*. In attendance are Liber and Diaz, the latter from Iberia, but both having their mantles thrown back, Spanish fashion, over the left shoulder. The two end compartments of the design seem to indicate a representation of the close of the day's sport. The chase is over, and the huntsmen are invited to repose, conjuring up visions of attendant houris clothed in gorgeous raiment. Such might have been the intention of the artist in delineating the forms and features of six Asiatic ladies with bejewelled arms and necks, quaintly attired, and with an extravagance of head-dress that would puzzle a coiffeur of our own times. According to M. Tissot, these indescribable females may have been pictorial representations of Numidian female divinities. This remarkable series of mosaics gives some insight into Roman life and customs in North Africa at the close of the fourth century, and bears striking testimony to the peaceful condition of the country in the declining years of the Empire. Sixteen centuries have passed since Pompeianus presided over this lordly retreat, as a patron of the turf and a lover of sport in all its aspects. A few years after his decease the disturbing influence of the invading Vandals must have rendered the maintenance of such an establishment an absolute impossibility, and one can picture

Africa under the later Emperors

the lifework of this distinguished Roman neglected, abandoned, and finally becoming a mere hunting-ground for Vandal or Byzantine, Arab or Moor.

Honorius takes rank as a long-ruling Emperor, sharing the distinction with Augustus and Constantine. For the last fourteen years of his reign he was associated with the youthful son of his brother Arcadius, bearing the name of Theodosius II. Their joint rule was not marked by any disturbing events in North Africa, except the slight rising already referred to, and consequently the inscriptions bearing their names are mostly of a complimentary character. At Kalama, for instance, a dedication commences with the customary phraseology, *Beatissimis temporibus dominorum nostrorum Honori et Theodosi semper et ubique vincentium*,[1] and at Bisica the wording of an inscription bears testimony to a sense of tranquillity and contentment during their reign.[2]

POLLENTES IN FINE IMPERIO
D · D N · N HONORI ET THEODOSI PPS · IMP AVG
ADMINISTRANTE FELICE INNODIO VC AMP
PROC · PAVSICVM FIRMO VC LEG SVO PERMI
HILARIO VA SIIA VETVSTAS CVM SIRA

Pollente sine fine imperio dominorum nostrorum Honori et Theodosi perpetuorum semper imperatorum Augustorum administrante feliciter Innodio, viro clarissimo, amplissimo proconsule provinciæ Africæ vice sacra judicante cum Firmo viro clarissimo legato suo permittente Hilario vices agente prætorio Africæ . . . . cum straturis.

Theodosius II., as the successor of his father, who ruled over the Eastern provinces of the Empire, took no part in African affairs, although he may be credited with the postponement of the invasion of the country by Vandals. This was effected by bribes and promises. When the former failed and the latter had no prospect of fulfilment, Theodosius was powerless. The invaders crossed the Straits, crept along the southern shores of the Mediterranean, and before twelve years had passed by, Genseric their king was firmly established on the throne at Carthage. With Valentinian III., son-in-law of Theodosius, the family of Theodosius came to an end, and with the fall of the

---

[1] *C.I.L.* No. 5341. De la Mare, *Explor.* tab. 181.
[2] *C.I.L.* No. 1358. This inscription is not very legible. The interpretation given is by Wilmanns. *Vide* Davis, *Ruined Cities in Africa*, p. 388.

dynasty the Empire fell too. North Africa has no record of the career of this last of Roman princes, although his name appears on two imperfect inscriptions in the form of dedications to the joint Emperors. Inscriptions terminate also, bringing to a close the series of historic memorials which had continued uninterruptedly to mark the development and success of the colony of North Africa during a period of nearly 600 years. A century elapses before these faithful records of national life begin to appear again in somewhat consecutive form. In the interval the Vandals have been swept away, leaving behind them nothing but marks of ruin and destruction. Petty kings, or rather chiefs of the more powerful native tribes, aided by bands of mercenary adventurers, have established themselves in the mountain strongholds, much in the same way as the Kabyles of our own day have acquired a semblance of authority over large tracts of fertile country not easy of access. These little kings have left a record of their presence on several slabs that have been brought to light. The inscription given on page 281, relating to *Masuna rex gentium Maurorum et Romanorum*, may be cited as the most perfect, the date being A.D. 468. Any reference to later memorials is beyond the scope of this outline of Roman African history, but inscriptions commence once more in the renowned days of Justinian and Theodora (A.D. 534–565), when the Byzantine dynasty was asserting its supremacy, and they terminate for ever under Constans II., who closed an uneventful career A.D. 668. The last of the imperial dedications in Africa appears on a large block of white marble, which served as a lintel to the entrance-door of a Christian basilica at Thamugas, and is of the reign of Heraclius II. or Constans II. The wording runs thus: *In temporibus Constantini* (*i.e.* Heraclii II. or Constantis II.) *Imperatoris Bel Gregorio patricio, Joannis, dux de Tigisi, offeret domum Dei Armenus.*[1] Gregorius was the exarch or governor of Africa, whose remarkable career has been already referred to in the description of Sufetula on page 124.

[1] *C.I.L.* No. 2389. Some doubt has been expressed as to the meaning of the word *Bel*. Wilmanns is of opinion that it is an abbreviation of *Bellicio*. Renier and others read the letters Fl. (*Flavio*), *I.R.A.* No. 1518. Tigisis was on the slopes of the Aurès mountains, not far from Lambæsis and Thamugas.

FRONT OF A MARBLE CIPPUS
(from the Museum at Philippeville).

CONCLUSION

No country ever occupied by the Romans possesses, at the commencement of this twentieth century, more remarkable monumental remains or a greater wealth of inscriptions than North Africa. They are there to tell their own tale of national progress of a civilising people, of Emperors good and bad, of munificent citizens, of scholars eminent in philosophy and skilled in rhetoric, of men and women in all ranks of life obedient to the laws, loyal to their rulers, and leaving behind them a pleasant memory to be faithfully recorded on imperishable stone. If the popularity of any one of the Emperors can be tested by the number of dedications in his honour, some two or three will head the list without fear of contradiction; while of others, who were raised to the throne at the will of the legions and passed rapidly across the stage as mere adventurers, it will be seen that inscriptions are but few, and in some cases their very names have been erased by an aggrieved or dissatisfied populace.

The difficulties which beset the Romans in their career of conquest, at the close of the second Punic war, arose in a great measure from the general configuration of the country, which seemed fatal also to the native races in their attempts to expel the invader. The three zones of country, separated by high mountains, never impassable, but presenting natural difficulties in the transport of large bodies of disciplined troops, may be said to represent three distinct regions. On the north was the broad stretch of sea—the *mare sævum* which, for so many generations, proved an insuperable barrier to Roman advancement, and on the south the sea of sand—the mysterious desert stretching across the Equator, and unfit for habitation by

European races. To these peculiar features of North Africa may be attributed the partial success which attended the rising of frontier and desert tribes at all periods of the Roman occupation, fully sufficient to account for difficulties experienced by the Roman legions in suppressing a long series of tribal revolts. Till the time of Trajan, colonisation by the Latin race was confined mostly to the towns already peopled by Carthaginians or the descendants of old Phœnician traders. The accession of this princely ruler marks a starting-point in the history of Roman Africa. Under the twelve Cæsars progress had been checked by the almost insuperable difficulties attending the invasion of an unknown country, peopled by races whose habits of life and methods of warfare had nothing in common with the more advanced civilisation of the people of Italy, and the islands under Roman domination. Trajan seems to have been born at the right time. His noble bearing and distinguished generalship, coupled with administrative abilities of a high order, roused the enthusiasm of his subjects to a degree unknown since the days of Augustus. The African provinces reaped a full share of benefits from the career of such a ruler. Colonisation was attended with marked success. Cities and towns sprang up at the Emperor's bidding. Native tribesmen found themselves unmolested, their forms of religion and habits of life undisturbed, and encouragement given to a free interchange of commercial products. Under the Antonines the good work still progressed, was checked for a time under the rule of the worthless Commodus, and reached its climax in the strong hands of Septimius Severus. Inscriptions innumerable bear ample testimony to the condition of the African population at this period, and monumental remains, which still greet the traveller in some of the less trodden parts of this fair land, bear ample evidence of the presence of large communities

[1] It is nearly twenty-five years since Captain Roudaire published his report on the Chotts or lakes forming a large portion of the southern boundary of North Africa. (*Etude relative au Projet de Mer Intérieure*, Paris, 1877.) His investigations seemed to show that the *Palus Tritonitis* of the ancients, into which Ulysses sailed, is the stretch of water separating Djerba from the mainland, rather than the inner lake behind the Oasis of Gabès, marked *Palus Tritonitis* on every map and chart, both ancient and modern, and that in prehistoric times all these chotts were united and formed of themselves an inland sea. (*Vide* G. Boissière, p. 25 *et seq.* Also Sir R. L. Playfair, *Travels*, p. 271.)

Conclusion

enjoying the full benefits of civilised life. Carthage, the metropolis of the East; Cæsarea, the enlightened capital of the West; Hadrumetum, the flourishing city of the Byzacene; Saldæ, the beautiful city on the hills; and Leptis, on the shores of the Great Syrtes, took high rank among the commercial ports on the borders of the Mediterranean. And in the interior, Cirta, the capital of old Numidia; Sitifis, the seat of commerce at the crossing of the great Roman highways; Lambæsis, with its vast military population, presenting scenes of activity in times of peace or frontier disturbances; Thamugas, the city of delight, where Roman citizens loved to congregate and to make their last resting-place when life's work was over; Calama, Uthina, Thugga, Sufes, and Sufetula—each and all compared favourably with similar cities and towns in Italy, Spain, and Gaul, and have left equally enduring marks of a long career of wealth and prosperity.

If we turn to inscriptions relating to municipal life, we find that obedience to ruling authority and loyalty to the Emperor are seldom wanting. The discipline which was maintained in Rome till the fall of the Western Empire was equally potent in the provinces. We find the same degrees of magistracy, the same laws so adjusted as not to press too heavily on the old-world traditions of native races, the same gods and ranks of priesthood, and the same public-minded spirit which prompted Roman citizens in all parts of the Empire to ennoble the country of their adoption by works of munificence or general utility. And memorials of men and women in every walk of life are with us also, bearing unmistakable testimony to the existence of contented and well-ordered communities. The expressions may often seem to us exaggerated in these prosaic times, but any one who is accustomed to read the well-known lettering will not fail to note that the ties of family and friendship were rarely forgotten, and that the employment of superlative expressions of endearment and regret was but the utterance of the heart in the hour of grief or bereavement.

In this closing stage of our inquiry it may be desirable to ascertain, on the basis of monumental remains and inscriptions, whether the achievements of Roman citizens in these African provinces, either in literature or art in their various branches, may be classed as of African growth, and how far the subjugation of the country may, at any period of the Roman occupation, be said to have been complete.[1]

In previous chapters allusion has been made to Carthage and Cirta as the great centres of scholarship, proving as attractive to students in literature and philosophy as the university towns of our own day in Great Britain or other European countries. A long roll of names, mostly bearing the stamp of Italian origin, has been transmitted to us by various contemporary writers. Some of these distinguished African scholars were descendants of settlers in the early days of colonisation, and may fairly lay claim to be classed as Africans; while others were of a rambling order, passing from Athens or Corinth, Alexandria or Rome, to take part in some educational movement, or to exhibit their skill in some school of rhetoric or philosophy.

The intimate commercial relations between Carthaginians and Greeks, prior to the Roman occupation, tended to the spread of Hellenism in the coast towns of North Africa; while the establishment of Greek merchants in the chief cities of Numidia gave an impetus to the general use of Greek among the better educated classes. Micipsa, the Numidian, favoured the intercourse with Greeks, and induced merchants from the islands of the Mediterranean to settle permanently in his dominions. Juba II., again, gave exceptional encouragement to the literature and arts of Greece, and, in the course of his long and prosperous reign, made Cæsarea, his capital, a renowned centre of culture and refinement. At a still later period, under the Antonines, Greek was the accepted language of the coast towns. Latin had made little progress, and the Punic tongue largely prevailed among the peasantry and labouring classes. From Aurelius Victor we learn that the Emperor Septimius Severus, a native of Leptis, spoke Punic and Greek. He

[1] The Romans certainly occupied some of the oases in the Desert. At Géryville in south-western Algeria, the same parallel as El-Aghuoat, are traces of Roman occupation; also at Besseriani (ad Majores), not far from Chott Molghigh, where a stone bearing the name of Trajan was found. (Duruy, *Histoire des Romains*, vol. v. p. 478.)

Paulinus Suetonius, familiar to us as Roman governor of Britain in the time of Vitellius, crossed Mount Atlas with an army and encamped near the desert-river Ger in south-east Morocco. The name of Ger is still preserved. *Eph. Epigr.* vol. v. fasc. 3 and 4, No. 1043.)

Conclusion

expressed himself easily in the latter, but his knowledge of Latin was slight. This spread of Hellenism continued till about the middle of the third century, when Roman colonisation had so far advanced as to render the use of the Latin tongue an absolute necessity; and in the age of St. Augustine the use of Greek must have been exceptional, the language awaiting a revival under the Byzantine Emperors after a lapse of 150 years. It is reasonable, therefore, to find the literature of North Africa bearing this stamp of Hellenism, and the chief authors of the first three centuries of the Christian era transmitting their thoughts in Greek characters. King Juba II., Apuleius of Madaura, Fronto of Cirta, and Tertullian of Carthage, representing different periods and different schools of thought, may be selected from the long list of African writers who preferred to express themselves in Greek rather than in Latin. And at a later period we find such eminent authors as Lactantius and Julius Africanus writing their compositions also in Greek, at a time when Latin had asserted itself as the general language in every provincial town. But in the great teaching centres at Carthage, Hadrumetum, Cirta, and Leptis, which were largely frequented by students of African origin, the arts of writing and declamation were taught in Latin and Punic as well as in Greek, Punic largely prevailing.[1] The result was the formation of a literary style of heterogeneous kind, with Greek as a basis, a large admixture of Punic and Libyan expressions, and the free use of Latin words and idioms transported from the other side of the Mediterranean. But the Greek was not the Greek of Æschylus or Sophocles, nor was the Latin the language spoken by Virgil or Horace. In a word, it was essentially of African growth, and, to use the words of an eminent modern writer, it possessed an originality that was remarkable. Perhaps the writings of Apuleius are more familiar to us, even in their translated form, than those of any other African author, and if they have aroused a larger share of critical enthusiasm than has fallen to the lot of any other literary genius of that time, it is due to the versatile talents which made Apuleius pre-eminent among Africans. Whether as romancer, philosopher, orator, writer, or dreamer, Apuleius stands alone, and, as the author of *The Golden Ass*, will always

[1] *Vide* J. Toutain, p. 168; also G. Boissier, *Le Journal des Savants*, Jan. 1895.

take rank as one of the fathers of romance. Among other African writers who assisted in creating an African literature, Apollinaris of Carthage, the learned grammarian of world-wide reputation ; Fronto of Cirta, skilled in rhetoric and debate ; Aulus Gellius, the renowned author of *Noctes Atticæ* ; Severus of Leptis, the grandfather of the Emperor Septimius ; Florus, the poet and rhetorician, and Aurelius Victor, the historian stand out conspicuously in the ranks of Roman literature. Macrobius also, a contemporary of St. Augustine, and Capella, a poet and romancer and a native of Madaura, merit a place in the records of African literature. Mention should also be made of Terentianus, the Moor, whose works in prose and verse are still extant, and his rival compatriot Juba, whose work on the metric art established a high reputation among authors at the beginning of the third century.[1]

The stamp of originality impressed upon so many literary creations in North Africa is conspicuous by its absence in all that relates to the artistic products of the country. Neither in painting, sculpture, architecture, nor any branch of the decorative arts are there any indications of the influence exercised by climate, habits of life, or national sentiment. Religion in its many aspects, with a long array of deities attached to various forms of almost forgotten creeds, and legendary history, with its many links of association with the primitive inhabitants of the world, failed to arouse the imaginative faculty. The ideal played no part in the arts of Africa. Monumental remains and fragments of sculpture are numerous enough, but the art was not of Africa. There is nothing to remind us of the soil or the daily life of an ancient people. There is nothing, in fact, of African growth and, to quote the words of an intelligent writer on this subject,[2] there is abundant proof of sterility of imagination in all that relates to the artistic products of a great and prosperous people. In testimony of this assertion, the Punic sculptors failed to originate anything in human form to represent their conception of their most ancient divinities. 'When the Latin name of Saturn was substituted for the Punic name of Baal, and when the custom of modelling human repre-

---

[1] B. Ten Brink, *Jubæ Maurusii de Re Metrica Reliquiæ*. Utrecht, 1854. Also Paul Monceaux, *Les Africains*, p. 390.

[2] J. Toutain, p. 113 ; also *Mélanges de l'Ecole Francaise de Rome*, 1892, p. 97.

sentations of deities became recognised in the country, it was Græco-Roman art which supplied the ideas. But the Cronos of Greece and the Saturn of Italy had few attributes in common with the Phœnician Baal. The first two were symbolised by the scythe and the serpent, and the last by the crescent and the disc. Instead of conceiving a new type, such as Alexandrian art had produced in its representations of Zeus-Ammon, of Serapis and Isis, African art was content with adding to the bust of Saturn figures of Helios and Selene, personifying the Sun and Moon. In their language the deity was spoken of as one, though in their art it was triune.' The reason for this absence of artistic proclivities is not far to seek. The race which preceded the Roman was anything but artistic. The fine arts never flourished at Carthage, and certainly every exploration, either on the site of the city itself or of the numerous *emporia* on the coast, favours this statement. As a tributary of Egypt for a long period the Carthaginians, in spite of their wealth and power, were satisfied with borrowing from their master the skilled products of a neighbouring country. And in later years, when Carthage had to contend with Greeks in the fair island of Sicily, resplendent with temples and palaces, embellished with sculpture of the best period of Greek art, and rich in works of jewellery and specimens of the plastic art, Hellenism exercised an irresistible attraction, testified in a measure by Carthaginian coins which have been transmitted to us almost as perfect as on the day when they were minted. These two consecutive influences, Egyptian and Greek, have left their mark on the numerous remains which may still be studied in the galleries of the Louvre or in the museum on Carthage hill, where decorative forms associated with Egyptian and Hellenic art may be seen side by side

It is reasonable to assume that Punic Carthage, at the time of the second Punic war, presented to the Romans an aspect somewhat similar to that of other towns bordering on the Mediterranean colonised by Greeks, and that the temples and public buildings which adorned the streets of the great metropolis were the works of Greek artists encouraged to settle in this prosperous corner of North Africa. The appearance of other towns on the coast, peopled by Carthaginians and Greeks and the descendants of old Phœnician trading families, is also a matter of pleasant conjecture. Nor can any reliable opinion be formed of the appearance of the walled city of Carthage of Roman times, although there is abundant evidence to prove that, at the close of the second century, Carthage was second only to Rome and Alexandria in its external display of wealth and magnificence. Fortunately we can speak with absolute certainty of the condition and grandeur of many of the chief towns already mentioned in these pages, and can compare their public edifices and adornments with those of other countries peopled by Romans. But originality is wanting. Græco Roman art, rooted in the golden days of the Republic and in full flower in the active reign of Augustus, became the servant of the Roman in every country of his adoption. North Africa presented no exception to this order of things. Moulded to his own ends and infused with the dominating spirit which characterised his race, the arts of Rome were transplanted to the most distant provinces of the Empire, bearing the same impress of change, progress, and decline as in the metropolis itself. In every branch of art, whether in sculpture, painting as displayed in the decorative forms of mosaic, or in architectural design, the same monumental remains await our coming, the basilica, the amphitheatre, the triumphal arch; the aqueduct and the fountain; the bridge, the temple, and the tomb. They stand before us as examples of dignity of conception. unerringness of line, justness of proportion, fitness of purpose, and soundness of construction. Purity of style is too often wanting. But as memorials of a great people they bear the impress of that strength of character and unswerving purpose which made the Roman name so conspicuous among nations of earlier as well as later times. It may be said of the triumphal arch, the glory of the Empire, symbol of power and progress, that it is a mere monument of the past, for triumphing Cæsar with his spoil-laden legions needs it no longer; of the great *Thermæ*, which in the later Empire became part of the national life, the club and the café for all classes of citizens, that their value departed with the people who originated them; of the aqueduct, that its stately aspect has for ever given place to more prosaic forms. The Basilica has been superseded by the Mart, the Exchange, the Court of Justice. Even the colonnade and the portico, which the Roman made his own, and which are still amongst the beautiful of architectural forms, have had their day, though, let us hope, to return again in the cycle of recurrent change. Granted that the fashion of all these things has passed away, we must admit that the spirit which prompted them is with us still. The growth of nations, the revolutions in public and social life during a period of wellnigh fifteen centuries, have failed to dim the Roman name, or to break the spell of his compelling genius. His laws, his language, his literature, his festivals, even his calendar, keep their ground. And in architectural forms do not the Christian cathedrals, or even the simple village church with its nave and aisles, its arcaded lines and its apsidal choir, remind us daily of their Roman prototype, the basilica of the Cæsars? The student goes forth to realise the dream of his youth, the world of antiquity. He bends his steps towards Rome, not the Rome of the Pope, but the Rome of imperial Cæsar, for therein lies the spirit of the Roman. The antiquary, in these far-off isles of Britain, unearths and brings to light a pavement of mosaic, a stretch of wall, a fragment of pottery, and the interest of a county is in a blaze—kindled by the spirit of the Roman. The traveller in a distant land is attracted by some chiselled stone lying neglected by the wayside. He marks its familiar letters, and, forgetful of aught else, strives to decipher the time-worn sentences; for on him likewise the genius of Rome has laid a spell. The vital force in all that the Roman originated, or adapted to his own ends, has no parallel in the history of mankind.

It is difficult to ascertain from the latest Latin authors, or from Byzantine and Arab writers, whether the boundaries of Roman administration were definitely fixed, and whether the subjugation of the country was ever regarded as complete. Fortunately, archæology comes to our aid, and, as the useful handmaid of history, elucidates many points arising out of these questions. The remains of a clearly defined line of fortresses and military posts stretching across the mountain ranges of the Tell, and along the desert frontier from Cyrene to the confines of Western Mauritania, bear ample testimony to the nature of the defensive measures adopted by the Romans against invasion from the west and south, and to a feeling of insecurity in the presence of native races so little desirous of cultivating more civilised ways of life. Till the close of the Empire these frontier strongholds were mostly occupied by veterans, whose services to the State in times of raid or insurrection are recorded in several inscriptions still extant. From the time of their first encounter with the Berbers of the hill country or the rude warriors from the Desert, the Romans must have recognised the almost insuperable difficulties in waging irregular warfare with unorganised tribes, having no seat of government and no settled habitations—here to-day and gone to-morrow, the hillsman secure in some inaccessible mountain retreat, the man of the Desert lost to sight in a whirlwind of sand as he scampered across his trackless domain. This sense of insecurity seems to have been never absent from the Roman mind, and was particularly apparent at a late period of the Empire, when Diocletian attached the province of Mauritania Tingitana to the diocese of Spain, as a means of checking the piratical raids of Moorish corsairs on both shores of the Mediterranean. It was also indicated by the unusual authority given to the commander of the legion in Africa, who, from the time of Caligula, received his orders direct from the Emperor, and exercised more power than the governor of the province. Exceptional circumstances demanded exceptional forms of government, and the defensive measures found necessary for the protection of large communities enjoying all the privileges of civilised life redound to the credit of the Roman world; yet, looking back at the six centuries of work accomplished by the Romans in their attempt to make North Africa a prolongation of Italy, one is forced to admit that the subjugation of the country was never complete, and that the native races were never conquered.

The climatic condition and the general aspect of the country in the early days of Roman occupation were much as they are in our own time, except, perhaps, on the southern frontiers overlooking the great Desert. But with the development of Roman civilisation a new order of things changed the face of the land. Recognising the value of natural resources, and bending the elements to his indomitable will in the service of mankind, the Roman colonist controlled the watercourses, constructed gigantic reservoirs to meet the necessities of a thirsty soil, encouraged forestry, and converted a region of desolation into a garden of cultivation. And this is amply borne out in the statements of Arab authors of the seventh century, who are profuse in their praise of the fair land which had fallen into their hands. From Carthage to Tangier, stretching a thousand miles from east to

Conclusion

west, the whole country was clothed with timber, and in many parts of the south olive woods were so dense that you could travel from village to village under a roof of foliage.[1]

It may be asserted, with an equal show of truth, that the condition of North Africa as a colony in the present day, and in full recognition of the enlightened policy of the French, as masters of the larger portion, bears a strong resemblance to that which prevailed under the broad but sterner rule of the Roman Emperors. We hear of the same occasional disturbances on the frontiers, the same forced submission of the hill tribes, the same difficulties in guarding the outposts from the dangers of tribal revolt, and the same racial antagonism to the methods and habits of civilisation. The Libyan gave place to the Phœnician as a commercial necessity, and surrendered the command of the coast without appeal to arms or the sacrifice of human life. The Carthaginian, in his turn, converted the factories and storehouses of his ancestors into temples and palaces, and a country of traders became the most formidable nation of the old world. The achievements of the Romans are a landmark in the history of mankind, and can never be ignored. Then came the destructive Vandals, followed by the hybrid Byzantines, and with their final expulsion by Arabs the history of antiquity may be said to have come to a close. To-day is but the yesterday of sixteen hundred years ago. 'The Arab has replaced the Phœnician' (as M. Paul Monceaux has observed),[2] 'and the Frenchman has replaced the Roman. But that is all.' The primitive races—the ancient Berbers of the Desert or the mountain ranges, are still in possession, preserving their old traditions of tribal and social life, and speaking almost the same tongue

---

[1] The region known as Byzacena, now forming the southern portion of Tunisia, was covered with olive woods. The prosperity of the country was largely due to the enormous quantity of oil shipped to Italy and other countries. As an instance of the value of this product it is stated that when Sufetula, under the rule of Gregorius, was captured by Arabs, the general commanding the victorious army was amazed at the amount of treasure that had fallen into his hands. 'Whence comes this enormous wealth?' he asked. Looking about him as though in search of some hidden object, a citizen picked up an olive and, laying it before the general, told him that this little fruit was the cause of all their prosperity, adding that the Byzantines, who had no olives in their country, were their best customers. (*Vide* Ibn Abd el Hakem, *Histoire des Berbères*, transl. by De Slane, i. p. 306; also Paul Bourde, *Les Cultures Fruitières*, Tunis, 1893.)

[2] Paul Monceaux, *Les Africains*, p. 3.

as their ancestors did some three thousand years ago.[1] The Numidian, the Moor, and the Getulian are there also, cultivating their olives in the land of their forefathers, tending their sheep on the broad plains of the Metidja or Chelif, or moving silently from place to place, like true sons of the Desert.

Reflections such as these, quickened by personal acquaintance with the undying memorials of a great people, give an interest to their achievements in every part of an old-world Empire. It is good for us, as citizens of a later Empire, enjoying inestimable privileges inseparable from a far higher range of civilisation, to think over these things, in a spirit of gratitude to the Roman world for services rendered in the cause of human progress. The civilising work of the Romans in this fair land of North Africa will always be a pleasant memory, and will provide for generations to come an inexhaustible field for study and research.

[1] The old Carthaginian idiom has completely disappeared, but the Libyan or Berber dialect is still spoken by some of the Desert tribes, little altered, though with the addition of many words and expressions that are either Latin or Neo-Punic. (M. J. Toutain, *Les Cités Romaines de la Tunisie.*)

MOSAIC SLAB IN THE MUSEUM AT CONSTANTINE
(Byzantine period)

APPENDICES

APPENDIX I

LIST OF ABBREVIATIONS USUALLY FOUND IN ROMAN INSCRIPTIONS AND NOTICED ON MEMORIAL STONES IN NORTH AFRICA.

A. C. *armorum custos.*
A. P. *anno provinciæ.*
A. P. C. *ager publicus Cirtensium.*
B. B. *bonis bene.*
B. B. M. M. *bonis bene, malis male.*
B. M. *bene merenti.*
B. M. P *bonæ memoriæ puella.*
B. M. V. *bonæ memoriæ vir.*
B. Q. *bene quiescat.*
C. A. *curam agente.*
C. F. F. *carissimæ filiæ fecit.*
C. J. C. *Colonia Julia Carthago.*
C. M. V. *clarissimæ memoriæ vir.*
C. S. F. P. N. C. *consularis sexfascalis provinciæ Numidiæ Constantinæ.*
D. *depositus ; dedit ; designatus ; domo ; duplarius.*
D. D. *decreto decurionum ; dedit dedicavit ; donum dedit.*
D. D. P. P. *decreto decurionum pecunia publica.*
D. M. E. *devotus majestatique ejus.*
D. M. S. *Diis manibus sacrum.*
D. N. *dominus noster.*
D. N. M. Q. E. *devotus numini majestatique ejus.*
D. S. F. *de suo fecit.*
D. S. P. *de suo posuit.*
E. O. B. Q. *ei ossa bene quiescant.*

E. V. *egregius vir.*
F. C. *fieri curavit ; faciendum curavit.*
F. D. *filio dulcissimo ; filiæ dulcissimæ ; fecit dedicavit.*
F. K. F. *filio carissimo fecit.*
F. P. D. M. P. *filius patri dulcissimo matri piissimæ ; filius parentibus de meo posuit.*
G. P. R. F. *genio populi Romani feliciter.*
H. B. *homo bonus.*
H. E. *hic est.*
H. E. B. Q. *hic est bene quiescat.*
H. E. F. *hæres ejus fecit.*
H. E. S. *hic est situs.*
H. M. F. *honestæ memoriæ femina.*
H. M. M. *honesta missione missus.*
H. O. B. Q. *hic ossa bene quiescant.*
H. P. *hæres posuit.*
H. Q. B. *hic quiescat bene.*
I. O. M. *Jovi optimo maximo.*
L. A. P. *libens animo posuit.*
L. D. D. D. *loco dato decurionum decreto.*
L. L. V. S. *lætus libens votum solvit.*
L. P. P. P. *loco publico pecunia publica.*
M. B. *malis bene.*

M. D. M. I. *Mater deum magna Idæa.*
M. F. *memoriam fecit.*
M. K. *mater castrorum.*
M. L. *miles legionis.*
M. V. P. P. *maritus uxori piissimæ posuit; uxori piæ posuit.*
N. M. Q. E. D. *numini majestatique ejus dicatissimus.*
O. B. Q. T. *ossa bene quiescant tibi.*
P. A. *provincia Africa.*
PA. ET MA. *pater et mater.*
P. N. *præses noster; Numidiæ.*
P. D. D. P. P. *posuerunt decreto decurionum pecunia publica.*
P. F. K. F. *pater filio carissimo fecit.*
P. N. C. *præses Numidiæ Constantinæ.*
P. P. *primus pilus.*
P. P. M. S. *præses provinciæ Mauritaniæ Sitifensis.*
P. P. N. *præses provinciæ Numidiæ.*
P. P. P. *parentes pii posuerunt.*
P. S. D. N. *pro salute domini nostri.*
Q. *Quæstor.*
Q. M. C. *qui militare cœperunt.*
Q. Q. *quinquennalis.*
Q. R. Q. T. I. T. E. Q. N. A. LE. *fecit.* The concluding lines of a dedication to a *virgo sancta*, age 18, found near Hydra. The meaning of these initial letters has not yet been ascertained.
S. A. S. *Saturno augusto sacrum.*

S. C. F. C. *senatus consulto faciendum curaverunt.*
SEX. F. P. N. *sexfascalis provinciæ Numidiæ.*
S. P. *sua pecunia; sumptu proprio; sumptu publico.*
S. P. D. D. D. *sua pecunia dono dedit dedicavit.*
S. P. F. C. *sua pecunia faciendum curavit.*
S. S. *sumptu suo; suis sumptibus; supra scripta.*
S. T. L. *sit terra levis.*
S. T. T. L. *sit tibi terra levis.*
S. V. *se vivo.*
T. F. I. *testamento fieri jussit.*
V. A. *vixit annis.*
V. C. *vir clarissimus.*
V. E. *vir egregius.*
V. H. *vir honestus.*
V. L. A. S. *votum libens animo solvit.*
V. O. *vir optimus.*
V. P. *vir perfectissimus; votum posuit.*
V. P. A. *vixit piis annis.*
V. P. A. V. P. *vir perfectissimus agens vicem præsidis.*
V. P. F. *uxor piissima fecit.*
V. P. P. P. N. *vir perfectissimus præses provinciæ Numidiæ.*
V. S. I. *vice sacra judicans.*
V. S. L. A. F. *votum solvit libens animo feliciter.*
V. V. V. *vale, vale, vale.*

APPENDIX II

LIST OF THE PRINCIPAL KNOWN TOWNS IN THE AFRICAN PROVINCES OF THE ROMAN EMPIRE, OR THE SITES OF OTHERS WHICH HAVE BEEN IDENTIFIED BY INSCRIPTIONS.

Provincia Byzacena abbreviated thus:	P.B.
,, Mauritania Cæsariensis abbreviated thus:	P.M.C.
,, Mauritania Sitifensis ,,	P.M.S.
,, Mauritania Tingitana ,,	P.M.T.
,, Numidia ,,	P.N.
,, Proconsularis ,,	P.P.
,, Tripolitana ,,	P.T.

Roman Name	Modern Name	Province
Abuzza	Henchir Djezza	P.P.
Acholla	El Alia	P.P.
Ad Aquas	Bordj Medjana	P.P.
Ad Fratres	Nemours	P.M.C.
Ad Majores	Besseriani	P.N.
Ad Medias	Medeah	P.M.C.
Ad Mercuriam	Ain Chabro	P.N.
Ad Piscinam	Hammâm	P.N.
Ad Regias	Arbal	P.M.C.
Agbia	Hedjah	P.P.
Altava	Lamoricière	P.M.C.
Althiburus	*Hr. Medeina	P.P.
Ammædara	Hydra	P.B.
Aphrodisium	Phradise	P.P.
Apisa	Hr. Ain Tarf	P.P.
Apollonia	Mersa Souza	P.T.
Aquæ Cæsaris	Hr. el-Hamescha	P.N.
Aquæ Calidæ	Hammâm Righa	P.M.C.
Aquæ Regiæ	Hr. Bubuscha	P.B.
Aquæ Sirenses	Hammâm ben Hannia	P.M.C.
Aquæ Tibilitanæ	Hammâm Meskoutin	P.N.
Aquæ Flavianæ	Hr. Hammâm	P.N.

* Hr. Abbreviation of Henchir, signifying ruins or remains of antiquity.

312 Roman Africa

Roman Name	Modern Name	Province
Aræ	Tarmunt	P.M.S.
Arsacal	Ain Kerma	P.N.
Arsenaria	Arzeu	P.M.C.
Assuras	Zanfour	P.P.
Aubuzza	Hr. Djezza	P.P.
Aurelia Vina	Hr. el-Meden	P.P.
Ausum	Akbou	P.M.C.
Auzia	Aumale	P.M.C.
Avitta	Bou-Flis	P.P.
Babba	Narouja	—
Bagai	Ksar Bagai	P.N.
Barca	Tolometa	P.T.
Berenice	Benghazi	P.T.
Bescera	Biskera	P.N.
Bida	Djamäat-es-Saharidj	P.N.
Bisica Lucana	Testour	P.P.
Bulla Regia	Hammâm Darradji	P.P.
Cæsarea	Cherchel	P.M.C.
Calceus Herculis	El-Kantara	P.N.
Capsa	Gafsa	P.B.
Carpis	El-Mraissa	P.P.
Cartenna	Tenes	P.M.C.
Carthago	Carthage	P.P.
Casæ	El-Mâdher	P.N.
Castellum Medianum	Bordj Sebbalat	P.M.C.
Castellum Tingitanum	Orléansville	P.M.C.
Castra Cornelia	Kalat el-Oued	P.P.
Castra Nova	Mascara	P.M.C.
Castra Severiana	Hadjar Roum	P.M.C.
Cedia	Hr. um Kif	P.N.
Cella	Hr. en Naam	P.B.
Cellæ	Kherbet Zerga	P.M.S.
Chilma	Gilma	P.B.
Choba	Ziama	P.M.S.
Chullu	Collo	P.N.
Chusira	Kissera	P.B.
Cirta	Constantine	P.N.
Cissi	Dellys	P.M.C.
Civitas Celtianensium	El-Meraba	P.N.
Civitas Urusitana	Hr. Sudja	P.B.
Clupea	Kelibia	P.P.
Columnata	Touknia	P.M.C.
Cuiculum	Djemila	P.N.
Curubis	Kourba	P.P.
Cydamus	Ghadâmes	P.T.
Cyrene	Grenna	P.T.
Diana Veteranorum	Zana	P.N.
Darnis	Derna	P.T.
Equizetum	El Gueria	P.M.S.
Furnis	El Msaadin	P.P.
Furnis Limasa	Hr. Boudja	P.P.
Gemellæ	Mlili	P.N.
Gigthis	Hr. Bou Ghâra	P.T.

Appendix II 313

Roman Name	Modern Name	Province
Gilva	Aghbal	P.M.C.
Giufis	Hr. Mecherka	P.P.
Goris	Hr. Dräa el-Gamra	P.P.
Gurza	Kala'at Kebira	P.B.
Hadrumetum	Susa	P.B.
Hippo Diarrhytus	Bizerta	P.P.
Hippo Regius	Bone	P.N.
Horrea	Ain Zada	P.M.S.
Horrea Cælia	Hergla	P.B.
Icosium	Algiers	P.M.C.
Igilgilis	Djidjelli	P.M.S.
Iomnium	Taksebt	P.M.C.
Kalama	Guelma	P.N.
Lamasba	Hr. Meruâna	P.N.
Lambæsis	Lambessa	P.N.
Lambiridis	Kherbet Uled Arif	P.N.
Lares	Lorbes	P.P.
Lemellef	Kherbet Zembia	P.M.S.
Leptis Magna	Lebda	P.T.
Leptis Parva	Lemta	P.B.
Lixus	El Araisch	P.M.T.
Macomades Majores	Ksûr el-Ahmahr	P.N.
Macomades Minores	Mahres	P.B.
Mactaris	Mukther	P.P.
Madaura	Mdaourouch	P.N.
Malliana	Milianah	P.M.C.
Mascula	Ain Khenchla	P.N.
Masculula	Hr. Gergûr	P.P.
Mastar	Ruffach	P.N.
Materna	Mateur	P.P.
Maxula	Rades	P.P.
Megalopolis	Soliman	P.P.
Membressa	Medjez el-Bab	P.P.
Mesarfelta	El Uthaia	P.N.
Milevum	Mila	P.N.
Mons	Kasbait	P.M.S.
Murustaga	Mostaganem	P.M.C.
Mustis	Hr. Mest	P.P.
Muzuc	Hr. Khaschoun	P.B.
Naro	Hammâm el-Lif	P.P.
Naragarra	Sidi Yûsef	P.N.
Neapolis	Nebeul	P.P.
Neferis	Hr. Bou Beker	P.P.
Nepte	Nefta	P.B.
Numerus Syrorum	Lalla Maghnia	P.M.C.
Œa	Tripoli	P.T.
Oppidum Novum	Ain Khadra	P.M.C.
Phua	Ain Fua	P.N.
Pomaria	Tlemçen	P.M.C.
Portus Divinus	Oran	P.M.C.
Portus Magnus	St. Leu	P.M.C.
Quiza	Pont du Cheliff	P.M.C.
Rapidi	Sour Djouab	P.M.C.

Roman Name	Modern Name	Province
Rubræ	Hadjar-Roum	P.M.C.
Rusazus	Azzouza	P.M.C.
Rusgunia	Medina Takious	P.M.C.
Rusicada	Philippeville	P.N.
Ruspina	Monastir	P.B.
Rusucurium	Tagzirt (?)	P.M.C.
Rusubeser	Zeffoun	P.M.C.
Sabrata	Zourara	P.T.
Saddar	Ain el-Bey	P.N.
Safar	Ain Temouchent (?)	P.M.C.
Saldæ	Bougie	P.M.S.
Sarra	Hr. Bez	P.B.
Satafis	Ain Kehira	P.M.S.
Scillium	Kasserin	P.B.
Segermes	Hr. Harât	P.B.
Septem Fratres	Ceuta	P.M.T.
Seressitum	Hr. el-Abuab	P.P.
Serteis	Kherbet Sidra	P.M.S.
Sicca Veneria	El-Kef	P.P.
Siga	Takenbrit	P.M.C.
Sigus	Zigania	P.N.
Sila	Sidi el-Abassi	P.N.
Simittu	Chemtou	P.P.
Sitifis	Setif	P.M.S.
Subzuar	Sadjar	P.N.
Sufazar	Amoura	P.M.C.
Sufes	Sbiba	P.B.
Sufetula	Sbeitla	P.B.
Sullectum	Salecta	P.B.
Tabaria	Mohammedia (?)	P.P.
Tacape	Gabes	P.T.
Tagaste	Souk-Ahras	P.N.
Tagura	Taoura	P.N.
Tanaramusa Castra	Berouagia	P.M.C.
Taphrura	Sfax	P.B.
Telepte	Feriana	P.B.
Temda (?)	Temda	P.N.
Tenelium	(?)	P.N.
Tepelte	Hr. Blaiet	P.P.
Teuchira	Taoukra	P.T.
Thabraca	Tabarca	P.P.
Thaca	Zactoum	P.B.
Thacia	Bordj Messaoudi	P.P.
Thala	Thala	P.B.
Thamugas	Timegad	P.N.
Thapsus	Dimas	P.B.
Thenæ	Hr. Tina	P.B.
Theveste	Tebessa	P.N.
Thibaris	Hr. Amâmet	P.P.
Thibica	Hr. Bir Magra	P.P.
Thibursicum	Teboursouk	P.P.
Thignica	Ain Tunga	P.P.
Thimburus	Hr. Kusch Batihia	P.P.

Appendix II

Roman Name	Modern Name	Province
Thubba.	Hr. Tobba	P.P.
Thuburbo Majus	Hr. Kasbat	P.P.
Thuburbo Minus	Tebourba	P.P.
Thubursicum.	Khamisa	P.N.
Thugga.	Dougga.	P.P.
Thunigabensis	Hr. Ain Laabed	P.P.
Thysdrus	El-Djem	P.B.
Tibilis .	Announa	P.N.
Tiddis .	El-Kheneg	P.N.
Tigis	Taourga	P.M.C.
Tigisis .	Ain el-Bord	P.N.
Timici .	Ain Temouchent (?)	P.M.C.
Timida Regia	Sidi Ali-Sedfini	P.P.
Tingis .	Tangiers	P.M.T.
Tipasa .	Tefaced.	P.M.C.
Tipasa .	Tefesh .	P.N.
Tisurus .	Tozer	P.B.
Tubuna.	Tobra	P.N.
Tuburnicus	Ain Tubernok	P.P.
Tubusuptus	Tiklat	P.M.S.
Tucca.	Hr. El-Abiod.	P.M.S.
Tuccabor	Tukâber	P.P.
Tunes .	Tunis	P.P.
Tuniza .	La Calle	P.N.
Turris .	Telmina.	P.T.
Turris Hannibalis.	Mahadia	P.B.
Uccula .	Hr. Durât	P.P.
Ucubis .	Hr. Kaussât .	P.P.
Uppenna	Hr. Schigarnia	P.B.
Usilla .	Inchilla .	P.B.
Usinaza.	Saneg .	P.M.C.
Uthina .	Oudena.	P.P.
Utica	Bou Chater	P.P.
Uzappa .	Sidi Abd el-Malek.	P.B.
Uzelis .	Udjel	P.N.
Vaga	Beja	P.P.
Vallis	Sidi Median .	P.P.
Vazaivi .	Ain Zoui	P.N.
Verecunda	Marcouna	P.N.
Vicus Augusti	Sidi Bou Khahila .	P.P.
Vicus Augusti	Hausch Sabra	P.P.
Villa Magna.	Zaghouan	P.P.
Vina	Hr. el-Mden .	P.P.
Volubilis	Ksar Faraun .	P.M.T.
Zabi	Beschilga	P.M.S.
Zama Major .	Hr. Djâma	P.P.
Zama Regia .	Sidi Amor Djedidi	P.P.
Zarai	Zraia	P.N.
Zattara .	Kef Bu Ziûn .	P.P.
Zilis	Azila	P.M.T.
Zuccabar	Affreville	P.M.C.
Zucchara	Ain Djougga.	P.P.

APPENDIX III

CHRONOLOGY OF THE PRINCIPAL EVENTS IN NORTH AFRICA DURING THE ROMAN OCCUPATION, AND, SUBSEQUENTLY, TILL THE INVASION OF THE COUNTRY BY ARABS.

Battle of Zama and defeat of Hannibal by P. Cornelius Scipio Africanus . . . . B.C. 202
Extraordinary career of Masinissa, the greatest of Numidian kings, commencing B.C. 212, and terminating . . . . . B.C. 148
Commencement of the third Punic War and the siege of Carthage . B.C. 149
Destruction of Carthage by the Romans under P. Cornelius Scipio Æmilianus . . . . B.C. 146
Caius Gracchus sent from Italy 6,000 persons to colonise North Africa and to found the city of Junonia on the site of Punic Carthage . . . . B.C. 122
Rise of Jugurtha, grandson of Masinissa, his seizure of the kingdom of Numidia, and commencement of the Jugurthine War . . B.C. 111
Defeat of Jugurtha by C. Marius and close of the war . . . B.C. 106
Death of Jugurtha and subsequent division of the kingdom of Numidia . . . . B.C. 104
Kingdom of Cyrene bequeathed to the Romans by Ptolemy Apion B.C. 97
Export of Numidian marbles to Rome first recorded . . . B.C. 78
Rivalries of Julius Cæsar and Pompey brought into the field Juba I., King of Numidia and great-grandson of Masinissa, who embraced the cause of Pompey in Africa, about . . . . B.C. 50
Julius Cæsar landed in Africa to subdue the Pompeian faction and fought a decisive battle at Thapsus, when the armies of Metellus Scipio, Cato, and Juba were defeated . . . . B.C. 46
North Africa from the borders of Egypt to the Atlantic Ocean became subject to the will of Rome . . . . . . B.C. 46
Sallust, the historian, appointed Roman governor of Numidia . B.C. 45
Juba II., son of Juba I., made subservient King of Mauritania by the order of Augustus . . . . B.C. 25
Commencement of the rebuilding of Carthage by the order of Augustus, who sent out 3,000 colonists to assist the natives in their work . . . . B.C. 19
Rise of Tacfarinas, the Numidian, who wages destructive war against the Romans, which continues for seven years. . . A.D. 17

Appendix III

Death of Tacfarinas, close of the rebellion, and submission of native tribes	A.D. 24
Mauritania made a Roman province by Caligula	A.D. 37
Death of Juba II., son of Juba I., closes the line of recognised native kings of Mauritania	A.D. 40
Galba, afterwards Emperor, proconsul of Africa	A.D. 46
Vitellius, afterwards Emperor, proconsul of Africa	A.D. 49
Vespasian established the third legion Augusta at Theveste	A.D. 72
Nerva established a colony of veterans at Sitifis	A.D. 97
Foundation of the city of Thamugas under Trajan, and great spread of colonisation in North Africa	A.D. 100
Insurrection of Moors under Q. Lusius Quietus suppressed	A.D. 117
Hadrian's first visit to the African provinces, and supposed date of the commencement of the aqueduct of Carthage	A.D. 122
Alleged second visit to Africa	A.D. 125
Permanent establishment of the third legion Augusta at Lambæsis	A.D. 125
Moors invade Numidia, but are suppressed	A.D. 138
Spread of education in Africa, and rise of Carthage, Cirta, and other cities as great teaching centres	A.D. 140
Death of Antoninus Pius, under whose rule of twenty-three years the provinces of Africa enjoyed great prosperity	A.D. 161
Joint rule of Marcus Aurelius and Lucius Verus	A.D. 161–169
Moors cross the Straits of Gibraltar and invade Bætica	A.D. 170
The rule of Commodus uneventful in North Africa	A.D. 180–192
Pertinax, a native of Hadrumetum, proclaimed Emperor	A.D. 192
Septimius Severus, a native of Africa, born at Leptis, subdues all rivals and ascends the throne as sole Emperor	A.D. 198
Great prosperity in North Africa and spread of colonisation	A.D. 200
Severus persecutes Christian communities in Africa and suffers Perpetua and others to be delivered to wild beasts in the amphitheatre at Carthage	A.D. 203
Caracalla raises to the rank of citizens all free inhabitants of the Empire	A.D. 216
The rise of Macrinus, a native of Africa, his assumption of the purple, and his death the following year	A.D. 217
Heliogabalus, a great-grandson of Bassianus, high priest of the Temple of the Sun at Emesa in Syria, proclaimed Augustus at the age of fourteen	A.D. 218
Alexander Severus, a native of Phœnicia, born in the Temple of Alexander the Great at Arka, proclaimed Emperor	A.D. 222
Maximinus, a Goth, with the assistance of Capellianus, Roman governor of Mauritania, assumes the purple and ravages North Africa	A.D. 235
Popular rising against the tyranny of Maximinus, and proclamation of Gordian as Cæsar Imperator	A.D. 236
Death of Gordian I. and of his son Gordian II.	A.D. 238
The great amphitheatre at Thysdrus probably commenced	A.D. 239

Gordian III. reigned successfully for six years and restored tranquillity in Africa. Assassinated by orders of Philip the Arab, who proclaimed himself Emperor . . . . . . A.D. 244
The thousandth anniversary of the foundation of Rome celebrated with great rejoicing throughout the Empire, and by the construction of many public works in Africa . . . . . A.D. 247
Philip the Arab murdered by his own soldiers . . . . . A.D. 249
Persecution of Christians in Africa under Decius . . . . A.D. 250
Æmilianus, a Moor, alleged to have been raised to the purple in the Isle of Djerba, and acknowledged Emperor by the Senate after the death of Decius . . . . . . A.D. 251
Continued persecution under Valerianus and his son Gallienus . A.D. 256
The rising of the Quinquegentians, or Feud of the Five Peoples, causes great devastation in North Africa . . . . . A.D. 260
Successful campaign of the Emperor Probus against the Marmarides on the eastern borders of Roman Africa . . . A.D. 280
Diocletian divides the Empire and allots the African provinces to Maximianus . . . . A.D. 284
Final suppression of the rebellion of the Quinquegentians . . A.D. 303
Abdication of Diocletian and temporary abdication of Maximianus . . . . A.D. 304
Rapid spread of Christianity throughout North Africa . . A.D. 305
Commencement of the Donatist schism, which was political as well as religious, in the reign of Constantius . . . . . A.D 305
The city of Thamugas, as well as other large towns in Numidia, suffered from the Donatist heresy . . . . . . A.D. 323
Constantine the Great convoked the Council of Nicæa in Bithynia, when 318 bishops attended and condemned the doctrines of the Donatists . . . . A.D. 325
Constantine the Great laid the foundations of Constantinople . A.D. 330
Julianus, the Apostate, receives the submission of the African provinces on the death of Constantius . . . . . A.D. 361
Rebellion of Moors under Firmus, who was defeated by Theodosius, father of Theodosius the Great, about . . . . A.D. 370
Restoration of many public buildings in North Africa in the reign of Valentinian and Valens . . . . A.D. 364-375
Rapid spread of Christianity in Africa under Theodosius the Great, who died . . . . A.D. 395
Rising of Gildon, a Moor and brother of Firmus, at that time military governor of Africa in the reign of Honorius . . . A.D. 397
Defeat of Gildon by Stilicho, a Vandal captain . . . . A.D. 398
St. Augustine created bishop of Hippo . . . . . A.D. 395
St. Augustine convenes a Council at Carthage, when 566 bishops were present . . . . A.D. 411
Bonifacius appointed governor of Africa . . . . . A.D. 422
The African provinces enjoyed peace and prosperity till the death of Honorius . . . . A.D. 423
Invasion of Africa by Vandals under Genseric . . . A.D. 429

Appendix III

Bonifacius defeated by the Vandals at Hippone . . . . A.D. 431
Carthage taken by surprise by the army of Genseric and the Vandal
   kingdom founded in North Africa . . . . . . A.D. 439
Valentinian III. abandons to the Vandals the Proconsular Pro-
   vince, Byzacena, and a portion of Numidia . . . . A.D. 442
All North Africa in the possession of the Vandals . . . . A.D. 476
African Council convened by Himeric, king of the Vandals. 474
   sees sent representatives. The bishops suffered terribly and
   were deprived of all their possessions . . . . . A.D. 484
Hilderic, the Vandal king, favours Christianity, recalls the bishops,
   and recognises Boniface as Primate of Africa . . . . A.D. 524
Belisarius, the Byzantine general, lands at Capoudia (Caput Vadia),
   not far from Thysdrus, and defeats Gelimer and the Vandal army A.D. 533
Solomon, his successor, chases the Vandals from Africa . . A.D. 534
Destruction of Thamugas by Moors . . . . . . A.D. 535
Solomon constructs fortifications outside all the principal towns, but
   destroys the public buildings of the Romans . . . . A.D. 539
Heraclius I. proclaimed Emperor 610, died . . . . . A.D. 641
North Africa overrun by Arabs . . . . A.D. 646
Gregorius, governor of Africa, resisted the Arabs, and was defeated
   near Tripoli. Sufetula, his capital, fell into the hands of the
   invaders . . . . A.D. 647
Destruction of Carthage by Hassan . . . . . . A.D. 698
Queen Kahina, the Joan of Arc of Numidia, resists the Arabs, and
   defeats them near Thamugas . . . . A.D. 703
She entrenched her army in the amphitheatre at Thysdrus and
   subsequently engaged Hassan in a decisive battle at the foot of
   the Aurès mountains, and was defeated . . . . . A.D. 705
All North Africa submits to the followers of Mahomet, and Islamism
   is firmly established . . . . A.D. 750

INDEX

ÆMILIANUS, the Moor, his short reign. Inscriptions relating to him, 239
Æsculapius, Temple of, at Lambæsis, and its remains, 159
African legion first located at Theveste, 44; removed to Lambæsis, 162
Agathocles, the Sicilian, invades North Africa, 3
Albinus, Clodius, memorial of, 198
Algerian onyx, its varieties and where found, 76
Amphitheatre at Thysdrus, its construction and arrangement, 231; its use as a fortress, 233; the principal ones compared, 234
Apollodorus, the architect, 62; the story of his disgrace, 119
Apuleius of Madaura, 132; his career and remarkable gifts, 134; notice of his principal works and account of his trial, 135-139
Aquæ Tibilitanæ, a remarkable spring; legend relating to it, 146
Aqueduct of Carthage, 109; its construction, 114; legend relating to it, 115
Army, the Roman, in the time of Marcus Aurelius, 162
Assuras, monumental remains of, 203
Augustine, St., Bishop of Hippo, 245
Augustus, dedication to, at Mascula, 42
Aurelian, Emperor, memorial of as *Restitutor Orbis*, 248

BAGRADAS, river, its peculiarities; legend of Regulus and his army, 20
Bassianus, the founder of a dynasty, 207; his pedigree, 219
Bocchus, king of Mauritania, and his treacherous conduct, 15
Boundaries of Roman Africa difficult to define, 305
Bulla Regia, its remains, 71
Byzacene, the region so called, 58

CÆSAR, Julius, victory at Thapsus, 17
Capellianus, Roman governor of Mauritania, incites the natives to revolt, 223
Caracalla, his arch at Theveste, 47; his rule in Africa, 205; inscriptions relating to him, 207
Carinus, Emperor, memorials of, 251
Carpitana, name of a town recorded in an inscription, 64
Carthage, Punic, destroyed, 13; magnificence of Roman Carthage, 24; heights of buildings in the city, 24; the aqueduct, 109; its construction, 114; a great intellectual centre, 131; its renowned scholars, 141
Carthaginians store their rain-water, system adopted, 110
Carus, Emperor, memorials of, 251
Castella, described, in various parts of North Africa, 168
Castrum at Lambæsis described, 166
Christianity, rise of in Africa, 242; leaders of, 243
Cirta, capital of Numidia, 8; made a seat of government by Augustus, 26; tomb of the silversmith, 80; the birthplace of Fronto, 142; its schools, 128; renamed by Constantine, 274
Cisterns, Punic, at Carthage, 112; Roman and others in the country, 110
Claudius, M. Aurelius, Emperor, his short reign, memorial of, 247
Cleopatra Selene, wife of Juba II., 26
Coloniæ explained, 36
Colonisation of North Africa, first attempted by C. Gracchus, 33
Commagena, an auxiliary force raised in that country employed in Africa, 188
Commodus, Emperor, his worthless rule, 187; his name erased, 189
Concrete construction explained, 22; its application, 114
Configuration of North Africa, a bar to complete occupation, 297

Y

Constans, son of Constantine the Great, his rule in Africa, inscriptions relating to him, 274
Constantine the Great, he defeats Licinius and becomes sole emperor, 267 ; inscriptions relating to him and his sons, 270-273
Constantius Chlorus, Emperor, merits of, his rule influenced by his wife Helena, 261
Constantius, son of Constantine the Great, memorials of, 275
Cornelia, Salonina, wife of Gallienus, Emperor, memorial of, 241
Cothon, meaning of the word, 21
Crispina, wife of Commodus, memorial of, at Thamugas, 194
Cyrene, its foundation, 4 ; transferred to the Romans by Ptolemy Apion, 18

DECIUS, persecution of Christians in Africa, 237 ; inscriptions relating to him, 238
Dioceses explained, 258
Diocletian, his remarkable rise, 253 ; inscriptions relating to him, 259 ; persecution of Christians in Africa, 263 ; division of the Empire, 266
Domitius, L. Alexander, governor of Africa, proclaims himself Emperor, 265

EDUCATION, spread of, in Africa in the second century, 128
Egrilianus, C. Cornelius, his munificence at Theveste, 48
El-Kahina, the Joan of Arc of North Africa, 233
Emesa in Syria and its Temple of the Sun, 213
Epitaphs of worthy men and women, 151

FAUSTINA the younger, memorials in her honour, 192
Fertility of the soil of North Africa attested by Pliny the Elder, 57
Firmus, a distinguished Moor, heads a revolt against Valentinian and is defeated, 280
Fronto of Cirta, his friendly relations with Marcus Aurelius, 143 ; his career, 145 ; memorial at Kalama, 145

GALBA, afterwards Emperor, proconsul of Africa, 41

Gallienus, son of Valentinian, memorial of, 241
Gallus, Emperor, successor of Decius, inscriptions relating to, 239
Genseric, invasion of North Africa, 245
Geta, inscription relating to him, 204
Getulians, 5
Gordian I. proclaimed Emperor at Thysdrus, 223 ; his defeat by Capellianus and suicide, 223
Gordian II., his short career, 223
Gordian III., several memorials in his honour, 224-227 ; a promoter of art, 228
Gracchus, Caius, his attempts at colonisation unsuccessful, 14, 33
Gratianus, Emperor, inscriptions relating to him, 286
Gregorius, governor of Africa, 91 ; his defeat by the Arabs, 124 ; inscription relating to him, 296
Gyaris, island of, 150

HADRIAN, his first visit to Africa, 105 ; second visit, inspection of the camp at Lambæsis, 107
Hadrumetum, an ancient port, 65
Helena, mother of Constantine the Great, memorial of, 262
Heliogabalus, his contemptible reign, 211 ; inscription bearing his name, 212
Herennius and Hostilianus, sons of Decius, memorials of, 238
Hippo Diarrhytus, its rise as a colony ; peculiarity of its currents, 64
Historians, the principal ancient authorities on North Africa, 103
Honorius, his weak rule, 289 ; memorials of, 290

ICOSIUM, the ancient Algiers, an inscription mentioning it, 42
Inscriptions, self-laudatory, 80, 82, 130 ; the last Roman one, 296

JOL, afterwards Julia Cæsarea, a Phœnician port, 26
Juba I., his sad end, 17
Juba II., his distinguished career, 25 ; his patronage of literature and the arts, 26 ; his existing sepulchre described, 27
Jugurtha, his remarkable career, 15
Julia Cæsarea, capital of Juba II., its monumental remains, 31
Julia Domna, 49 ; her extraordinary influence, 201 ; memorials in her honour, 202, 203

Index

Julia Mæsa, her distinguished position, 208
Julia Mammæa, 208; her influence over her son, Alexander Severus, 217
Julianus, the Apostate, memorial of, 278

KALAMA and its remains, 146
Khomair country and its people, 70
Kleber near Oran, its marble quarries, 76

LAMBÆSIS, the camp at, 166; its arrangements, 167; inscriptions both military and civil, 172-181
Latifundia explained, 14
Legion, the third Augustan, its services, 165, 171; its temporary disgrace, 90; reconstituted, 165
Leptis Magna, its antiquity, 6; birthplace of Septimius Severus, 140; a place of renown, 198
Licinius, Emperor and supporter of Paganism, opposes Constantine the Great and is defeated, 267
Livia, wife of Augustus, dedication to, at Zama, 42
Longevity, many examples of, 83
Lucius Domitius Alexander, governor of Africa, incites a revolt; inscription relating to him, 265

MACRINUS, the Moor, assumes the purple, 210
Mactar, ruins of, 79
Madaura, the birthplace of Apuleius, 132
Magistrates, gifts and money payments on their election, 99
Magnentius, the usurper, a memorial of, 275
Magnia Urbica, wife of the Emperor Carinus, memorial of, 251
Marble quarries in North Africa, 72, 75, 76, 77
Marcia Otacilia, wife of Philip the Arab, memorial of, 236
Marciana, wife of Septimius Severus, a memorial of, 200
Marcius Turbo, the general, his victory over Lusius Quietus, 107
Mascula, a seat of Christianity, 88
Masinissa, his remarkable career and foundation of a powerful kingdom, 12; his supposed sepulchre, 29
Masuna, a Moorish king, memorial of, 281
Mauritania, its frontier undefined, 273; divisions of under Claudius, 32; and under Diocletian, 53

Maxentius, son of Maximianus, raises the standard of revolt in Africa, 266; defeated by Constantine, 269
Maximianus, his joint rule with Diocletian, 257; inscriptions relating to him, 258; his abdication, 260; his reassumption of power, 266
Maximinus, his revolt and defeat, 220-225
Maximus, an upholder of Paganism, raises the standard of revolt in Africa and is defeated by Theodosius, 287
Medjerda, vagaries of the, 20
Medrassen, the tomb of Numidian kings, described, 30
Memmia, second wife of Septimius Severus, 218
Memorials of good women, 151; and of students, 130
Meninx, island of, its celebrity, 240
Milliaria, their origin, 68; the Miliiarium Aureum, 69
Milvian bridge, an inscription relating to it, 272
Monasteria, meaning of, 65
Municipia explained, 35

NATIVE troops in the Roman army in Africa, 184
North Africa, division of, 32; configuration of the country, 38
Numerianus, son of Carus, memorials of, 251
Numidia contributes to the success of the Romans, 10
Numidian marble, when first used, its transport, 75

ŒA, its prosperity and monumental remains, its associations with Apuleius, 133
Onyx, Algerian, 76
Orbiana, wife of Alexander Severus, her banishment to Cæsarea; memorial of, 216
Ostia, its importance under the Empire, and present condition, 59

PACCIA Marciana, wife of Septimius Severus, memorial of, 200
Pertinax, Emperor, memorials relating to him, 195
Philæni, legend of the, 6
Philænorum Aræ, site of, 5
Philip, the Arab, murders Gordian III., 235; his rule, inscription relating to him, 236

Pisé, method of building with, described, 114

Plautilla, wife of Caracalla, mentioned in an inscription, 202

Pliny the Elder in praise of fertility of soil of North Africa, 57

Pliny the Younger, his intimacy with Marcus Aurelius, 60

Pompeianus, a governor of Africa, his country seat, and its interesting remains, 292; inscription recording his name, 291

Pontifex Maximus, origin of the title explained, 224

Præcilius of Cirta, his tomb and remarkable epitaph, 81

Præses explained, 255; inscription recording the use of the title, 257

Prætorian guard : temporary disbandment, 199; their despotism and cruelty, 225

Prætorium at Lambæsis described, 186

Prefect of the Prætorian guard, a man of high distinction, 259

Priscus, Marius, proconsul of Africa, tried for corrupt practices, 61

Probus, Emperor, memorial of, 250

Proconsuls, corrupt practices, 60

QUADI, and their tactics, 163

Quietus, Lusius, governor of Mauritania, 107

Quinquegentians, their rebellion, 245; defeated by Maximian, 258

REGULUS, M. Attilius, his attack on the Carthaginian fleet, 3

Reservoirs in North Africa: one near Kairouan described, 111

Roads, classes of, 40, 66; superintendents of, 67; principal roads at end of second century, 182

Romans, our indebtedness to them, 305

Romanus, governor of Africa, brought to trial and condemned, 282

Rome, the thousandth anniversary in time of Philip the Arab, 235

Rufus, L. Passienus, honoured with a triumph, 42

SABINA, wife of Hadrian, 119

Sabinia Tranquillina, wife of Gordian III. : memorials of, 227

Saldæ, and its water supply, 112

Sallust, proconsul of Africa, 25

Saltus, meaning of, 189; the principal ones, 191

Scillium, its monumental remains, 82

Scipio Africanus and the close of the second Punic war, 11

Septimiana explained, 214

Septizonium explained, 203

Severus, Alexander, 213; inscriptions relating to him, 214; subject to his mother's influence, 217

Severus, Septimius, his powerful rule, 199; inscriptions, 200-203

Sexfascales, inscription relating to, 284

Sicca Veneria in the time of Constantine, 276

Sigus, an old Numidian city, 84

Simittu : Trajan's bridge, 72; its renowned marble quarries, 74

Sitifis, its rise and prosperity, 51

Sittius, Publius, his services, 34

Sœmias, Julia, mother of Heliogabalus, 208; memorial of, 212

Soldiers, privileges of, 170; their services in times of peace, 171; memorials of, 173-185

Solomon, the Byzantine general, 46

Sophonisba, story of, 8

Students, memorials of, 130

Sufes, a noted town, 123

Sufetula, its rise and prosperity, 123; its last days, 124; monumental remains and inscriptions, 126

Syphax, his wayward career, 7; his defeat, 9

TACFARINAS, the Numidian: his struggles with the Romans, 34; his defeat after seven years' war, 35

Tacitus, Emperor, merits of, 249

Temple at Theveste converted into a canteen, 51

Thabraca, its position and remains, 69; island of, 70

Thamugas, its foundation, 88; later history, 91; monumental remains, 92; inscriptions, 100

Theodosius, the general, his successful campaigns, 287

Theodosius the Great, memorials of, 289

Theodosius II., 295

Theveste, its history, 44; the basilica, 45; other monumental remains, 46-51

Tholus, meaning of, 47

Thysdrus, the town of, 229; its amphitheatre described, 230; subsequent history, 233

Tiberius, dedication to, 43

Tibilis, its extensive remains, 146

Trajan, his interest in the provinces of the Empire, regulates the corn supply from Africa, 55; his benevolence, 85

Index

Tripoli, monumental remains of, 156
Triumph, explained by Gibbon: triumphal arches, their origin, 49

UTHINA, remains of its theatre, 234
Utica, its antiquity, 19; structural remains: causes of its decay, 20

VALENTINIAN, his rule in Africa, 280; the Emperor's joint rule with Valens: inscriptions relating thereto, 284; restores public buildings in Africa, 285
Valerianus, memorial of, 241
Vandals, record of their expulsion from Africa, 45

Verecunda, its inscriptions, 147
Verus, the Emperor, and his joint rule with Marcus Aurelius, 156
Vespasian establishes third Augustan legion at Theveste, 41, 44
Veterans, establishment of, 35
Vicarius, the term explained, 258
Vitellius, proconsul of Africa, 41
Volussianus, son of Gallus, memorial of, 239

ZAGHOUAN, description of its monumental remains, 116
Zama Regia, its position, and battle of, 10

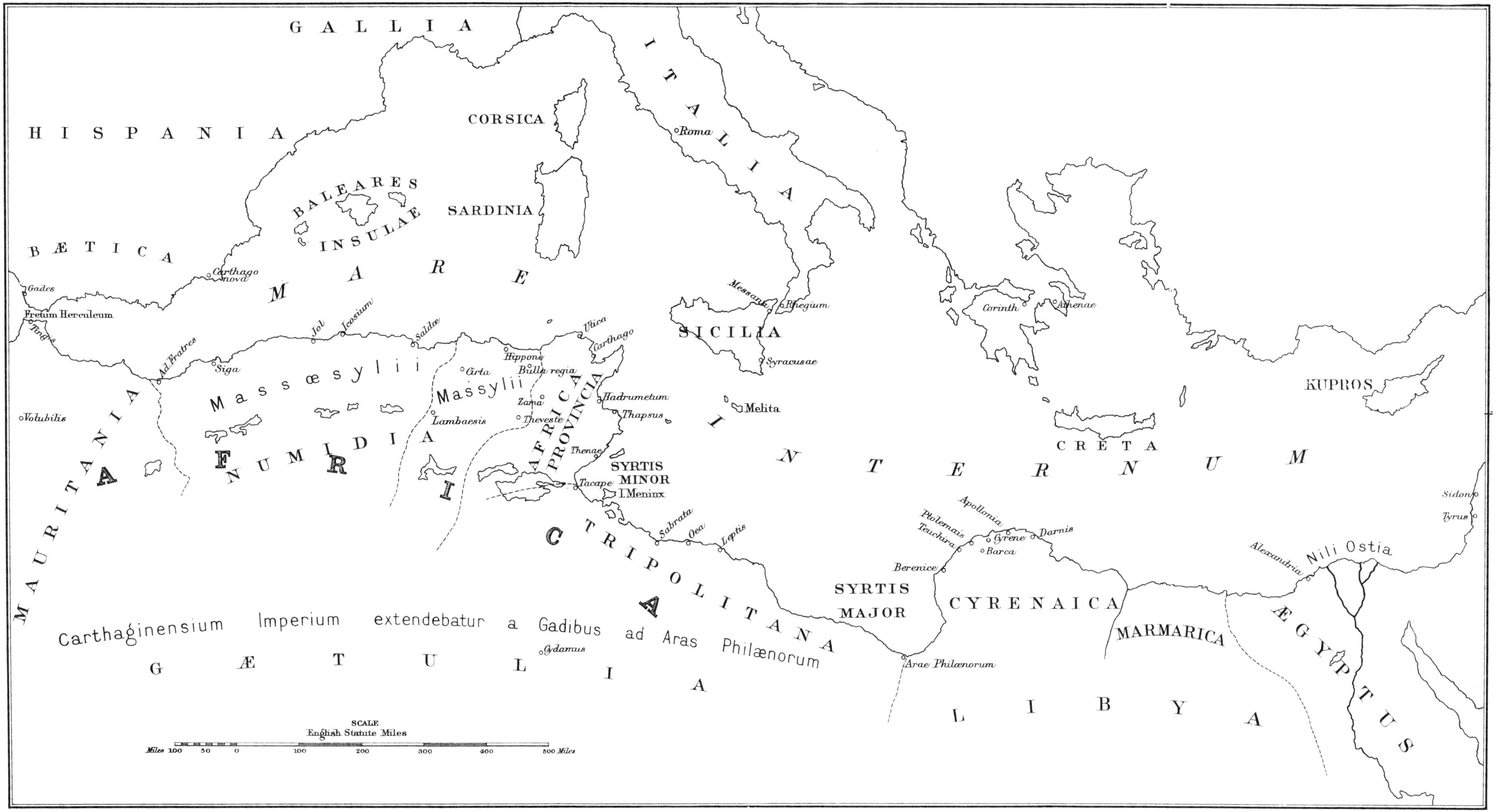
GALLIA
HISPANIA
ITALIA
CORSICA
SARDINIA
BALEARES INSULAE
BÆTICA
Roma
Carthago nova
Gades
Fretum Herculeum
Tingis
MARE INTERNUM
Messana
Rhegium
SICILIA
Syracusae
Melita
Corinth
Athenae
CRETA
KUPROS
Jol
Icosium
Saldæ
Utica
Carthago
Ad Fratres
Siga
Hippone
Bulla regia
Cirta
Massæsylii
Massylii
Zama
Lambaesis
Theveste
Hadrumetum
Thapsus
AFRICA PROVINCIA
Volubilis
MAURITANIA
AFRICA
NUMIDIA
Thenae
SYRTIS MINOR
Tacape
I. Meninx
TRIPOLITANA
Sabrata
Oea
Leptis
Ptolemais
Teuchira
Apollonia
Cyrene
Barca
Darnis
Berenice
SYRTIS MAJOR
CYRENAICA
MARMARICA
Alexandria
Nili Ostia
Sidon
Tyrus
ÆGYPTUS
Arae Philænorum
Carthaginensium Imperium extendebatur a Gadibus ad Aras Philænorum
Cydamus
GÆTULIA
LIBYA
SCALE
English Statute Miles
Miles 100 50 0 100 200 300 400 500 Miles